Histories of the Sacred and Secular, 1700-2000

Series Editor
David Nash
Department of History
Oxford Brookes University
Oxford, UK

This series reflects the awakened and expanding profile of the history of religion within the academy in recent years. It intends publishing exciting new and high quality work on the history of religion and belief since 1700 and will encourage the production of interdisciplinary proposals and the use of innovative methodologies. The series will also welcome book proposals on the history of Atheism, Secularism, Humanism and unbelief/secularity and encourage research agendas in this area alongside those in religious belief. The series will be happy to reflect the work of new scholars entering the field as well as the work of established scholars. The series welcomes proposals covering subjects in Britain, Europe, the United States and Oceania.

Editorial board:

Professor Callum Brown (University of Glasgow, UK)
Professor William Gibson (Oxford Brookes University, UK)
Dr Carole Cusack (University of Sydney, Australia)
Professor Beverley Clack (Oxford Brookes University, UK)
Dr Bert Gasenbeek (Humanist University, Utrecht, Netherlands)
Professor Paul Harvey (University of Colorado at Colorado Springs, USA)

More information about this series at
http://www.palgrave.com/gp/series/14868

Lisa McClain

Divided Loyalties? Pushing the Boundaries of Gender and Lay Roles in the Catholic Church, 1534-1829

palgrave
macmillan

Lisa McClain
Department of History
Boise State University
Boise, ID, USA

Histories of the Sacred and Secular, 1700-2000
ISBN 978-3-030-10313-2   ISBN 978-3-319-73087-5 (eBook)
https://doi.org/10.1007/978-3-319-73087-5

© The Editor(s) (if applicable) and The Author(s) 2018
Softcover re-print of the Hardcover 1st edition 2018
This work is subject to copyright. All rights are solely and exclusively licensed by the Publisher, whether the whole or part of the material is concerned, specifically the rights of translation, reprinting, reuse of illustrations, recitation, broadcasting, reproduction on microfilms or in any other physical way, and transmission or information storage and retrieval, electronic adaptation, computer software, or by similar or dissimilar methodology now known or hereafter developed.
The use of general descriptive names, registered names, trademarks, service marks, etc. in this publication does not imply, even in the absence of a specific statement, that such names are exempt from the relevant protective laws and regulations and therefore free for general use.
The publisher, the authors and the editors are safe to assume that the advice and information in this book are believed to be true and accurate at the date of publication. Neither the publisher nor the authors or the editors give a warranty, express or implied, with respect to the material contained herein or for any errors or omissions that may have been made. The publisher remains neutral with regard to jurisdictional claims in published maps and institutional affiliations.

Cover illustration: *Escape of Lord Nithsdale* © Classic Image / Alamy Stock Photo

Printed on acid-free paper

This Palgrave Macmillan imprint is published by Springer Nature
The registered company is Springer International Publishing AG
The registered company address is: Gewerbestrasse 11, 6330 Cham, Switzerland

For Doug, Sue, and Kim McClain,
with love and gratitude for your support and encouragement all these years

Preface

Since his election in 2013, Pope Francis I has engaged the estimated 1.2 billion Catholics and innumerable non-Catholics worldwide with his frank, inclusive talk on issues as diverse as poverty and homosexuality. At a time when many seem confused by the Church's apparent willingness to reconsider its traditions regarding some issues—such as divorce—but not others—such as women's ordination—*Divided Loyalties? Pushing the Boundaries of Gender and Lay Roles in the Catholic Church, 1534–1829* provides history, context, and insight revealing how ordinary Catholics and the Catholic Church have successfully navigated such challenges and controversies before without undermining the faith, family, or society. It takes readers into a long-ago world of gender confusion and religious questioning by scandalous nuns, Catholic rogues, and "Apostolic Viragoes" in the British Isles after King Henry VIII famously broke with the Roman Catholic Church to marry Anne Boleyn in 1534. For the next three centuries, Catholicism was illegal in the British Isles. In the frequent absence of churches, priests, and sacraments, Catholics experimented with gender roles and expanded religious roles for ordinary Catholics in a desperate attempt to save souls. *Divided Loyalties?* reveals the history of Catholics worshiping in an illegal, underground faith who would do what they had to do to be good women and men AND good Catholics. And the Catholic Church was on board … to a point.

Filled with richly detailed stories, this book explores how Catholics created and tested new understandings of women's and men's roles in family life, ritual, religious leadership, and vocation. Engaging personal narratives, letters, trial records, and other stories reveal how far ordinary

Catholics would go to get their needs met and how far the Catholic Church would bend its rules on gender and laypeople's roles in the Church to sustain Catholics struggling to keep their faith alive. In the many generations that passed between Henry VIII's break with Rome and full Catholic emancipation in the British Isles in 1829, Catholics had time to set limits, loosen them, and face the consequences.

This is history, but the lessons learned inform our contemporary discussions not only about gender and lay roles in the Church but also about divine power and authority itself. The primary aim of this book is to explore the Catholic Church's long-term, ongoing process of balancing gendered and religious authority. My intent is not to take sides in any debates but to introduce historical evidence and a framework for interpreting developments. As a historian specializing in both the history of Catholic Christianity and gender studies, I firmly believe it is incumbent upon scholars to provide a clear sense of why these stories of past lives and events matter—to find meaning in a narrative, not simply because it reveals new, scholarly insights into the past, but because it connects to themes of humanity and society that bridge centuries.

I am grateful to the many friends and colleagues who gave of their valuable time to wrestle with ideas over tasty beverages and to critique and edit this work, providing encouragement and direction: particularly Doug Sims, whose fine editorial talents helped craft the final text; members of the Group for Early Modern Studies at Boise State University—Steve Crowley, Matt Hansen, Janice Neri, Mac Test, and Jim Stockton; Brady Jones; Karen Wadley; Sue McClain; Dane Johns; and students in my Boise State University graduate seminar on gender and sexualities—Shiann Johns, Steve Humiston, Marsha Hunter, Victor Higgins, Tim Syreen, Julie Okamura, Chelsee Boehm, KayCee Babb, Tristan Kelly, Roy Cuellar, and Tim Reynolds.

I would also like to acknowledge the generosity of the Idaho Humanities Council that helped fund travel with a Research Fellowship, and the assistance of Pat Fox and the archival staff at the Harry Ransom Humanities Research Center at the University of Texas at Austin.

Last, but certainly never least, I am deeply indebted to my immediate family, Doug, Anna, and Will, for their patience, love, and support.

Boise State University, Boise, ID   Lisa McClain

Contents

1 Introduction: Devout Outlaws — 1

Part I Pushing the Boundaries of Gender — 11

2 The New Normal — 13

3 Disobedient Women — 41

4 Wodehouse's Choice — 79

5 Amending the Marriage Contract — 117

Part II Pushing the Boundaries of Religion — 155

6 The "Good Catholic" — 157

7 Sharing the Job: Cooperation Between the Priesthood
   and Laity   195

8 Where the Catholic Church Draws the Line: Mary
   Ward vs. the Catholic Priesthood   235

Index   275

CHAPTER 1

Introduction: Devout Outlaws

Mary Ward broke the law, and she knew it. She and her companions—known as the English Ladies—were Catholics.[1] Together, they practiced an illegal faith in the Protestant British Isles in the seventeenth century, during the religious conflict and violence of the Reformation era. However, the English Ladies did more than worship behind closed doors. They deceived the authorities. They disguised themselves to evade arrest. They taught and encouraged others to practice an outlawed religion. They assisted renegade priests working underground on behalf of the Roman Church. In doing so, these women risked imprisonment and even execution.

Yet it was not only the laws of England that Ward transgressed. Ward and the English Ladies sought to serve the Catholic Church in a new way, a way not yet approved by the papacy. Similar to nuns, these devout women understood themselves as called to a religious vocation. Unlike nuns, they wanted to live and work free from the cloister so they could care for the spiritual needs of Catholics worshiping covertly in their homeland. Despite such seemingly good intentions, the papacy suppressed Ward's Institute of English Ladies, bringing the organization to an abrupt, unpleasant end. With his 1631 papal bull, *Pastoralis Romani Pontificis*, Pope Urban VIII not only suppressed the Institute but gave it "sharper

© The Author(s) 2018
L. McClain, *Divided Loyalties? Pushing the Boundaries of Gender and Lay Roles in the Catholic Church, 1534-1829*, Histories of the Sacred and Secular, 1700-2000, https://doi.org/10.1007/978-3-319-73087-5_1

censure" than was usual because of the serious dangers posed to Christians by these women's activities. He declared the Institute null, void and of "no authority or importance." The English Ladies were "extinguished," "removed entirely from the Church of God. We destroy and annul them, and we wish and command all the Christian faithful to consider them and think of them as suppressed, extinct, rooted out, destroyed and abolished" (Wetter 2006, 213–18; also 129–37).[2] The papacy even imprisoned Ward briefly for heresy and kept her under surveillance for years after her release (67–103). She and the English Ladies were devout outlaws.

Considering such scathing language, it is surprising to find Urban VIII, less than a decade later, assuring Mary that she was not a heretic and providing her a pension. He communicated secretly to keep Ward's Institute house in Munich open although her Institute no longer existed (Rapley 1990, 213–14n35). Urban asked his nephew, Cardinal Francesco Barberini, to provide a letter of introduction for Ward and her companions to Queen Henrietta Maria of England. Ward was going back to Protestant England to work for the Catholic cause but this time with papal knowledge and support. Barberini's 1638 letter praised Ward as "much esteemed in Rome both for her well known qualities and piety." He encouraged Henrietta Maria to receive Ward, showing "all kindness she can to her and her company" (Chambers 1882, 2:452). Urban's envoy in England, Count Carlo Rossetti, welcomed Ward enthusiastically, reporting that he had been commanded to "serve her in all he could" (Kenworthy-Browne 2008, 65). What was simultaneously so objectionable and yet so laudable about Ward and her Ladies that would explain such an "about face"?

On the surface, it seems obvious that these unmarried women's attempts to serve God and the Church without being enclosed in a convent forced Urban's hand. Ward and the English Ladies clearly appeared to violate church law. Moreover, accusations coming out of England portrayed these women as driving a contentious wedge between Catholics who differed in their opinions of the women and their work. Women disguising themselves, traveling and living independently, and interacting with virtual strangers —it was scandalous, almost unthinkable. At best, critics found the women's efforts vain and useless. At worst, naysayers gossiped about these "whores" and "galloping nuns" (*Godfather's Information* 1623; Dirmeier 2007, 1:763–64; Chambers 1882, 1:318–19, 2:169–70, 183–87). The social conventions of gender did not support women who assumed the freedom that these English Ladies did.

Some scholars view Ward as a proto-feminist pioneer for refusing to be enclosed in a convent, while others prefer to see her as a conservative Catholic woman whose attempts to avoid enclosure unintentionally challenged gender biases (Wetter 2006; Strasser 2004; Lux-Sterritt 2011; Ellis 2007; Harriss 2010; Rapley 1990, 3–9, 28–34). Neither of these interpretations of Ward quite unravel the puzzle posed by Ward's unusual status. If this woman's unconventional activities were so divisive among English Catholic clergy and laity, Urban VIII should not have been so willing to smooth the way for her return to England. Her gender hadn't changed. She and her companions still lived together outside a convent. The pope clearly intended them to work among prominent Catholics, serving Catholic interests. If the original objections to Ward and the English Ladies were truly grounded in disagreements over these women's lack of enclosure, their adoption of non-traditional gender roles, or the types of public, pious works that the women performed, why encourage Ward's return, where she would presumably continue to cause divisions among Catholics? What was really going on here?

The Bigger Issue

Ward's tussle with Urban VIII illuminates more than one woman's failed attempt to found a new form of women's religious life. Her story opens a window through which to examine the ongoing process by which societies balance gender and religious priorities. Historically, across societies, across faiths, and across continents, groups and individuals have been willing to alter their traditional gender expectations and gendered economic, social, and religious roles to meet pressing, immediate needs. From craftswomen who stepped up to fill labor shortages after the Black Death to female citizens who took up arms during the French Revolution, times of instability and change are often associated with re-negotiations of gender roles. One of the best-known recent examples is the U.S. and Great Britain's use of women's labor outside the home in World War II, in fields as diverse as manufacturing (Rosie the Riveter) and intelligence gathering and analysis (the code breakers at Bletchley Park). Although most individuals had been socialized to believe that women were not supposed to fill such roles (in fact, were incapable of doing such work), the times seemed to demand it. Governments needed women's labor because they had recruited the majority of able-bodied men to fight. At war's end, however, employers and governments dismissed the majority of these women. It was not because their work had been unsatisfactory. Women had proven themselves capable and invaluable. Instead, it was because the need evaporated. The war was over.

Once crises end, the presumption is that men and women return to traditional gender roles—"the way things used to be"—in home, society, and work force, even if some individuals prefer the new roles. Surely everyone understood that the violation of gender norms was a temporary measure, acceptable only to address a short-term, emergency situation? But what of women who had been challenged, even fulfilled, through their higher status, highly valued efforts and wished to continue?

Of late, tensions between gender norms and religious needs are rising, and not only within Christian denominations. For example, many fundamentalist Islamist groups such as ISIS and Boko Haram have traditionally appealed to particular interpretations of sharia law and nature (*kodrat*) as restricting women's work and movements to the private, domestic sphere (Shehadeh 2007). Despite these oft-stated values, these same organizations have reportedly been recruiting and training Muslim women for public and militant roles, such as Boko Haram's use of female suicide bombers in Cameroon in 2015. This is likely because women are less likely than men to attract the suspicion of authorities and more likely to be allowed to pass through security checkpoints with a minimum search (Bloom 2007). Groups of individuals, both large and small, male and female, prove willing to transgress customary gender norms and religious roles to meet a perceived greater need.

As such examples indicate, our assignment of individuals into gender roles has never been set in stone. Numerous times, gender roles based upon social, cultural, legal, or religious mores or divine or natural laws have been overturned by the very political, social, and religious authorities that created them; and this raises many questions and concerns. Under what circumstances is it acceptable to transgress gender norms? Are there limits, and if so, what are they and who determines them? How do the majority accept what was previously taught as improper and insupportable (if not unnatural and sinful) as suddenly palatable, even admirable? And, after the greater immediate need is satisfied, what next? The gendered and patriarchal structures imbedded within societies, religions, and cultures do not change simply because women's efforts were used to bridge temporary gaps in labor, religion, or service to the state in times of necessity. The memory of women's achievements and capacities will likely fuel future efforts to expand gender opportunities for both men and women, but the duration of these conflicts is typically too short (often less than a decade) to produce long-term changes to institutions and widely shared societal attitudes and practices.

In contrast, we have a historical anomaly in Mary Ward's world. The religious clashes of her lifetime were part of larger Catholic-Protestant conflicts in the British Isles that officially lasted almost 300 years and arguably much longer. As a result, any changes to gender and religious roles undertaken in response to the needs of the times had sufficient time to gain a foothold among Catholics in the British Isles. Many generations passed between Henry VIII's break with the Roman Catholic Church in 1534 and the Roman Catholic Relief Act of 1829 which legally ended the long process of Catholic emancipation in the British Isles. Catholics had time to test balances and boundaries between gender norms and religious needs in different situations. Catholics had time to set limits or loosen them.

By the nineteenth century, when the government officially lifted restrictions on Catholicism, Catholics had lived with their new gender and religious roles for generations. Turning back the clock to embrace earlier attitudes and practices would not have been easy or automatic. Yet these cultural changes were evolutionary rather than revolutionary. They took place as a result of the struggle of Catholic leaders to meet the needs of a beleaguered religious population and of individual Catholics to reconcile themselves to the demands of their situations. This meant that it did not require a conscious effort on anyone's part to reshape ideas about religion and gender.

By integrating the puzzle of Pope Urban VIII's harsher-than-usual suppression of Ward's Institute into this much larger story about broader, overlapping gendered and religious concerns, the contours of almost three centuries of gender and religious change emerge, a change precipitated as a largely unintentional byproduct of Catholic efforts to reclaim the British Isles for Rome and sustain an illegal minority faith. The first part of this book examines changing gender roles and the many ways in which both women's *and men's* understandings of what was appropriate, natural, and divinely created for each sex transformed as they struggled to practice Catholicism in a Protestant state. A brief historical overview of religious reforms and gendered traditions in the British Isles is provided in Chap. 2. Chapter 3 explores how Catholic women, traditionally taught to be quiet, modest, and obedient, carved out new roles for themselves as leaders and lawbreakers as they struggled to uphold an underground faith in their homes and beyond. Chapter 4 investigates how Catholic men—many of whom occasionally bowed their heads before Protestant priests to avoid impoverishment—understood and re-created their masculinity in new ways under these circumstances. Chapter 5 continues by scrutinizing Catholic women and men in relationship with one another to discover the subtle adjustments in gender and religious roles necessitated within marriage by religious conflicts.

Examining such issues from the perspective of gender alone is valuable but provides an incomplete picture of the transformations occurring among Catholics in the British Isles. Gender and religious norms have long supported and reinforced one another within a larger patriarchal system. Neither "trumps" the other in some hierarchy of importance. Individuals and societies negotiate men's and women's gender roles within a web of other issues and concerns, including religion. Similarly, religious leaders, institutions, and believers negotiate religious roles within a web of other priorities and pressures, including gender.

The second part of this book thus alters the perspective of inquiry to explore the same conflicts and concerns through a primary lens of faith. Chapters probe how different religious roles evolved to meet the needs of Catholics living in a Protestant state and how gender was interwoven throughout such transformations. For example, just as Catholics created new understandings of what it meant to be good women, men, wives, and husbands, so did they need to create new definitions of what it meant to be a good Catholic, the subject of Chap. 6. In addition, just as the Church saw religious advantages to softening strict borders between gender roles, so did it blur traditional boundaries between lay and priestly roles, as Chap. 7 explores. Need, again, drove such evolutions, as the Catholic Church adjusted to the challenges of its status as an illegal faith and the realities of upholding an underground church. Gender, of course, was intimately embedded within these changes, and the concluding Chap. 8 weaves the broader lessons learned at the intersections of religion and gender throughout the book into an answer to the conundrum of Mary Ward's treatment. It also provides a framework through which to interpret broader controversies concerning gender and lay roles in the Catholic Church in Ward's day and our own.

Although this book is not about Mary Ward, we will meet her many times along the way. Her story will be joined with many others, such as the layman Francis Wodehouse's tale of unusual physical suffering brought about by the conflict between his masculine and religious priorities. We will examine the lives and choices of religious men and women such as Henry Garnet, Gertrude More, and Lucy Herbert, whose letters and spiritual writings coupled with trial records and monastic chronicles reveal a tapestry of intentional and unintentional re-negotiations of gendered and religious roles. These new interpretations of the lives and experiences of better-known Catholics couple with those of less well-known believers, such as the Dublin women who rose up against Protestant authorities the day after Christmas, provoking a street riot.

History is, at its heart, about storytelling. When enough stories accumulate, patterns emerge that scholars can then interpret and contextualize. Bringing together what otherwise might appear to be three centuries worth of anecdotal or insignificant snippets of Catholic experiences reveals such patterns of evolving gender and religious norms. We can begin to identify circumstances under which it was acceptable for Catholics to transgress gender and religious mores, the limits to such transgressions, who drew them, and why. We begin to understand the rationalizations that a majority of Catholics made to transform what had previously been taught as unacceptable, unnatural, and even sinful into something admirable. Even after the Catholic Church's emergency situation in the British Isles dwindled following Catholic Emancipation in 1829, the Church could hardly expect Catholics of the nineteenth century simply to return to gender and religious roles as they had been in the sixteenth century. Too much had changed.

Gender and Religious Roles Today

The primary aim of this book is to explore issues surrounding the Catholic Church's long-term, ongoing process of balancing gendered and religious authority. As in so many other historical situations, a crisis or great need led to changes in the range of available gender and religious roles. As Ward's attempts to create a new female religious organization demonstrate, some women sought to create new roles for women in the Catholic Church and British society. As many other examples throughout this book testify, men did the same. Contrary to oft-expressed fears, society did not collapse, government and church did not crumble, and the world did not end with the redrawing of gender boundaries.

These events are part and parcel of a long-standing discussion not only about women's and men's natural or God-given roles but also about divine power and authority itself. The earliest Christians and Church Fathers argued over such issues and took centuries to agree upon a hierarchical structure of authority that has since been revised or reinterpreted many times. This hierarchy eventually excluded women, but it also excluded certain types of men. In Ward's era, both clerics and laypeople expressed concerns over perceived subversions of authority made by men and women, laypeople and clergy, Catholics and Protestants. Who exercises authority, what legitimates it, and who submits to it and how? All of these issues are addressed herein.

Although these disputes occurred hundreds of years ago, they are debates that continue in related forms even today within the Catholic Church, other faith traditions, and secular societies worldwide. These are not dry theological or philosophical dialogues but vibrant discussions of embodied beliefs. People of faith are questioning traditional gender and lay roles taught within their religious affiliations. They view this not as rebellion but as part of what it means to be engaged, faithful believers. In seeking greater connection with the divine and meaningful ways to serve their faith, they intentionally or unintentionally press up against existing boundaries, just as Mary Ward did. Although such "transgressions" have frequently been viewed with fear and stigmatized as potentially disruptive, dangerous, and destructive to traditional orders, three centuries of Catholic experiences in the British Isles reveal positive consequences and strengthening of religious culture that can result from extending gender and religious roles beyond custom and tradition.

NOTES

1. The institute did not operate with an official name at this time. Although later known as the Institute of the Blessed Virgin Mary, Mary Ward's organization went by various titles during her lifetime, such as the Institute of English Ladies and the English Virgins.
2. The bull was first drafted in 1628. Orders to suppress the Institute's houses on the continent were communicated to nuncios by *Propaganda Fide* as early as October 1629; however, such orders were never communicated to Ward. Ward continued to believe that efforts to suppress the houses were a mistake and not originating from the pope until she was shown a published copy of *Pastoralis Romani Pontificus* after her imprisonment and release. By 1631, the suppression was largely complete.

WORKS CITED

Bloom, Mia. 2007. "Female Suicide Bombers: A Global Trend." *Daedalus* 136, no. 1: 94–102.

Chambers, M.C.E. 1882. *The Life of Mary Ward (1585–1645)*. 2 vols. Edited by Henry James Coleridge. London: Burns & Oates.

Dirmeier, Ursula, ed. 2007. *Mary Ward und ihre Gründung: Die Quellentexte bis 1645*. 4 vols. Corpus Catholicorum 45–8. Münster: Aschendorff Verlag.

Ellis, Pamela. 2007. "'They Are but Women': Mary Ward (1585–1645)." In *Women, Gender and Radical Religion in Early Modern Europe*, edited by Sylvia Brown, 243–63. Studies in Medieval and Reformation Traditions, 129. Leiden: Brill.

Godfather's Information, or Certaine Observations Delivered me by Mistress Marie Allcock, the First Minister of Mistress Wardes Companie at Leeds (Liege) Yea the First of All Who Was Publicklye so Called. 1623. n.p.

Harriss, Patricia. 2010. "Mary Ward in Her Own Writings." *Recusant History* 30, no. 2: 229–39.

Kenworthy-Browne, Christina, ed. 2008. *Mary Ward 1585–1648: A Briefe Relation with Autobiographical Fragments and a Selection of Letters*. Rochester, NY: Boydell and Brewer for the Catholic Record Society.

Lux-Sterritt, Laurence. 2011. "Mary Ward's English Institute and Prescribed Female Roles in the Early Modern Church." In *Gender, Catholicism, and Spirituality*, edited by Lux-Sterritt and Carmen M. Mangion, 83–98. London: Palgrave Macmillan.

Rapley, Elizabeth. 1990. *The Dévotes: Women and Church in Seventeenth-Century France*. Kingston, Ontario: McGill/Queen's University Press.

Shehadeh, Lamia Rustum. 2007. *The Idea of Women in Fundamentalist Islam*. Gainesville, FL: University Press of Florida.

Strasser, Ulrike. 2004. "Early Modern Nuns and the Feminist Politics of Religion." *The Journal of Religion* 84, no. 4: 529–554.

Wetter, M. Immolata. 2006. *Mary Ward: Under the Shadow of the Inquisition*. Translated by M. Bernadette Ganne and M. Patricia Harriss. Introduction by Gregory Kirkus. Oxford: Way Books.

PART I

Pushing the Boundaries of Gender

CHAPTER 2

The New Normal

Mary Ward (1585–1645) was born into a changed world. To understand these changes is to understand her story. Henry VIII's break from Rome in 1534 marked the first defection of a major European country from papal authority in the Reformation era, and the Catholic Church during her lifetime was under new pressures. Henry cut spiritual, legal, institutional, and financial ties to the Roman Church throughout England, Ireland, and Wales. Catholic churches became Protestant ones. Rites were changed. Monasteries were dissolved. Catholic property reverted to the state. Catholic priests became Protestant ones or they lost their offices. Despite Henry's eldest daughter Mary I's resumption of ties with the Catholic Church during her brief reign (1553–1558), his younger, Protestant daughter, Elizabeth, severed them again soon after taking the throne. Within two years, Elizabeth I's government passed the Acts of Supremacy and Uniformity (1559) and the Irish Act of Uniformity (1560), which, together, again removed England, Ireland, and Wales from papal authority. Scotland, then an independent monarchy, also severed ties with Rome in 1560. Lowland Scots accepted the Calvinist/Presbyterian theology of the Scottish Kirk with rapidity while Catholicism remained illegally entrenched in the relatively inaccessible Highlands until the government's destruction of the clan system in the mid-eighteenth century

© The Author(s) 2018
L. McClain, *Divided Loyalties? Pushing the Boundaries of Gender and Lay Roles in the Catholic Church, 1534-1829*, Histories of the Sacred and Secular, 1700-2000, https://doi.org/10.1007/978-3-319-73087-5_2

(Mullett 1998; Heal 2003; Walsham 2014; Dawson 2007). Protestantism was thus established as the only legal religion of the British Isles. It would remain so for the next 270 years.

Catholic worship continued clandestinely, however, during these three centuries. Men left their homes to train for the priesthood at newly established Catholic seminaries on the continent and began returning in 1574 as part of a Catholic quest to reclaim the British Isles, especially England and Ireland, for Rome (Mullett 1998, 51–53, 59–60; Murray 2009, 5–19, 261–321). England, Wales, and eventually Scotland—each Catholic for almost a millennium before Protestant reforms—became mission fields, lands to be converted. Ireland, which never lost its Catholic majority, did not need to be reconverted so much as continuously supplied with priests and leadership to serve an underground church that was a poorly kept secret from Protestant authorities. This story is well known. Priests often stayed in the manor houses of wealthier Catholics, using them as bases of operation to serve surrounding communities. Lacking physical churches, tithes, and administrative support, missionary priests served their flocks from the margins, hiding from Protestant authorities while providing spiritual comfort and the sacraments to Catholics and attempting to reconcile Protestants to the Catholic Church (McClain 2004, 20; Mullett 1998, 19–21; Kaplan 2007, 172–97). It was this work that Ward and the English Ladies felt called to join.

Not Quite Nuns

Mary Ward grew up amidst these political and religious changes, spending her childhood in several Catholic households trying to adjust to "the new normal." Missionary priests served these homes, providing spiritual comfort and the sacraments (Lux-Sterritt 2006, 196–201; Peters 1994, 28–54).[1] Increasingly certain that she was called to the religious life yet living in a country where there were no longer any Catholic convents, Ward crossed the English Channel in 1606 when she was 21 years old, hoping to be accepted at one of the many continental convents welcoming Catholic women and girls from the British Isles. She initially joined a Flemish house of Poor Clares, the female branch of the Franciscan order, and later founded an English house of the same order. Ward's religious life changed at age 24 after she received a series of divine revelations beginning in 1609 in which she said God called her to explore a different type of women's religious vocation based on the example of the Society of

Jesus. "Take the name of the Society," these visions told her (Kenworthy-Browne 2008, 146; Simmonds 2008, 120–35). These visions would alter her personal journey, the mission, and the future of the Catholic Church.

However, Ward had a problem. Women's and men's opportunities throughout much of the British Isles were based upon interpretations of divine law, natural law, and English common law which together circumscribed a set of roles and expectations for each sex. Theologians based divine law on interpretations of Judeo-Christian scripture that helped prescribe the character and place of each sex in divinely created hierarchies of family and society (i.e., Gen 2:7–25; Luke 1:26–56, 2:1–20). Such beliefs defined women as subordinate to male authority and inherently sinful, yet ideally chaste, modest, and out of the public eye.

Natural law, in contrast, was based on philosophers' inference of universal principles about human nature gleaned from their observations of human behavior. Its proponents, most notably Aristotle, created binding moral rules based on those principles. Perceived differences in physical and mental character between men and women justified women's subordination to men and "naturally" legitimated their lesser status and rights in society.

English common law then translated divine and natural understandings about both men and women into a legal system that upheld traditional gender roles, judged moral and ethical issues, and conferred or denied rights and privileges based on gender. Common law placed an unmarried young woman under the legal authority of her father or other male guardian. If a woman married, she did not enjoy legal rights and status in her own right but rather was "covered" under her husband's rights as if they were one person in a complex and sometimes contradictory system known as coverture. An unmarried adult woman, whether spinster or widow, was permitted to exercise limited legal rights but not to the extent a man could (T.E. 1632). A woman inspired, as Ward was, to pursue a new way of life could not simply do so.

Just as women could not act as men did within worldly society, neither could women pursuing a religious calling act within the Catholic Church as men could. Since 1298, Pope Boniface VIII's decretal, *Periculoso*, required all nuns—also known as women religious—to stay enclosed behind convent walls, in what is known as mandatory claustration. Although enforcement of this strict ideal was never absolute, this was not some little-known, antiquated rule that Ward could ignore. The Council of Trent (1545–1563), the Catholic Church's influential Reformation-era council held to determine correct Christian belief and practice and to reform abuses, had recently confirmed *Periculoso* and the values behind it. Female religious needed to be isolated to protect them from heresy, temptation, and opportunities for sin, especially sexual sin, to which their womanly natures allegedly inclined them (Makowski 1999, 1–8, 23–28, 31, 38–40, 104, 121, 126–27; Waterworth 1848, 240–41). Yet the Church had tolerated other small groups of pious women living communally yet unenclosed, such as the beguines, *beatas*, *klopjes*, and Ursulines (Makowski 1999, 122–23; Kooi 1995, 80; 2012, 26–28, 111, 124). Why not one more? With such precedents, Ward hoped that she and her colleagues might obtain an exception to strict enclosure, especially considering the great need and Rome's desire to reclaim the British Isles.

Requesting papal approval, Ward asked that her Institute of English Ladies bypass *Periculoso* and traditional episcopal hierarchies to exist, as the Jesuits did, under the direct jurisdiction of the pope and free from any cloister as a form of "mixed life." Her ladies would be more than laywomen but not nuns. They sought to blend elements of lay and monastic life into something new. They would live together out in the world under the authority of the Roman Church. They would follow a regular routine of communal prayer, ritual observances, and religious discipline. They would adopt conservative, distinctive dress appropriate to the secular world but would not wear nuns' habits. They would be led by a female superior, an "abbess." And while English Ladies made the traditional three monastic vows of chastity, obedience, and poverty, they took such vows privately, not publicly and solemnly before church authority as nuns did. The primary purpose of such a mixed life would be to sustain and relieve distressed Catholics and promote the salvation of others through educating young girls or "by any other means that are congruous to the times," "in any place," for the "propagation" of the Catholic Church (Chambers 1882, 1:376–78, 384).

Violence and Its Aftermath

The Church certainly seemed to need and want such help. In particular, Catholic leaders went to great lengths to reclaim the two largest and most influential kingdoms—England and Ireland—for Rome. In the first decades of Elizabeth's reign, they considered seizing power through violence. In his 1570 papal bull, *Regnans in excelsis*, Pope Pius V released all

Elizabeth's subjects from their loyalty to their heretic queen, removing any taint of sin should they rebel. Influential Catholics living in her realm or in exile in continental Europe schemed to topple Elizabeth from the throne and replace her with a Catholic monarch. The usual candidate was her cousin, Mary Queen of Scots. Open insurrections, such as the Northern Rising of 1569, and behind-the-scenes plots, such as the Throckmorton and Babington Plots, ended in failure and eventually with Mary's beheading at Fotheringay Castle in 1587. In the 1580s and 1590s, the papacy openly supported Catholic Spain's efforts to invade the British Isles, most notably the failed Spanish Armada of 1588 and a later, smaller armada sent to support an Irish rebellion in 1595, which also failed. Philip II (1527–1598), King of Spain and former King of England during his marriage to Mary I, hoped to depose Elizabeth and return her realm to Catholic loyalty. Some Irish Catholics encouraged such plans, even inviting the Spanish monarch to place one of his relatives on the throne of Ireland (Mullett 1998, 57). This move would have the double benefit of reconciling Ireland to Rome and removing Ireland from English control.

After Elizabeth's death in 1603 ended the Tudor monarchy, the Stuart monarchs faced a declining threat from violent Catholic extremists. With his accession to the English crown as James I, the Protestant James VI of Scotland united the crowns of England, Scotland, and Ireland. Initially, Catholics sought to remove him. Following the failure of the 1603 Main and Bye Plots to depose or kidnap James, and the much better known Gunpowder Plot of 1605 in which Guy Fawkes and other conspirators planned to blow up king and Parliament, Catholic attempts to overthrow the Protestant monarchy fell off sharply. None had worked, and all had resulted in increased persecution of Catholics and harsher enforcement of the laws against them. Catholics began to conclude that reconversion would be a long, drawn-out process, if it occurred at all.

However, if not a return to Roman jurisdiction, what then? What was Catholic presence in the British Isles to look like? Although the Catholic Church named cardinals and bishops as ecclesiastical leaders over the British Isles, there were no public, clearly defined Catholic parish, episcopal, or diocesan structures or administrations. There were no ecclesiastical courts to enforce discipline. There was little property or funding. With the many priests arriving on mission, it was not always clear who was in charge. Should it be the secular priests—those who chose a life free from the monastery and who promised obedience to a bishop? Alternatively, should it be the regular priests—those ordained clerics who also had taken monastic vows and followed a rule (or *regula*) of one of the religious orders, such as the Jesuits or Benedictines? Priests were divided over whether to operate as though the institutional hierarchies of the medieval era were still in place or to embrace the idea of the British Isles as a true mission field—a blank slate upon which no concrete rules were written. Heated conflicts erupted over who had authority over whom, as will be discussed further in Chap. 8. On this issue, the secular priests and the Jesuits in particular disagreed. As the secular priest, John Mush, complained, "Verily, here is nothing but most lamentable confusion, debates & factions among both clergy and people" (Tierney 1841, 4:clxxix–xxx). Even in Ireland, which boasted a majority Catholic population, enthusiastic bishops, and underground monastic activity, secular and regular priests competed with one another for influence and the loyalties of the laity (Mullett 1998, 65–69, 120–36, 185–93).

In this environment of changing Catholic expectations and uncertain leadership, Ward began pursuing her plans for the Institute. Stumbling into these conflicts, Ward's plan encountered opposition from the very Catholics she hoped to serve. Church approval was a lengthy process lasting many years, and while religious officials debated the merits of Ward's vision, she and the English Ladies were already at work. Ward travelled back to England and was joined by other women to help with the mission. Beginning in 1609, members lived together in London in a house kept by the Institute. Others stayed with Catholic families—wealthy and poor—in the countryside. Their activities consisted primarily of underground evangelization. They educated girls, catechized families, and performed acts of charity. They persuaded and prepared people to turn or return to the Catholic faith, finding priests for reconciliation and the sacraments when the time came (Mother Mary Margaret 1955, 28–29; Chambers 1882, 2:25–38). The women supported missionary priests by providing safe places for them to stay and by funneling Christians to them (Chambers 1882, 1:44). Most of this was done surreptitiously, as the practice of Catholicism was illegal, even in Ireland where Catholics outnumbered Protestants. Support of Catholic priests, especially Jesuits, was punishable by fines, imprisonment, and possibly death under the charge of treason (McClain 2004, 21–25, 204–8).

A Knock on the Door in the Night

Protestant authorities knew all about Catholics' underground activities, and from the 1570s through the eighteenth century, successive parliaments passed laws of increasing severity impacting Catholics in England,

Ireland, Wales, and Scotland.² These parliaments hoped to curb Catholic practices, hamstring the mission, and eventually erode Catholic loyalties. Rather than criminalizing Catholic religious beliefs, per se, these laws prosecuted Catholics for betraying the monarch and state by acting in the interests of a foreign power—the papacy. Nowhere was the equation of Catholicism with treason more clearly stated than in the long title of one of the last penal laws passed during Elizabeth's reign, the "Act for the better discovery of wicked and seditious persons terming themselves Catholics, but being rebellious and traitorous subjects" (35 Eliz I, c. 2). Reconciling anyone to Catholicism, as the English Ladies would do, became a treasonable offence, as did carrying or circulating papal bulls and Catholic religious objects such as crucifixes and rosaries. The government ordered Catholics living abroad to come home. It became illegal and punishable by death just to *be* a priest ordained after 1559 in the British Isles. Those who harbored or assisted priests were to "suffer death, loss, and forfeit as in cases of one attainted of felony" (13 Eliz I, c. 1 & 2, building upon 35 Henry VIII, c. 2; also 27 Eliz I, c. 2; 29 Eliz I, c. 6; 3 and 4 James I, c. 4, 5; 7 James I, c. 6).

Protestant efforts to smoke out Catholics and encourage conformity to the state church also included the Recusancy Acts, a set of civil laws rather than criminal ones. Subjects who recused themselves from weekly Church of England, Church of Ireland, or Church of Scotland services—hence the term, *recusants*—faced increasingly stiff fines. The government restricted Catholics and other dissenters from practicing certain professions and often preferred to fine Catholics rather than imprison them. Parliaments held during the reign of the perpetually cash-strapped James I, for example, increased fines to such high levels that many Catholics who recused themselves could not afford to pay. The makers of the law anticipated these financial realities and wrote the law to allow the government to seize two-thirds of a recusant's land for non-payment of fines (3 James 1, c. 4). Even if the recusant died, heirs could not reclaim the land until they paid all the arrears. The government repealed the Recusancy Acts in 1650 during the Commonwealth period, but the penal laws continued in effect until 1829, supplemented by further fines, confiscations of property, and restrictions on economic opportunities and political participation.

These laws significantly hampered male missionaries' efforts to convert and minister to Catholics and avoid detection. The government's enforcement of these laws waxed and waned depending on where one lived in the British Isles and whether there was any perceived threat of foreign invasion or domestic rebellion, but being Catholic always carried risks. Even when the "threat level" was low, the risks never disappeared. Recusants and potential converts had to weigh the costs of Catholicism and of helping Catholic clergy. Priests needed to be particularly careful. Priest hunters, called *pursuivants*, and law enforcement officials learned how to identify male missionaries by their dress, mannerisms, speech, possessions, and company they kept. They learned the travel patterns that missionaries used to sneak into and around the country. They learned the homes and families with which missionaries would be most likely to stay. They became good at their jobs.

Consequently, many Catholics enjoyed only sporadic access to priests and sacraments throughout the seventeenth century while frustrations and fears over salvation grew, particularly in England, Scotland, and Wales. Catholics dreaded the unexpected knock on the door that might be the priest hunters arriving with a warrant to search. Some families built ingeniously disguised hiding places in their homes to conceal any priests or incriminating Catholic books and objects from such scrutiny. Poorer Catholics might construct small, hidden outbuildings on their property to hide visiting priests. Pursuivants eventually discovered these ruses, too. Inevitably, a number of priests and laypeople were arrested, imprisoned, fined, and sometimes executed (Kaplan 2007, 123). The Catholic Church has canonized or beatified almost 300 English, Welsh, Irish, and Scots martyrs taken in these ways. The number of Catholics arrested, imprisoned, and fined was much higher.

Many Catholics began looking for ways to convince the monarchy of their loyalty to the crown. By and large, throughout the seventeenth century, the government refused to listen. Catholics' very practice of their religion made them lawbreakers. Protestants were taught to view Catholics with suspicion, as lying, criminal, disloyal subjects, especially after the Gunpowder Plot, the Irish Rebellion of 1641, and later when the majority of Catholics supported Charles I and the losing Royalists in the Civil War.

In this environment of suspicion, women such as Ward and the English Ladies who served the Catholic cause often possessed advantages over men. Reflecting widely accepted attitudes about women based on natural law, the authorities presumed women were less likely and less capable of planning treason or political rebellion. In addition, under common law, women were not considered fully responsible for their actions in the way that men were. If Protestant authorities searched their homes, some women claimed that Catholic items found there did not belong to them but to men and that they, being women, were not acquainted with the uses of such things. If the authorities arrested a woman for breaking the Catholic penal laws, they typically released her or gave her a lighter punishment than a man would have received. Convicted recusant women, even those originally sentenced to death, were likely to be reprieved (Chambers 1882, 2:34; Petti 1968, 44–80; Stone 1892, 110, 138–39; Blundell 1933, 29; SP Dom 12/168/6; *CSP Dom* 14/98/26, 27, 35, 36, 40). The Protestant government only executed three women under the penal laws despite their disproportionately high activity on behalf of the Catholic cause.

Under such circumstances, would the Catholic Church approve of women undertaking new types of work in support of its missionary activities in the British Isles—work that was desperately needed, that men found increasingly difficult to perform safely and effectively, but that women could accomplish with less risk? Ward believed so. Catholics in the British Isles and in Rome gradually learned to accommodate their expectations and efforts to the realities of practicing Catholicism illegally in a Protestant country.

Catholic leaders had already made exceptions to well-known religious laws and conventions to make Catholic worship, the mission, and the salvation of souls possible. One of the most obvious accommodations was to Catholic understanding of religious space. Without churches, priests often found themselves marrying, baptizing, burying, and absolving Catholics of their sins in unusual places, such as woods, fields, and jail cells (McClain 2004, 55–80; SP Dom 12/192/46; Chambers 1882, 2:28). The Church had always been willing to bend some of its rules in times of emergency, not as rejections of doctrine but as necessary, temporary, and justifiable suspensions of rules in particular situations (McClain 2004, 6). Various popes, such as Gregory XIII, also issued indulgences to inspire Catholics to work for the British Isles', particularly England's, reconversion (Bridgett 1899, 49, 99). Such leniencies occurred frequently under a variety of circumstances throughout Catholic Church history.

By 1590, the emergency situation had already lasted for decades with no end in the foreseeable future. Exceptions occurred on a larger scale and were gradually institutionalized. The papacy, for example, granted a special dispensation to missionary priests that allowed them to publish their books anonymously and without indicating the place of publication. Ordinarily, the Church banned such anonymity in publication, but it was considered too dangerous for these writers to publish using their names. Not only they but their families might face persecution. It was more important, Rome felt, to encourage authors to write and distribute books that might strengthen the Catholic cause in the British Isles than it was to enforce the usual decrees (Merrick 1947, 64–65; Waterworth 1848, 19–21).

Not all Catholics in continental Europe agreed with such accommodations, feeling that Catholics in the British Isles received special treatment. For example, in 1615, Mutio Vitelleschi, the newly elected General of the Society of Jesus, proved willing to bend Jesuit practice to the special circumstances in England to try to strengthen the effectiveness of the mission. The body of Jesuits that elected him, however, objected to such partiality, claiming that it contradicted the vision of their founder. The Spaniard Ignatius Loyola founded the Society of Jesus in 1534 as a means to combat heresy, especially Protestant heresy, in the early years of the Reformation. He viewed the Catholic Church's troubles as largely a problem of pastoral care that could be remedied by a new form of religious service. Although one of many new religious societies established in the sixteenth century, the Jesuits were distinctive in their organization and relationship to Rome. A former soldier, Loyola organized the Jesuits in quasi-military fashion as an all-male order, governed by a general, and answerable directly to the pope. Jesuits viewed themselves as warriors fighting for Christ, the pope, and the truth of Catholic Christianity. They were not tied to a church or monastery but ready to go wherever the church commanded them, leading people to Catholicism as good pastors of God's flock.

Loyola intended the Society of Jesus to transcend nationalities, Vitelleschi's opponents argued (Lockey 2015, 62–64). Jesuits were to unite spiritually to serve God, not divide themselves into groups such as English, Spanish, or French. Yet, what had the British done? Exactly that—they established particularly English, Irish, and Scots colleges in places such as the Low Countries, Rome, and Spain. These schools were run largely by English clerics. They hosted student populations that were predominately English, Irish, Welsh, and Scots, with the obvious intent to train these men to return home on mission and likely face martyrdom.

Vitelleschi was torn. He wanted missionary efforts in the British Isles to succeed, but he did not believe they could unless he authorized unpopular accommodations to standard Jesuit ideals. In the end, he risked the anger of his colleagues to encourage missionary goals. First, he asked the leaders of Jesuit provinces in which the schools were located to accept more

Englishmen and Irishmen than was traditional. Then, he elevated the English Mission first, in 1619, to vice-provincial status and later, in 1623, to a full province. He thereby allowed the English an unusual and controversial measure of autonomy as a nationally organized province and missionary effort (McCoog 1994, 16–17, 20, 24–25).[3] Vitelleschi was likely gratified when a large proportion, approximately one-fifth, of English students at these seminaries elected not only to be ordained to the priesthood but also to join the Society.

How Far Could the Boundaries of Gender Be Pushed?

Given this demonstrated willingness to compromise established policies to meet the needs of Catholics in the British Isles, where would the Catholic Church draw its limits about women and related expectations about gender? The Irish Jesuit Henry Fitzsimon, in 1609, in his *Words of Comfort to Persecuted Catholics*, noted how mutable attitudes and policies involving gender could be when religion was involved. Protestants such as the fiery preacher, John Knox, declared it unlawful for a woman to rule England when Catholic Mary I sat upon the throne but "in Queen Elizabeth's days that unlawfulness was lawful." Similarly, in Scotland, Protestants initially supported a woman—Catholic Queen Dowager Marie de Guise—as head of the church until their numbers increased enough for them to "change their doctrine" and remove her (Fitzsimon 1881, 23).

Catholic willingness to change gender expectations to meet religious needs was evident in the daily lives of ordinary Catholics. Lay Catholics often stepped in to fill the gaps left by an irregularly available priesthood, and some of these Catholics were women. Although it was not normally their role, Catholic women baptized children and arranged burials. They motivated neighbors, relatives, and poor people to reconcile with the Catholic faith. They taught and prepared them to receive Catholic priests and the sacraments at the soonest opportunity (McClain 2015, 445, 452–53; Mush 1849, 99). Such women were not trying to assume male or priestly roles. They were simply trying to serve God and their neighbors' souls as best they could in trying times. Mary Ward and her English Ladies can be seen as part of this larger phenomenon, seeking to institutionalize new types of women's participation in the work of the Church.

Henry Garnet, Jesuit superior in England from 1587 until his execution following the Gunpowder Plot in 1606, even appeared to entertain the idea of women taking a more active role in Catholic ministry, possibly having an approved role in administering the sacraments. It was a practical matter of need. There were so few priests in the British Isles that it was difficult enough to have one priest present, let alone another person approved to administer the sacraments. How could a priest himself receive the Eucharist if there was no one to give it to him? In 1599, Garnet addressed a letter to Marco Tusinga, one of the Jesuit Robert Persons's aliases, about his dilemma. Persons (1546–1610) was one of the instigators of the mission and one of its first missionaries. A polemical writer, diplomat, and perhaps the most influential promoter of the English Colleges on the continent, Persons was then serving as rector of the English College in Rome. In the letter, Garnet lamented the current state of affairs and ran through what he saw as his choices. At one point he observed that, "it was once the custom in England for women to minister in the public temples." He was not criticizing women's ministry in pre-Christian times, but rather seeming to consider this as an option having some tradition behind it. The tension between socially and religiously approved gender roles and immediate social and religious needs was apparent. Ultimately, Garnet informed Persons that he would ask the pope for a general permission for priests to administer the sacrament to themselves (*CSP Dom* 12/271/105). Although Garnet eventually discarded the option of women administering the Eucharist, he was not the last Catholic to entertain the possibility of expanding women's roles in this sacrament.

Perhaps nowhere was this tension between gender and religious roles played out more publicly than in Mary Ward's efforts to train women to aid the mission. She conceived the women's work as a complement to the work of male missionaries to save souls and work for her country's reconversion. In the early seventeenth century, the need for more workers in the mission field was obvious. The need for the Catholic Church to bend its rules in this emergency situation was already being felt, particularly among clergy struggling to meet the pastoral needs of Catholic believers (McClain 2004, 55–139; 2007, 77–96; 2013, 90–124). Ward envisioned the papacy approving her innovative Catholic female organization to help meet these pressing needs. Her Institute of English Ladies, modeled upon Loyola's Society of Jesus, would work undercover to help meet the spiritual necessities of Catholics worshipping clandestinely within Protestant England.

Reports concerning Ward's Institute written by both Catholics and Protestants indicate that the English Ladies were having some measure of success on the mission. Institute numbers grew. Forty women had joined by 1612. By 1616, Institute houses were opening across Europe. By 1628, the Institute would span from Liège to Naples to Prague and number approximately 200 members (Rapley 1990, 28; Wetter 2006, 162n2).

Gendered attitudes about women actually facilitated the English Ladies' work on the mission and allowed them to reach groups—such as the poor—who historians often describe as underserved by the mission. For over two decades, Ward and her English Ladies eluded discovery and punishment more easily than male missionaries. They taught, served, performed charitable acts, and prepared laypeople for reconciliation and the sacraments. They got away with it so often because ingrained gendered stereotypes about women did not allow the authorities to comprehend what Catholic women working in this capacity would look like or do (Walker 2000, 1–23; 2004, 228–42; Bowden 2010, 297–314; Bowden and Kelly 2013). Authorities searched either for "galloping girls" (a pejorative term describing flighty, uncontrolled women who shunned many gender expectations) or nuns. Ward's English Ladies were neither. The authorities could not find what they were looking for, thus allowing Ward's English Ladies to work relatively undetected in England for almost 20 years (McClain 2015, 447–48).

Following their papally-supported return to England in 1639, Ward and her colleagues established themselves in London. They continued to live together chastely and modestly, thinking of themselves as a family with Ward as their head. They educated Catholic girls and performed charitable acts. In many ways, their efforts on behalf of Catholics after the suppression look quite similar to their earlier Institute work. In 1642, after the outbreak of the Civil War, Ward and many of her companions journeyed northward and established another household of chaste, modest women near York. The war came to their doorstep when Parliamentary and Royalist armies struggled through the Siege of York in 1644. Ward fell ill and died shortly thereafter in January 1645. Her work, however, continued. Decades after her death, English Catholic women revived a form of Ward's Institute that would spread across continents by the nineteenth century, a legacy which will be discussed in the final chapter (Wallace 2011, 134).[4]

BROKE CATHOLIC MEN AND THE NEW NORMAL

After Ward's death, the very real needs of Catholics in the British Isles continued in an era of uncertainty lasting through the eighteenth century. Protestants might turn a blind eye to the Mass they knew their neighbor hosted next door behind locks and shutters; or they might not. It remained illegal to be a priest in the British Isles. The penal laws remained on the books, and the authorities enforced them in some years but not in others. Restrictions on Catholics' education and livelihoods increased. Depending on where and when one lived, Catholics might face disarmament, disenfranchisement, fines, and limitation on land ownership and inheritance. In addition, the stigma of treason was difficult to dispel. Catholic hopes rose and fell with political developments.

In this environment, women such as Ward were not the only ones struggling to reconcile the demands of both their faith and their gender. Men, too, have a gender. Catholic men restricted by the penal laws often found it difficult to fulfill the traditional duties expected of them *as men*.

William Blundell (1620–1698) referred to such challenges when he took up his pen and opened his notebook in the mid-1640s, just as Mary Ward's life neared its close. Blundell was an impoverished rural gentleman trying to support his large Catholic family in Little Crosby in Lancashire. Married at the age of 15 to Ann Haggerston, William eventually fathered 14 children, 10 of whom survived infancy. Commissioned as a captain of dragoons when he was 22, Blundell was permanently disabled in 1642 during his first battle fighting for Charles I under the Royalist banner in the English Civil War. A musket shot to the thigh shattered his femur and allegedly shortened one of his legs by three inches, requiring him to wear a special high-heeled shoe for the remainder of his life. He spent the next five decades at home, in jail, or in exile. Throughout this time, he collected his correspondence, receipts, and personal musings into a private notebook or commonplace book (Blundell 1933, 4–16, 31, 37; Baker 2010).

Blundell's story takes us forward from Ward's death and the Civil War years to the end of the seventeenth century and introduces the idea of an evolution in gender and religious roles for Catholic men that occurred in tandem with debates and adjustments regarding Catholic women's roles. Blundell's revelations highlight the tensions many men experienced as they struggled to remain good Catholics while providing for their families. Their challenge was that it was almost impossible to do both. Between the penal and recusancy laws, as well as occasional extra taxes, fines, and sequestrations of Catholic property, many Catholic men such as Blundell were broke. For example, the government fined Blundell heavily for his recusancy and sequestered his property when he could not pay. He became financially dependent, forced to borrow money from women—his two sisters—and from Protestant men to keep his family financially afloat. He was often in jail or forced into hiding. In the midst of these losses and absences, Ann, his wife, provided the family's main financial support. She petitioned and was granted legal rights to one-fifth of the Blundell property to maintain their family. Even after William was able to repurchase his land from the government, he was perpetually in debt (Blundell 1933, 31–32, 40). Was William or any other Catholic man truly still head of his household if he was restricted from providing for his family—one of the primary responsibilities of masculine headship?

Despite such handicaps, Catholic men in the British Isles continued to work and hope for better times, hopes that would remain largely unfulfilled until the later eighteenth century. The coronation of Charles II in 1660, for example, raised Catholic hopes for toleration including William Blundell's. This event is known as the Restoration because it restored the Stuart monarchy following the beheading of the last king, Charles I, and the Interregnum. Blundell joined Charles II's entourage on its triumphant return from exile, and his notes from this period exude an ebullient optimism that Charles would ease the plight of Catholics (Blundell 1933, 92–93). Indeed, Charles II tried to persuade Parliament toward greater leniency (Mullett 1998, 76). His Protestant opposition generally triumphed, however, passing legislation such as the Test Act of 1673, which effectively barred Catholics from many social or economic opportunities, such as the holding of public office and military service. In 1677, Blundell wrote his Protestant cousin, Sir Roger Bradshaigh, a Member of Parliament, pleading with him not to vote to levy special taxes upon Catholics. All Catholics, as good subjects, Blundell wrote, would cheerfully pay their general taxes in support of the Crown; and if a foreign power, including Rome, attacked on any pretense, Catholics could be counted upon "to pay, to pray, and to fight" for the defense of the realm (Blundell 1933, 184–85). Blundell insisted that Catholics were good men to be counted among all other good men. The government did not listen.

When Charles II's successor, his brother, James, Duke of York, revealed he was Catholic, many Protestants conditioned to believe in a Catholic threat panicked, and the pressures on Catholic men increased. Protestants believed the lies of Titus Oates, who in 1678 claimed to have evidence that Catholics were again plotting to overthrow the Protestant monarchy and rebel against their Protestant neighbors, just as they had tried to do under Elizabeth I and James I. Before Oates's poor character and the flimsy nature of his evidence were exposed, the government tried and executed over two dozen Catholics as traitors (Greaves 1992). These were the last English and Irish Catholic martyrs made during the penal times.

A Man and His Sword

Anti-Catholic hysteria over this "Popish Plot" increased persecution of Catholics in many urban and rural areas, including Blundell's Lancashire. In 1679, the government seized Blundell's sword and required him to put up a bond for his good behavior. To say that he resented it would be an understatement. His sword was clearly more than a mere weapon in his eyes. It symbolized his ability to protect his family and his status as a free man. He wrote to a friend, John North, a Catholic bookseller in Dublin, describing his sword as his "trusty" longtime companion that had been with him when he had sacrificed the use of "his limbs, his lands, and his liberty," doing a man's duty serving his king in the Civil War. Now this new king's men were stripping him of his sword, "yet I hear no personal charge against me, nor do I fear any at all except purely on the account of the religion I have always professed" (Blundell 1933, 203). Six months later, he was still ranting about his sword in another letter to Ireland, to his son-in-law, Richard Butler. "I know no reason at all, besides the Will of my Superiors, why I should be compelled" to post bond and give up this sword. He had done everything the government had asked of him:

> It was in the noblest cause imaginable that I lost the use of my limbs. I was in my younger days 4 times made a prisoner for my Loyalty. I paid my ransom twice. I was then no less than 10 years sequestered. After I had been plundered of all and when I was compelled to purchase my own lands with the money which I took upon interest: when this was done, I paid ... a tenth part of my revenues. (204)

So much had been taken from him—basically beggaring his family—all to prove he was an obedient subject. And how had his loyalty been repaid? The government had now stripped him of his means to defend his family after denying him the means to provide for them. How dare they take his sword after all he had sacrificed and done to prove himself loyal. He prayed to carry this cross with patience (204).

Catholic hopes rose again during the brief reign of James II from 1685–1688. After withstanding attempts to block his succession, James gained the crown after his brother's death. James worshipped openly as a

Catholic and pursued a measure of toleration for Catholics while publicly vowing to uphold England's constitution and the Protestant state churches of England, Ireland, and Scotland. He suspended the enforcement of the penal laws and used his royal prerogative to dispense with the Test Act, allowing Catholics to serve openly in public office as well as in the army. In 1687, he issued a Declaration of Indulgence granting freedom of worship to Catholic and Protestant dissenters. Catholic optimism soared! Exiled Catholics returned from abroad, and the Catholic religious orders conspicuously opened chapels and schools. Blundell mentioned his satisfaction in being able to use the court system and carry his sword again. He was a full man before the law once more (243–44, 246).

Catholic jubilation proved short-lived after such a visible Catholic presence frightened many Protestants, who continued to distrust Catholics and Catholicism. Although James's efforts at greater religious toleration were ad hoc measures and not actual repeals of the penal laws, Protestants feared what James might do if given sufficient time and opportunity. This unease grew with the birth of an heir, James Francis Edward, in 1688. Protestants realized their Catholic king could be succeeded by another Catholic king and that either monarch might return the realm to Rome's authority. This simply would not do.

James II's brief reign and the open Catholic presence he tolerated ended with his forced abdication in 1688 in favor of his Protestant daughter, Mary, and her husband, William of Orange. A group of Protestant leaders invited William to invade England an exact century after Protestants had opposed Spanish King Philip II's attempts to invade England with the Spanish Armada. James's government collapsed, and he fled to the continent with his family in a virtually bloodless coup known as the Glorious Revolution. William III and Mary II ruled jointly and, in 1689, Parliament passed the Toleration Act, extending a limited religious tolerance to all Protestant faiths that embraced the doctrine of the Trinity. Catholics, however, were conspicuously excluded from this tolerance (Kaplan 2007, 243–46).

Restrictions on Catholics grew in the immediate aftermath of the Glorious Revolution. William and Mary's government limited their ability to carry arms, inherit and buy land, and practice law. These were limitations that disproportionately impacted men. When the Protestant government confiscated arms and horses from Catholics in 1692 and 1694, Blundell chafed over the indignity. They took his sword again! Although he was now a sickly man above 70 years of age, his government still feared him as a potential traitor. He was even named as a conspirator in a fictitious Jacobite plot to restore James to the throne, an accusation quickly proven to be without substance (Blundell 1933, 269–74).

The Protestant Ascendency

Catholics in Ireland such as the Butlers—the family of Blundell's daughter and son-in-law—were particularly hard hit by new political and economic restrictions. In contrast to the Scots who had embraced Protestantism *before* their union with the English monarchy, many Irish despised Protestantism as a foreign import of the English crown. Quarrels over religion exacerbated pre-existing linguistic, cultural, and political discord. Loyalty to Catholicism became linked to one's loyalty to Ireland, a form of opposition to English dominance. In the first decades of the Reformation, particularly during Elizabeth I's reign, English reformers worried about alienating the tenuous loyalties of nominally English families who had resided in Ireland for centuries, known as the Old English. Leaders often exercised religious authority in Ireland hesitantly or irregularly. The same cannot be said of their secular authority. Successive English governments in the sixteenth and seventeenth centuries deprived Catholics in Ireland of their land and bestowed it on incoming English adventurers and colonists. This was true for lands belonging to Gaelic Irish, also known as the Old Irish, as well as the Old English. Although James II might have been expected to champion his co-religionists' claims against such injustices during his reign, he did not. He may have been Catholic, but he was first and foremost King of England, and he protected English interests in Ireland.

Ireland's Catholics rebelled in 1641, helping precipitate the outbreak of the English Civil War, and they did so again after the Glorious Revolution in support of James II against William and Mary in what is known as the Williamite War. The deposed James finally pledged to emancipate Ireland's Catholics and restore Irish lands to their original owners when he needed Catholic support to reclaim his crown. From 1688 to 1691, Ireland's Catholics fought for James. They lost.

If it was difficult for a Catholic man such as Blundell to maintain his family in England, it was even more difficult for most Catholic men in Ireland to do so. Blundell's son-in-law, Richard Butler, suffered heavy fines, confiscation of lands, and periods of imprisonment from the Titus Oates Plot in 1678 through the Williamite War. His wealth was greatly reduced.

His son, Edmund Butler—William and Ann Blundell's grandson—provided new perspective on such material loss and its relationship to manhood. Edmund languished in jail after being captured while leading an assault on Londonderry in 1689 as part of the Williamite War. As an eldest son, he could expect to inherit the bulk of his father's possessions and status, yet he understood how the penal laws had impoverished his family. He accepted that he was not going to inherit much in the way of material wealth. As Edmund wrote to his grandfather in July 1694, jail was unpleasant, as one would expect, but "when I consider that imprisonment may in a manner be termed my inheritance, my father, my grandfather, and almost all my ancestors having undergone it for my Master's [i.e., God's] sake, I think I have no reason to repine at my lot." It was better than having conformed to Protestantism out of cowardice or base desires (Blundell 1933, 259–60). He replaced the worldly legacy he would have inherited had his family not been Catholics with the spiritual wealth gained by witnessing for the Catholic faith. He restored his masculine honor and family pride by enduring, even embracing, persecution.

The Irish eventually made peace with William and Mary, who promised increased toleration for Catholics in the Treaty of Limerick, but any clemency proved short-lived. Between 1695 and 1727, Protestant landowners in Ireland pressed for both the English and Irish Parliaments to pass a series of harsh laws—known as the Penal Code—against Irish Catholics. The new Penal Code went further than existing laws, prohibiting Irish Catholics from voting, holding office, receiving a university education, practicing law, and wearing swords. The laws also restricted land purchases and inheritance rights. In sum, Catholics may have been the religious majority in Ireland, but they were effectively subjugated economically, politically, and socially by the Protestant government in what is known as the Protestant Ascendency.

A New Dynasty and a New Struggle for Catholic Emancipation

The eighteenth century, which saw a transition from the Stuart to the Hanoverian monarchy after the death of Anne (r. 1702–14), thus began a time of great change for Catholics throughout the British Isles. The specifics will be explored in greater detail in subsequent chapters; for now, it is sufficient to note that by approximately 1750, most Catholics in England, Wales, Ireland, and Scotland sought accommodation with the Protestant monarchy and their state churches, striving to appear as unthreatening as possible while carving out social and economic spaces for themselves (Mullett 1998, 159–96). In contrast to seventeenth-century fears, the majority of Protestants now tended to accept Catholic claims of political patriotism. Despite a politically active Catholic community in exile and brief, unsuccessful rebellions in 1715 and 1745 designed to place the Catholic Stuarts back on the throne, the Protestant Hanover monarchs George I (r. 1714–27) and George II (r. 1727–60) acknowledged the loyalties of the vast majority of Catholics within the realm and avoided blanket national persecutions (Glickman 2009, 54). Overt anti-Catholic sentiment and enforcement of the penal laws gradually declined. As long as Catholic practices were invisible to the public eye, they were tolerated. As a 1776 Protestant report out of Dundee, Scotland, explained, there was "a congregation of papists or those of the Church of Rome who have a priest … but keep not open door, these having no tolleration, though they are winked at" (Mullett 1998, 178–80; also Kaplan 2007, 8, 142–43, 195–97).

However, while Catholic numbers grew and the sacraments became more readily available in many areas, these were still uncertain times. The penal laws were still on the books, and there were limits to Protestant toleration. Just because Catholics generally lived in peace with their neighbors now did not mean that they could count on doing so in the future. Enforcement of the penal laws had always been sporadic, so there was always an underlying fear that any new crisis might spur new persecutions (Williams 1960, 263; Mullett 1998, 136–37; Kaplan 2007, 96–98, 355). In light of their continuing vulnerability, some Catholics laid low, hoping to remain invisible to public scrutiny. Other Catholics, however, refused to isolate themselves from public affairs. Through a variety of pamphlets, novels, histories, and treatises, these Catholics placed their illegal faith directly in the public eye to debate and demonstrate Catholics' political loyalties and sense of national identity (Glickman 2009, 6–18, 53–86, 122–57, 222–57).

By the end of the eighteenth century, during the reign of George III (r. 1760–1820), Catholics fought to repeal prejudicial laws once and for all. Between 1778 and 1791, prominent Catholics formed a Catholic Committee to advocate for emancipation. They initially supported a limited lifting of restrictions on Catholics with the first Catholic Relief Act in 1778. The government granted some of their requests, in part to allow Catholics into the army to fight for the crown against colonial rebels in the Americas. Such tolerance, however, provoked anti-Catholic rioting, first in

Edinburgh in 1779 and then in London in 1780, known as the Gordon Riots, incited by the propaganda of Lord George Gordon, President of the Protestant Association of London. A second Catholic Relief Act of 1791 repealed restrictions and penalties more extensively, extending to Catholics the liberties given to all other Nonconformists a hundred years earlier through William and Mary's 1689 Act of Toleration (18 George III, c. 60; 31 George III, c. 32; Kaplan 2007, 352–53). In 1800, the Scots Catholic Alexander Geddes believed that Catholics throughout the British Isles had engaged in over 200 years of their own "secret reformation," purging themselves of the worst dogmas and dangerous loyalties and beliefs that had so aroused Protestant fears (Geddes 1800, 217–18). Only later in the nineteenth century with the Roman Catholic Relief Act of 1829, however, did the British government commit to removing more fully the anti-Catholic stigma that had become acculturated in the British Isles over almost three centuries since Henry VIII's break with Rome.

By this time, Mary Ward had been in her grave 164 years and William Blundell, 131 years. Much had changed. Protestantism had spawned new faiths in the British Isles, such as John Wesley's Methodism. The Jesuit order had been suppressed (1773) and reinstated (1815) by the papacy. Some British subjects, such as the Deists, rejected institutionalized Christianity, while others rejected religion and God altogether. England, Ireland, Scotland, and Wales were now united as Great Britain. The Tudors gave way to the Stuarts who, in turn, passed the crown to the Hanovers. The English Civil War, Glorious Revolution, French Revolution, and many other domestic rebellions, colonial revolts, and foreign wars had threatened the monarchy and its interests. Industrialization and related economic and socio-demographic changes unsettled many individuals and communities.

In spite of such profound change, many of the Catholic Church's needs remained similar to those during Ward's and Blundell's lifetimes. Catholicism remained illegal, and the penal laws remained on the books throughout this time. Catholics still faced political, economic, and social disadvantages for recusancy. Although some Protestants winked at Catholic worship conducted behind closed doors, others did not. Catholics never knew when what had been tolerated informally would no longer be found acceptable; and while some Catholics—particularly those in urban areas of England and Ireland—could attend an occasional Mass and find a priest for confession, baptism, or burial, other Catholics could not. Priests still faced imprisonment and exile in many areas of the British Isles.

Although the details of the crisis fluctuated through decades and centuries, the need for someone or something to relieve Catholics did not evaporate until the early nineteenth century.

Throughout this time, dominant gender roles throughout society changed little, despite occasional challenges (Mendelson and Crawford 1998, 201). During the instability of the Civil War and Glorious Revolution, for example, some women carved out public roles by writing, publishing, petitioning, and rioting. Predictably, most opportunities dried up soon after the conflicts ended (Hughes 2012; McDowell 1998; Wiseman 2006; Gillespie 2004). Even following the widespread economic, political, and social transformations of the eighteenth century, divine law, natural law, and common law continued to circumscribe women's submission to male authority. The law of coverture still subsumed women under the legal identities of their fathers or husbands. Women were still not held fully responsible for their behaviors and were still punished more lightly under the law than men. The arguments and evidence used to justify women's subordination often changed, but the conclusions about the need for women's obedience remained. This was true for women across social ranks (Tague 2002, 7, 18–48, 219). Similarly, while economic, social, and political upheavals limited many men's opportunities to get ahead, groups of men such as laborers, university students, and highwaymen experimented with alternative ways a man might establish a masculine reputation. Such men attempted to assert new types of manhood, but they never displaced or superseded traditional masculine values and patriarchy (Cohen 1996; Shepard 2003; Mackie 2009).

Admittedly, this amalgamation of Catholic histories of such diverse areas into one larger narrative is somewhat misleading, yet it is necessary and enlightening. England, Ireland, Scotland, and Wales—considered collectively here as the British Isles—boast separate histories, identities, cultures, and languages. Religious and political balances varied over time and within each kingdom and region. The papacy certainly devoted a disproportionate amount of its efforts to reclaiming England and Ireland in comparison to the interest it showed in Scotland and Wales. The robust opportunities to practice Catholicism in Western Ireland in the 1590s would likely have been envied by Catholics in Edinburgh, while Catholics in northern Wales or the Scottish Highlands would probably not have traded places with Catholics near London at the time of anti-Catholic persecutions during the Popish Plot in the late 1670s or the Gordon Riots in 1780 (Mullett 1998, 51–55, 65–67; Glickman 2009, 158–90).

Despite such differences, these regions were joined by the shared pressures of centuries of Catholic-Protestant conflict in the Reformation era. Catholics throughout the British Isles lived under similar laws. They faced similar prejudices, persecutions, and uncertainties. They shared similar goals and often worked together across political boundaries to revive and sustain the Catholic faith and a Catholic presence throughout the British archipelago. They lost the public, institutional presence, property, and wealth of their faith. They had to fight to justify their religious beliefs and practices and their political loyalties. They had to prove their path to salvation was the right one, whereas once it had been presumed to be the only one.

Moreover, inhabitants of the British Isles, no matter their nationality or faith, shared similar beliefs about gender. Although they might disagree about many things, a Scots Calvinist like John Knox and an English Catholic like Archpriest William Harrison could agree that both divine and natural laws created women as subordinate to men and prohibited women from leading in matters of religion. Neither a typical Welsh goodwife nor an Irish fishmonger would have challenged a husband's right to lead in all matters, especially religion, within his own home or questioned a wife's obligation to submit to his headship.

Although such parallels are represented herein with sensitivity to historical differences, England has primacy of place as the driving force behind the religious events and changes occurring throughout the Isles. Wales had been annexed and united to England since 1284, but Henry VIII (himself of Welsh origin) incorporated Wales formally under the English crown by 1542. He also elevated Ireland from a Lordship to a Kingdom in 1542, declaring himself king. Approximately 60 years later, in 1603, James VI of Scotland inherited the English crown after the death of his cousin, Elizabeth I. He united the hereditary crowns of England and Scotland and ruled from England as James I. Decisions made by the Protestant crown and Parliament at Westminster thus precipitated many of the choices made in Edinburgh and Dublin as well as in the countryside of Wales, Ireland, and Scotland (Armitage 2000; Bradshaw and Roberts 2003).

BACK TO THE PUZZLE

This brief, yet necessary, odyssey through the history of the British Isles now comes to a close. We can now return to the stories that are the heart of this book, more comfortable in the context in which such lives were lived—all of which, of course, brings us back to the original conundrum introduced in the last chapter. As this condensed history reveals, the Roman Church had a great desire to reclaim or at least sustain Catholicism in the British Isles. If Ward's Institute of English Ladies was reasonably successful in its efforts on the mission and if the Roman Catholic Church was willing to go to great lengths and bend its own rules to maintain Catholicism in the British Isles, why did Urban VIII suppress Ward's Institute? A need was clearly there, and the women appeared to be filling it. In addition, even more surprisingly, after having "extinguished," perpetually abolished, and every other synonym for destruction he could think of to "remove [the Institute] entirely from the Church of God" (Wetter 2006, 213–18), why did he facilitate Ward's return to England less than a decade later, asking his most influential associates—a queen, a papal envoy, a count—to assist her and her companions?

To answer this question, we must take a closer look at both women's and men's gender roles, their relationships with one another, and their various attempts to remain good Catholics despite the many pressures to conform to Protestantism. And what of the Church's role in this? As the Catholic Church struggled to adjust to "the new normal"—its position as an illegal, underground church—to what extent would Catholic priests and Church leaders support changes to gender and religious roles in the British Isles? Piece by piece, chapter by chapter, we will add the stories necessary to solve the puzzle of the harsher-than-normal suppression of Mary Ward's Institute. In the process of examining these three centuries of gender and religious change, we will also have built a foundation upon which to answer the bigger issues raised about gender and religious authority up through the present age. Who exercises religious authority, what legitimates it, and who submits to it and how? The answers may surprise you. We'll begin with the women …

Notes

1. The quality of histories of Ward varies between enthusiastic hagiographical accounts and rigorous scholarship wherein authors interpret critically the primary sources written by Ward and her supporters that were clearly biased in her favor. The full texts, many of them translated, of primary documents by and relating to Ward contained within Chambers (1882) are authoritative and invaluable. Only recently has a full body of documentation relative to Ward and her Institute become easily accessible to scholars, most notably

in Dirmeier (2007), some of which duplicates texts provided by Chambers. Both resources are used throughout this book. Other important materials include the *English Vita*, or the *Briefe Relation*, a biography written shortly after Ward's death, most likely by Winifred Wigmore and/or Mary Poyntz, two of Ward's closest companions; an *Italian Vita*, possibly also by Poyntz or Elizabeth Cotton at a later date from Rome; and Ward's incomplete *Italian Autobiography*. I will be using Kenworthy-Browne's reprint and edited versions (2008). A biography/autobiography of 50 painted images known as *The Painted Life* is extant and displayed at www.congregatiojesu.org/en/maryward_painted_life.asp and the Convent of the Congregation of Jesus in Augsburg, Germany. Letters and other documents have been preserved in archives of the Congregation of Jesus at the Bar Convent, York; Munich; Nymphenburg; and Bamburg. Vatican archival material reflecting the Roman Church's attitudes toward Ward and the Institute became available with the opening of Inquisition archives in 1998.
2. Irish recusants were subject to the same penalties as English recusants (Burton et al. 1911).
3. A Jesuit Irish mission was officially begun in 1598 and lasted until the suppression of the Society of Jesus in 1773. Ireland was not raised to provincial status until 1860, after the re-establishment of the order.
4. By 1900, approximately 6000 followers were educating 70,000 girls in 200 schools worldwide without credit to Ward. Leo XIII's Constitution *Conditae* of 1900 and subsequent Regulations of Canon Law in 1901 finally made it possible for women to live as religious under simple vows, paving the way for more diverse forms of religious life for women.

WORKS CITED

Armitage, David. 2000. *The Ideological Origins of the British Empire*. Cambridge: Cambridge University Press.

Baker, Geoff. 2010. *Reading and Politics in Early Modern England: The Mental World of a Seventeenth-Century Catholic Gentleman*. Manchester: Manchester University Press.

Blundell, William. 1933. *Cavalier: Letters of William Blundell to his Friends 1620–1698*. Edited by Margaret Blundell. London: Longmans, Green and Co.

Bowden, Caroline. 2010. "The English Convents in Exile and Questions of National Identity c. 1600–1688." In *British and Irish Emigrants and Exiles in Europe, 1603–1688*, edited by David Worthington, 297–314. Leiden: Brill.

Bowden, Caroline and James E. Kelly, eds. 2013. *The English Convents in Exile, 1600–1800: Communities, Culture and Identity*. Burlington, VT: Ashgate.

Bradshaw, Brendan and Peter Roberts, eds. 2003. *British Consciousness and Identity: The Making of Britain, 1533–1707*. Cambridge: Cambridge University Press.

Bridgett, T.E. 1899. *Our Lady's Dowry: How England Gained that Title.* London: Burns & Oates Ltd.
Burton, Edwin, D'Alton, Edward, and Kelley, Jarvis. 1911. "Penal Laws III: Ireland." In *Catholic Encyclopedia.* New York: Robert Appleton Company.
CSP Dom (Calendar of State Papers, Domestic Series) of the Reign of Elizabeth I. 1863–1950. Public Record Office, series 2. London.
Chambers, M.C.E. 1882. *The Life of Mary Ward (1585–1645).* 2 vols. Edited by Henry James Coleridge. London: Burns & Oates.
Cohen, Miche'le. 1996. *Fashioning Masculinity: National Identity and Language in the Eighteenth Century.* London: Routledge.
Dawson, J.E.A. 2007. *Scotland Re-Formed, 1488–1587.* Edinburgh: Edinburgh University Press.
Dirmeier, Ursula, ed. 2007. *Mary Ward und ihre Gründung: Die Quellentexte bis 1645.* 4 vols. Corpus Catholicorum 45–8. Münster: Aschendorff Verlag.
Fitzsimon, Henry. 1881. *Words of Comfort to Persecuted Catholics. Written in Exile, Anno 1607. Letters from a Cell in Dublin Castle, and Diary of the Bohemian War of 1620.* Edited by Edmund Hogan. Dublin: M.H. Gill & Son.
Geddes, Alexander. 1800. *A Modest Apology for the Roman Catholics.* London: Davis, Taylor and Wilks.
Gillespie, Katharine. 2004. *Domesticity and Dissent in the Seventeenth Century.* Cambridge: Cambridge University Press.
Glickman, Gabriel. 2009. *The English Catholic Community 1688–1745: Politics, Culture and Ideology.* Studies in Early Modern Cultural, Political, and Social History. Woodbridge, Suffolk: The Boydell Press.
Greaves, Richard L. 1992. *Secrets of the Kingdom: British Radicals from the Popish Plot to the Revolution of 1688–1689.* Stanford: Stanford University Press.
Heal, Felicity. 2003. *Reformation in Britain and Ireland.* Oxford: Oxford University Press.
Hughes, Ann. 2012. *Gender and the English Revolution.* London: Routledge.
Kaplan, Benjamin J. 2007. *Divided by Faith: Religious Conflict and the Practice of Toleration in Early Modern Europe.* Cambridge, MA: Belknap Press for Harvard University Press.
Kenworthy-Browne, Christina, ed. 2008. *Mary Ward 1585–1648: A Briefe Relation with Autobiographical Fragments and a Selection of Letters.* Rochester, NY: Boydell and Brewer for the Catholic Record Society.
Kooi, Christine. 1995. "Popish Impudence: The Perseverance of the Roman Catholic Faithful in Calvinist Holland, 1572–1620." *Sixteenth Century Journal* 26, no. 1: 75–85.
———. 2012. *Calvinists and Catholics During Holland's Golden Age: Heretics and Idolaters.* New York: Cambridge University Press.

Lockey, Brian C. 2015. *Early Modern Catholics, Royalists, and Cosmopolitans: English Transnationalism and the Christian Commonwealth.* Transculturalisms, 1400–1700. Burlington, VT: Ashgate.

Lux-Sterritt, Laurence. 2006. "Mary Ward's English Institute: The Apostolate as Self-Affirmation?" *Recusant History* 28, no. 2: 192–208.

Mackie, Erin. 2009. *Rakes, Highwaymen and Pirates: The Making of the Modern Gentleman in the Eighteenth Century.* Baltimore: The Johns Hopkins University Press.

Makowski, Elizabeth. 1999. *Canon Law and Cloistered Women: Periculoso and Its Commentators, 1298–1545.* Washington, D.C.: Catholic University of America.

McClain, Lisa. 2004. *Lest We Be Damned: Practical Innovation and Lived Experience among Catholics in Protestant England, 1559–1642.* New York: Routledge.

———. 2007. "'They Have Taken Away My Lord:' Mary Magdalene, Christ's Missing Body, and the Mass in Reformation England." *The Sixteenth Century Journal* 38, no. 1: 77–96.

———. 2013. "Troubled Consciences: New Understandings and Performances of Penance among Catholics in Protestant England." *Church History* 82, no. 1: 90–124.

———. 2015. "On a Mission: Priests, Jesuits, and 'Jesuitresses' and English Catholic Missionary Efforts in Tudor-Stuart England." *The Catholic Historical Review* 101, no. 3: 437–62.

McCoog, Thomas M. 1994. *English and Welsh Jesuits, 1555–1650, Part 1: A-F.* Records Series. Southampton: Catholic Record Society, LXXIV.

McDowell, Paula. 1998. *The Women of Grub Street: Press, Politics and Gender in the London Literary Marketplace 1678–1730.* Oxford: Clarendon Press.

Mendelson, Sara and Patricia Crawford. 1998. *Women in Early Modern England, 1550–1720.* Oxford: Clarendon Press.

Merrick, M.M. 1947. *James Duckett: A Study of His Life and Times.* London: Douglas, Organ.

Mother Mary Margaret. 1955. *The Wedge of Gold: The Life of Mary Ward (1585–1665* [note: Ward died in 1645]) *Foundress of the Institute of the Blessed Virgin Mary.* York: Herald Printing Works.

Mullett, Michael. 1998. *Catholics in Britain and Ireland, 1558–1829.* New York: St. Martin's Press.

Murray, James. 2009. *Enforcing the Reformation in Ireland: Clerical Resistance and Political Conflict in the Diocese of Dublin, 1534–1590.* Cambridge: Cambridge University Press.

Mush, John. 1849. *The Life and Death of Margaret Clitherow, the Martyr of York, now First Published from the Original Manuscript.* Edited by William Nicholson. London: Richardson & Son.

Peters, Henriette. 1994. *Mary Ward: A World in Contemplation*. Translated by Helen Butterworth. Leominster: Gracewing.

Petti, Anthony G., ed. 1968. *Recusant Documents from the Ellesmere Manuscripts*. Records Series. St. Albans: Fisher Knight for the Catholic Record Society, LX.

Rapley, Elizabeth. 1990. *The Dévotes: Women and Church in Seventeenth-Century France*. Kingston, Ontario: McGill/Queen's University Press.

Shepard, Alexandra. 2003. *Meanings of Manhood in Early Modern England*. Oxford: Oxford University Press.

Simmonds, Gemma. 2008. "Women Jesuits?" In *The Cambridge Companion to the Jesuits*, edited by Thomas Worcester, 120–35. Cambridge: Cambridge University Press.

SP Dom (State Papers, Domestic Series). Public Record Office, Kew.

Stone, J.M. 1892. *Faithful unto Death: An Account of the Sufferings of the English Franciscans during the 16th and 17th Centuries, From Contemporary Records*. London: Kegan Paul, Trench, Trübner & Co.

T. E. 1632. *The Lawes Resolutions of Women's Rights: Or, the Lawes Provision for Women*. London: John Grove.

Tague, Ingrid H. 2002. *Women of Quality: Accepting and Contesting Ideals of Femininity in England, 1690–1760*. Woodbridge, Suffolk: Boydell Press.

Tierney, M.A. 1839–1843. *Dodd's Church History of England from the Commencement of the Sixteenth Century to the Revolution in 1688*. 5 vols. London: Charles Dolman.

Walker, Clare. 2000. "Prayer, Patronage, and Political Conspiracy: English Nuns and the Restoration." *The Historical Journal* 43, no. 1: 1–23.

———. 2004. "Loyal and Dutiful Subjects: English Nuns and Stuart Politics." In *Women and Politics in Early Modern England, 1450–1700*, edited by James Daybell, 228–42. Burlington, VT: Ashgate.

Wallace, David. 2011. *Strong Women: Life, Text and Territory 1347–1645*. The Clarendon Lectures in English 2007. Oxford: Oxford University Press.

Walsham, Alexandra. 2014. *Catholic Reformation in Protestant Britain*. Burlington, VT: Ashgate.

Waterworth, J. trans. and ed. 1848. *The Canons and Decrees of the Sacred and Oecumenical Council of Trent*. London: Dolman.

Wetter, M. Immolata. 2006. *Mary Ward: Under the Shadow of the Inquisition*. Translated by M. Bernadette Ganne and M. Patricia Harriss. Introduction by Gregory Kirkus. Oxford: Way Books.

Williams, J.A. 1960. "Benedictine Missions in Wiltshire in the Seventeenth and Eighteenth Centuries." *Downside Review* 78: 263–73.

Wiseman, Susan. 2006. *Conspiracy and Virtue: Women, Writing and Politics in Seventeenth Century England*. Oxford: Oxford University Press.

CHAPTER 3

Disobedient Women

Catherine Holland was a liar, and she was proud of it. In this woman's autobiographical account of her conversion to Catholicism, she described her years of living a double life, bragging about how well she deceived everyone. She hid contraband items in her room. She read banned books. She snuck away from the house to meet lawbreakers. When she feared she was close to being caught, she covered her tracks. Eventually she ran away to begin a new life of her own choosing (Holland 1925). Catherine Holland was willful, deceptive, and defiant and showed no small measure of satisfaction in being so. She was a disobedient woman.

Like Mary Ward, Holland was a Catholic woman pushing the boundaries of proper gender and religious behavior in her era. Yet unlike Ward and the English Ladies, most Catholics lauded Holland's behavior. Holland may have been a disobedient woman, but she was a good Catholic. She rejected Protestantism and eventually became a nun. The Catholic Church held up women such as Holland as heroic exemplars for the faith. Behavior that Catholics never would have condoned from women in a Catholic country could become a source of pride for those living in a Protestant one. By exploring a variety of such confrontations between gender and religious authority in this and subsequent chapters, we can begin to identify patterns in how ordinary Catholic women and men pushed against

© The Author(s) 2018
L. McClain, *Divided Loyalties? Pushing the Boundaries of Gender and Lay Roles in the Catholic Church, 1534-1829*, Histories of the Sacred and Secular, 1700-2000, https://doi.org/10.1007/978-3-319-73087-5_3

traditional definitions of proper male, female, and Catholic behavior. And as the Catholic Church struggled to maintain its presence, doctrines, and authority in the British Isles, we see where the Church would draw its line in the sand.

For almost 300 years, Catholic women from the British Isles such as Ward and Holland struggled to be both good women and good Catholics, walking a tightrope strung between the contradictory dictates of their gender roles and the Catholic faith. The first prescribed obedience, humility, modesty, and subservience to male authority, while the second counseled resistance and disobedience to Protestant authority. How was it possible for a woman to be simultaneously obedient *and* disobedient? Subservient *and* rebellious? It may have seemed an impossible task. Holland, Gertrude More, and Mary Ward—the lay and religious women whose transgressive actions and ideas are explored in this chapter—were among the many Catholic women who tried to balance these opposing expectations while creating new models of Catholic womanhood.

As explained in the previous chapter, women were not simply free to create a new way of religious life or a new relationship to male authority. Prior to Protestant reforms, divine law, natural law, and English common law combined to create a set of roles and expectations for women's behavior. For example, if a woman wanted to understand how to be pleasing to God, she sought the advice of her priest. Priests counseled women not to trust in their own faulty judgment, but to rely on the Church to interpret God's will for women. Then Protestant reforms and penal laws made Catholic priests scarce, leaving Catholic women with no authorities to interpret God's will for them.

If women wanted to re-negotiate this relationship, they needed a recognized, external authority to legitimate their efforts. They found that authority in the idea of "conscience." Many Catholics in this era understood conscience not as individual preference or judgment, but as the voice of God communicated directly to the believer's heart through the Holy Spirit. To follow one's conscience was to be directed by God in how to follow God's will and law above all else (*Gaudium* 1965, #16; Lockey 2015, 291; Aquinas 1947, I–II: 109:3). To act against conscience was a sin (Persons 1754, 233–41, 283, 355–61, 423–29, 621–22). A woman who claimed that God inspired her to act in a particular way asserted that her behavior was justified by God's will. In contrast to well-known Protestant appeals to conscience, however, these Catholics did not *replace* a priest's or the Church's mediation with conscience. Instead, they utilized conscience *in addition* to traditional reliance upon the clergy, the saints, and the Catholic sacraments for salvation. It was one more tool in an already powerful arsenal. Conscience gave women the confidence to face hardships that endangered their reputations as good women or good Catholics. Strained or combative family relationships, financial struggles, conflicts with male clerics, government persecution, even execution—all became endurable with a woman's belief that she was following God's will and was thus pleasing to him. Conscience validated women's disobedience to any authority other than God.

In many cases, the Catholic Church supported and encouraged women's appeals to conscience. Rather than castigate women such as Holland for defying male authority, the Church praised their efforts to strengthen the faith in the beleaguered British Isles. In such informal, unintentional ways, women and the Church redefined women's relationship with the Church. Women's confidence in the power of conscience grew as they received the Church's validation.

As the harsh suppression of Ward's Institute shows, this redefinition of gender and religious roles was not without controversy inside the Church. When priests eventually became available, some women chose to seek guidance from both priests *and* conscience. These women had to choose which source of authority to follow if priestly advice conflicted with divine inspiration. This could cause friction between women and the Catholic clergy that had long taught women to mistrust their own judgment and that expected women's unquestioning obedience.

For women to challenge such long-standing, widely accepted patterns of authority and submission appeared to confirm society's and religion's worst fears about women's natures. Women such as Holland and Ward resembled the easily tempted, deceptive, and insubordinate caricatures lampooned in controversial pamphlets of this era that were part of a well-known debate over gender roles, commonly known as the "Fight for the Breeches." Who wore the pants—men or women?

To be clear, these women were not trying to pursue an early feminist agenda or seeking some modern sense of personal empowerment. They did not question the truth of the Catholic faith or attempt to overturn the doctrine that gave clergy authority over their salvation and souls. Instead, they used divine inspiration as revealed to them through conscience to begin rewriting their places within family, society, and the institutional structure of the Catholic Church.

Unusual circumstances offered Catholic women in the British Isles the opportunity to re-draw the boundaries of their social roles. Almost three centuries of great need compelled women and the Catholic Church to work together in non-traditional ways, gradually and unintentionally changing the expectations for women's social and religious behavior. Through the stories of Catherine Holland, Gertrude More, and Mary Ward, we begin to see the outlines of this process, as well as where the Church would place its limits on women's efforts to redefine their place in society and the Church.

The Lying Daughter

Catherine Holland was a teenager living abroad in the Catholic city of Bruges in what is today Belgium when she first snuck out of the house to explore a Catholic church. She had been born in 1637 in Norfolk into a Protestant family of privilege and authority. Because of his wealth and status, her father, John Holland, could afford to move his family out of harm's way during the Civil War and its aftermath. As a result, Catherine spent much of the 1640s and 1650s on the European continent. It was here that she was first drawn toward Catholicism. It was also here that she began to lie and defy her father's God-given authority. The Holland conflict was hardly unique. We just happen to have an excellent record of it by her own hand (Holland 1925, 271–306).

It was the early 1650s. Holland was 16 years old, and she admitted she had been fairly unconcerned with religion up until that point in her life, her parents giving her conflicting messages on the subject. John and Althea Holland had a "mixed marriage." John was fervently Protestant while Althea was Catholic. John Holland insisted that their children be raised in the Protestant faith, encouraging Catherine to imitate her mother in all things *except religion*. Although Catherine often expressed frustration with her mother's unwillingness to defy her father openly, she also recounted her mother's secretive attempts to prod her children toward a Catholic path. Althea, obedient to her husband's authority, would school her children in Protestant prayers, but later, she "would often be saying in my hearing there was but one Truth and, that out[side] of that [Truth], there was no Salvation; and would often admonish me to pray to God to bring me to that Truth" (273, 276).

Holland grew up conflicted. "Now between the suggestions of my mother and the instructions of my father, which were so contrary one to the other … I knew not which to choose, troubled I was but had nobody to speak unto." She recalled her youthful aversion to Protestant teachings, claiming it "went against my Conscience to learn [them]," although she admitted she had little understanding of what conscience was at such a young age. Unable to confess her dilemma to a Protestant cleric or seek guidance from a Catholic one, she ignored religion altogether. She was, in her own words, a vain teenage girl interested in dancing, music, games, and other diverting entertainments. She became willful, enjoying lying to her father to get her own way. Yet at the same time, her conscience continued to trouble her (273–76).

About this time, Holland began, as she termed it, "stealing away" to Catholic churches, Masses, and other rituals, seeking answers to her many questions. "Often did I venture to steal out to Church although I did not know what to do there; nor did I understand what was done." Catholic churches looked, sounded, smelled, and felt different from the Protestant ones she was used to visiting and "moved Devotion more than any Thing I had seen" (273–76). She was determined to figure out this new way of worship on her own, as she did not feel she could trust anyone else enough to ask for guidance or instruction.

She found answers to some of her many questions in books she bought and cached away. Eventually, she taught herself the *Ave Maria* prayer and acquired some rosary beads, which she "ty'd next me and kept very secret" to keep them hidden from the rest of her family. She would bring them out from under her clothing at night to pray "with much Satisfaction." She monitored her own speech and behaviors around her family, knowing without a doubt that she could not show any inclination toward Catholicism at home. For three years in Catholic Bruges, she vacillated between her admitted pride at navigating this unfamiliar religious path that inspired and excited her and fear over her father's wrath if he discovered her secrets and disobedience. The strain was so great that she contemplated suicide (275–77).

Prior to the Restoration, the court-in-exile of the future Charles II migrated throughout Europe. When the court eventually settled in Bruges in 1655, John Holland decided that his family would be better off in Protestant Holland. Catherine found herself in Bergen op Zoom, a town with no Catholic churches of which she was aware (Kaplan et al. 2009). Still in her late teens, living with her family, attending the sober Protestant Dutch Reformed Church, and closeted about her attraction to Catholicism, she gave up. She put aside religion and threw herself once again into worldly pleasures. "There was no Sport without me, I being the Ringleader of all the Farces and sportive Fooleries" (278).

By the time her conscience again prompted her to act, her father had brought her back to Protestant England, and Catherine was a pampered but dissatisfied young woman of almost 20 years. It was 1657, and with no Catholic churches into which she could slip, she began to "steal away" into the woods to ponder the divine and her relationship to it. "Who am I? Why am I? What is this World? Who made it? Where is God? How is he to be found and comprehended?" she asked (279). Ordinarily, clergymen and society in general discouraged laypeople, and particularly women, from contemplating such abstractions and complexities on their own. There were doctrinal truths to uphold, and laypeople were prone to error if left unguided.

But Holland was not rejecting priestly counsel; it was simply unavailable. Catholic clergy had guided Holland to a certain extent through the many Catholic books she had purchased and devoured, but this exchange could never be interactive (McClain 2004, 53–54, 249–51). Holland had to resolve any questions about meaning and interpretation for herself. She eventually trusted God to help her do so. She recalled, "One Time above all the rest I remember being in the Fields all alone deeply engaged in these pensive Thoughts. I had a great War within myself." What if, she wondered, there was no God, no soul, any of it. It was all made up, "the Invention of cunning politic Men for to keep People in Awe, and for the better Government of Nations, who must be kept in Fear with Something besides Moral Laws" (Holland 1925, 279). She allowed herself to address her myriad of doubts and ask whatever blasphemous questions might arise. In hindsight, she thought it a wonder "I did not break my brain, considering how young I was ... weak and ignorant, and nobody to give me a solution or inform me." Holland unknowingly explored a key conflict between gender and religion and the role each plays in propping up and legitimating the other within the larger system of patriarchy. This internal debate took her several years to work through to her satisfaction, and Holland admitted, "I had almost lost all Religion and turned Atheist" (280–81).

Her conscience eventually spurred her to convert to Catholicism formally after she returned to Holland in 1659 to live with her mother. She described her tipping point. Closeted in prayer, she found herself unable to stand until she had resolved this issue within herself. She faced her doubts, strengthened by conscience, conviction, and God's grace. Deep down, she knew, "There is no fooling with God ... I then at that very same Time renounced the Protestant errors, and the religion that I was brought up in, and resolved to embrace the Catholic Truth and to break through all oppositions whatsoever" (282). She referred repeatedly afterward to the unusual courage, interior strength, and "Assurance" she felt from following her conscience (282–83, 285–88, 292). She felt the "forcible Hand" of God leading her to his will. To deny conscience was to deny God's will and felt like being tortured "on the Rack, and torn several ways" (287, 288). "From this time I stood my Ground and fell back no more" (283). There was no priest by her side. She chose for herself, her guidance coming directly from God, from clergy through religious books she had read, and from her own prayers.

Though her efforts might seem courageous to modern readers, by the standards of her own era Catherine Holland was a disobedient and deceptive daughter, Christian, and subject. Although now a determined Catholic, she lived in a Protestant country and had to continue to attend Protestant services, thereby flouting both Catholic and Protestant church leaders. She contemplated defying the paternal authority of her father "whom I both loved and feared" (283), knowing the dissension her conversion would cause within her family. Her father would be furious and likely blame her mother, even though Catherine felt that Althea had given her scant support. In fact, her mother's unwillingness to disobey her father meant she couldn't be relied upon to intervene on Catherine's behalf. So, she continued to lie, becoming so depressed that Althea wrote to John in England, conveying deep concern. John wrote to Catherine, asking her to tell him what was wrong (285–86).

Catherine used this opportunity to overcome her fears, "let forth the Secret," and tell her father the truth. She cloaked her disclosure with words of obedience. "I set Pen to Paper, and very resolutely told him that seeing he did so earnestly command, I would as ingenuously obey" (285). Her father had commanded her to tell him what was wrong. She, being an obedient daughter, would give him precisely what he asked for, while revealing her intention to disobey him in religion. She emphatically proclaimed the falsity of Protestantism. Her conscience so impelled her to convert that "neither Fire nor Sword should alter my mind" (285–86). Certainly her father would not be able to do so. She, a woman, had determined all these things while relying primarily on God's counsel.

While she waited for her father's return letter, she told her mother the truth as well. Although her mother was ecstatic that Catherine had embraced Catholicism, her support was as insubstantial as Catherine feared. Negotiating between the demands of gender and religion, Althea chose to meet society's expectation of a "good wife," obeying her husband while remaining a Catholic within her heart. Such marital conflicts and choices will be explored in greater depth in Chap. 5. John wrote back a "thundering letter, wherein he wished he had not been so curious" about Catherine's state of mind. He commanded Althea not to aid her in any way and ordered Catherine not to reveal her religious leanings to anyone until he could get home and talk some sense into her. Althea told Catherine that all she could do was continue to pray for her (286–87).

While Catherine recognized her obligation to be an obedient daughter, she chose to prioritize Catholicism, balancing gender and religion differently than her mother did. The entire household soon learned of her conversion, and she puffed up a bit, believing "All did admire I dared to write to him in such resolute Terms considering in how great Awe I otherwise stood of him" (288). Calmed in conscience and buoyed by faith, she negotiated from a position of assurance, no longer fearing her father. For example, Catherine agreed to keep up the pretense of her Protestantism only if John agreed that she did not have to partake of Protestant communion. Fearful that Catherine would leak the family secret, he agreed (286–88).

Their relationship as father and daughter soured. Catherine decided that she would obey her father in all matters other than her faith. When he returned home, she would be first at the door to greet him, first to serve him in all things. John Holland reacted by shunning his daughter, responding to her with "a deaf Ear and a dumb Mouth" (289). For two to three years, he resorted to a combination of scorn, threats, and entreaties, and made a great show of favoring Catherine's sister instead.

Then Holland began making plans to run away and join a monastery where she could finally satisfy her conscience. She sent letters asking for aid to a convent of English Augustinian nuns she remembered from Bruges nine years previously. She began a clandestine correspondence with the nuns under her parents' noses which lasted for years, both in Bergen op Zoom, as well as back in England, where the family returned to live following Charles II's Restoration to the throne in 1660.

Holland described her intention to become a nun both as a way to satisfy her conscience and to give her father and the world "the slip when they thought they had me most fast." She tricked her father into believing her Catholic convictions were "blown over," but all the while she planned her escape. "Whilst I seemed to do nothing," she bragged, "I did act most, and made in my heart a firm Resolution not to rest plotting until I had found a way to convey myself privately away to some Monastery, to have any Liberty of Conscience" (290). Holland's gleeful description of her laywoman's path to conversion and eventual monastic profession occasionally makes it difficult to determine whether pride or conscience motivated her disobedience. It seems likely that religious conscience inspired the content and form of her defiance, while her willfulness fueled her obvious satisfaction in successfully following God's plan for her.

While in London preparing to abscond to Bruges, Holland was finally able to find the priestly counsel and Catholic community she had craved for so long. Her family's new lodgings were in Holborn, a neighborhood with a substantial Catholic population (McClain 2004, 143, 147–49). The back door of her family's home even opened to Fetter Lane, a street where Catholics, including two Jesuits, lived. She now had priests to answer her questions and guide her. Holland visited Catholic homes secretly and used various go-betweens to convey her letters, including a "good honest simple wench" who she "befriended to do the deed" (Holland 1925, 292). After a couple of close calls, in which her father almost intercepted her letters, she credited God's will with the miraculous keeping of her secrets (291–93).

Despite her initial pleasure at these new opportunities, Holland was ultimately disappointed by the priests and chose to follow her conscience rather than their authority. She even criticized their poor efforts to aid her soul. For example, Fr. Edward Leedes, the provincial of her new Jesuit neighbors, ordered them not to support her efforts to escape. All they were allowed to do was pray for her, as her mother had done. Holland claimed that Leedes was more worried about getting the Jesuits in trouble with the Protestant government than he was about her religious needs, so she would make her own way, with God's help (298–99).

First, however, she decided to write this Jesuit provincial who had so little zeal for saving souls and give him a piece of her mind. She composed:

> A sufficient long tart Letter; and amongst other Things I did ask him; if his reverence did think that his holy Father St. Ignatius or St. Francis, or any of the former Saints, would have by so strange a Command as he had imposed upon his Subjects, have left a Soul in so great a Danger as he had made his leave mine: and this through a little Fear and human Respect? ... Although Men forsook me, God would not. (299)

For her to presume to write with such sharpness to a Jesuit leader showed her lack of experience with Catholic authority. She had been so long without clerical direction that she had become increasingly comfortable expressing her understandings of God's will through conscience.

Holland's comfort with her own religious knowledge contributed to her willingness to critique how Catholic clerics operated, but she still supported the existence of their institutional authority. She was more critical of the Anglican clergy. Although she was still attempting to fool her father into believing that she had abandoned her religious concerns, John asked the Bishop of Winchester, (likely Brian de Uphaugh) to come to discuss religion with his daughter to settle any concerns she might have about the truth of the Protestant faith. Althea risked offending John by warning Catherine of the bishop's impending visits, thinking that she could arrange to be away from home to avoid any uncomfortable confrontations.

Catherine's response provides insight into how Catholic women in the British Isles may have seen their disobedience as a strength rather than a shame. She told her mother that she wanted to hasten the bishop onto the field of battle. The bishop might disdain having to dispute with a mere girl, but she wasn't afraid to stand up to him! When they met, she essentially unmanned her opponent, describing him as faint and lacking in vigor (293–95). In contrast, by following her conscience, she viewed herself as a warrior and champion of her faith, a typically male role discussed in more detail in Chap. 6.

When the bishop advised her to turn to scripture for the truth of Protestant doctrine, she did not appeal to the authority of Catholic theologians to interpret those scriptures but relied on her own knowledge. She responded that the scriptures, if taken literally, contained too many contradictions, which bred confusion and heresy. Her implication was that the bishop's faith was just such a heresy. The bishop responded, "Show me," thinking, Holland surmised, to confound his "effeminate Defendant; but I, no whit daunted" found an example from Proverbs that the bishop could not answer (296). "I was informed afterwards, that the Bishop told my Father, there was no good to be done with me." She was too obstinate a woman (297). In Holland's mind, however, she had triumphed.

Right to the end, Holland understood her disobedience to her parents, the government, and Protestantism as part of a greater obedience to God's will as shown to her through conscience. God's will legitimated Holland's rejection of customary female submission and modesty. It authorized her unfeminine combativeness and deceptiveness. In 1663, right before she finally arranged her departure for the English Augustinian convent, she described herself as acting the part of a "Counterfeit Protestant and vain worldling" (298) in an effort to cheat the world right up to the day before she departed for Bruges. While she put on this performance, she wrote letters, visited her Jesuit neighbors, arranged an annual maintenance for herself of £30 to support her at the convent, got her personal possessions out of her parents' home, and made travel plans to Dover and across the English Channel. She deceived everyone and thought she did it well. The day she departed, she left a letter for each of her parents. In her father's, she begged his blessing and forgiveness, assuring him that she would have been an obedient daughter if not for her conscience and love of God. Then she tricked her family again by pretending to take a book out for a walk in the garden. She walked away for good (299–302).

Within days, Catherine Holland was in Flanders, welcomed by Prioress Mary Bedingfield. She made her profession as a nun on September 7, 1664. Shortly thereafter, her spiritual director commanded her to write the story of her conversion. While the existence of her detailed record may be exceptional, Holland's struggles as a laywoman were not. Most Catholic laywomen lacked clerical guidance but experienced a pull to fulfill God's will. With or without clerical interpreters, they relied upon conscience to understand God's intent and purpose for their lives. In the end, women decided for themselves. They chose their spiritual paths to a greater degree than most women had been able to do prior to the Reformation, while wrestling with seemingly irreconcilable differences between gender and religious expectations. They used conscience—God's will as revealed to them through the Holy Spirit—to redraw the boundary lines of their submission to gender and religious authorities as part of their Catholic faith.

After so many years relying on God, conscience, and self to negotiate the intersections of faith and gender and so many disappointments when she sought counsel and support from other Catholics and clerics, one wonders how well Catherine Holland adjusted to convent life. Obedience to male and female superiors may not have come easily. The convent *Annals* chronicle her death on January 6, 1720. They describe her as possessing great spirit and humor, but also as having "much to overcome in her nature, and the struggle between nature and grace was sometimes very apparent." If she thought her own will conflicted with God's in a given situation, she would tell herself, "Come Kate along with me," and go take a discipline, some type of penitential act (Durrant 1925, 305–6). If such a record is accurate, it reflects Holland's understanding of her own challenges as an individual and a woman; her commitment to divine will as revealed to her through conscience; and her community's acceptance of her, largely with good grace and forbearance.

Misunderstood: The Story of a Disobedient Nun and Her "Meddling" Superiors

The nun, Gertrude More (1606–1633), had no less a commitment to following God's will, but she would have to fight to receive a similar level of acceptance within her convent and the Catholic Church. More boasted an irreproachable Catholic pedigree as the great-great-granddaughter of the statesman, author, and martyr, Sir Thomas More. Born in Essex as Helen More, she left England for the continent where she adopted the name Gertrude upon her profession as a Benedictine nun. Later, she became one of the principal founders of the English Benedictine convent at Cambrai. Although situated in Flanders in what is today France, this was a religious house populated primarily by English and Welsh nuns and girls under the spiritual jurisdiction of the men of the English Benedictine Congregation, a community of monks in exile. Girls and women such as More would most likely have grown up in the British Isles amid Catholic struggles. Much of their worldview was already formed before they knocked at the convent doors. After arrival, More and other nuns typically did not integrate into local Catholic communities but, instead, recreated islands of British community, culture, values, and interests on the continent. As scholars such as Caroline Bowden and Clare Walker have emphasized, nuns such as More faced quite similar gender and religious pressures as did women living back in the British Isles (Walker 2004; Bowden 2010). Thus, although they lived on the continent, their stories are part of the history of Catholics from the British Isles.

More admitted later in life that she had not even wanted to become a nun. She only professed because she had been afraid to disappoint her spiritual father, Dom Benet Jones (Weld-Blundell 1910, 1:281–83). After a beginning filled with discontent, she eventually found her calling as a contemplative—a monastic who increasingly detached herself from the world to focus on her interior life with God. One of her convent companions praised More's gift "to direct and animate souls in their way towards God."

> Indeed, it cannot be imagined how great a comfort and encouragement she was to us all in these times ... for her example and words were so moving and so efficacious, and proceeded from a heart so inflamed with the Divine love and zealous of God Almighty's honour, that if a soul were even so much dejected as that she was ready to fall or faint, they were of force to raise her up again and move her to confidence and courage. She had such a feeling and compassion of souls when she did see them in peril and danger of being drawn into fear or dejection of mind that she made little account of all she suffered, so that they might be animated and comforted by it. (Weld-Blundell 1910, 1:295–96)

As her last spiritual director, the Benedictine ascetic and mystic, Augustine Baker, observed in his "Life of Dame Gertrude More," "What madness, then, would it not be for anyone to withdraw her from this way of life, and to put her into another fashioned by human ingenuity and skill ... Surely no one, no Superior or Director, would withdraw her unless in ignorance of the course she was pursuing" (1:47). Yet, as we shall see, this was precisely what some clerics attempted. As Baker admitted, "By natural disposition, it is true, Dame Gertrude was little inclined to subject herself to anyone ... In consequence, her life in religion was anything but pleasant" (1:48–49).

In contrast to Holland's public testament of her life as a Catholic laywoman, Gertrude More wrote for herself, as in her "Apology for herself, and her Spiritual Guide," to ease her frustrations and comfort herself in her fears (2:209–90). After her grisly death from smallpox at the age of 27, Baker, her most supportive spiritual director, found her writings in her cell. He combined these writings with his knowledge of More and statements he took from her sisters after her death to write her life story. Within this text, he preserved and published many of her private writings *verbatim*, despite their critique of his own male clerical privilege.

When More professed as a nun, she did the two things required of all female monastics: she took a formal vow of obedience, and she dedicated her life to a relationship with God. When her vow interfered with conscience and her union with God, More began questioning the premises and limits of nuns' obedience to male superiors. Unlike Catherine Holland, who might be supposed to have relied so strongly on conscience because she had so little access to priests, More did not lack for clerical guidance. By contrasting More's views with those of Baker and her fellow nuns, we can see not only how one woman re-negotiated her relationships with God and the clergy but also how such changes could spread among other

Catholic women to provide alternatives to women's traditional gender and religious roles. More claimed that religious women had the right to make decisions about how to perfect their souls based on what God revealed to them through conscience instead of being expected to follow the instructions of male superiors blindly (Bilinkoff 2005).

More's challenge to the limits of monastic obedience sprang from her disgruntlement that few of her convent's usual practices advanced her faith. The traditional prayers left her "cold as a stone" (1:28). The spiritual practices suggested by her first spiritual directors or in books failed to resonate with her. She complained that her superiors refused to listen to her about this problem (1:174–5, 187, 2:217). Both sides grew frustrated.

Thanks to the controversial Baker, who proved an understanding spiritual director, More eventually moved beyond the strict routines and approved practices of her convent. After witnessing her hard work and discipline in pursuit of a contemplative life, Baker grew to trust More's piety and connection to God (1:189–93). He then accommodated her religious practices to her strengths and weaknesses, adhering to the spirit of the *Rule of St. Benedict*. He allowed her to search out forms of prayer that resonated with her. He taught her to trust in conscience, instructing her how to determine whether an inspiration she felt originated from the Holy Spirit or from her own will. Unless given a direct command by her superiors, he advised her to trust the voice of conscience and act in the way that she felt would provide her the most spiritual profit. In other words, he provided her with spiritual tools and then let her be. Baker found, "It is not surprising, then, that once having found this way, which consists principally in finding the Divine inspirations, she should be most averse to relinquishing it for any other, believing all other ways to be insufficient for her needs" (1:49; also 77–78, 84–88, 91, 98–100, 102–13).

Baker was careful to let readers of More's life story know that this woman was not a typical nun and that what was beneficial for her should not be presumed useful for all other nuns. He reminded readers that he never forgot that More and her sisters were women with physical, mental, and spiritual weaknesses which always "had to be taken into account" (1:99–100). However, at the same time, Baker acknowledged that More was far from unique. He proposed that women's souls that were similar to hers would benefit from his more hands-off approach to spiritual direction. Baker believed that each person should "follow their own call from God … though it should appear to be strange to others, even as Dame Gertrude did" (1:82–83; also 1:49, 54, 77–79, 109–11).

Under Baker's supervision, More went on to develop a deep contemplative faith and trust in God's guidance above all worldly authority. As she described it, it was precisely her "want of doubt" that led to conflict with her superiors. "They infer that she slighteth ... her superiors, as not fit to govern her; so ignorant do they think she doth esteem them." If her superiors would only speak with her, she wrote, they would see this was untrue (2:217). More consoled herself that she was still orthodox. She found support for her path in scripture, the writings of Church Fathers, and from the pens of more recent theologians and holy persons such as Teresa of Ávila and John of the Cross, each of whom lived with superiors who did not support them. "A soul will always find contradiction from some Superior or another," More mused, "and yet if the soul live in her interior as she should, it will be no impediment to her progress ... These souls, though they might seem to others to have deviated from true obedience, yet the results showed they were far from such a fault" (2:284; also 1:81, 2:282–83).

Perhaps unsurprisingly, More developed a reputation as a disobedient nun for her ability and willingness to criticize how confessors and spiritual directors exercised authority over women. She distinguished between the spiritual help such men provided and the guidance that could only come from God. Both were important but achieved different outcomes. To attain salvation, Christians should follow directives from the Church and its priests. To attain spiritual perfection, however, Christians should follow God directly (2:240).

The nuns lived under the spiritual jurisdiction of the English Benedictine men at Cambrai. Priests of this order would have visited the nuns frequently to provide the sacraments and serve as superiors and spiritual directors. Even if More and some of her sisters followed God through their consciences, they still owed obedience to God's earthly representatives. More refused to "neglect, omit, put off, or perform badly anything of my Superior's commanding or ordaining" (2:216; also 1:298–99, 2:217–20, 225). She and the other nuns were not trying to shirk their yoke.

More wanted to follow both God and his priests, but sometimes their instructions conflicted. Just as Holland negotiated her obligations to paternal authority, More challenged the blind obedience many clerics expected and praised in religious women.

> O misery, that all this should be fathered upon holy obedience, that most noble of virtues! Who sees not that this is turning religious obedience (in those who

simply desire to perform it) to a policy abominable to be thought of or named! Oh my God! Was this thy meaning when we vowed ourselves to Thee? Or, rather, didst not Thou say, 'Be wise as serpents and simple as doves?' Thou didst not say, 'Be so foolish under pretense of blind obedience that thou shalt not know thy right hand from thy left.' (2: 247–48; also 255, 259, 261–68)

More did not reject monastic obedience. She praised it as the highest virtue. It was obvious to her, however, that blind religious obedience perverted women's true obligations, causing misery. She knew religious women who obeyed their spiritual directors' every suggestion and command and yet told her that they were strangers to God, perhaps to an even greater degree than they had been before entering the convent (2:261–62).

More argued that the sanctity and perfection of the religious orders of her day were a far cry from past ages. What better proof of this could there be than that there were more monks and nuns than ever before in history, "yet none will deny that the world was ever so much without Saints, since Christ's time." This proved to More that if Catholics wanted the monastic life to improve their souls, they would have to reject the "blind obedience [to Superiors] which is so much extolled and commended by all" (2:264), along with the prescribed regimens of communal prayer, and the efforts to live laudably among their peers and superiors that so many religious seemed to think was enough (2:255, 283). God must want something more of her and others, and her male superiors were not always directing them toward it.

More believed that God did not intend female religious to abandon reason as they entered the convent door. Nuns were to remain wise yet innocent, continuing to trust their own discernment. She made it clear that she took a vow of obedience to God, not to men. "Woe be to those … that have confidence in men rather than God!" (2:244) Should she and her sisters "place our peace upon that which is changeable as the moon—to wit, the humours and opinions of Men?" (2:245) Unlike changeable, fallible men, God was immutable and perfect. Thus it was God to whom she owed her obedience (1:302, 2:229–30, 244–47, 277, 285).

More maintained that alongside the many good male superiors and spiritual directors were many poor ones who, although they might be good men and priests, were harming the spiritual growth of religious women under their care. In doing so, they strayed from their profession and wronged not only the nuns but God. She criticized the "invincible ignorance" (2:260), defectiveness, and lack of aptitude of male superiors in this latter category who only "pretend ... to have some experience of a spiritual life" (2:212). "It is incredible the martyrdom that a contemplative soul hath to undergo when under [such a man's] charge; and a ... miracle it will be for her ... to hold to the instructions proper for her" (2:235; also1:152, 2:234–37, 257–58, 281, 286). Such clerics, she claimed, often designed a spiritual program of devotion for nuns based upon the readings and pious practices that had furthered the clerics' own faith. What worked for them should work for all. They tied down nuns' souls, never inquiring what their calling might be or to what practices they felt drawn (1:297, 2:151–53, 210, 229–30, 275–76, 281).

In re-defining the boundaries of spiritual men's authority, More concluded that she should confess to a priest who exercised jurisdiction over her and that she ought to observe and fulfill all obligations of her monastic Rule. That being done, "what warrant, I pray you, will she need (after her conscience is once well settled) from Confessor or Superior?" (2:244) Beyond these basic obligations, most other issues were incidental—that is, not absolutely required by her Rule, doctrines, or other formal decree— and thus somewhat negotiable. Spiritual growth took place within, and God through the Holy Spirit had provided each soul with the knowledge of how to attain spiritual perfection so that souls had no need of men to teach it to them (2:240–41, 244–47, 257–58, 266, 285). For example, she frequently chose to ignore the advice of some spiritual directors, choosing not to perform devotional acts they recommended if they contradicted her conscience—her understanding of God's will—and contributed little to her soul's perfection.

Although this may appear as disobedience to clerical authority, neither More nor her spiritual director, Baker, saw her as being insubordinate when she chose to ignore a priest's advice because she was not disobeying a direct command. As all human beings were fallible, she wrote, each soul should have enough sense to observe for itself what God was calling it to do "as she may distinguish the sun from the moon" (2:290; also 1:174–75, 181–82, 187, 192–93, 2:218–19, 259, 281–82). In addition, as Baker had authorized her to choose according to her conscience, in theory she was obeying his religious authority even when disregarding that of others.

If a superior kept insisting on her compliance over such minor issues of religious practice and life, More would obey only after she had her say. She would request a hearing before "competent" authority (1:50; also 51–52) where she could explain what she understood God's will to be for her and her sisters. Then, if formally commanded to perform or halt a certain practice, she would comply. The tension between the monastic humility expected of her and More's need to stand firm against power and authority when bowing to it would violate her conscience is clear. On the one hand, More contended that it was improper for nuns to "contend, complain or justify" themselves to superiors. She believed that an exception to this rule existed, however, when "justice doth requireth a simple relation of the truth to Superiors when the good of her own soul (or other souls) in the house requires it" (2:236). When a nun felt that unquestioning submission would violate her conscience, she *should* contend, complain, or justify herself. Otherwise, she risked denying God's will. More described how she would consult God first and then approach her superiors humbly, charitably, and without anger—conforming to expectations for nuns' demeanor—but, once standing before her superiors, she expected to speak and be heard. In directly confronting the "opposition and contradictions we find and feel from our Order" (2:250), More consoled herself that God gave humans such trials for a purpose, "for our own good" (2:150). No one was her enemy "because in all things we will regard God, who permitteth such difficulties to happen to us, that our fidelity to Him may thereby be tried; and so we do not regard with aversion the party who afflicted us" (2:149–50). She and her sisters should be patient and wait for a resolution in God's own time (2:217–19, 224–25, 236, 257, 259, 266).

Some of More's superiors found her presumptuous, forward, and a danger to her peers and to clerical privilege. They felt disrespected by her criticisms of their spiritual guidance and rejection of their authority. Even more disturbing, her ideas were spreading to other nuns (2:217, 260). Some religious men placed the blame upon Augustine Baker. His superiors formally examined his methods and the Cambrai nuns' practice of them, essentially placing Baker, More, and her sisters on trial (1:136–41, 2:210–11, 218, 220). Although his accusers admitted that his spiritual direction appeared potentially profitable, they believed that it posed dangers for women. Simply put, they did not trust women's consciences. Women's prayer life should be made "safe and sound" for their own protection (1:138; also 2:212). In her private writings, More believed that these critics looked upon these issues "with no other intention but to carp" (2:211). Those who misunderstood the divine call to contemplation "will make both themselves, and others also with them, to lay the defect (which was only in them) upon the unfitness of instructions for women. For it will seem to them that [these things] cannot possibly be practiced by women without perils and dangers unspeakable" (2:250).

Embedded within such concerns for the nuns were anxieties over male clerical privilege. For example, nuns under Baker's spiritual direction, including More, had taken it upon themselves to shift their schedule of prayer. Their accusers charged that this independent action and other novelties in prayer and religious life introduced by Baker were unsuited to women's nature (1:138, 152, 187–88, 2: 210–12, 249–50, 258). However, they also labeled the nuns "enemies to the government of their Superiors" (2:212–13).

From the nuns' perspective, they acted according to their consciences, spurred by God's will, to perfect their souls. Their superiors had been retarding their spiritual growth by not allowing sufficient time for "two serious recollections" of mental prayer each day to which the nuns felt drawn. The nuns simply shifted their daily schedule around so they could have this dedicated time without neglecting other prayers and duties. In their own eyes, they were balancing their obligations to their order with what God called them to through conscience. Their critics, however, tarnished the nuns' reputations and discouraged prayer by publicly "disgrac[ing] those who are in that course of prayer, and to affright those who come after … for they are there pointed out in plain terms to be enemies of the government of Superiors" (2:211–14).

In the end, Baker's superiors approved his methods and form of prayer for the women (Sweeney 1861, 66). The Catholic Church could accommodate this challenge and modification to its gender and religious order. This conflict highlights the different points of view expressed in these re-negotiations of women's roles and male authority, and how the Church might reconcile them.

As this inquiry made clear, however, it was not only More who had begun re-defining women's monastic obedience but other nuns within the house at Cambrai. After her death, Baker asked someone he described as an unnamed, unlearned woman of credit and talent—likely another nun—to write down what she could recall about More and her influence within her religious house (1:281–304). This writer attested that she and many others at Cambrai would affirm More's God-given gift of encouraging her sisters to seek God's inspiration directly. Not all her sisters were capable of pursuing the contemplative path, but among those who were, More could not bear to see a sister deterred. This writer described More standing up for her own liberty of spirit and that of other nuns who could not, or would not, stand up to male clerical authority as she did. In situations in which a spiritual director tried to convince a sister to disregard her conscience and follow his instructions rather than God's call, More "interpose[d] herself to receive the blows in safeguard and defense of those that were weak and not able to bear them," trying to eliminate hindrances to her sisters' spiritual growth (1:296; also 1:295, 297, 2:250–52). Women, More claimed, were in particular danger of being swayed from God's path and onto the priest's path:

> Wherefore, for the most part, those under them, if they be poor, simple women (however good may be their spirit) live miserable, dejected lives; for it is the only way these directors can bring their politic and absolute government about. Ordinarily, they do it under this pretense, saying there is no way to make this or that soul humble, but to bring her into such fear that she dare neither speak, think, nor do anything without their approbation. (2:246–47)

If the woman bent to priestly authority, the cleric declared her happy and encouraged other women to emulate her. If the woman's conscience appeared conflicted or troubled, the cleric explained that she was "suffering for justice" (2:247, also 258–59).

More observed with frustration that it was always the woman who was deemed wrong and never the cleric. If a woman refused to follow his guidance, she had gone astray. If she was anything less than sober and serious, he judged her not ready for a spiritual life. Instead, she charged, it was the spiritual director who was at fault, neglecting his subject's divine call (2:275–76, 279). More, her anonymous sister reported, told her sisters:

> God bless and deliver us from those ways and directions [i.e., from a spiritual director] that will make a soul afraid to have recourse to God, that would darken and obscure our reason so far that we should not be able to discern and observe His inward speaking to our souls nor dare to turn ourselves towards Him or to pray in any other manner but how and when we are warranted by men, and take all things at second hand from them. (1:297)

They should employ their reason to challenge any spiritual directives that distanced them from God. They were fully capable of discerning God's will without a male interpreter.

And some sisters listened. The writings of this unnamed colleague demonstrate how some members of More's religious house, even unlearned ones, began criticizing their former unquestioning acquiescence to their male superiors and re-defining the boundaries of their monastic obedience as More had. This anonymous author was careful to distinguish between the Church, which she praised, and the advice of its representatives, which she deemed poor (1:297). Instead, God served as the best spiritual guide (1:303). This writer explained with nuance how God would not excuse a female religious who went against her conscience and disregarded divine inspiration in order to follow a superior's advice. The only circumstance in which a nun might do so was when a superior had explicitly disallowed or disapproved it, echoing More's need for a more formal directive to be made before she obeyed against her conscience (1:298–99).

While More and her sisters appear to challenge religious women's obedience to male clerical authority in these contexts, Baker repeatedly swore that More's obedience to God and priests was absolute (1:50–52, 190, 191). It was, however, conditional. More would obey after a formal hearing before a competent authority, followed by a direct command to obey. She felt free to disregard more informal "advice."

Moreover, More understood her obedience to priestly authority in new ways. She obeyed God's representatives not in their own right or for their own merit—merit she often doubted—but as a form of obedience to God (1:191, 2:149–50, 210, 224, 267–68). By continuing to revere and obey superiors she believed to be misguided or flatly wrong, she saw herself as cooperating with a larger divine plan, even if she could not understand its particulars. She thus upheld the necessity of obedience while re-interpreting who, when, and why she obeyed.

More's obedience, however, was more than a surface conformity to superiors whom she actually resented. She could have adopted such a veneer of compliance—indeed, it would have been easier than the path of confrontation she followed. She knew that it was "possible to comply with our external obediences, and perform them so well that the Superior shall hold me in good esteem, and be able to discover no great defect in our performance of them." Yet there was no spiritual profit in such deceptions, she maintained (2:224). A Christian could not pretend obedience and humility to one's superiors because God knew the believer's heart and would not excuse duplicity. "Better it is to obey in a manner never so imperfect than to contend and withstand Superiors under what pretense soever" (2:218; also 1:295-96). More would neglect nothing owed to her superiors and perform all obligations to the best of her ability with as good a will as she could. Only then was she working toward perfecting her soul.

But it was not easy. More grappled with her anger and frustration in her private writings as she strove to perfect herself. Convent chronicles are filled with formulaic descriptions of patient, resigned nuns suffering from illness and pain, and More was no exception. The sisters who cared for More as smallpox rotted her flesh and flies devoured her facial tissue wrote to Baker that she "was resigned to death" (1:260), she died properly "in the exercise of patience, silence, interiors solitude, resignation" (1:267), and she "gave signs of as great resignation and confidence in Almighty God as could be seen in anyone" (1:270). She had such "great patience" (1:270) that she was "Job upon the dunghill" (1: 271).

However, More cultivated a higher degree of forbearance—literally, the patience of the saints—in her attempts to perfect her soul. The tension between her desire to obey and her frustration with the clerical "meddlers" who "mislike[d] her proceedings or misinterpret[ed] them" (2:235) is evident in her personal writings. It would be a miracle, she proclaimed, if she could hold on to her obedient, willing heart and piety while feeling that her superiors were putting her and her sisters through a form of martyrdom. Yet, like Holland, she found courage and strength in following her conscience. She was certain that God intended such challenges for her eventual good and that patience would carry her through these trials, making her insensible to unkindness and injury and bringing her to peace in God's will. She committed herself to this daily struggle because, if done properly, she would find comfort "in that one thing which is alone necessary": the love of God (2:229; also 2:149–50, 230, 236, 266).

In turning directly to God in love, More and her sisters changed the extent of nuns' reliance on traditional forms of clerical mediation between God and believers. In fact, as More lay dying at the age of 27, she requested the Eucharist—the literal body and blood of Christ—but was denied because her illness made her liable to choke on it. Instead, she was offered a confessor, presumably to perform the last rites and absolve her of sin before her death. She refused, saying, "No, I will see no man." Although she could not receive Christ in the external forms of body and blood, God was with her internally. She needed nothing more (1:248–49).

Gertrude More's influence survived her, and 17 years after her demise, another Cambrai sister, Barbara Constable, furthered More's vision, penning a 400-page manual, *Advice for Confessors*. This nun dared to recommend to confessors how they might better care for souls. Whereas most of More's criticisms of clergy were made privately, Constable made a public call for change. She restructured the relationship of male confessors and convent women, confining the men's influence on the nuns' spiritual lives to the absolution for sin, as More had suggested years earlier (Gertz 2013).

Nuns such as these placed such strong trust in conscience—interior knowledge of God's law and will—that they, like Catherine Holland, redefined the boundaries of gendered and religious obedience. Unlike Holland, they did so within the monastic environment rather than the secular world. The Catholic Church could more easily laud Holland for her lay defiance of worldly and Protestant authority, but it would eventually embrace nuns such as Gertrude More and the challenges they posed to Church tradition, along with the new relationships they furthered between women, God, and Church authority. Yet Mary Ward and her attempts to build new relations between women and the Church remained outside the pale.

The Chattering Hussy and Galloping Girl

Mary Ward did not want to get married, no matter that her father, Marmaduke Ward, had found her the perfect husband. What fault could Mary possibly find with Edmund Neville, heir of the Earl of Westmoreland? However, Mary wished to become a nun, and her father, like John Holland, could not compel his daughter's obedience. Frustrated at her refusal to honor his paternal male authority, Marmaduke hoped that she might obey clerical male authority, and so took her to speak with her confessor, Richard Holtby. Surely a priest would make Mary see reason.

Her two primary authority figures—both male, one a layman and one a cleric—teamed up against Mary. The girl and the priest sat, discussing her future at length. It became obvious to Mary that her father had filled the priest in on all the details of their familial conflict. Holtby initially encouraged Mary to honor her father's plan. She could do much more good for the "whole Catholic body" in England and serve God better, Holtby argued, by marrying Neville than by leaving England to become a nun (Chambers 1882, 1:93). In Ward's own words from *The Italian Autobiography*, "His words were of weight ... I did not dare do what he prohibited as unlawful" (Kenworthy-Browne 2008, 125; also Chambers 1882, 1:90–96). Ward, like most Catholic women, was accustomed to accepting her confessor's advice as the will of God. Yet her desire to become a nun also felt like God's will. Should she accept her confessor's advice or follow her conscience? To what higher authority could Ward appeal to resolve this dilemma?

Since Holtby was Christ's representative, she decided to go over his head. In her autobiographical writings, Ward described how she prayed to Jesus to take up her cause with Holtby and how Jesus answered. While Holtby was celebrating the Eucharist, he allegedly spilled the chalice of wine. The priest, interpreting this as a sign of God's displeasure in his counsel to Mary, reversed himself and supported her choice to become a nun (Kenworthy-Browne 2008, 8–9, 125).

This was a turning point in Ward's life: God would serve as her primary spiritual director, not a priest, and God sometimes showed her a path different from the ones laid out for her by male clerics. For example, in 1609, while in London and making her home at St. Clement's Churchyard in the Strand, her spiritual director counseled her to join the Discalced Carmelites, a strict, reformed order founded by the Spanish contemplative nun, Teresa of Ávila. Ward related how soon afterwards "something supernatural befell me," a visionary experience.

> I was abstracted out of my whole being, and it was shown to me with clearness and inexpressible certainty that I was not to be of the order of St. Teresa, but that some other thing was determined for me ... I did not see what the assured good thing would be, but the glory of God which was to come through it showed itself inexplicably and so abundantly as to fill my soul in such a way as that I remained for a good space without feeling or hearing anything but the sound, 'Glory, glory, glory.'(139–40)

But what she would do now if her confessor commanded her to join the Discalced Carmelites?

Like More, Ward needed to negotiate a new type of balance between her commitment to follow her conscience and her reverence and obedience for Christ's anointed representatives. Unlike More, she did so as a laywoman, not as a nun. At first, she hoped that there might be a way to satisfy both God and the priest, but she could not find it. She either displeased God by not fulfilling his will as revealed to her directly or she affronted God by defying his representative. Ward finally concluded that she would follow God's revealed will for her, even if it meant opposing the wishes of a priest. As a sign of this commitment and recognition of its difficulty, Ward remembered, "I put on a hair cloth,"—a rough, abrasive garment typically made from horse or goat hair—under her clothing for some time. The chafing and itching served as a persistent reminder of the importance of making the right choices for the right reasons as she navigated between conscience, priestly directives, and her own will (139–40, also 130).

Unlike Holland and More, Ward's story is not about accommodating either convent life or lay life to the competing pulls of traditional gender and religious expectations. As discussed earlier, Ward and the English Ladies wound up as not quite nuns but more than laywomen. They wanted to lead a "mixed life," combining the best of convent and lay life to create a new model of Catholic women's activism to aid the Catholic mission.

Gender, lay, *and* religious expectations would need to change if Ward was to fulfill her vision. Although their efforts to combine elements of both lay and monastic lifestyle and practice appear different from Holland's and More's respective challenges to lay and religious authorities, Ward and the English Ladies had to confront many of the same intertwined social and religious fears about women. Ward relied on many of the same justifications for her disobedience as Holland and More did—her interior assurance that she could recognize and should fulfill God's will and the imperfections of human and clerical guidance. Her Ladies fulfilled God's will and law by demonstrating their love of God and their neighbors through saving souls on the mission and educating girls and women. However, like More, Ward and her companions believed that traditional forms of masculine lay and clerical authority limited women's ability to serve God. As Ward saw it, there was a need, and God asked her to help fill it by living a mixed lay and monastic life. In doing so, Ward and the English Ladies created a new niche for Catholic women's service to the faith for over 20 years before the papacy suppressed the Institute. Moreover, their well-known and hotly deliberated challenges to enclosure motivated other Catholic women to enter the debate, questioning women's existing roles and supporting new ones.

Ward was certainly not the first Catholic woman to confront the tensions between laywomen seeking greater opportunities for service to the faith and the Roman Church. Many earlier women, most notably Catherine of Siena (1347–1380), engaged in such work. Catherine traveled throughout the Italian peninsula teaching, preaching, and converting, viewing herself as one among many heirs to Mary Magdalene and the first disciples. (Catherine of Siena 1940, 42). When some observers criticized her for preaching and teaching, she dictated a letter in which she defended her actions:

> We have been put [here] to sow the word of God and to reap the fruit of souls. Everyone must be solicitous of his own trade: the trade which God has given us is this one; so we must exercise it and not bury this talent, for

> otherwise we would deserve great reproof; but we must act in every time and place, and in every creature ... I have come here for no other reason than to eat and taste souls and to draw them out of the devil's hands. I want to give my life for this, a thousand lives if I had them. And for this reason I will come and go according to what the Holy Spirit will make me do. (39)

Despite such apparent similarities to Ward's aims and in contrast to the Church's condemnation of Ward's activities, the Church generally supported Catherine in her work. This is likely because Catherine pursued her non-traditional vocation at a time when the Roman Church faced no serious challenges to its authority, as it did during the Reformation. Timing, it seems, mattered.

Like Catherine of Siena and Catherine Holland, Ward viewed her loyalty to God as justifying her resistance to the authority of her father, priest, and government. Fortunately, her confessor did not insist that Ward join the Discalced Carmelite order, and later that year, Ward travelled to St. Omer, in what is today northern France, with a group of like-minded young women to discover the work to which God drew her in conscience. In doing so, Ward and her Ladies began to engage in practices that many critics, both Catholic and Protestant, considered disobedient and possibly downright dangerous. Regardless of their good works, they were not nuns, and they overstepped society's obvious limitations upon women's behavior (Chambers 1882, 1:319). Although both clerics and laypeople had similarly criticized other groups of unenclosed pious laywomen who served the Church—such as beguines and *klopjes*—for transgressing women's proper roles, the difference between these situations and Ward's appears to be one of degree. In working for their neighbors' salvation, Ward and her English Ladies went where other women typically did not, illegally crossing national borders and clearly breaking laws. Whereas women were supposed to be silent, the English Ladies counseled, taught, and were rumored to preach. In the *English Vita*, one of Ward's closest companions surmised that Ward was sometimes so courageous and fearless in her work for souls that she forgot her sex, meaning that she forgot the restrictions and behaviors normally associated with women (Kenworthy-Browne 2008, 15).

When returning to England to serve the mission, the women engaged in stealth and subterfuge just as men on the mission did, but because society believed that women were inclined to deviousness, the English Ladies' deceptions were held up as evidence of the inappropriateness of their work. For example, a common stratagem was for a Lady to disguise herself as a poor person. In such attire, a Lady could hide in plain sight. It was also easier for her to meet and gain the trust of other poor people whom she might convert (Kenworthy-Browne 2008, 20, 77–78, 122; Chambers 1882, 1:43, 217, 2:34–36).

The English Ladies also camouflaged their communications. They wrote letters in lemon juice, which would remain invisible until the paper was heated. They used false names in their correspondence, sometimes *male* names (Chambers 1882, 2:496–500; Orchard 1985, 105). Ward and her companions continued such tactics even after the suppression of the Institute. When the Catholic Church briefly imprisoned Ward in Munich, she went into jail prepared with a good supply of lemon juice, knowing that her mail would be inspected. She sent out secret missives on whatever paper was available, such as pages of books and food wrappers (Chambers 1882, 2:350–51). Worthy of mention is a letter Ward wrote from London to one of her colleagues in Rome in 1639 after the pope facilitated her return to England. Ward disguised the message to appear as an embroidery pattern, an innocuous scrap of womanly creativity. It was a large circle of paper, inscribed in ink, "This is the full measure of the embroidery, may be a straw-breadth less, and if done by Christmas will serve." Ward wrote in lemon juice on the other parts of the paper, beginning "God knows if what I write will be … read," but identifying political friends, requesting vestments, plays, and books, and speculating about opening a school in London (2:466–67).

Detractors referred to such sly practices, accusing the English Ladies of wanting to deceive people, even into thinking that they were nuns or priests. Popular anxieties fed such criticisms, steeped in the fearful and negative rhetoric about women popularized by the early modern debate over the worth of women and the "Fight for the Breeches." The accusations often became quite outlandish. For example, rumors circulating about Ward had her traveling around England and Flanders in a luxurious carriage-and-four calling herself a duchess. She was said to preach out in public streets in front of an altar. Her Ladies were alleged to be prideful, licentious, overly loquacious, and indecorous. Detractors alleged that the English Ladies would go to inns "to gain souls" and were thought to be courtesans or whores. The women themselves were "chattering hussies" and "galloping nuns." The women's efforts were vain, useless, and detrimental to Catholic efforts and interests at home and on the continent (*Godfather's Information* 1623; Chambers 1882, 1:318–21, 2:37–39, 169–170, 183–87).

These accusations were rooted in fear of what unsupervised women might do in society (Ellis 2007; Lux-Sterritt 2011; Gallagher 1999). Indeed, closer examination of the criticisms show that the women posed not just a danger to the gender order but to the religious order as well. William Harrison, Catholic Archpriest of England, in a memorial written just before his death in 1621 and eventually delivered to Rome, called the English Ladies a "great shame and disgrace to the Catholic religion" (Chambers 1882, 2:186), who by their bad reputations simply gave the Protestants more ammunition in the fight against Rome. Who were such women to undertake such activities, he questioned, "as if [the Catholic faith] could not be supported or propagated otherwise than by idle and garrulous women"? (2:185) Yet in the midst of his gendered criticism, religious issues came to the fore. Harrison was appalled that "such vain designs of weak women, supported by no ecclesiastical authority" had proven so successful (2:183; also 184–87). Like More and her companions who changed the prayer life at Cambrai without permission from their superiors, Ward and the English Ladies were viewed as pursuing their new agenda without proper clerical guidance or authorization.

Ward certainly did not reject clerical direction. She, like More, praised the many good spiritual directors from whom she and her Ladies benefitted: men such as Bishop Jacques Blaes of St. Omer and the Jesuits Roger Lee and John Gerard (Chambers 1882, 1:409–11; Kenworthy-Browne 2008, 133–35). Like Augustine Baker, these clerics used their authority to encourage women's spiritual capacities and efforts to fulfill God's will. For example, Lee exhorted the English Ladies to a more active religious life on New Year's Day 1612. It was not enough to sit comfortably in contemplation of God, praying for the good of their own souls. Lee prodded the women to extend themselves for the salvation of others' souls using the sweat of their brows, even their blood, should God ask it (Chambers 1882, 1:323).

Although valuing spiritual direction, Ward's certainty that God communicated with her directly and purposefully meant that she would uphold God's will over all else. Churchmen such as Blaes agreed that the Holy Spirit directed Ward, guiding her actions and her Institute and its works. Blaes even wrote an open letter to this effect dated 1615 (1:319–26; also Kenworthy-Browne 2008, 18). Although Ward and Blaes did not call it conscience, it was the same conscience that Holland and More upheld, and which some English Ladies explicitly invoked (Kenworthy-Browne 2008, 131, 142; Chambers 1882, 1:471; Wetter 2006, 47–53). This assurance gave Ward and her Ladies confidence to stand up not only to Catholic clerics but also to Protestant authorities on numerous occasions, whether under arrest in England or under siege by Parliamentary forces during the English Civil War (Kenworthy-Browne 2008, 23, 66–71; Chambers 1882, 1:436–43, 2:482, 487; Mother Mary Margaret 1955, 42).

Like More, Ward's willingness to redraw the boundaries surrounding longstanding Catholic beliefs about women's obedience and roles within the Church inspired other women to do the same. Foremost was Ward's insistence that a mixed life, combining communal piety with active service, was not only possible for some women but was God's will for them, even if it contradicted current Church law. Mary recalled how, as a youth, she had only been offered two choices for her future: marriage and family or a life enclosed in a convent (Chambers 1882, 1:208). Through divine inspiration, Ward discerned broader possibilities for the good her women could do for the souls of their neighbors, but she didn't see how they could do it from behind a convent grate.

In her proposal for her Institute, known as the *Ratio Instituti* (*Scheme of the Institute*), presented to Pope Paul V in 1616, she argued that the urgencies of the times, the "need of spiritual laborers" in her homeland, and the glory of God warranted an exception to religious women's enclosure in convents.

> We propose to follow a mixed kind of life, such a life as we hold Christ our Lord and Master to have taught his disciples, such a life as His Blessed Mother seems to have lived and to have left to those following her, such a life as appears to have been led by Saints Mary Magdalene, Martha, Praxedes, Prudentiana, Thecla, Cecilia, Lucy and many other holy virgins. (1:376–78, also 1: 208, 224)

She and her Ladies had to be out in the world, talking and interacting with people if they hoped to draw people away from worldly interests, toward God and the Catholic faith. This was God's will.

Ward influenced other women, not just her Ladies, to see the value of women performing such work and to question enclosure. In her narrative of her experiences on mission in Suffolk in the early 1620s, a sister of the Institute known as Dorothea related more than one conversation in which the mistress of the home in which she was staying would defend the work of the English Ladies, challenging the pronouncements of missionary priests about the need for women to live behind convent walls. Dorothea recalled one conversation in which she and the mistress of the home sat with a group of men that included a visiting Benedictine priest named Palmer. Not knowing that Dorothea was an English Lady, Palmer began speaking disparagingly about Ward and the alleged shameful behaviors of the women of her Institute.

It was not Dorothea who rose to the Institute's defense but the mistress. She questioned the necessity of religious women's enclosure. "I see not why such women may not as well to God's honor live in the world, to labor for the conversion of souls," the woman asserted (1:38). She had obviously given the matter some thought, as she outlined certain conditions that would need to be met for women to live this type of life. Candidates for such work should be women of particular character and training who could work profitably for the souls of others. They would need to be part of a community, bound by obedience. They would have to undergo a lengthy period of self-mortification and demonstrate virtue before being sent out on such work, not assuming the work for themselves. The mistress reasoned that,

> Although it is true that Our Blessed Savior commended a contemplative life in Mary Magdalene, yet did He neither forbid nor disapprove a mixed life, and I have heard divers of good judgment commend, if not prefer, this, if as in these gentlewomen [the English Ladies] contemplation be mixed with action. (2:37–38)

Like Ward, this woman looked to God for justification of this course of action. Surely it was reasonable for proven, devout women to serve God more actively in a mixed life directed by the Church. As God had not disapproved it, she did not see why the Church should.

Ward justified the legitimacy and value of the women's efforts by contrasting God's authority with the fallibility of priestly authority in an oft-cited set of speeches she gave to her Ladies in St. Omer in 1617 (1:407–14). She had just returned from a year spent in England only to find her colleagues disturbed and discouraged. In her absence, a confessor had told them that their efforts were ultimately in vain because they were only women. Ward told them not to be deceived by such poor spiritual counsel. Their faults had nothing to do with their womanhood.

> There is no such difference between men and women that women may not do great things, as we have seen by example of many saints ... And I hope in

God it will be seen that women in time to come will do much ... Wherein are we so inferior to other creatures that they should term us 'but women?' ... As if we were in all things inferior to some other creature which I suppose to be a man! Which I dare to be bold to say is a lie, and with respect to the good Father may I say it is an error ... If they would not make us believe we can do nothing, and that we are but women, we might do great matters. (1:409)

Instead, women's challenges were due to imperfections shared by both men and women. If her Ladies experienced doubt in their abilities or purpose, it was the result of putting too much faith in their imperfect human confessor rather than in God's truth, which was eternal and available to all Christians, male or female.

As More encouraged her sisters at Cambrai, Ward encouraged her Ladies to trust themselves to discern God's will. While some men might not believe that a woman could apprehend God, she knew differently through her own experience. Ward in no way absolved her women of their obedience to male clerical authority, but she did suggest that they use conscience to take a more critical view of their relationship to it. God's will must be done (1:411–14).

One woman, however, apparently misinterpreted Ward's intentions and God's will, resulting in the greatest act of disobedience associated with the Institute. By examining this transgression—which not inconsequentially occurred just before the publication of the papal bull suppressing the Institute—we can begin to see the boundaries of the Church's forbearance regarding women's experimentation with gender and religious roles. Ward's closest companion, Winefrid Wigmore, defied the orders of a papal representative in an effort to protect Ward's Institute, and she ordered other members of the Institute to do the same. This seemed to confirm society's and the Church's greatest fears about the dangers of the Institute and its expanded religious role for women. As Archpriest Harrison had suggested, it was reasonable to fear that if the Church slackened the reins on women, they would make mistakes. If the Church allowed women the level of self-governance and mobility Ward requested, women would defy male religious authority. They would fall into error and lead others into wrongdoing. Women needed the "sound and solid judgment" of the male priesthood not only for their own protection but to protect other Christians from the women's potentially heretical influence (1:185).

Wigmore was one of Ward's oldest friends. The two reportedly met as young women when the Wards stopped at Coughton Court in Warwickshire. While there, both Mary and Winefrid attended a Mass celebrated by Jesuit Superior Henry Garnet and later walked the grounds getting acquainted. They quickly discovered their similar interests in faith, ritual, and spiritual books (Mother Mary Margaret 1955, 18–19). Their friendship would last a lifetime. Wigmore was one of the first English Ladies and held posts within the Institute over several decades, frequently serving as Ward's secretary. She returned with Ward to England after the suppression and was with Ward when she died.

Wigmore's devotion to Ward perhaps helps explain her poor judgment in rejecting absolute obedience to Church authority. In 1629, papal representatives tried to close three Institute houses, those in Trier, Liège, and St. Omer. In 1630, Ward, who was in Rome lobbying for the Institute, sent out letters to the women of the Institute instructing them not to obey the orders of these priests as they did not come directly from the pope or with his knowledge. Until the pope issued a final decision on the future of the Institute, Ward hoped that the Institute would be allowed to continue, and these men on their own had not the authority to shut it down (Wetter 2006, 32–35; Chambers 1882, 2:xxi–ii). Based on this communication, Wigmore, at Trier, resisted a papal nuncio's efforts to close the house, but then went further. The Jesuit rector of the English College in Liège, Fr. Stafford, in a September 1630 letter to the General of the Society, Mutio Vitelleschi, reported that Wigmore maintained that members of the Institute were more bound to obey Ward as general superior of the Institute than they were to obey the pope. They could even defy an excommunication (Wetter 2006, 41). That Wigmore made such assertions is not in doubt. Why she made them is unclear. Ward herself swore obedience to the pope and the Catholic Church. Wigmore's rash, undiplomatic words and actions, however, made it appear as if Ward and others intended to resist papal authority (37–58).

Wigmore's mistake likely contributed to the harshness of the Institute's suppression, and it certainly seemed to validate the fears of Ward's critics and Institute naysayers. Women's increasing trust in themselves to discern God's will was not permission to do as they wished, ignoring or disobeying clerical commands. Women could not rewrite their place in the Church according to their own wills. Conscience had to be disciplined and discerning. The voice of God communicated through the Holy Spirit authorized women to act according to God's will, not their own. Only then could the Church support women's challenges and changes to traditional understandings of women's gendered and religious roles. The Church was drawing its limits.

Bold Humility

When the Catholic Church held up Catherine Holland as an exemplar, it may have appeared as if the Church was de-emphasizing women's submission by condoning her many forms of disobedience. When Gertrude More and her Cambrai sisters criticized some male clerics and chose to ignore their advice, it may have appeared as if women were rejecting Church authority. In addition, when Mary Ward and the English Ladies ignored Catholic rules about mandatory enclosure and exceeded social limits on women's public behavior for over two decades before the Institute's suppression, it may have appeared as if they were abandoning religious and gender norms.

Appearances, however, can be deceiving. In reality, each of these women succeeded in balancing many of the contradictory expectations placed upon them by society and the Catholic Church. They could be both subservient *and* resistant, obedient *and* disobedient, humble *and* bold. These women supported their submission *as women* to both spiritual and worldly authorities as they reconstructed the very foundations of the relationship between women and the Catholic Church. They did this not by rejecting Catholicism, as Protestants did, but by sacrificing for it and attempting to strengthen it during a time of great need. Nor did they reject womanly submission to male authority more generally. Each of the authorities with whom they wrestled was male and supported by divine and natural law. Catholic women were going to continue to be the most obedient daughters, wives, laypeople, and nuns they could be with one important caveat: they would do so as long as their obedience did not offend the will and law of God as revealed to them through conscience. These women made little distinction between the voice of God and conscience. They were functionally the same.

These women saw themselves as following a long-standing hierarchy of obedience. No Catholic would have disputed that women owed submission to God first, followed by the Church and its representatives, the sovereign, and men within their households. Before the Protestant Reformation, this hierarchy was united by the same faith and forms of worship, creating a mutually supportive framework of gendered and religious relationships.

During the conflicts of the Reformation era, however, believers often had to make choices about which religious, government, or familial authority to obey. Holland and Ward chose to ignore their fathers' directives, prioritizing obedience to the Catholic Church and to God. Holland and More chose to limit their obedience to Christ's representatives on earth in certain situations in order to be obedient to God first. In addition, through their staunch fidelity to the Catholic Church and to God, Holland, More, and Ward all disobeyed the Protestant government.

Christian conscience was not a new concept, particularly in the Reformation era. What was new was the increasing number of women willing to trust in their own abilities to understand what God called them to do within a Catholic framework. Women had traditionally been counseled not to depend on their faulty judgment. As Ward noted, the majority of Catholic women were habituated to rely on priestly mediation to tell them what God willed. Without regular access to priests for almost three centuries, however, women increasingly had to rely on their own discernment. What was also new was their commitment to act according to this interior assurance, even when it thwarted the plans of fathers, husbands, priests, or monarchs. Women accepted their role as women to submit, but they increasingly chose or re-prioritized which authorities they would submit to and in what ways.

Women's obedience became less passive. Each woman's greatest act of disobedience was to insist on a greater voice in how her soul would be saved or perfected. Women were not seeking personal authority but spiritual benefit: for themselves, the Church, and God. Women would construct more intimate relationships with God and question any obstacles to such unions.

Above all, each woman's continued submission to authority appears as a great exercise in bold humility. Each woman submitted to God's authority absolutely rather than her own or a priest's will. Such humility should not be confused with powerlessness or meekness. These women's humility came from an interior strength in the face of overwhelming social and religious pressures. That fortitude was grounded in their confidence in and obedience to God.

Through the exceptional and detailed records of their thoughts, motivations, and actions, Holland, More, and Ward reveal how Catholic women could approach their challenges to lay and clerical male authority with great deliberation and forethought. These were not the frivolous and impetuous women portrayed in popular and religious tracts. It would have been much easier for them to submit to parental, clerical, or government authority and avoid the conflicts associated with the process of renegotiating their gendered and religious obedience.

Instead, some Catholic women chose the harder path, aiding and upholding their faith while supporting the Catholic Church in an era of religious division and conflict. The unusually well-documented experiences of Holland, More, and Ward provide a window into understanding the many other Catholic women such as Dorothy Vavasour, Alice Oldcorne, and Margaret Clitheroe, who left fewer marks in the historical record but who also cited their consciences as justifying their disobedience to traditional authority (Hirst 1913, 100–1, 105–6, 111, 112, 117; Mush 1849, 167; Myerscough 1958, 153). Many of their stories appear in later chapters.

These women struggled to create new paths whereby they could be good Catholic women because it had become so difficult to meet society's traditional expectations of women while simultaneously remaining devout Catholics. To do so required a certain degree of experimentation with women's traditional roles in lay and religious life. Each of these women pursued spiritual truth within the Catholic faith and saw herself as supporting its work and purpose. Catholicism was the vehicle through which these women embraced change, opening new spaces and opportunities for women within an old system. Faith justified the radical changes they made in their lives—such as Holland's—and the challenges they made to different authority structures—such as More's—as they embraced God in new ways. Because these experiments took place over almost three centuries, Catholics acculturated themselves to both the process and the results. Even after religious toleration decreased the need for women to take up these new roles, Catholic men and women would have been used to them.

Within limits, the Church supported these developments. Because of the importance the Church placed on women's continued Catholic loyalties in the Protestant British Isles, the Catholic Church gave women the opportunity to challenge and experiment with traditional forms of gendered and religious authority. The Catholic Church, however, did not alter its opinions about women and their natures in this era. Actions such as Holland's and More's were not behaviors the Church likely would have condoned had these women lived in a Catholic country. But then, would women have thought or needed to make them in such a country? Furthermore, Church support had its limits. The English Ladies—particularly Wigmore—pushed boundaries and the Church pushed back. Women could seemingly question their obedience to male clerical authority as More did, and criticize the clergy as Constable and Holland did, but not to the extent that Ward and her companions did. Where the Church drew the line will be defined more precisely in a later chapter.

However, the women were not alone in their efforts. Men, too, such as Augustine Baker, played a part in these changes. As the next chapter reveals, many Catholic men faced a struggle parallel to that of Catholic women. They wanted to be seen as good men and good Catholics in a Protestant-run society that made it almost impossible to be both. However, because Catholic men's relationships to authority were different than women's, their confrontations with gender and religious expectations take their own path, to which we will now turn.

Works Cited

Aquinas, Thomas. 1947. *Summa Theologica*. Translated by the Fathers of the English Dominican Province. New York: Benziger Bros.

Bilinkoff, Jodi. 2005. *Related Lives: Confessors and their Female Penitents, 1450–1750*. Ithaca, NY: Cornell University Press.

Bowden, Caroline. 2010. "The English Convents in Exile and Questions of National Identity c. 1600–1688." In *British and Irish Emigrants and Exiles in Europe, 1603–1688*, edited by David Worthington, 297–314. Leiden: Brill.

Catechism of the Catholic Church. n.d. Part 3, Section 1, Chapter 1, Article 6. http://www.vatican.va/archive/ccc_css/archive/catechism/p3s1c1a6.htm. Accessed July 15, 2015.

Catherine of Siena. 1940. *Le Lettere di S. Caterina da Siena*. Edited by Piero Misciattelli. Florence: C/E Giunti-G. Barbera. L. 121, 2:200–1. Translated by Karen Scott in "St. Catherine of Siena, '*Apostola*.'" *Church History* 61, no. 1 (1992): 34–46.

Chambers, M.C.E. 1882. *The Life of Mary Ward (1585–1645)*. 2 vols. Edited by Henry James Coleridge. London: Burns and Oates.

Durrant, C.S. 1925. *A Link Between Flemish Mystics & English Martyrs*. Preface by Francis Cardinal Bourne. London: Burns, Oates and Washbourne.

Ellis, Pamela. 2007. "'They Are but Women': Mary Ward (1585–1645)." In *Women, Gender and Radical Religion in Early Modern Europe*, edited by Sylvia Brown, 243–63. Leiden: Brill.

Gaudium et Spes. 1965. Point 16. http://www.vatican.va/archive/hist_councils/ ii_vatican_council/documents/vat-ii_cons_19651207_gaudium-et-spes_en. html. Accessed February 12, 2016.

Gallagher, Lowell. 1999. "Mary Ward's 'Jesuitresses' and the Construction of a Typological Community." In *Maids and Mistresses, Cousins and Queens:*

Women's Alliances in Early Modern England, edited by Susan Frye and Karen Robertson, 199–219. Oxford: Oxford University Press.

Gertz, Genelle. 2013. "Barbara Constable's Advice for Confessors and the Tradition of Medieval Holy Women." In *The English Convents in Exile, 1600–1800: Communities, Culture and Identity*, edited by Caroline Bowden and James E. Kelly, 123–38. Burlington, VT: Ashgate.

Godfather's Information, or Certaine Observations Delivered me by Mistress Marie Allcock, the First Minister of Mistress Wardes Companie at Leeds (Liege) yea the First of All Who Was Publicklye so Called. 1623. n.p.

Hirst, Joseph H. 1913. *The Blockhouses of Kingston-upon-Hull, and Who Went There. A Glimpse of Catholic Life in the Penal Times, and a Missing Page of Local History*. Introduction by Francis J. Hall, 2nd ed. London: A. Brown & Sons Ltd.

Holland, Catherine. 1925. "Conversion of Sister Catherine Holland." In *A Link Between Flemish Mystics & English Martyrs*, by C. S. Durrant, preface by Francis Cardinal Bourne, 272–305. London: Burns, Oates and Washbourne.

Kaplan, Benjamin, Bob Moore, Henk van Nierop, and Judith Pollmann, eds. 2009. *Catholic Communities in Protestant States: Britain and the Netherlands c. 1570–1720*. Manchester, UK: Manchester University Press.

Kenworthy-Browne, Christina, ed. 2008. *Mary Ward 1585–1648: A Briefe Relation with Autobiographical Fragments and a Selection of Letters*. Rochester, NY: Boydell and Brewer for the Catholic Record Society.

Lockey, Brian C. 2015. *Early Modern Catholics, Royalists, and Cosmopolitans: English Transnationalism and the Christian Commonwealth*. Burlington, VT: Ashgate.

Lux-Sterritt, Laurence. 2011. "Mary Ward's English Institute and Prescribed Female Roles in the Early Modern Church." In *Gender, Catholicism, and Spirituality*, edited by Lux-Sterritt and Carmen M. Mangion, 83–98. London: Palgrave Macmillan.

McClain, Lisa. 2004. *Lest We Be Damned: Practical Innovation and Lived Experience among Catholics in Protestant England, 1559–1642*. New York: Routledge.

Mother Mary Margaret. 1955. *The Wedge of Gold: The Life of Mary Ward (1585–1665* [note: Ward died in 1645]) *Foundress of the Institute of the Blessed Virgin Mary*. York: Herald Printing Works.

Mush, John. 1849. *The Life and Death of Margaret Clitherow, the Martyr of York, now First Published from the Original Manuscript*. Edited by William Nicholson. London: Richardson & Son.

Myerscough, John A. 1958. *A Procession of Lancashire Martyrs and Confessors*. Glasgow: John S. Burns & Sons.

Orchard, M. Emmanuel. 1985. *Till God Will: Mary Ward Through Her Writings*. Foreword by Mother Teresa of Calcutta. Introduction by James Walsh. London: Darnton, Longman and Todd.

Persons, Robert. 1754. *A Christian Directory, Guiding Men to Their Eternal Salvation*. Liverpool: John Sadler.

Scott, Karen. 1992. "St. Catherine of Siena, '*Apostola*.'" *Church History* 61, no. 1: 34–46.

Sweeney, James Norbert. 1861. *The Life and Spirit of Father Augustine Baker*. London: Catholic Publishing and Bookselling Co., Ltd.

Walker, Clare. 2004. "Loyal and Dutiful Subjects: English Nuns and Stuart Politics." In *Women and Politics in Early Modern England, 1450–1700*, edited by James Daybell, 228–42. Burlington, VT: Ashgate.

Weld-Blundell, Benedict, ed. 1910. *The Inner Life and Writings of Dame Gertrude More*. 2 vols. Glasgow: R. & T. Washbourne, Ltd.

Wetter, M. Immolata. 2006. *Mary Ward: Under the Shadow of the Inquisition*. Translated by M. Bernadette Ganne and M. Patricia Harriss. Introduction by Gregory Kirkus. Oxford: Way Books, 2006.

CHAPTER 4

Wodehouse's Choice

In his autobiography, the Jesuit William Weston related the intriguingly titled story of "The Man with Brass Bowels" to demonstrate the torment and discomfort suffered by some Catholics who conformed to the Church of England. Elizabeth I had spent part of the summer of 1578 making a royal progress through Norfolk. At the completion of her sojourn, Elizabeth ordered all Catholics who had not yet attended Church of England services to do so or suffer the consequences of breaking her laws. Francis Wodehouse of Breccles, Weston's "Man with Brass Bowels," explained how he wrestled with this choice.

> That proclamation of the Queen … did not touch me lightly. On the contrary, it lay like a load on my mind. It was not a matter merely for myself, not just a question of imprisonment. My wife, my children, my whole family and fortune were concerned. At a single blow, all would be gone together. Yet, if I submitted, I would have to face perpetual disgrace in the eyes of decent men: and not that only, but infamy and the stigma of cowardice as well, and, before God, the assured and inescapable jeopardy of my soul. (W. Weston 1955, 148–51)

This story spotlights the almost impossible challenges faced by Catholic men such as Wodehouse who tried to fulfill society's traditional expectations of men while simultaneously remaining devout Catholics. Frustrated,

Wodehouse first mentioned his family and fortune. He was a prominent squire, with a well-recognized duty to lead and support his family and household (Jessopp 1913, 226, 239, 245). If he refused to attend Protestant services, he would forfeit a substantial amount of his wealth in fines to the state. If jailed for recusancy, he would be branded a criminal, unable to head his household or fulfill his masculine responsibilities.

If he followed the queen's command and conformed and attended Church of England services just this one time, he could save it all. To do so, however, would lose him a different type of masculine reputation—his religious reputation as a Catholic man. Fellow Catholics, men whose opinions mattered to him, would think him a coward and bad Catholic; and his capitulation would certainly displease God, endangering his soul. Wodehouse had a serious choice to make.

Wodehouse's dilemma is significant because the conflict he faced—between the fundamentally incompatible demands of traditional masculine social roles and religious faith—was experienced by many men throughout the British Isles (Glickman 2009, 58–59). Being born male did not guarantee a man's reputation for masculinity. Manhood had to be learned and earned, and thus could be lost (Cohen 1996; Neal 2008). In the Reformation era, religion assumed a more prominent place in this economy of masculinity, forcing a re-valuation of what constituted masculine capital and making it more difficult for Catholic men to earn it.

As the choice facing Wodehouse reveals, men began to debate masculine priorities and reorganize masculine hierarchies in this era of Protestant/Catholic tensions. Some traditional proofs of masculinity became inaccessible to Catholic men so they had to create new ones. Resembling the pressures faced by Catholic women discussed in the previous chapter, Catholic men were asked to submit to social, religious, and governmental authority in new ways that challenged their understandings of masculinity and restructured their relationships with the Church, government, other men, and women. Eventually, Catholic men would construct new definitions of masculinity that allowed them to be good men, Catholics, and subjects, but only after it became clear that traditional definitions of manhood no longer worked for many of them.

How to Be a Man

There was no one way to "be a man" in the British Isles in this era. Different groups of men—distinguished by age, social rank, socioeconomic class, and profession, among other factors—observed and upheld different standards of masculinity (Shepard 2003, 1–11). What these varying definitions shared was the need for men to prove their manhood to other men. This required a man to assume a particular position in society after proving that he possessed manly skills, as opposed to the traits of women, boys, or even beasts. There was no one way to supply this proof, but it usually involved tests. A man of rank had to demonstrate leadership, honor, and courage while cementing his place in society through marriage and the support of legitimate heirs. A cleric or man of learning fought battles with words and knowledge to triumph over opponents and gain status. Acts of self-mastery and self-denial—especially over sexual urges—were indicators of true manhood among such men. A craftsman had his own trials in which he showed mastery of his profession. Passing such tests eventually conferred full masculinity upon him by allowing him to head his own household. Young men or poor men developed their own tests to prove their manhood to one another as they waited for the time they could prove themselves men to broader society (Karras 2003; Shepard 2003; Murray 1999).

One of the highest praises a man could receive was to be recognized as a "true" man. A true man was one who was mature, moderate, and controlled in his personal life and in his relationships with others: in speech, action, emotion, and in his sexual relations. However, a true man was also expected to be genuine and transparent, his outward persona matching his inward thoughts and character. True men of any social status could therefore trust one another despite their differences (Neal 2008, 13–55, 150–56, 175–82, 243).

Before the Reformation era, men of good reputation sought to be seen as God-fearing Christians who fulfilled their duties as laypeople or clergy. After Protestant reforms, religion intersected with lay and clerical masculinities in new ways. Both Catholics and Protestants, for example, tied gender to religion by attempting to emasculate men of the opposing faith. When the Protestant government executed Catholic men for treason, they literally emasculated them, cutting off and burning their genitalia as part of the standard dismemberment upon the scaffold. Catholic and Protestant men also accused one another of being immoderate, inconstant, immoral, and untrustworthy men *because of their religion*. For example, when the Scottish Benedictine Alexander Baillie scathingly disparaged Protestants as "unhallowed offspring" and "sedicious and counterfeat Christians," he entered the confessional controversies between Catholics and Protestants in the early seventeenth century (Baillie 1628, preface to the reader, A3v, 16, 40, 42, 140). Protestant men, Baillie asserted, were trouble-making men. Whether he realized it or not, Baillie's references to dubious parentage, lack of respect for lawful authority, and fakery all touched upon issues impacting gendered reputation in the sixteenth and seventeenth centuries regardless of issues of religious belief and practice.

Religion was very much a lens through which Baillie and other Catholics viewed their own gender and that of their Protestant adversaries and vice versa. A man of the opposing faith was hardly a man at all (Strange 1649, 7; Baillie 1628, A5r, A6r, 27–28, 38–39, 42, 224). During the English Civil War, in particular, rivals articulated their political and military differences through language combining gender and religion. Parliamentarians decried Royalists as effeminate, debauched, and popish, implying unmanly subservience and immoderation. Cavaliers challenged Parliamentarians' control over their wives by labeling them cuckolds (Hughes 2012, 90–99). Through this mixing, the religion one professed joined qualities such as social rank, age, politics, and occupation as a prime determinant of a man's reputation. Like Wodehouse, Catholic men in the British Isles needed to re-negotiate relationships between their manhood, their faith, the state, and one another. Their stories provide insights that can be applied to men of other faiths as well.

As Wodehouse understood, a key component of masculinity was good husbandry. A man's reputation, his sense of manhood, indeed, the very order of society, all depended upon his ability to "husband," to manage and govern his "substance." He must be seen as mastering all who lived, and all that went on, within his household. Pastor Justus Menius represented this view when he declared in *Erynnerung* in 1528, "A husband has two functions: first, he should rule over his wife, his children, and servants and be head and master of the entire house; second, he should work and produce enough to support and feed his household" (quoted in Hendrix 2008, 71; also Whately 1617, 46–50, 73–76). A man who failed at this was considered unfit for greater community responsibility.

Catholic men, however, could impoverish their families through their loyalty to Rome. The 1581 Act of Persuasions raised fines for non-attendance at Protestant services four hundred-fold, from one shilling per week to £20 per week for four successive absences. Anyone who heard a Mass could be fined 100 marks, over £66, each month. Under the act, few Catholics could afford to avoid Protestant services without risking financial ruin and thus failing to fulfill their traditional duty of husbanding their resources. They faced Wodehouse's choice: refuse to attend Protestant services and face financial distress or conform to maintain their substance and lose their reputations among men whose opinions they valued.

Just as laymen such as Wodehouse needed to reframe their understanding of their husbanding responsibilities, so did Catholic clerics and monastics. One way such men had traditionally demonstrated their masculinity to other men was through husbanding church property. In addition to its churches, shrines, and monasteries, the Catholic Church had also historically controlled businesses, endowments, and large amounts of agricultural and pastoral lands. However, in the first decades of reform in the British Isles, monarch and government converted Catholic churches and cathedrals into Protestant houses of worship. Henry VIII dissolved over 1300 religious houses in England, Wales, and Ireland in the 1530s and 1540s, selling off their buildings, endowments, and other properties.

Both laymen and clerics would need to craft new expectations of how a Catholic man properly maintained his substance. For laymen who chose to absent themselves from Protestant services, the Jesuit martyr Robert Southwell (1561–1595) redefined Catholic husbandry when he told laymen to go ahead and impoverish their families because they would be doing so to maintain God's substance rather than their own worldly wealth. In his practical guide for lay householders, *Short Rules of a Good Life*, intended to encourage Catholic constancy in the face of hardship, Southwell asserted that each householder was a "bailiff, tenant or officer" in his relationship with God. God was "his landlord," and he must govern what he was given in God's best service (Southwell 1973, Chap. 1, lines 94–97, 104–5). Southwell instructed householders to view the husbanding of household wealth as intersecting with their spiritual responsibilities:

> See into the offices of the house and survey the household book. But if I have the government of it wholly in mine own hands, I must do it oftener, having regard that waste and lavishing be avoided, frugality used, and behaving myself in the demeaning of temporal things, rather as a steward or bailiff of another's goods than an owner of mine own, seeing that in truth I must at my dying day be liable to God [for] how I have spent every farthing. (Chap. 6, lines 184–94)

Southwell recognized that his readers would likely be called to make significant sacrifices of their material comforts and social positions but argued that such worldly affairs were secondary to their "principal business" of service to God and salvation of souls (Chap. 1, lines 32–33, 43–7). Some lay Catholics evidently took such instructions to heart, as when the recusant layman William Wiseman told the Jesuit John Gerard that he would make choices for his family and possessions by viewing them as God's treasure rather than his own (Gerard 1959, 47).

As a consequence of Protestant reforms, however, Catholic clerics in the British Isles no longer possessed the sacred spaces and other properties that had been so central to their religious masculinity. What was left for them to husband? Moreover, the loss of church buildings and monasteries was also the loss of privileged masculine space. Men's status rose as they acquired access to certain spaces within a church building, to jobs husbanding that space, and to the rights to conduct high-status rituals within that space (Coon 2011, 83–85, 98–215, 247). Clerics needed new ways to prove their manhood and male status to other men.

Most priests and friars living in the British Isles now depended on laypeople for financial support and to provide them with space in private homes. Clerics might spend a day, a week, months, or years in a layman's home. This created tensions between competing ideas of masculine authority. Within his home, a layman had the right to rule as master. This mastery included responsibility for each soul under his roof. Laymen knew their duty as heads of household to teach Christian values and set the standard of prayer and piety for the rest of the house (Murphy 1737, 42–43; Gerard 1959, 48). To allow religious disorder within one's household was perhaps the worst transgression of which a man could be guilty (Crawford 1993, 42, 50, 126–27).

However, male clerics, upon entering a home, often expected to act as heads of household in both spiritual and worldly matters, as they would have done in churches or monasteries. Priests had long described themselves as spiritual fathers over subordinate clerics and parishioners, a role analogous to that of secular men fathering and supporting children (McLaughlin 1999, 27, 31). Now, in lay homes, they saw themselves as father figures whose authority in all matters should be respected. They often reorganized household routines and expenditures in addition to leading worship (Southwell 1973, *Short Rules*, Chap. 3; Chambers 1882, 1:40; Gerard 1959, 43, 48, 51, 166–68).

In prior centuries, one's worldly father and one's spiritual father generally did not live in the same household. One could balance the authority and commands of each, albeit with occasional difficulties. The movement of Catholic worship from public to private spaces changed this relationship. With multiple father figures living in the same space and expecting to exercise similar types of authority over the same people, it was unclear what man filled which roles or who possessed authority in which situations. A household could not have two heads (Gouge 1622, fol. 2v).

It became important to re-negotiate how male authority functioned within the household, particularly in the numerous cases in which laymen kept priests permanently in residence (Southcote 1872, 23–26; Bedingfeld 1912, 38–39; Willaert 1928, 13–14). If one were wealthy, problems could be avoided by simply setting priests up in a household separate from one's own. Anthony Browne, 2nd Viscount Montague, did this by buying a house on Drury Lane in London for the purpose of harboring priests (Willaert 1928, 42).

Few Catholics could afford such expense. In the best cases, laymen and priests cohabited amicably and supported one another's efforts, possibly becoming friends. The lay Catholic Swithin Wells, for example, opened his household to priests who celebrated Mass there two to three times a day. Wells also served as their guide, escorting them across the country to other laymen's homes (Challoner 1839, 1:247–48). The Lancashire recusant William Blundell apparently enjoyed an excellent relationship with the Jesuit John Walton who resided with the Blundell family in the early 1650s. After Walton's health forced him to leave Lancashire for a warmer climate, Blundell corresponded with the priest for years, assuring Walton that his old room still waited for him (W. Blundell 1933, 40, 52–53).

In more challenging situations, however, conflicts over masculine authority arose. Household members exploited the uncertainty about who was in charge to play one man off against another. Marital tensions arose as wives obeyed priests instead of husbands. Children who wished to pursue religious vocations on the continent appealed to priests to overrule their fathers' orders that they remain and marry (Gerard 1952, 161–62; Mush 1849, 94–97, 116–22; Hamilton 1904, 159; Kenworthy-Browne 2008, 8–9; Mawhood 1956, 232–38).

Some priests worked actively on their end to lessen confrontations and discomfort over their presumption of authority. When John Gerard joined the Wiseman household at Braddocks (or Broadoaks), in Essex, he had some changes to the house and its routines he wanted made. To avoid trouble, he communicated his wishes in advance so that all the adjustments could be made prior to his arrival. "I had no wish to become a source of contention," he recorded, "and I waited a full two months before I moved in" (Gerard 1959, 48, 166).

Tensions could be complicated further if more than one priest resided in a home. Gerard was sensitive to such situations and took steps to avoid conflict. Before he arrived to stay at the home of Sir Nicholas Drury at Lawshall (or Losell) in Suffolk, from the summer of 1589 to the winter of 1591, he became aware that a chaplain had already been living with the family for some time. He did not want to step on this man's toes. Knowing that he had Drury's full confidence, Gerard took any changes he wanted made to Drury, who then proposed them to the chaplain as if they came from himself and not Gerard. All thus went smoothly (43).

Priests could also challenge the masculine reputations of other laymen in a household through inattention or insensitivity. Southwell, in *Short Rules*, clearly expected that he or any other cleric would exercise a high degree of authority in whatever home they resided. This was appropriate as such clerics were the spiritual superiors within the household, working for the good of souls within. Yet the normally perceptive Southwell displayed startling ignorance about the loss of status a male householder would face by following the priest's directions to behave "as a well-nurtured child behaveth himself toward his natural father" when submitting to a resident priest (Southwell 1973, Chap. 3, lines 19–23; also 2–3, 26–30). Southwell's instructions effectively stripped the householder of the masculine status and authority he had earned as head of his household.

Southwell's blindness to the emasculating impact of his words and attitude is on greater display in "An Epistle of Robert Southwell unto his Father," Richard Southwell, dated October 22, 1589. He described himself as a most respectful, grateful, obedient son, writing out of concern for the soul of an aging father near the end of his life. It grieved him that he was a priest who did much to benefit the spiritual health of others but had not had the opportunity to help the man to "whom he [was] indebted to for his very life and being" (Southwell 1973, lines 72–76; also 12–14, 36–39, 64–65, 153–55). He would try to make amends by steering his father down a better path.

Southwell continued by emphasizing his father's feebleness. "Your force languisheth, your senses impair, and your body droopeth, and on every side the ruinous cottage of your faint and feeble flesh threateneth fall" (lines 164–66). After characterizing his father's life as one of poor husbandry that had achieved little up to this point, he noted that "your tired ship beginneth to leak and grateth often upon the gravel of your grave" (lines 513–15; also 115–20, 179–91, 434–40, 448–56). Clearly Southwell thought there was no time to lose!

In a traditional family hierarchy, it should have been the father, Richard, who counseled the son, Robert, based on the status conveyed by his age and authority. To encourage his father to reverse this order of precedence, Robert re-conceptualized their relationship. As a missionary priest and Jesuit, he had been far from home for many years. He equated himself to scriptural figures such as Tobias and Esau (lines 76–86). Like them, he had journeyed far and come home bearing a great gift for his father: in Southwell's case, spiritual knowledge and authority. Southwell legitimated his inversion of the family's masculine hierarchy by turning to scriptural examples such as David, who was chosen by God over his own father and older brothers to do great works (lines 90–99).

Although assuring his father that he meant no dishonor or disparagement, Southwell clearly claimed the right to judge him. He promised to feed and cure his father, as he himself had been fed and cured by God. He would thus both rule over and support his father. To effect this, Southwell first maintained that both he and his father were equal in the eyes of God. They were brothers rather than father and son. However, more than a brother, Southwell claimed he was a "father to the soul that is a son to the body" (lines 130–31). As a priest, he served as a vice-regent of God, and his father should be "a dutiful child" and yield to him (line 535; also 521–37). He would be a father to his own father by using his labor to unburden Richard Southwell of his sins, thus saving him from spiritual death (lines 83–86, 109–14, 136–40). Yet, adding to the confusion over masculine roles, Robert simultaneously portrayed this as a duty of a son to his father. He begged his father to forgive him if he was overstepping, but too much was at risk (lines 521–37, 562–69, 577–82).

Southwell was right. The stakes were high, but not only for religion and salvation. For a variety of reasons—fear of inability to husband, competing male authority in some homes, loss of certain ways to prove religious masculinities—masculine hierarchies were destabilized because of their conflicts with religious priorities. Catholic men needed new ways to demonstrate their masculinity and piety to fortify their positions as worldly men and men of faith.

Carrots and Sticks

Unlike society's expectations for women's overarching obedience and submission before men's authority, society expected men to assert their masculine prerogatives in some situations while submitting in others.

Within the complex systems of male hierarchies, virtually all men had to submit to other men in some ways. Apprentices submitted to their masters. Youths submitted to their elders. Soldiers submitted to their commanding officers. Laymen submitted to clerics. Subjects submitted to their monarch. It was the tension between assertiveness and submission that stymied Catholic men such as Wodehouse.

Deferring to the monarch in matters of religion was nothing new in the British Isles, where the sovereign was presumably responsible for the care of souls. However, prior to 1534 there had been only one religion. Submission generally involved matters of right practice or belief within a shared faith. A violation might garner the miscreant a one-time fine or public penance. In the new environment of confessional division, the stakes rose. Nonconformity meant multiple financial forfeitures, long terms of imprisonment, and possibly death. In the past, violations were defined as heresy and handled in church courts. Now they were prosecuted in secular courts as secular crimes, such as treason.

The law employed both carrots and sticks to convince Catholic men to go to Protestant services against their religious inclinations. Sometimes coercion was physical, as when Protestant soldiers forced recusants to church under threat of death or when groups of toughs dragged Catholic prisoners in Manchester's "House of Rogues" to Protestant services. In such situations, both Catholics and Protestants often ended up bloodied (*CSP Dom* 16/460/56; Pollen 1908, 52; Murphy 1737, 33–39; Hirst 1913, 108, 116, 125–27). Social rewards for conformity were also used. If a man wanted government office or preference at court, he generally had to submit and take oaths agreeing to beliefs he did not hold. Other tactics, such as the mandatory use of the English language in all church services, eliminated the use of Latin from rituals while also silencing the Cornish and Welsh liturgies that men in those regions had used in their Catholic services prior to reforms (Ellis 1974, 72, 75–76).

Financial pressure was frequently exercised to great effect. In addition to facing debilitating fines, recusant men lost economic opportunities. They were barred from holding public office and could find it difficult to practice a trade or profession. Apprenticeships with Protestant masters became difficult to obtain and hold. Some Protestants refused to patronize Catholic-owned shops. In addition, while Catholics might study at university, they could not receive degrees unless they swore Protestant oaths.

In each case, Catholics had to make tough choices involving trade-offs of male status or authority. Many Catholic men submitted to varying degrees because, like Wodehouse, they feared losing their substance. Subtle resistance, however, was possible in the midst of apparent submission. Men's conformity could mean occasional, strategically planned church attendance—just enough to avoid persecution and fines. Authorities thought they had John Moore of Goosnargh in the diocese of Chester dead to rights in 1634 when they charged him with recusancy and of having attended Catholic rites of baptism, marriage, and burial, in addition to possessing and distributing Catholic books. Moore may well have been guilty of all those things, but he had conformed enough for the churchwardens at Goosnargh to certify that he went to church and so escaped the charges (HCCP 1634/16).

Church attendance did not, of course, mean acceptance of Protestant teachings. Some men read their Catholic psalters during Protestant services, much as they would have done at Mass. Others stuffed their ears with wool or prayed their rosaries kept in pockets (Bossy 1975, 130–31; SP Dom 12/240/295; Haigh 1975, 219, 277; Hirst 1913, 116).

A common pattern was for the male head of household to attend Protestant services while women, children, and servants remained faithful Catholics back at home. Public conformity could gain a man with Catholic sympathies considerable worldly preferment and opportunity. For example, although four of Welshman William Herbert's sisters married into prominent Catholic families and another became prioress of the English Augustinian nuns at Bruges, Herbert conformed and served in the House of Lords (Durrant 1925, 317–18). Similarly, Sir John Throckmorton served as Lord President of Wales while protecting his wife and son, who were both recusants (Loomie 1978, 140). Protestant officials as high as the lords of the Privy Council complained of how men who were really Catholics filled important decision-making offices, even though they paid no attention at church and their wives, children, and servants never darkened the church's doors (Add. MS 32092, fols. 218r–219v).

Such men were among those known as "church papists": individuals whose loyalties were with the Catholic Church but who nominally conformed to avoid trouble. This pattern of male-head-of-household conformity coupled with female recusancy repeated itself in the families of gentlemen and craftsmen, yeomen and laborers (Walsham 1993; HCCP 1624/19; Morris 1877, 3:248–51; W. Weston 1955, 37; Chambers 1882, 1:40). For example, Welsh schoolmaster Morgan Lewis conformed to keep his position at the Royal Grammar School at Abergavenny, Monmouthshire, while his wife, Margaret Pritchard, held tight to the

Catholic faith at home (Kenny 1963, 460–61; Gillow 1885, 4:205). Marye Cole, a 23-year-old unmarried woman of Middlesex, testified in April 1593 that her father, Robert Cole of Heston, conformed, though she and her mother were both in jail for recusancy (Petti 1968, 62).

But Catholic men who conformed were failing to fulfill certain aspects of their traditional masculine responsibilities. Men were supposed to lead their households in right religion. While a man attended services of a faith in which he did not believe, a woman, usually his wife, and possibly another man—a priest if one were available—would be leading his household in Catholic observances in his place.

This choice, as Wodehouse feared, could cost men a portion of their masculine and religious reputations among their peers. This was the most visible part of the trade-off of conformity, as the young Catholic nobleman Sir Anthony Babington understood. Sir Francis Walsingham, Elizabeth I's principal secretary and spymaster, approached Babington, flattering him that he had the skills to "make his mark in the state" (W. Weston 1955, 102). Walsingham offered Babington worldly advancement if he would demonstrate his loyalty to Elizabeth and turn over information on Catholic plots and priests. Babington took his choice to the Jesuit William Weston. Weston sympathized with Babington, telling him:

> There is no way I know which will get you out of the snare set for you. If you accept his offer, you deny your religion; if you hold him off and reject his advances, you expose yourself to inevitable death; and you cannot dissimulate and waver between the two without endangering your salvation; nor, if you did, would you keep for any length of time your Catholic name among Catholic gentleman. (102–3)

The threat of losing the esteem of his fellow Catholics obviously bothered Babington. He protested that everyone who knew him knew he was a Catholic even if "occasionally, I have acted and spoken rather more freely than I should." Weston assured the young man that no one doubted his faith, nor would they as long as Babington continued "to act in the manner that people rightly expect of a Catholic. On the other hand, if you take a chance and say or do anything which Catholics are afraid even to suggest to their most loyal and close friends, you cannot avoid suspicion and a bad name" (101–3). Babington made his choice, refusing to conform. He was later arrested as part of a plot to assassinate Elizabeth I and rescue the Catholic Mary Queen of Scots from imprisonment and place her on the English throne. Babington was convicted of treason and executed in September 1586.

Other recusants suffered in less dramatic ways. Recusant men were poorer than they would have been had they conformed because of fines, exactions, and lost economic and social opportunities. Catholic men publicly attested time and again that they paid these costs willingly as loyal Catholic subjects. Diaries and private correspondence from the seventeenth and eighteenth centuries—such as William Blundell's—tell a different story, showing that many men resented the penalties as unfair and burdensome (Blundell 1933, 184–88, 202–4, 212–17; Stuart Papers, 47/48).

The severity of financial hardship varied. Edward Southcote of Staffordshire, for example, was still able to serve three courses per meal per day. He complained, however, in a letter to his son, Philip, about how the number of dishes per course had decreased from 20 dishes on his grandfather's table to a mere five on his own. The family would have been much wealthier without the special taxes and fines assessed on Catholics (Southcote 1872, 42–43, 49–50).

Other Catholic men were more hard-pressed. Blundell wrote to his cousin, Thomas Massey, a Jesuit, on August 11, 1673, berating him for wastefulness. This was evidently a long-running dispute.

> Good cozen,
> Your last [letter] and your last but one (contrary to my frequent requests and your promise) were in needless double paper. I think it hath happened a score of times that the needless double paper of your own hath cost me 9d. or a shilling, whereas it would single have cost but 3d., or, if covered by your single paper, but 6d. at the most. If what you are to write require it, I will willingly pay for a whole dozen of sheets. I do only complain now (as often before) of *needless* paper. (Blundell 1933, 155)

By this time, Blundell had over three decades of experience cutting corners in the household expenses to maintain his wife, 10 surviving children, and their growing families.

Catholic men employed various strategies to cut their losses due to fines, sequestrations, and the like. Some recusant men illegally attempted to protect their wealth by converting it into movable property that they could conceal. Protestant officials were alert to this practice, and some Catholic men were caught. Other men asked Protestant men to front for them in financial transactions, especially those relating to property. For example, rather than give up a portion of property to the government, a Catholic man would transfer ownership or control of the property to a third party, often a Protestant friend, who could be trusted to give it back when circumstances were favorable (Blundell 1933, 40–43, 49–51, 70–71, 94). The downside of such attempts to preserve one's masculine reputation by protecting one's substance was that they involved unmanly activities such as deception, crime, and becoming obligated to other men.

Some men who faced Wodehouse's choice tried to mitigate the financial trade-offs of recusancy by husbanding their resources in new ways. Sir Richard Weston (1591–1652) and his wife, Grace, were resolute Catholics who regularly hosted Mass in an old family chapel. Weston's religious fidelity was strong enough to weather the tumultuous decades of the Civil War and Interregnum periods without compromise with the Church of England (Harrison 1899, 121, 131–33). During those decades, he tried to offset the heavy financial penalties he suffered for his faith by providing for his family through more efficient management of the rather poor land of Sutton Place, Guildford (Harrison 1899, 120–22, 126–30; SP Dom 23/193/825).

Weston was passionate about finding new ways to improve his land's productivity. He fled to Flanders at the beginning of the Civil War not only to escape the conflict but also to educate himself about Flemish agricultural techniques that might improve crop yields. He returned in 1643 and set about innovating on his manor. In 1645, Weston anonymously published a small book known popularly as *Brabant Husbandrie,* detailing how landowners could boost agricultural productivity by adopting Flemish methods, such as the introduction of clover and turnips as field crops and the use of canals and locks for irrigation. Weston also constructed the first canal in England. Within a decade, his book was reissued twice—this time identifying Weston as author—and landowners throughout the island were successfully incorporating his ideas (Hartlib 1651; Harrison 1899, 123).

Weston clearly envisioned this text as fulfilling his masculine duty to provide for his family and husband his substance well. In the reissued editions, Weston addressed his sons, identifying the treatise itself as his legacy, a last will and testament that his sons should execute. His guidance would show them how to improve an estate while benefiting the public good, surely the noblest way for a man to increase his wealth, one that made a man worthy of praise and honored by his neighbors. He paraphrased Cato, writing that, "it is a great shame to a man, not to leave his inheritance greater to his successors than he received it from his predecessors" (Hartlib 1651, A3r–v). Indeed, not to do so was tantamount to committing high treason—an interesting foil to the usual accusations made against

Catholics at this time (Hartlib, A3r–4r; Harrison 1899, 124–25). While other men fought in the Civil War, proving themselves men through tests of courage and strength, Weston focused on different proofs: better husbanding of property and family in the name of public service. In this way, Weston sought to preserve his masculine status as a Catholic man.

Husbandry was not just a worldly pursuit but a religious responsibility as well, Weston claimed. It was, first and foremost, commanded of men by God and the most common endeavor among men. It was natural. It was holy. Before beginning, his sons should "lay the foundation of [their] husbandry upon the blessing of Almighty God," asking God's aid in all their labors, because God was the source of this newfound prosperity toward which their father would guide them. This truth, he said, was the "quintessence and soul of Husbandry" (Hartlib 1651, A4r). Nineteenth-century chronicler Frederic Harrison observed that other than Weston's quotations from the Vulgate Bible, these views could easily have come from any Puritan, and he expressed surprise that a Catholic Royalist penned them at the apex of the Civil War (Harrison 1899, 125).

For this was a masculine and religious ideal that men of different faiths could agree upon. Samuel Hartlib, the man who reissued Weston's treatise, was a Puritan. Prior to publishing the second edition in 1651, Hartlib wrote to Weston twice, asking for confirmation that Weston was the author (Harrison 1899, 123). Many people, Hartlib attested, still sought copies of the book, and he felt honored to publish it. He heartily praised the book, claiming that their countrymen were beholden to Weston for his "Industrie and Ingenuitie" and for "such an improvement in their Husbandrie" (Hartlib 1651, A2r).

The Puritan Hartlib's enthusiasm for publishing the Catholic Weston's work might seem unusual in light of well-known religious animosities between the two faiths. One explanation is that a treatise on agricultural improvements had little to do with religion. Yet Hartlib clearly viewed Weston's treatise through a religious lens. In his letter to Weston, Hartlib apparently recognized how odd his promotion of a Catholic's writings would seem, but conveyed his certainty that it was the duty of all Christian men to oblige one another without partiality.

Hartlib seemed to view his publication of this work as a bridge across confessional divides. He pre-empted Protestant criticism by appending a dedicatory epistle of his own to the 1652 edition, addressed to members of the Commonwealth's Council of State. In it, he linked masculine and religious obligations in support of his publication of this book. It was the duty of all men *as men* to imitate Christ by serving mankind. Weston's treatise clearly did this by serving the public good so well. Hartlib touted the benefits of impartial love extended in service to all people and supported his views with quotations from scripture. Such advancement toward the Kingdom of Christ was more important than any outward considerations (R. Weston 1652, A2r–A4v).

Weston still paid a price for refusing to conform outwardly as men such as Herbert did. In 1651, he was reported for delinquency in paying his recusancy fines, and the government sequestered his estate. He was, however, able to reclaim part of his property before his death, with the help of Protestant allies (Harrison 1899, 128–29).

Deception, Disguise, and Dissimulation

As the choices facing Babington and Wodehouse made clear, however, the decision of whether to conform involved more than financial hardship. If a man conformed, he endangered his standing with his Catholic peers. If he became a recusant, he risked his reputation within broader Protestant society.

Recusants repeatedly heard themselves classed with thieves, rogues, and murderers. In 1650, the government passed a law that offered the same reward for the arrest of a Catholic priest as it did for a highwayman (Blundell 1933, 40). Catholics were often imprisoned with such lawbreakers, as if their crimes were equivalent. Some Protestants jeered at, provoked, and assaulted Catholics, who, after all, were not "true" men (W. Weston 1955, 202).

As unjust as such generalized aspersions and attacks may have been, Catholic men who considered themselves honest did engage in unlawful behaviors to protect themselves, their families, and their property. As mentioned previously, some men hid property from the government so it could not be seized. Rather than risk imprisonment, other men fled into hiding or led their households in flight from the authorities. It was not uncommon for Catholics to learn about an impending search in advance, through gossip about Protestant men meeting or the arrival of official-looking documents to men in authority. The Protestant Bishop of Hereford complained to the Earl of Salisbury in a letter of June 22, 1605, that when a search was made for Catholics in his area, they had all fled into the woods or over the Welsh border into Monmouthshire. The searchers visited villages in a 30-mile radius. Again and again, they found plenty of evidence of Catholic practice, in the form of images, books, and altars left behind, but all the people were gone except the occasional elderly woman or child. Obviously, everyone had been forewarned (SP Dom 14/14/52).

Other Catholics responded by cloaking their appearances, behaviors, and intentions in ways that harmed their reputations as true men if they were discovered. Many Catholic clerical writers, such as William Weston, urged Catholics to be honest about who they were as Catholics, even if they risked punishment (Weston 1955, 102–3, 120). Yet the very nature of such men's work on the mission made such honesty and transparency impossible. Secrets needed to be kept to protect the missionaries and those who aided them. A significant consequence of such stealth was that Catholic men opened themselves up to criticisms of dishonesty. Such men gave false names to their Protestant neighbors, within their correspondence, or when stopped by authorities, and clearly were not who they appeared to be. At Jesuit Superior Henry Garnet's arraignment as one of the Gunpowder Plot conspirators, authorities highlighted the many aliases Garnet used—Walley, Darcy, Roberts, Farmer, and Phillips—and used them to attack his masculine reputation. "Surely," his accuser asserted, "I have not commonly knowen(sic) or observed a true man, that hath so many false Appellations" (*True and Perfect* 1606, O1r, T1v–T2r).

Lay Catholics and clerics seeking to avoid arrest wore disguises that gave a lie to their identities. Catholic priests, for example, wore disguises to sneak into England, Scotland, Ireland, and Wales, and to avoid detection once there, as the Jesuit Thomas Holland did after his return to England in 1635. Skilled at changing his appearance, he could alter his hair, beard, and clothing to assume various guises, such as those of a merchant, servant, or man of rank. As he spoke fluent French, Spanish, and Flemish, he would disguise himself as a foreigner and speak in broken English if anyone questioned him (Foley 1877, 1:546–65).

The Jesuit John Gerard explained how he always dressed as a "gentleman of moderate means" in order to move undetected through Protestant society. Once caught and imprisoned, however, he wore a Jesuit gown and cloak. Protestants angrily called him a hypocrite. "Why didn't you go about in these clothes before?" they taunted. "Instead you assumed a disguise and assumed a false name. No decent person behaves like that" (Gerard 1959, 105).

The Franciscan missionary Henry Heath tried to have it both ways: wearing his habit while being disguised. Before setting off for England, his superiors tried to give him an outfit of secular men's clothing. He refused.

Instead, Heath left Douai in his friar's habit. When he arrived at Dunkirk, before setting sail across the English Channel, he hired a tailor to transform his habit into a suit of laymen's clothing and his monk's cowl into a sailor's cap. He was still, technically, wearing his habit. Emphasizing the continued religious nature of his seemingly secular apparel, he used the lining of his cap as a place to store Catholic writings he wanted to smuggle into England. Despite his subterfuge, he was arrested in England soon after his arrival (Stone 1892, 158; Challoner 1839, 2:138).

Catholics tried to justify their actions by finding precedents for a man's use of disguises and deceptions. In defending such practices, Gerard directed his examiners to the example of St. Raphael, who "took a disguise and a false name, and his incognito helped him to do the work which God entrusted to him" (Gerard 1959, 105; also 38). However, while these justifications eased practitioners' minds that what they were doing was not sinful, they failed to convince others that these were honest and decent men.

Laymen trying to avoid arrest, assist the missionaries, or thwart Protestant authorities might employ disguises and deceptions as well (HCCP 1596/7; HCCP ND/11; Foley 1877, 2:497). Some of the more interesting examples involve men assuming female dress or identities to avoid detection. Part of proving oneself a man, recall, was to separate oneself from behaviors and actions common to women. In these cases, men risked their reputations as men in two distinct ways: through their lack of transparency and by deliberately adopting female personas. During the Civil War, for example, Blundell became "Cicely Burton" in his correspondence. Reminiscent of Mary Ward's lemon-juice letter hidden within a needlework pattern, he circulated military intelligence for the Royalists disguised as discussions of women's crafting. As one editor of Blundell's letters speculated, "We shall never know whether in those times of danger, William Blundell haunted his home, which no doubt was closely watched by unfriendly eyes, actually in female disguise or whether the alias was only made use of in case his letters were intercepted" (Blundell 1933, 20–21, 24, 26).

William Maxwell, Earl of Nithsdale, did cross-dress to avoid his impending execution in 1716, as detailed in this book's cover illustration, *Escape of Lord Nithsdale*. A Scots Catholic, Lord Nithsdale was sentenced to death for his leadership role in the Jacobite Rising of 1715 and jailed in the Tower of London. Winifred, Lady Nithsdale, a Welsh Catholic, detailed how she planned and executed his escape in an undated letter to her sister, Lucy Herbert. The night before his scheduled execution,

Winifred visited her husband, bringing a maid along. William exchanged clothing with the maid and left the prison dressed as a woman at his wife's side, undetected. He fled to the continent, first to France and later to Rome, again employing a disguise, but this time eschewing female garments for the livery of a servant to the Venetian ambassador. Winifred and their daughter joined him later, but only after Winifred put herself at risk by riding to Scotland to secure documents that protected her family's property claims (Durrant 1925, 318–324). In both these cases, men temporarily adopted female identities to deceive and evade religious and political authorities.

Laymen also practiced deception with their property. Catholics constructed secret, illegal chapels within their homes or on their lands. They hired Catholic architects to create ingenious hiding spaces in which priests could conceal themselves in case Protestant authorities searched the home. They buried forbidden items, such as altar stones and Catholic images, on their property. Household account books camouflaged payments to priests, the observance of Catholic fast days, and the purchase of seemingly ordinary household items, such as candles, for rituals (McClain 2004, 55–80; *Selections* 1878, xl, xlvii, liv, lxii, 207, 354; Blundell 1933, 158). Catholic homes and lives often disguised as much as they revealed, and Protestant neighbors and authorities either suspected or knew this for certain.

As such examples demonstrate, few parts of Catholic life could be taken at face value, and therein lay the problem with keeping one's reputation as a "true" man. As much as neighbors of different faiths might want to trust one another, they often knew they were not seeing the whole story. Who knew what lurked beneath the ordinary dress of a passerby—the hair shirt of a Catholic penitent? Was the peddler on the road really carrying fabric and notions for sale, or was this man really a Catholic priest, concealing Massing items beneath the bonnet, fabric, and other quotidian items in his trunk (Batt 1639, 2, 6–7; MacGregor 2015)? Some Catholics smuggled other Catholics in and out of the British Isles and fostered a black-market trade in Catholic books, relics, beads, and other objects. Still others were rumored to be secret agents for the papacy, corresponding in secret codes using invisible ink. Catholics engaged in forbidden rituals and celebrated marriages and baptisms in secret corners. Even Catholics imprisoned in jails were involved in such deceptive and criminal activities. Critics decried Catholic "legerdemain Tricks" and "Masquerade." They depicted Catholics as charmers or as buffoon actors, "Jack Puddings," up on stage, claiming that only the credulous person would be taken in by their acts (Wake 1689, A2r, A3r–v; *Five Scarce Tracts Belonging to the Popish Controversy* 1751, 3–4, 6; *Collection of the newest* 1689, 11–12).

The two related practices of dissimulation and equivocation contributed to this reputation for deceit and probably did more to damage the masculine reputations of Catholic men than did any actual criminal behaviors. Dissimulation, quite simply, is pretending not to be what one really is. For example, Catholics who feared prosecution pretended outwardly to be Protestants while continuing to be Catholics at heart. In essence, they lived a lie. Equivocation, on the other hand, tried to avoid an outright lie. When equivocating, a person used wording that was intentionally misleading although technically not a lie. It was explained as the withholding of the truth from someone who was not entitled to it and to whom the person being questioned was not obligated to divulge it. As Southwell discussed in his "Defense of Equivocation," Catholics typically used equivocation when questioned by Protestant authorities. It might involve answering a direct question with a "yes" or "no," while providing a mental reservation to oneself that contradicted or altered the obvious meaning of what had just been attested aloud (Gerard 1959, 134, 175, 250–53).

Although Catholics in the British Isles were not thinking about issues of masculinity when they employed dissimulation and equivocation, both practices challenged the ideal of the "true" man. Upholding this masculine ideal mattered more than ever in an era of religious division. As the anonymous author of the eighteenth-century *A Dialogue Concerning the Extent of Humane Reason in the Concern of Religion, & Determination of Matters of Faith: between C. L. of ye Ch. Of England, & J. R. of ye Catholic Church* conveyed, even if two people did not agree about their religion, each should be clear and candid in explaining their beliefs and sincere and honest in their dealings (Recusant MS B1048, 3–4). In that way, as in past times, men could trust one another despite their differences.

This valuing of the true and transparent within individual men also applied to entire groups of men, such as laymen and priests, and paralleled many of the larger doctrinal conflicts between Protestantism and Catholicism that were couched in terms of true faith versus false faith. The Catholic Church claimed that truth should always be visible, just as God's Church should always be visible (Hay 1783, 330; Vane 1649, 188–90). If the Protestant Church was the true church, where had it been for the past 1500 years? Protestantism was mere fashion. It possessed "weake, unstedfast, tottering foundations." If Protestantism had no firm foundation and was not true, then men who practiced it were false men—unsettled, uncertain, and inconstant (Strange 1649, 19). Protestant theologians defended their faith against charges of novelty by claiming that their faith only seemed new. God's truth was established centuries ago and simply hidden from view since the first centuries of Christianity until Protestants recovered it. Catholic polemical writers dismissed such claims, repeatedly emphasizing how the Catholic Church's continual visibility signaled its legitimacy (Martin 1978, pref. [unnumbered pages] 1–5; Challoner 1735, xi, 8, 16–17, 125; *Old Fashion* 1778, 128).

In this larger doctrinal debate, the Catholic Church's stance was that what was legitimate was not hidden. Of course, Protestants used this same standard to judge individual Catholic men and their actions. Catholics plotted in secret. They hid. They used false names and disguises. In contrast, as Sir Walter Mildmay asserted in a speech before the Star Chamber on May 16, 1582, the Protestant government was open and visible, charging such men in a public forum, where everyone could see and hear what was said and done (Petti 1968, 13–14).

While equivocation and dissimulation provided valuable short-term gains for Catholics by helping them avoid prosecution, they ultimately backfired by creating an overall impression that Catholics—especially men—were liars. Protestant accusations of Catholic dishonesty have been well-analyzed by historians, but Protestant critiques not only impugned the reputations of Catholics as subjects or as Christians, they also tarnished their reputations *as men*. It was no accident that Protestants repeatedly placed Catholics in the same group of dishonest individuals as thieves and rogues. All were false men, and, thus, all were dangerous. This impression would take decades, if not centuries, to overcome.

Dissimulation and equivocation contributed greatly to a general atmosphere of distrust among men. Believers of both faiths derided false men, counterfeit men, yet Catholic accounts of heroism in the face of persecution attempted to defend the counterfeit in their own actions while disparaging it in Protestants' (Holland 1925, 297–98). Similarly, Protestant authorities assumed that Catholics would be equivocating and dissimulating, so they felt justified in engaging in similar practices to ensnare Catholics, thus further diminishing everyone's ability to ascertain whether a man was "true" or not, regardless of faith. For example, Babington Plot informer Robert Poley was a Protestant in service to Lady Sydney, Walsingham's daughter. Poley went undercover as a Catholic to expose the plot against Elizabeth I's life. Southwell and William Weston both derided how Poley pretended to be all the right things to be welcomed and trusted by Catholics, and they called into question the masculine reputations of those Catholics foolish enough to fall for Poley's tricks, calling them "green wits," immature men who were precipitous, rash, and bold, caught fast like "silly fishes" on Walsingham's hook (W. Weston 1955, 85, also 81–84, 100–1). What appalled Southwell most, however, was how Poley disguised his true intentions beneath the cloak of religion (Southwell 1595, 2–3, 14–18). Of course, could not the same be said about Catholics who equivocated or dissimulated? In the end, no one could trust what someone looked like, what someone said, or who someone said they were.

Both Catholic and Protestant men expressed frustration at the situation they had allowed to develop (Bain 1894, 59/1/556; *Collection of the Newest* 1689, 8). Catholic men such as William Weston expressed astonishment at the strange concatenation of lies and truth that was brought to bear against Catholics accused of crimes. Government authorities arrested Weston in 1586 on suspicion of being involved in Anthony Babington's treason. Unable to connect Weston to the plot, authorities produced evidence of other treasonous activities that would keep Weston in jail. One witness, Weston described, bore false testimony against him, but "as I listened to this, I could not help but be astonished. A great part of what he said was true." Weston had to pick his way carefully through the witness's minefield of testimony, finding and exposing a number of falsities. He argued that if part of the testimony was a lie, the remainder must be suspect. "A man who had no hesitation in telling lies could not be trusted not to lie in everything he said" (W. Weston 1955, 89). Of course, this would be the same rationale Protestants used to brand Catholic equivocators as liars.

In the first decades after Elizabeth's Act of Uniformity, the Jesuit Weston and other men developed a standard of truthfulness in answering Protestant authorities. If one could tell the truth without endangering others, one did so. If telling the truth put others at risk, one should refuse to answer. Weston questioned his accusers' right to interrogate him about such issues, claiming that his clerical privilege protected him from their inquiries. He never denied his own Catholicity, but he told his accusers that he could not answer them without sin. He refused to swear on a Bible, claiming that his word as a priest was as binding as any oath (W. Weston 1955, 120–21).

Indeed, during these early decades, many Protestant authorities did trust the words of Catholic priests. For example, when the keeper of Wisbech Castle prison needed to move 36 jailed priests to a new location four days away, he was too cheap to pay a sufficient number of soldiers to guard the prisoners. According to one of the priests, Thomas Bluet, the priests promised to make the trip as scheduled without attempting escape. The keeper trusted them, and the priests kept their word. Other jailers placed similar trust in their charges, allowing them to leave prison temporarily as long as they promised to return, sometimes even allowing them a copy of the jailhouse key. Everyone knew that Catholic laypeople were breaking rules in the jails right and left, but surely the priests could be trusted (*CSP Dom* 12/283/70, 14/91/20; SP Dom 12/217/61, 12/265/135, 16/22/111).

Gradually, this blanket trust in priests diminished, as the lines between truth and falsity blurred with the growing use of equivocation in the early seventeenth century. The falsity and equivocation of Catholic men played a starring role in the trials of the Gunpowder plotters, especially in the March 1606 trial of Jesuit Superior Henry Garnet. The published transcript of Garnet's trial began with the indictments of the main conspirators, liberally peppered with terms like "traitorous" and "treason." The indictment described how the conspirators rented a house adjacent to Parliament and moved twenty barrels of powder into the cellar "for the traitorous effecting of the Treason, and traitorous purposes aforesaid." Afterwards, these conspirators "traitorously did meete" with other conspirators to plot what the indictment claimed was possibly the worst crime ever conceived, concocted by men so false they were more beastly than human (*True and Perfect* 1606, B1v).

The prosecutors lumped the priest, Garnet, in with these men by including a transcript of his separate trial with the published record of their indictment. Garnet emerged as the poster child for Catholic duplicity. In his arraignment, he became, according to Cecil, the concealer of the plot, a man who exemplified how "horrible Treasons haue bene couered vnder the mantle of Religion" (Y2v–Y3r). Garnet allegedly knew about the plot in advance but did not notify authorities. Garnet defended himself, claiming that one of the conspirators revealed the plot to him under the seal of confession. Although he could not reveal what he heard, he insisted that he wrote to Rome asking them to caution James about a possible attack.

Then, under questioning, Garnet equivocated. He denied having conversations that prosecutors later proved had occurred. He was hardly the first Catholic to equivocate. Other clerics such as Gerard and Southwell had upheld the method, and Garnet himself had written a treatise defending equivocation (Gerard 1959, 134, 174–76, Appendices D & E, 250–53). In fact, his accusers placed a copy of his own treatise in front of Garnet during his interrogation. Attorney General Edward Coke and other members of the Privy Council, such as Cecil, exposed Garnet's equivocation at trial and pulled every weapon out of their rhetorical arsenal to discredit Garnet as a false man. Garnet's lies and secrets linked him as a "rotten roote of that hideous and hateful tree of Treason." His "false tongue" was iniquitous. His crafty deceit was akin to that of the early heretics. The secrecy of his actions made him devilish. Garnet, the priest, was unchaste and adulterous because his lies were like bastard children, conceived by a heart and tongue that were not in accord (*True and Perfect* 1606, N2v–O1r, T2r–v, T3r, Y2v, Y3r). Coke harshly condemned Garnet and all Jesuits as hypocrites who censured other Christians for lying while justifying their own lies when the need arose (Y4v).

Despite Garnet's downfall, equivocation and dissimulation spread among lay Catholics, accompanied by Protestant suspicions and critiques of Catholic manhood (SP Dom 14/80/84, 14/87/15; Wake 1689, A1r–A2r, A3r–v). Protestant authorities subsequently strengthened rules and the jail facilities themselves to confine Catholics—even priests—more securely (SP Dom 14/80/78). Some Protestants believed that the papacy provided a dispensation that did not define equivocation as a sin in these circumstances in the British Isles (*CSP Dom* 12/245/131; *True Speeches* 1679, 8; Corker 1682, 197; 30 Chas. II, 2, c. 1 and 1 W. & M., 1, c. 8). Catholic priests, by conversation, letters, and treatises, instructed laypeople in how to equivocate and dissimulate. Of course, not all priests agreed, and their conflicting advice left some lay Catholics confused about what was permissible to say or do (McClain 2004, 255–68).

As Catholic men sought to maintain their masculine reputations under myriad pressures, one of their greatest challenges was overcoming this perception that all Catholic men were dishonest. Eventually realizing the long-term damage equivocation caused to both masculine and religious reputations, Catholic men began to publicly denounce the practice to convince Protestants that they were truthful, loyal subjects and happy to be so. John Fenwick, one of five men executed in 1679 for the Titus Oates plot, in his last speech, said:

> As to what is said and commonly believed of Roman Catholicks, that they are not to be believed or trusted, because they have Dispensations for Lying, Perjury, Killing Kings, and other the most enormous Crimes; I do utterly renounce such Pardons [and] Dispensations. (*True Speeches* 1679, 8)

Three other men executed in connection to the plot, the Jesuit John Gavan and laymen Richard Langhorne and William Howard, made similar assertions, asking listeners to accept their plain words at face value. All three men claimed that Catholics did not believe in such deceptions (*True Speeches* 1679, 6; Langhorne 1679, 3; Corker 1682, 186, 197). Pope Innocent XI officially condemned equivocation the same year.

Of course, the logical problem was that a Catholic could proclaim such honesty while equivocating. As a commentator in an "Animadversion" on Fenwick's and Gavan's speeches noted, such protestations of plain speaking might have been accepted from a man recognized for truth and sincerity but could not be taken at face value from Catholic men. "Their Credit is utterly blasted by their Doctrine," which allowed for falseness and insincerity under the guise of truth-telling. This author, approximately 70 years after Garnet's trial, dragged Garnet's equivocation back into the public eye, using it to explain how equivocation worked and why people could not accept the words of a Catholic, especially a Jesuit, as truthful, even at the hour of his death (*True Speeches* 1679, (separate pagination) 1–4, 7–8, 10, 15). In other words, Garnet lied then; these Catholics lied now.

Catholic leaders in the eighteenth century attempted to reclaim their reputations as true men by rejecting the formerly acceptable practices of dissimulation and equivocation. John Hornyold, Vicar Apostolic for the Midlands in England, confronted such issues in the introduction to *The Real Principles of Catholicks or a Catechism for the Adult*, first published in 1749. Cursed are we, Hornyold proclaimed, if we publicly claim a belief using anything but the ordinary sense and understanding of the words or if we use any equivocation or mental reservation in publicly asserting these beliefs (Hornyold 1821, xi). Scottish bishop George Hay, Vicar Apostolic for the Lowlands of Scotland who helped revive Catholicism in urban areas such as Edinburgh and Aberdeen, addressed the long-term harm done by equivocation and dissimulation in *The Sincere Christian Instructed*. When the full truth of a matter is discovered, as eventually it almost always is, Hay wrote, it appears as if the Church condones its members not telling the full truth. This gives enemies of the Church ammunition to use in discrediting the faith. It also, he noted, sets a bad example within the Catholic faith for youth and those of weaker understanding. Men should deal plainly and simply with one another and with God, without subterfuge or double-dealing (Hay 1783, 317–18, 321–22, 325–26). In *A Letter Addressed to the Catholics of England by the Catholic Committee* in 1792, Catholic Committee members asserted that Catholics no longer followed the exhortations of earlier popular Catholic writers such as Robert Persons and Nicholas Sanders to equivocate. Contemporary Catholics, the writers avowed, were loyal (4).

Catholic men, such as Henry Englefield of Sunny-Earley, Shinfield, near Reading, complied with the new directives not to equivocate, thus attempting to fulfill the older definition of true manhood by being open and transparent. Englefield registered with the government as a Catholic, he said, to avoid the hatred and mistrust that typified attitudes about Catholics. In plain terms reminiscent of Catherine Holland's attempts to prioritize her obligations to her father and her faith, Englefield explained what his loyalty looked like. He promised active obedience to his sovereign in all things inoffensive to God and non-resistance to the government in all other circumstances. He could not, he said, swear oaths according to the Test and Abjuration Acts because he would be bearing false witness, a violation of the Ten Commandments. The reason for his unwillingness, he explained, was that he believed in the real presence of Christ in the Eucharist. To swear an oath against the real presence would be perjury (Estcourt and Payne 1885, 8–9). Just as Holland understood herself as a good daughter despite her refusal to submit to her father in all things, Englefield presented himself as a "true" man although his loyalty to his sovereign was not absolute.

Second-Class Subjects

Men such as Englefield wanted to be seen as good men and good Catholics, but they also wanted to be seen as good subjects, worthy of the rights and status granted all men by their sovereign. It was well over two centuries before Catholic men attained this goal. Just as the transparency of the true man was believed to sustain the traditional gender order, religious transparency was thought to uphold the social order and political stability. Protestant pastor and theologian Richard Baxter (1615–91) reflected the views of many Protestant subjects when he preached to the House of Commons less than a month before the Restoration in 1660 that a papist simply could not be fully loyal to the sovereign because he could not serve two masters. One was ultimately loyal either to Rome or to the monarchy. A loyal subject must cease being Catholic.

Protestant authorities no longer viewed Catholic men as "true" men, and thus felt justified in passing laws that limited their customary liberties as male subjects of the crown. In addition to restricting public service and other employments, some laws limited Catholic men's movements and their ability to bear arms. Such constraints went to the core of these men's gender and religious identities, forcing them to craft new understandings of themselves and their relationships with men, women, and authority.

The government restricted Catholics' movements during times of domestic unrest or foreign threat, constraining them to within five miles of their homes. Protestants feared that Catholics would form a "fifth column," rising in support of the pope or a Catholic leader against the Protestant monarch. As the deputy lieutenants of Cornwall wrote to the Earl of Pembroke in December 1625, they were fully aware "of the dangerous contageon that may grow in this kingdom by those kind of Jesuited Papists more to be feared than Pestilence" (SP Dom 16/11/52, 52i). If Catholics wanted to go further abroad, for business or family reasons, they had to request special passes.

Likewise, when rumors of domestic or European threats reached a fever pitch, Protestant authorities stripped Catholic men of horses and arms they were otherwise allowed to possess. Authorities were supposed to leave some weapons deemed appropriate for Catholic men to defend their homes, such as bows, arrows, and pole arms, which were neither carried by men of status nor overly useful in close-quarters combat (Kempe 1836, 294). Particularly insulting was that the government sometimes sold confiscated arms, armor, and horses, so that the owners could not reclaim their property later. During the year of the Spanish Armada, 1588, for example, the Privy Council directed the Lords Lieutenant of the various counties to sell weapons taken from Catholics to Protestant militiamen who needed them, in order "to arm the Queen's true subjects." Money from the sales was to be given to the original owners, but this did little to soften the insult to their masculinity (Petti 1968, 31, also 101–2, 201, 283–305, 309–33).

Men valued their arms and mounts highly, as symbols of their manhood and their freedom. Swords, armor, and horses were not mere items to be replaced. Catholic men such as William Blundell felt their loss. As discussed in Chap. 2, Blundell proclaimed that when he fought for his king during the Civil War he wore his sword as a free man. When under house arrest, he wrote to his "Governor" on December 24, 1647, asserting that he had a pass to wear it signed by Sir Thomas Fairfax, leader of the Parliamentary army. As a Catholic, Blundell was imprisoned in his own house and needed another man's permission to carry the symbol of his free manhood (Blundell 1933, 26–27).

But these issues went deeper, to the core of a man's leadership within his household. After stripping many Catholic men of their ability to maintain their families financially, the government was also setting limits on Catholic men's ability to protect their families. If he was unable to perform these functions, was Blundell still truly the head of his own household? Blundell and other men had to work within such limitations as *de jure* but not *de facto* heads of household, as will be discussed in depth in the next chapter.

The following story illustrates the complexities of the situation. In 1647, the Parliamentary army quartered three of Fairfax's troopers in the Blundell home in Little Crosby. They were supposed to pay Ann Blundell, as property owner, for their keep. Ann, as William's wife, possessed the legal right to one-fifth of the family property after the government took the rest in penalties for William's recusancy, as discussed in Chap. 2. All three soldiers attempted to leave without paying, promising to send her money as soon as the constable paid them their wages (26–27).

Ann was understandably nervous about ever recovering a penny. Although she was legally entitled to the money, as a woman she had no way to compel the soldiers to pay her. She appealed to her husband. Though he had no legal rights in the matter and was under house arrest, William did have a sword. He organized four servants and three neighbors to help him stop the soldiers from taking their horses out of the Blundell stables until they paid Ann. Tensions escalated. Swords were drawn and sticks and stones brandished. Eventually cooler heads prevailed, and the men struck a compromise. They arranged for the constable of Crosby to pay what he owed the troopers directly to Ann, and the soldiers would send the remainder of what they owed later.

Ordinarily, a man exercising his well-recognized right to defend his property would raise few eyebrows. The problem was that Blundell, a Catholic man under house arrest as a potential threat to the government, had drawn a sword on three Protestant soldiers. Understandably nervous in hindsight, he picked up a pen and wrote to Protestant authorities to try to explain. He emphasized that he had only acted in defense of his wife's rights, claiming none for himself, other than the right to wear his sword by Fairfax's permission. He also asked whether there was a preferable way of handling the situation, considering that the soldiers were departing with no guarantee of returning (26–27).

Three decades after the stable incident, the government seized Blundell's weapon and required him to put up a bond for his good behavior during the fear generated by the Popish Plot in 1679. As discussed in Chap. 2, Blundell complained of this outrage at length to his friends and family. He had proven his manhood and his loyalty to his monarch, and this was how he was repaid? Then, 15 years later, when the government again confiscated arms and horses from Catholics in 1692 and 1694, Blundell was still sore over the continued indignity.

Blundell felt that he had demonstrated his loyalty time and again, counter to Baxter's assertions that it was impossible for Catholics to be loyal subjects. The anonymous author of a 1660 pamphlet entitled *The Good Catholick No Bad Subject. Or, a Letter From a Catholick Gentleman To Mr. Richard Baxter* objected and sought to prove his loyalty as well. The Catholic gentleman claimed that Baxter's choice—of being either a traitor to God or a traitor to the monarch—was a false dichotomy. He protested that he did not need, nor was he willing, to sacrifice either his faith or his allegiance to his sovereign. He challenged Baxter to prove that he, the author, was disloyal simply because he was a Catholic. If Baxter could do so, the gentleman promised he would back down (*Good Catholick* 1660, 2, 3, 6).

The author set up the controversy man to man, with phrasing reminiscent of a challenge to a duel. He had been injured, and he demanded satisfaction. He was entitled "to be righted," and because "no better Champion appears to defend me, think, I both may and ought to defend myself" (*Good Catholick* 1660, 3).

This gentleman contended that Baxter, men like him, and the law treated Catholic men as second-class subjects just because they were Catholic. Catholic men were denied a man's usual rights under the law. The author stood up against the injustices endured by many Catholic men who had complained for decades of their unsuccessful attempts to invoke their legal rights in a variety of situations: to protect their persons and property, to sue, to serve on juries, to witness, to mount a defense at trial, to execute a will, and to vote in Parliamentary elections. Catholic men accused of serious crimes, even murder, were presumed guilty because they were Catholics. Protestants who committed crimes against Catholics got away with it. Catholic men were targeted because of their religion, and their property was plundered. Sometimes they were killed (for examples, see *CSP Dom* 16/460/5, 16/460/52, 16/465/27, 16/457/48i; Murphy 1992, 172; Blundell 1933, 254–55). As a correspondent of Blundell's, J.W., shared, no one who absented themselves from state church services could use the courts to seek redress from any person who went to church. The law protected conformists. Everyone else was out of luck, including attorneys, according to J.W., who had so little business that they could not meet expenses (Blundell 1933, 173–75, also 187–88).

These rights mattered to Catholic men. William Aston, at 67 years old, decided to leave England because he had been unfairly indicted as a recusant. As he wrote to John Swinfen, MP for Tamworth, on November 1, 1676, he could not see the wisdom in living in a nation in which he was, by virtue of that indictment, "put out of the protection of my King and the laws of the nation" (Southcote 1872, 12). Some Catholics, such as John Caryll of West Harting, Sussex, found a way to work the system. Caryll temporarily conformed just long enough to bring suit before a court of law and then returned to recusancy (Myerscough 1958, 214–16). In the late 1680s, during the reign of James II when Catholics regained many of the rights they had lost, Blundell was proud to be able to bring lawsuits and carry his sword again. He exercised his rights as a full man before the law, at least for a short time (Blundell 1933, 243–44, 246).

The Catholic gentleman author of *The Good Catholick No Bad Subject* insisted that Baxter adhere to the crown's legal standards and treat Catholic men as full men in the eyes of the law. Innocence was presumed until an accuser proved guilt. Baxter had tarred the reputations of a large group of innocent men and denied them their birthright as subjects of the crown by his blanket accusation of treason without having met the burden of proof. The author even questioned the label "Papist" that Baxter used in his sermon to refer to Catholics. Many Protestants referred to Catholics as papists or "popish." These were hostile, anti-Catholic slurs. They implied a treasonous allegiance to the pope. Baxter, the author claimed, knew exactly what he was doing by using such a prejudicial term. Baxter wanted listeners to see Catholics not as Christians who were loyal to Christ but as men who owed "blind servile obedience" to a man, the pope. In this way, authors such as Baxter separated men into groups of worthy men entitled to certain privileges and protections and other men who were unworthy of such advantages. In this case, Baxter could convince others that Papists, because of their religion, were disloyal to their sovereign and unworthy of their birthright as English subjects (*Good Catholick* 1660, 4–5).

And yet it was his very Catholicity, the author claimed, that made him such a loyal subject:

> I am ready by Oath to confirm to all men in the face of heaven, That my loyalty to my sovereign is an indispensable duty from which no power

Spirituall or Temporal, Domestick or Forreign, under any pretense of Excommunication, Deposition, or any other whatsoever, can free me either wholly or in part; and til I am called upon to do it more solemnly, I here do in the mean time renounce all Dispensations, Absolutions, and whatsoever to the contrary ... I will by the grace of God, perform my Allegiance truly and fully as every good subject is bound to do. This is my Religion; this is what I have been taught in It concerning loyalty. (5–6)

Catholic men, in fact, claimed to be the best subjects, responsible for the country's greatness. As the anonymous author of the *Old Fashion Farmer's Motives for Leaving the Church of England* reminded readers, Catholic men of old were the very men who built the system of government and freedoms that Great Britain now enjoyed, such as Magna Carta and trial by a jury of peers (*Old Fashion* 1778, 128). Protestants were not convinced.

In the end, Wodehouse, the Man with Brass Bowels, made his choice. He decided to attend Protestant services, as some of his Catholic male friends encouraged him to do. Why risk everything if he could save it by just one trip to church? However, as soon as he entered the Protestant house of worship, Wodehouse described how his bowels began to torture him. It was as if they were on fire, sending flames higher into his heart and mind. He had an "unendurable hell" within him, but he would not leave the service. "To go out and leave the pestilential meeting when its business was only half through would avail me nothing, or rather place me in an even worse position than before." He'd already forfeited his Catholic reputation to go to the service. He wanted, therefore, to be sure that he got the financial advantages for which he had traded his religious honor. He suffered through the rest of the service and, as soon as it ended, went into the closest tavern. He downed mug after mug—reportedly eight gallons in all—trying to extinguish the hellfire within, but to no avail.

Returning home, he told his wife his woe. As a woman, the queen and government had not pressured her to attend Protestant services in the same way they had Francis. She sent for a Catholic priest, telling Wodehouse that only a priest had the power to channel the Holy Spirit to quench the flames and relieve his agony. According to Wodehouse, she was right. The priest resolved Wodehouse's intestinal difficulties, and afterwards Wodehouse resolved never to attend Protestant services again. He visited Edmund Freake, the Protestant Bishop of Norwich, to tell him so. Freake had Wodehouse immediately imprisoned. Wodehouse told

William Weston he did not mind the loss of freedom so much as the loss of his home and family (W. Weston 1955, 149–51). Weston, in turn, repeated the tale to strengthen Catholic men's constancy when faced with inducements to conform. While some details of this story must be taken with a certain skepticism, Wodehouse's circumstances and choices were real. They represent the struggle, passion, and determination of men to be true men and true to their chosen faith that reach beyond particular times and contexts.

Catholic men clearly faced a dilemma. Old understandings of Catholic masculinity—whether for laymen or clerics—no longer fit. They were left with Wodehouse's irreconcilable choice. If a layman chose to remain a loyal Catholic, he lost part of his masculine reputation. He failed to husband his substance, maintain and protect his family, and fully exercise the rights of a male subject. A priest or monk no longer husbanded the Church's substance, and his government branded him a treasonous criminal. Society no longer viewed either layman or cleric as a "true" man. However, if a man elected to keep his masculine reputation in society, he lost his religious standing. By conforming to the Protestant state church and fulfilling his time-honored obligations to maintain and increase his substance, he lost his good name among Catholics, failed to provide strong religious headship within his own household, and endangered his salvation.

Catholic men had to redefine Catholic masculinity. Although most surviving evidence concerns the struggles of impoverished men of middling or elite social rank, it is likely that Catholic men of humbler origins faced a similar need to renegotiate their masculinity in light of religious pressures. Men of all ranks needed to demonstrate their manhood to other men. They just employed different strategies to do so, particularly when their Catholicity made it difficult to prove their masculinity by traditional means. Like Catholic women, Catholic men needed to craft new standards for their gender that allowed Catholic men to rest in the knowledge that their reputations were secure both as good Catholics and as good men. To do so, they would select from among admirable attributes of Christians and traditional masculinity that were theoretically achievable and weld them into a new ideal of the Catholic man. Catholic men wanted to lessen the discomfort of Wodehouse's choice.

To this point, Catholic men's and women's efforts to satisfy gendered and religious expectations have largely been considered independent from one another: women such as Mary Ward faced one set of choices and challenges, while men like Francis Wodehouse and William Blundell dealt with another. Yet some of the most intriguing tests that men and women encountered occurred in their relationships with one another. The next chapter delves more deeply into the intimate details of the most common relationship between men and women: marriage. Just as Wodehouse shared his uncomfortable problem with his wife and a priest so they could search for solutions together, so did many husbands and wives, parents, laypeople, clerics, Catholics, and Protestants collaborate in arbitrating the seemingly irreconcilable demands of gender and religion in their interactions with one another. Their three centuries of experiences would re-negotiate relationships in marriage, the family, and the Church in this era, setting in motion a re-drawing of boundaries between personal, social, and religious authority that continues to this day.

WORKS CITED

Add MSS (Additional MSS). British Library.

Baillie, Alexander. (1628) 1972. *A True Information of the Unhallowed Offspring, Progresse & Impoisoned Fruits of our Scottish Calvinian Gospel, & Gospellers*. Reprint, Menston, Yorkshire: Scolar Press.

Bain, Joseph, ed. 1894. *The Border Papers: Calendar of Letters and Papers Relating to the Affairs of the Borders of England and Scotland, Preserved in Her Majesty's Public Record Office, London. Vol. 1, 1560–1594*. Edinburgh: H.M. General Register House.

Batt, Anthony. 1639. *A Short Treatise Touching the Confraternitie of the Scapular of St. Benedicts Order*. Douai: n.p.

Bedingfeld, Katherine. 1912. *The Bedingfelds of Oxburgh*. Privately Printed.

Blundell, William. 1933. *Cavalier: Letters of William Blundell to His Friends 1620–1698*. Edited by Margaret Blundell. London: Longmans, Green and Co.

Bossy, John. 1975. *The English Catholic Community 1570–1850*. London: Darton, Longman & Todd.

Challoner, Richard. 1735. *The Young Gentleman Instructed in the Grounds of the Christian Religion: In Three Dialogues Between a Young Gentleman and His Tutor*. London: T. Meighan in Drury Lane.

———. 1839. *Memoirs of Missionary Priests and Other Catholics of Both Sexes that Have Suffered Death in England on Religious Accounts from the Year 1577–1684*. 2 vols. Philadelphia: John Green.

Chambers, M.C.E. 1882. *The Life of Mary Ward (1585–1645)*. 2 vols. Edited by Henry James Coleridge. London: Burns and Oates.

Cohen, Miche'le. 1996. *Fashioning Masculinity: National Identity and Language in the Eighteenth Century*. London: Routledge.

A Collection of the Newest and most Ingenious Poems, Songs, Catches, &c. Against Popery. Relating to the Times. Several of Which Never Before Printed. 1689. London: n.p.

Coon, Lynda L. 2011. *Dark Age Bodies: Gender and Monastic Practice in the Early Medieval West.* Philadelphia: University of Pennsylvania Press.

Corker, James. 1682. *Stafford's Memoires, or, A Brief and Impartial Account of the Birth and Quality, Imprisonment, Tryall, Principles, Declaration, Comportment, Devotion, Last Speech, and Final End of William, Late Lord Viscount Stafford.* London: Langley Curtis.

Crawford, Patricia. 1993. *Women and Religion in England, 1500–1720.* London: Routledge.

CSP Dom (Calendar of State Papers, Domestic Series), of the Reign of Charles I, 1625–1649. 1964. Public Record Office, series 3. London: Longman, Brown, Green, Longmans & Roberts.

Dominicana: Cardinal Howard's Letters, English Dominican Friars, Nuns, Students, Papers and Mission Registers. 1925. Introduction by Bede Jarrett. London: Catholic Record Society, XXV.

Durrant, C.S. 1925. *A Link Between Flemish Mystics & English Martyrs.* Preface by Francis Cardinal Bourne. London: Burns, Oates and Washbourne.

Ellis, P. Beresford. 1974. *The Cornish Language and its Literature.* London: Routledge and Kegan Paul.

Estcourt, Edgar E. and John Orlebar Payne, eds. 1885. *The English Catholic Non-Jurors of 1715 Being a Summary of the Register of Their Estates [extracted from the Returns Made to the Commissioners by the Clerks of the Peace], with Genealogical and Other Notes, and an Appendix of Unpublished Documents in the Public Record Office.* London: Burns & Oates.

Five Scarce Tracts Belonging to the Popish Controversy. 1751. London: Reprinted for J. and J. Rivington, and S. Parker, Bookseller in Oxford.

Foley, Henry. 1877. *Records of the English Province of the Society of Jesus. Historic Facts Illustrative of the Labours and Sufferings of its Members in the Sixteenth and Seventeenth Centuries.* 7 vols. London: Burns and Oates.

Gerard, John. 1952. *Hunted Priest.* Translated by Philip Caraman. New York: Pellegrini and Cudahy.

———. 1959. *The Hunted Priest: Autobiography of John Gerard.* Translated by Philip Caraman. Introduction by Graham Greene. London: Fontana Books.

Gillow, Joseph. 1885–1902. *A Literary and Biographical History or a Bibliographical Dictionary of the English Catholics from the Breach with Rome, in 1534, to the Present Time.* 5 vols. London: Burns & Oates.

Glickman, Gabriel. 2009. *The English Catholic Community 1688–1745: Politics, Culture and Ideology.* Studies in Early Modern Cultural, Political, and Social History. Woodbridge, Suffolk: The Boydell Press.

The Good Catholick No Bad Subject. Or, a Letter From a Catholick Gentleman to Mr. Richard Baxter. 1660. London: John Dakins.

Gouge, William. 1622. *Of Domesticall Duties: Eight Treatises.* London: John Haviland for William Bladen.
Haigh, Christopher. 1975. *Reformation and Resistance in Tudor Lancashire.* Cambridge: Cambridge University Press.
Hamilton, Adam, ed. 1904. *The Chronicle of the English Canonesses Regular at the Lateran at St. Monica's Louvain.* Edinburgh: Sands & Co.
Harrison, Frederic. 1899. *Annals of an Old Manor House: Sutton Place, Guildford.* London: Macmillan and Co., Ltd.
Hartlib, Samuel. 1651. *Samuel Hartlib His Legacie: Or an Enlargement of the Discourse of Husbandry Used in Brabant and Flaunders.* London: Printed by H. Hills, for Richard Wodenothe at the Star under St. Peters Church in Cornhill.
Hay, George. 1783. *The Sincere Christian Instructed in the Faith of Christ from the Written Word in Two Volumes.* Dublin: P. Wogan.
HCAB (High Commission Act Books). Borthwick Institute. York.
HCCP (High Commission Cause Papers). Borthwick Institute. York.
Hendrix, Scott H. 2008. "Masculinity and Patriarchy in Reformation Germany." In *Masculinity in the Reformation Era*, edited by Hendrix and Susan C. Karant-Nunn, 71–94. Sixteenth Century Essays & Studies Series 83. Kirksville, MO: Truman State University Press.
Hirst, Joseph H. 1913. *The Blockhouses of Kingston-upon-Hull, and Who Went There. A Glimpse of Catholic Life in the Penal Times, and a Missing Page of Local History.* Introduction by Francis J. Hall. 2nd ed. London and Hull: A. Brown & Sons, Ltd.
Holland, Catherine. 1925. "Conversion of Sister Catherine Holland." In *A Link Between Flemish Mystics & English Martyrs*, edited by C. S. Durrant. Preface by Francis Cardinal Bourne, 272–305. London: Burns, Oates and Washbourne.
Hornyold, Joseph. 1821. *The Real Principles of Catholics; or a Catechism by Way of General Instruction Explaining the Principal Points of the Doctrine and Ceremonies of the Catholic Church.* Dublin: R Coyne, Catholic Book-Seller.
Hughes, Ann. 2012. *Gender and the English Revolution.* New York: Routledge.
Jessopp, Augustus. 1913. *One Generation of a Norfolk House: A Contribution to Elizabethan History.* 3rd ed. London: T. Fisher Unwin.
Karras, Ruth Mazzo. 2003. *From Boys to Men: Formations of Masculinity in Late Medieval Europe.* Philadelphia: University of Pennsylvania Press.
Kempe, Alfred John, ed. 1836. *The Loseley Manuscripts.* London: John Murray.
Kenny, Anthony, ed. 1963. *The Responsa Scholarum of the English College, Rome, pt. 2: 1622–1685.* London: Catholic Record Society, LV.
Kenworthy-Browne, Christina, ed. 2008. *Mary Ward 1585–1648: A Briefe Relation with Autobiographical Fragments and a Selection of Letters.* Rochester, NY: Boydell and Brewer for the Catholic Record Society.
Langhorne, Richard. 1679. *The Speech of Richard Langhorn Esq; at His Execution July 14, 1679. Being Left in Writing by Him Under His Own Hand.* London: n.p.

Lansdowne MSS. British Library.
A Letter Addressed to the Catholics of England by the Catholic Committee. 1792. London: J.P. Coghlan.
Loomie, Albert, ed. 1978. *Spain and the Jacobean Catholics, volume 2, 1613–1624.* London: Catholic Record Society, LXVIII.
MacGregor, Neil. 2015. "A Pedlar's Trunk." *Shakespeare's Restless World.* http://www.bbc.co.uk/programmes/articles/ZVdDDvbcZCNYTFQpqP4ZZl/transcript-shakespeares-restless-world-programme-14. Accessed January 19, 2015.
Martin, Gregory. (1619) 1978. *The Love of the Soule. Made by G.M. Whereunto Are Annexed Certain Catholike Questions to the Protestants. With a New Addition of a Catalogue of the Names of Popes and Other Professors of the Ancient Catholike Faith: And a Challenge to Protestants to Shew (if they can) a Like Catalogue of the Names of the Professors of the Protestant Faith.* Reprint, Menston, Yorkshire: Scolar Press.
McClain, Lisa. 2004. *Lest We Be Damned: Practical Innovation and Lived Experience among Catholics in Protestant England, 1559–1642.* New York: Routledge.
McLaughlin, Megan. 1999. "Secular and Spiritual Fatherhood in the Eleventh Century." In *Conflicted Identities and Multiple Masculinities*, edited by Jacqueline Murray, 25–43. New York: Taylor and Francis.
Morris, John, ed. 1877. *The Troubles of Our Catholic Forefathers Related by Themselves.* 3 vols. London: Burns and Oates.
Murphy, Cornelius. 1737. *A True and Exact Relation of the Death of Two Catholicks, who Suffered for Their Religion at the Summer Assizes, Held at Lancaster in the year 1628.* London: n.p.
Murphy, Martin. 1992. *St. Gregory's College, Seville, 1592–1767.* Southampton: Catholic Record Society, LXXIII.
Murray, Jacqueline, ed. 1999. *Conflicted Identities and Multiple Masculinities.* New York: Taylor and Francis.
Mush, John. 1849. *The Life and Death of Margaret Clitherow, the Martyr of York, now First Published from the Original Manuscript.* Edited by William Nicholson. London: Richardson & Son.
Myerscough, John A. 1958. *A Procession of Lancashire Martyrs and Confessors.* Glasgow: John S. Burns & Sons.
Neal, Derek. 2008. *The Masculine Self in Late Medieval England.* Chicago: University of Chicago Press.
The Old Fashion Farmer's Motives for Leaving the Church of England and Embracing the Roman Catholic Faith. 1778. n.p.
Petti, Anthony G., ed., 1968. *Recusant Documents from the Ellesmere Manuscripts.* Records Series. St Albans: Fisher Knight for the Catholic Record Society, LX.
Pollen, J.H., ed. 1908. *Unpublished Documents Relating to the English Martyrs, vol. 1. 1584–1603.* London: Catholic Record Society, V.

Recusant MSS. Harry Ransom Humanities Research Center. University of Texas.
Selections from the Household Books of Lord William Howard of Naworth Castle. 1878. Durham: Surtees Society, LXVIII.
Shepard, Alexandra. 2003. *Meanings of Manhood in Early Modern England.* Oxford: Oxford University Press.
Southcote, Edward. 1872. *The Southcote Family: Memoirs of Sir Edward Southcote, Knight.* Edited by John Morris. Roehampton, England: St. Joseph's Printing Office.
Southwell, Robert. 1595. *An Humble Supplication to Her Maiestie.* England: n.p.
———. 1973. "Short Rules of a Good Life" In *Two Letters and Short Rules of a Good Life*, edited by Nancy Pollard Brown. Charlottesville, VA: The University Press of Virginia for the Folger Shakespeare Library.
SP Dom (State Papers, Domestic Series). Public Record Office, Kew.
Strange, Nicholas. (1613) 1649. Introduction to *A Missive to His Majestie of Great Britain, King James, Written Divers Years Since, by Doctor Carrier Conteining the Motives of His Conversion to Catholike Religion*, by Benjamin Carier. Reprint, Paris.
Stone, J.M. 1892. *Faithful unto Death: An Account of the Sufferings of the English Franciscans During the 16th and 17th Centuries, From Contemporary Records.* London: Kegan Paul, Trench, Trübner & Co.
Stuart Papers. Royal Archives. Windsor.
The True Speeches of Thomas Whitebread, Provincial of the Jesuits in England, William Harcourt, Pretended Rector of London, John Fenwick, Procurator for the Jesuits in England, John Gavan, and Anthony Turner, All Jesuits and Priests; Before Their Execution at Tyburn, June the 20th MDCLXXIX with Animadversion Thereupon; Plainly Discovering the Fallacy of all Their Asseverations of Their Innocency. 1679. London: H. Hills, T. Parkhurst, J. Starkey, D. Newman, T. Cockeril, and T. Simmons.
A True and Perfect Relation of the Whole Proceedings Against the Late Most Barbarous Traitors, Garnet a Iesuite, and His Confederates. 1606. London: Robert Barker.
Vane, Thomas. 1649. *A Lost Sheep Returned Home: Or the Motives of the Conversion to the Catholike Faith, of Thomas Vane.* 3rd ed. Paris.
Wake, William. 1689. *A Defense of the Missionaries Arts: Wherein the Charge of Disloyalty Rebellions, Plots, and Treasons, Asserted Page 76 of that Book, Are Fully Proved Against the Members of the Church of Rome, in a Brief Account of the Several Plots Contrived, and Rebellions Raised by the Papists Against the Lives and Dignities of Sovereign Princes since the Reformation.* London: Richard Wilde.
Walsham, Alexandra. 1993. *Church Papists: Catholicism, Conformity and Confessional Polemic in Early Modern England.* Woodbridge, Suffolk: The Royal Historical Society, The Boydell Press.

Weston, Sir Richard. 1652. *A Discours of Husbandrie used in Brabant and Flanders: Shewing the Wonderful Improvement of Land There; and Serving as a Pattern for Our Practice in this Commonwealth.* 2nd ed. London-stone: William Du-Gard.

Weston, William. 1955. *William Weston, the Autobiography of an Elizabethan.* Translated by Philip Caraman. London: Longmans, Green and Co.

Whately, William. (1617) 1768. *A Bride Bush or Directions for Married Persons: Describing the Duties Common to Both, and Peculiar to Each of them.* Reprint, Bristol: William Pine.

Willaert, H. 1928. *History of an Old Catholic Mission: Cowdray, Easebourne, Midhurst.* Preface by Hilaire Belloc. London: Burns, Oates & Washbourne, Ltd.

CHAPTER 5

Amending the Marriage Contract

Elizabeth Cary, Lady Falkland's marriage was in trouble. Her husband, Henry Cary, Viscount Falkland and Lord Deputy of Ireland, had abandoned her. Privately, he cut her off financially, kicking her out of their home and seizing most of their household goods. He took their children from her care. Publicly, he denounced her character, calling her a wily woman, practiced in snake-like subtlety. He accused her of violating her marital duty to him in unconscionable ways to his shame and ignominy. He wrote to King Charles I, begging him to grant him a divorce so he could be free from this woman and she from him (Wolfe 2001, 268, 277, 293–94).

Her crime? In 1626, after over 23 years of marriage, Elizabeth converted to Catholicism, and everyone knew it. For the next seven years until her Protestant husband's death in 1633, Elizabeth Cary chose to practice Catholicism openly. She lived among Catholics in defiance of her husband's wishes; petitioned the king and his Privy Council for the financial support that Henry refused to provide; and increasingly involved herself in the religious disputes of the day (McClain 2014, 69–89). In 1630, Elizabeth Cary proudly proclaimed her identity as both a Catholic and a woman in her published translation of French Cardinal Jacques Davy du Perron's treatise of religious controversy, *The Reply of the Most Illvstriovs*

Cardinall of Perron, to the Answeare of the Most Excellent King of Great Britaine, the First Tome (Cary 1630, epistle to the reader and dedication). Henry Cary became, in his own words, "notorious over all the Christian world for this defection of his Wife's" (Wolfe 2001, 293).

Theoretically, neither Cary spouse should have been able to get away with any of this. Society expected Henry, as a man, to exercise his natural and divinely ordered right to rule over his wife and to maintain her financially. Elizabeth's proper feminine role within marriage was to submit to her husband's authority on all issues, particularly on religious ones.

Despite their frequent protestations to the contrary, neither Cary conformed to expected gender norms within marriage, and their noncompliance was rooted in religion. Henry Cary railed in an April 1627 letter to Sir Edward Conway, Charles I's Secretary of State, that a husband's supremacy trumped a wife's preferences "so our Religion teacheth," yet Henry could not compel his wife to obey either his masculine or his religious authority (277). It was husbands, not wives, who bore the greater social stigma in such situations as men who failed to master their subordinates (Shepard 2003, 73, 83, 86; Whately 1617, 46–49; Rowlands 1985, 150–51). In the end, Henry abdicated his responsibility for his wife. Similarly, Elizabeth Cary told Charles I in a letter of May 1627 that she wanted to "avoid the semblance of what I so much hate, which is disobedience" (Wolfe 2001, 282). In a 1630 petition to the Privy Council for spousal maintenance, Elizabeth insisted that she was an obedient wife, "unwilling to oppose her lord" (356–57). Yet her actions belied her claims. She consistently privileged her loyalty to God, Catholicism, and her conscience above her submission to her husband. Elizabeth did not use her faith as an excuse to flout her husband's authority. Instead, the expectations she faced as both a wife and a Catholic proved irreconcilable. Neither Cary could easily make choices that fulfilled both the gendered and religious demands placed upon them by society and faith.

Elizabeth's conversion and later choices held far-reaching consequences beyond one husband's tarnished reputation. In addition to endangering Henry's career and his standing as a man, Elizabeth's public defiance of male, marital, and religious authority threatened the foundations of religious, social, and political order in the British Isles. Henry, for example, corresponded with both Charles I and Conway, begging Charles to intervene to force Elizabeth into obedience. This was not just about his own marriage, Henry stressed. "The honor of our Religion, and of his Majesty," indeed, the institution of matrimony itself were at stake (277, 293–94).

Surely Charles's kingdom was big enough that he could find some out-of-the-way place to stash Elizabeth where she could cause both him and the king little trouble, where they could both be free of her and the "scandal and shame" she caused them (318–19). Ultimately, despite all his efforts, Elizabeth Cary continued to live and act as she pleased, as a woman, a wife, and a Catholic, providing a very public alternative to the expected balance between gender and religion within marriage (McClain 2014).

Such marital challenges were hardly exclusive to the Carys, though the documentation of their troubles is exceptional for its quantity and details. As the public record attests, people gossiped, and both Carys encouraged this, corresponding avidly with friends and patrons, each seeking moral and financial assistance in their public battle. According to Heather Wolfe, Elizabeth Cary, in particular, was a master of the literary form of letter writing (Wolfe 2001, 226–27; 2007, 10). Although leaving less evidence, other couples of different social ranks struggled similarly with the fundamentally incompatible demands of gendered marital roles and faith during this era of religious divisions.

This was true even within unions in which both spouses were Catholic, as the Broughton, Lancashire, yeoman Richard Herst (d. 1628) and his wife discovered. According to a hagiographic account of Herst's martyrdom published in 1737, both Hersts were Catholic recusants, raising a family of six children with a seventh on the way. Richard Herst was plowing a field on the day the Bishop of Chester's men—Wilkinson, Norcross, and Dewhurst—came to arrest him. Norcross delivered the warrant to Herst, and Wilkinson struck Herst with a stick. A girl working in the field saw the trouble and ran for help. Herst's wife and servants rushed from the house, and both sides struck blows. During the fracas, Dewhurst fled across Herst's partially plowed field, where he fell on the uneven soil and broke his leg. The wound festered, and eventually Dewhurst died. The authorities called it murder, even though Dewhurst publicly swore that his fall was an accident. For the judge, Sir Henry Yelverton, Herst's Catholicism made his malicious intent and guilt a foregone conclusion. Persuaded by Yelverton, Herst's jury found him guilty and sentenced him to death (Murphy 1737, 33–37, 44).

Even when placing the hagiographic elements of this martyrdom in critical perspective, its portrayal of Herst's final wishes highlights Catholics' conflicting marital and religious responsibilities. Before his execution, Herst labored to reconcile his obligations as a husband with his duties as a Catholic. The authorities offered Herst his life if only he would swear an oath of allegiance to the king, an oath that the papacy forbade Catholics to swear. As a married man, he felt the pull to save himself at whatever cost so that he could fulfill his obligations to his wife and children. His job, he wrote, was to "preserve himself for their Sake" to be a "Help-mate" and comfort to his wife, sharing the struggle of raising their large family. As discussed in the last chapter, it was also his responsibility as their head of household to lead them in religion, to teach his family how to live virtuously, in accordance with God's law. He could do neither if he were dead. On the other hand, his obligations as a Catholic demanded he not compromise his faith and that he set a public example by bravely enduring his persecution. He needed to display loyalty, courage, and resolution on the scaffold to stand up for the Catholic faith against Yelverton's unjust imputation that all Catholics were wanton criminals (42–43).

Like the Carys, Herst could not be both a good spouse and a good Catholic by traditional definitions of such roles. In the end, he prioritized his faith above his marital and family responsibilities, dying on the scaffold at Lancaster on August 29, 1628. Before he died, he penned three letters to his priest. His first concern was for religion, the bias against it, and the health of his soul. His second care, however, was to ask the priest, his friends, and neighbors to take care of his family. "Be a Meanes to helpe my Wife, and my Children, to my poore Estate." Just hours before he climbed the scaffold, he wrote that his greatest worldly care was to ensure the continued maintenance and well-being of his family (64–67). However, his spiritual obligations outweighed his worldly ones.

As the experiences of couples such as the Carys and Hersts reveal, the boundaries of authority, obligation, and obedience in marriage fluctuated for both women and men depending on the social and religious priorities at stake. In some marriages, spouses were more likely to prioritize the demands of faith over expected gender roles. As a byproduct, husbands and wives began to share authority within marriage in new ways to meet their religious needs. If a situation did not directly concern a soul's health or other religious priority, however, spouses were more likely to fulfill their expected gender roles in marriage. In other unions, spouses typically privileged traditional gender roles over religious loyalties. Catholic women such as Catherine Holland's mother, Althea Holland—who obeyed her Protestant husband's demands that she attend Protestant services and catechize their children Protestant—and Catholic men such as William Herbert—who conformed to the law to keep his property and his ability to maintain his family—valued their faith but chose to uphold traditional marital roles and priorities. Both models—and probably many more—existed side by side, but it is Catholics' experimentation within marital relationships that is noteworthy because of the light it sheds on the intersections and negotiations of gender and religious priorities.

For almost 300 years, spouses sifted through competing priorities and dealt with the tensions they caused. Options were tried. Boundaries were tested, and some fell while others were reinforced. Husbands' and wives' attempts to mediate between gender expectations and the demands of faith were active and participatory. Yet they were also often unconscious, an unintentional byproduct of conflict. Individual and societal expectations about proper gender and religious behaviors within marriage subtly shifted each time a spouse made some sort of choice—such as Elizabeth Cary, Richard Herst, William Blundell, or Althea Holland made—that committed them to re-prioritizing the needs of either their gender or their faith. Spouses searched through unfamiliar territory for some sort of resolution that they rarely found. In the process, Catholics in the British Isles—some of them with their Protestant spouses—altered acceptable gender and religious roles within marriage; and just as they did during the Cary conflict, the neighbors watched and talked, sharing opinions and slowly changing attitudes about what marriage could and should be.

Tracking the Way to the Harlot's House

Protestant cleric and popular sermonizer William Gouge's 1622 warnings to society to protect the stability of the family at all costs sound familiar to modern ears. They parallel the fearful language used in some contemporary discussions involving changing gender roles, religion, and social order. Gouge urged that in order for the family and society to run smoothly, each person, especially husbands and wives, needed to know and perform their expected roles. As Gouge lamented, "Oh if the head and several members of a family would be perswaded every of them to be conscionable in performing their own particular duties, what a sweet society and happy harmony would there be" (Gouge 1622, fol. 2v). The family was the first authority structure from which all others, including church and commonwealth, proceeded. Any change in that foundation threatened authority and stability everywhere. Chaos would inevitably result (Shepard 2003, 70–77; Fletcher 1995, 411; Tague 2002, 95–106).

Despite their many other differences, Catholic writers agreed with the Protestant Gouge about the importance of maintaining men's and women's traditional roles within marriage. Both Catholics and Protestants repeated scriptural justifications such as Eph. 5:21–25; 1 Pet. 3:1–7; and 1 Cor. 7:3 that legitimated wives' subjection to their husbands in all things. The Catholic Church, indeed, referred to itself as the Spouse of Christ. Just as the Church must submit to Christ's authority in all things, a wife should submit to her husband's authority. Husbands, in turn, were to exercise their authority with love and wisdom (Challoner 1827, 326–27; Golding 1577, fols. 277v–283v; Fletcher 1995, 89).

Popular Catholic and Protestant speeches, sermons, and writings clearly spelled out the gendered roles expected of men and women within marriage (Gouge 1622, fol. 2v). The Puritan cleric William Whately (1583–1639) published a wedding sermon entitled *A bride-bush, or a Direction for Married Persons. Plainely describing the Duties common to both, and peculiar to each of them.* Whately entitled one prominent section, "On a man's keeping his authority." Above all, men proved and kept their masculine reputations among other men by actively exercising their authority over their households, wielding such authority like a sword, lest it become rusty from disuse. Men should direct their wives in what they desired to be done and what they forbade. They had the right to both reward and punish their spouses as they saw fit but should employ justice, wisdom, and mildness rather than violence and lead by positive example to assert their proper place in the household hierarchy (Whately 1623, 97–106; also Crouch 1637, B2r–B3v; Gataker 1620, 10).

But Whately went further, contending that the religious and gender orders upheld one another. Failure to exercise masculine authority over one's wife was a sin before God, with far-reaching chaotic consequences to divine and natural orders. It upset God's plan and turned nature upside down. Similarly, Whately informed wives of their obligation to recognize their God-given and natural inferiority to their husbands and to live that inferiority through obedience and reverence for their spouses. Anything less was "unwomanhood" that "tracks the way to the harlot's house" (Whately 1617, 38). Just as Catholic priests counseled women to distrust their own discernment and turn to male clerics for guidance, Whately instructed wives not to trust or exercise their own judgment over that of their husbands. A wife should be as biddable to her husband's will as a "well-broken horse." After all, Whately asked, "Why is she his wife if she will not obey?" And if a wife refused to obey and reverence her husband, why should her children or servants obey and reverence her (42–43)? In such writers' minds, all authority was linked. The failure of one link broke the whole chain. Whately gave the same justification for women's submission as Gouge had: "Out of place, out of peace," not only in one's household but in church and commonwealth as well (36). As Henry Cary had written to Charles I, a wife's refusal to respect her superior's authority created chaos and confusion among hierarchical relationships beyond the immediate marital one.

Of course, the reason that writers such as Whately and Gouge felt the need to hammer home the importance of husbands and wives fulfilling their socially defined and religiously legitimated gender roles within marriage was because so many spouses did not. Women, and wives in particular, were the focus of popular criticism as part of the well-known controversy debating women's nature, character, competence, and appropriate gender roles. This battle of the sexes, or "Fight for the Breeches" as it was known popularly, was fought in the public eye by women's detractors, such as John Knox (1558) and Joseph Swetnam (1615), as well as by their defenders, such as Rachel Speght (1617). In pamphlets, books, art, ballads, sermons, and other popular media, wives who stepped outside traditionally defined marital roles were described as dangerous, unnatural, even monstrous.

However, men's failure to fulfill their gendered roles as husbands was part of this debate as well. Popular ballads such as "Poor Anthony" simultaneously mocked and lamented the plight of husbands who could not control their disobedient and disrespectful wives. They also instructed men how to reclaim their God-given right to rule over their wives and restore proper order, often by violent means. Poor Anthony, for example, purposefully blinded his disobedient, shrewish wife by replacing her eye drops:

> But I had a Liquor I more did prize,
>   Made of Henbane and Mercury, steeped in whey.
> I dropped in, and anointed her Face
>   Which brought her into a most devilish case;
> For She tore and she ranted, and well she might,
>   For after that time, she never had Sight.
>
> I then did get her a Dog and a Bell,
>   To lead her about from Place to place;
> And now 'tis "Husband, I hope y' are well;"

> Before, 'twas "Cuckold" and "Rogue" to my face.
> Then blessed be that Henbane and Mercury strong,
> That made such a change in my Wife's tongue;
> You see 'tis a Medicine certain and sure,
> For the cure of a Scold, but I'll say no more. (D'Urfey 1700, 152–54)

The message from such entertainments was clear. A husband should not suffer his wife's failure to submit to his authority (Fletcher 1995, 118–20). As Whately had sermonized, a husband's most important responsibility was to keep his mastery over his household.

One of the most important aspects of a husband's authority in his home was his religious leadership. Each husband held the well-recognized responsibility for the spiritual well-being of every person under his roof. It was important to both Catholic and Protestant leaders that husbands ensure the religious loyalties of this and the next generations (Stanney 1617, 364–65; Whately 1623, 97–98, 109–12). The Jesuit Robert Southwell, in his *Short Rules of a Good Life*, explained to husbands how to exercise religious authority in a particularly Catholic context to create a devout household pleasing to God. As Southwell counseled, a husband's worldly concerns were important but secondary to his principal business, "the most weighty and important business and the most necessary matter wherein I must employ my body, mind, time and labor," which was service to God and the salvation of his own soul and those souls in his care (Southwell 1973, Chap. 1, lines 32–33, 43–47).

A husband's failure to lead effectively in religious matters was more serious than other lapses in marital duty. Whether from inattention, inadequacy, or dereliction of duty, a *faux pas* as religious head endangered souls. As the Jesuit Edward Scarisbrike (1639–1708/9) contended in his treatise encouraging membership in the Sodality of the Immaculate Conception to assist Catholics in their quest for heaven, thieves everywhere sought to steal one's salvation. It was not, however, the public thieves that one should fear most. Instead, it was the person within one's own household, the "domestic thief" of one's salvation, who was most to be feared. Just when a Catholic thought they had "barred the door" and were safe from corrupting influences, someone whom they would never suspect would figuratively open that door to ideas that would endanger all within (Scarisbrike 1703, 81). The head of household had to be vigilant within his own home to protect the salvation of those under his care.

'Til Death Do Us Part

It was difficult to exercise traditional forms of religious leadership within marriage because there were now so many different types of marriages in which faith and gender issues interacted in new and varying ways. When a Catholic married another Catholic, both partners might choose recusancy or one partner might occasionally conform and attend Church of England services to avoid fines. When a Catholic married a Protestant, the religious and gender issues involved would differ depending on which spouse practiced which faith. If two Protestants married, one spouse might convert later, as Elizabeth Cary did, changing the marital relationship unexpectedly.

If a Catholic wanted to marry another Catholic, the couple's first hurdle was to obtain a marriage celebrated by a Catholic priest. This challenged traditional expectations of the marriage ceremony itself. Many Catholic marriages, such as the future martyr James Duckett's to Ann Hart, never appeared on any official parish register (Merrick 1947, 62). In the absence of public Catholic churches, Catholics married off the books, when and where they could: in fields, in private homes, even in prisons (Longstaffe 1858, 71–72, 74, 113, 114, 140, 141). When questioned by Protestant authorities, some Catholics admitted their clandestine unions. John Harrison of Shropshire testified that he and his wife were married by an old priest while imprisoned in Newgate Prison (SP Dom 12/256/71, also 12/243/93). Sir Richard Cholmeley of Brandsby, Yorkshire, acknowledged under examination in 1607 that a Catholic priest married him and his wife in a field (HCAB 15 1606/7–1612, fols. 139–142).

A more notorious clandestine marriage involved Roger Widdrington, who led one of the most powerful Catholic families along England's border with Scotland in the first half of the seventeenth century. In 1633, the Court of High Commission of the County of Durham charged Widdrington with having married Rosamund Reeveley in secret in Scotland. It was not unusual for Catholics living near the border to choose to marry in Scotland. Crossing the border was not difficult, and the government's enforcement of the penal laws could be lax (McClain 2004, 219–25; Blundell 1933, 4).

In the course of their investigation, commissioners examined brothers Edward and John Hall, two of Widdrington's tenants. Both Halls testified that one morning about a year previously, Widdrington, Reeveley, and a few others showed up on horseback wanting the brothers to accompany them. As Widdrington was their master, Edward and John mounted up. The group rode over the border into Scotland to Cuthberthoope, where "about 11 o'clock in the daytime, there came a gentleman who was a stranger to [the Halls], being an old man," who met them in an open field. All their party dismounted, and "there the stranger took forth a book and called Mr. Widdrington and Rosamund together. Before he spoke anything, he asked [Edward] and his company if they knew any cause why these two might not be joined together, after which the stranger did marry Widdrington and Rosamund Reeveley." Edward Hall testified that he recognized what happened next as a marriage ceremony because it was in English, and he recognized the words as those used in his own marriage service. He said he thought that it must, therefore, be a service acceptable to the Church of England. Upon further questioning, however, he admitted that the older man said some words he could not understand at the end of the ceremony and that other members of the wedding party told him that the man was a Catholic priest. Following the ceremony, Edward attested that Roger and Rosamund returned to Widdrington's home just ten miles south of the border. The couple had lived there since as man and wife, and everyone recognized them as such. After the High Commissioners deposed the Halls, the case lingered for another year before being dismissed, likely due to Widdrington's influential position along the border (Longstaffe 1858, 68–70).

Most recusant families were not as powerful as the Widdringtons, however, and many Catholic men such as Richard Herst had difficulties fulfilling their responsibilities as husbands, heads of household, and loyal Catholics. As discussed in the last chapter, recusant men faced economic challenges in supporting their families because of fines, sequestrations of property, restrictions on livelihood, and the implicit bias that they were criminals because practicing their faith was against the law. Recusant men were frequently imprisoned. Some men, such as the Lancashire recusant William Blundell, fled into exile to avoid jail.

Despite such difficulties, many recusant husbands went to great lengths to fulfill their gendered marital and religious duties. While Herst had tried to ensure his family's economic and social stability within the Broughton community after his death, some jailed Catholic men tried to continue their religious leadership of their families even while absent—whether in jail, at war, on the run, or in exile. They could, for example, send letters home, filled with religious guidance to further the health of the souls still under their care. Sir Henry Bedingfeld, imprisoned in the Tower of

London during the English Civil War, described how he continued to care for his wife's spiritual state from afar. She would, he thought, be in difficulty without him and need "spiritual comfort in these most miserable times." As her soul was still in his care, he penned a book on Christ's passion and sent it to her, hoping that it would provide her guidance and peace. Inscriptions within this handwritten book suggest that family members continued to read his manuscript and benefit from Sir Henry's *in absentia* religious leadership, even after his death (Bedingfeld 1912, 58–59).

Many Catholic or Catholic-inclined heads of household chose to become church papists instead of open recusants. They nominally conformed to the Protestant state church while their wives and most children did not, as discussed in the last chapter. In a December 1592 letter to the Catholics of England, Cardinal William Allen counseled priests to be lenient toward these occasional conformers. Such men were afraid and only trying to save their wives and children from ruin. Allen was a Lancashire native who emigrated to the continent and founded the English College attached to the University of Douai in the Spanish Netherlands that became the first training ground for priests on the mission. Although he could not excuse conformity, he advised priests to absolve such sin easily, being "not hard, nor rough, nor rigorous" no matter how many times the church papist conformed (SP Dom 12/243/80). After all, it was easy to sit on the continent and condemn Catholics for occasional conformity when one did not have to deal first-hand with the penal laws.

In contrast to husbands' difficulties, wives such as Francis Wodehouse's wife often remained free and able to practice their faith at home. Because married women did not possess legal identity in their own persons but were "covered" under their husbands', the government did not consider them fully responsible for their actions, even when their choices violated the law. They typically avoided the worst consequences of recusancy and the moral discomfort of church papacy.

Over time, such circumstances wrought subtle changes in the dynamics of marital authority, providing wives more opportunities to share in the financial and religious leadership of the home. For example, Blundell voluntarily went into exile on the Isle of Man in 1646 and 1648 to avoid prison. While he translated polemical works from Latin into English and wrote a history of the island, Ann Blundell governed and maintained their large family back home (Blundell 1933, 19–20, 34). She again led their family through the challenges of the Interregnum in the 1650s. In addition to supporting the family with the one-fifth of the Blundell property she retained, as discussed previously, she served as *de facto* head of household during the four periods that Protestant authorities jailed her husband for recusancy.

Although society assumed that such instances of female household leadership were temporary, the practical reality was that women sometimes headed households long-term (Shepard 2003, 202–10). Husbands died or abandoned their families. Some women never married. Women in stable marriages typically made decisions for their families during men's frequent absences from home due to work, war, pilgrimage, incarceration, travel, or other need.

Catholic wives found themselves with not only informal responsibilities necessitated by their husbands' absences, but legal and property rights as well. When the government seized property from Catholic men to pay their fines, it allotted a portion—usually one-fifth—back to wives. Government officials recognized the state might wind up supporting families of impoverished Catholics if it did not allow them some provision, and they saw wives as lesser threats to the state than their husbands. Officials intended this portion to be sufficient to allow a woman, such as Ann Blundell, to provide for the family's material needs rather than a man, such as William. Thus, as an unintentional consequence of Protestant-Catholic conflict, Catholic women's roles within recusant marriages shifted, as they held legal right to family property and were often the day-to-day authorities in the household in the absence of exiled or imprisoned husbands.

This evolution in gender roles extended beyond worldly issues to religious authority as well. This was especially true within families where the husband conformed outwardly while his wife and children maintained Catholicism at home or where the husband was Protestant and the wife Catholic. Although husbands were legally responsible for ensuring the religious conformity of all members of their households, Members of Parliament threw up their hands in frustration in 1601 and refused to enforce the law. They said they preferred not to interfere in private family life. In reality, church papist husbands did not want to bring their wives to heretic services, and the government proved unable to compel them to do so. Parliament also confessed that, despite their best efforts, most Protestant husbands were incapable of changing their Catholic wives' religious consciences and nonconformity (Petti 1968, 208–10; Loomie 1978, 128; Bain 1894, 59/2/646; Rowlands 1985, 151, 154–56, 160). Again, in very practical terms, religious conflict altered the balance of gendered authority within families as the government essentially recognized that husbands such as Henry Cary either would not or could not enforce their natural and divine rights to lead in matters of religion within their own homes.

While husbands could still get into occasional trouble for their wives' and families' nonattendance at church, the government usually left them alone. After 1620, the perpetually cash-strapped Stuart kings were much more interested in harvesting recusancy fines than they were in prosecuting Catholic wives for recusancy or their husbands for permitting it. Throughout the public debacle that was their marriage after 1626, for example, the government never prosecuted either Cary, not Elizabeth for her recusancy or Henry for "allowing" it. The religious and gender issues involved still deeply concerned society and government, but individuals and families such as the Carys were left on their own to reconcile the conflict between the roles required by religion and gender.

Much of this renegotiation took place behind closed doors, and the balance between men's religious authority and women's submission began to shift. In the absence of regular priestly counsel and public Catholic churches, Catholic laypeople—male and female—exercised more authority over family religious life than did heads of household in countries where Catholicism was legal (Rowlands 1985, 162). For example, although families had long incorporated family prayers into their round of daily activities, home-based worship restructured Catholics' relationship to the liturgy and sacraments. If the numerous Catholic pastoral books circulating are any indication, Catholics in the British Isles had more types of liturgies, prayers, and devotional tools available to choose from than ever before (Blom 1982). These formed the crux of a family's daily worship regardless of whether a priest was available. As Richard Broughton encouraged in his *A new manual of Old Christian Catholick meditations, & praiers faithfully collected and translated, without any word altered, or added*, if true believers lacked a church or other place to assemble, they must remember from Matt. 16 that wherever two or three were gathered in Christ's name, he promised to be with them. They should sing, read, and pray together (1617, 25–26). Many Catholic families did this in their homes.

When priests were available, they frequently celebrated Catholic sacraments in a home setting. The Roman Church stood firm that Christians needed priests to mediate between God and humanity through the

Catholic sacraments to attain salvation (Vaux 1969, xxxiii–iv). Despite the difficulties and dangers, many Catholics, such as Ralph and Frances Huntley, went to great lengths to bring priests into their homes to perform the sacraments—especially baptism and the Eucharist. The Huntleys found priests to baptize all four of their children in their home (Longstaffe 1858, 114).

Protestant authorities knew of such goings-on but could only respond after the fact, as when they brought over 30 people before the Court of High Commission of York "suspected to relieve popish priests and to have mass" and having "children baptized by popish priests" in their homes (HCAB 9, fol. 174, also *CSP Dom* 12/263/55). Eventually, Protestant authorities began forcibly removing some children from Catholic homes to be raised Protestant (Underwood 2014, 75–112). Some parents compromised by having their children baptized Catholic first, to save their souls, but later having them christened in the Protestant state church (Myerscough 1958, 161). Because their children's names would appear in the official Protestant parish registers, parents hoped they would not be exposed as Catholics and their children would be protected.

Whether in a recusant, partially conforming, or mixed marriage, Catholic wives began to assume new and different forms of religious leadership within their homes, spaces over which women exercised much practical authority. A priest describing the religious routine of Grace Babthorpe of Yorkshire, wife of Sir Ralph, portrayed her as the parent that kept their children from going to Protestant services and that arranged to have each child christened Catholic (Chambers 1882, 1:40). Catholic men such as Robert de Grey of Merton in Norfolk and Edward Thornbury of Cheedle in Staffordshire admitted that they left certain aspects of ritual life to their wives' discretion, such as their children's baptisms.

This was a change from traditional Catholic baptism in which the father usually took a greater role than the mother, gathering godparents, family, and friends, and presenting his child at the church. In contrast, Grey said that his son was "christened by a midwife or by a priest, he knoweth not which" (Petti 1968, 44). Thornbury knew who the first of his son, George's, godfathers was but not the second. He knew his other two children had been baptized Catholic but could not say where. He "refereth that to his wife" (47–48). Recusant Joseph Hudlestone of Greystoke in Cumberland admitted in 1624 that a Catholic priest married him and his wife, Ellinor, but that he was not "instantly present" when each of their 16 children was baptized. He was confident, however, that they had been truly baptized according to the laws of God's church (HCCP 1624/18). He trusted that his wife and the priest had gotten the job done.

Although Catholic-inclined men who conformed to the Protestant state church were still nominally the heads of religion within their households, it is unlikely that they exercised the same religious authority as recusant men. They still attended clandestine Catholic marriages, christenings, and burials, and they still might harbor priests, but they did such things with the stigma of their occasional conformity hanging over them (HCCP 1634/16; Mush 1849, 68–71). As Wodehouse and the Jesuit William Weston knew, men who conformed lost some degree of status in the eyes of other Catholic men, and it is reasonable to suppose that they lost some measure of respect and authority in the eyes of their wives and families as well. For example, after Ann Lander of Yorkshire was jailed for recusancy, she learned that her husband, John, an attorney, had been arrested and imprisoned for mounting her defense. Part of his punishment was to be pilloried—displayed for the public's amusement and his own humiliation. He wrote Ann, telling her that he could not face the ignominy. He was going to conform. She wrote back, telling him in no uncertain terms that she intended to suffer whatever crosses came her way rather than risk offending Christ who had borne a cross for her. She hoped he would do the same. She convinced him to stand firm (Notes 1877, 323). Would Ann Lander have been disappointed in her husband's religious leadership had he followed through on his original intent to conform? Would she and their children have experienced his religious leadership differently knowing that he attended heretical services against his conscience while they remained loyal Catholics at home? Would a man's masculine reputation in the eyes of his household suffer for having bowed before the Protestant state and church? We lack the evidence to provide definitive answers to such questions, but it is reasonable to wonder how they might have impacted the interpersonal dynamics of marriages.

Irreconcilable Differences?

Mixed Catholic-Protestant marriages presented different challenges than all-Catholic unions, even ones in which a Catholic-inclined husband adopted a veneer of conformity. Both Catholic and Protestant clerics warned Christians not to marry outside their faith. Religious differences would add to marital tensions as spouses and their families argued over faith issues. Moreover, the beliefs of the "true" Christian could be tainted.

Also, what if one partner did not allow the other to freely practice their faith (Challoner 1827, 329–30; Kaplan 2007, 291–93)?

Despite clerics' attempt to discourage such unions, social, financial, and perhaps romantic considerations induced some families to pursue mixed unions with their eyes wide open. In some cases, the clerics' fears were realized, as the sister of Mary Ward's Institute, Dorothea, related in her narrative of her missionary work in rural Suffolk in the early 1620s. She described the plight of a gentlewoman "who had not received any sacraments in six or eight years, by reason she had married a heretic, who used her very ill." Dorothea was expectedly critical of this husband and feared for the woman's spiritual well-being after such a lengthy sacramental drought. She reported, "I travelled eight miles to get a priest" to ease the woman's parched soul (Chambers 1882, 2:35).

Weston, however, described several mixed marriages in which the partners lived amicably, working around their religious differences. When closely examined, however, such "work arounds" unintentionally renegotiated the boundaries of gendered authority in the home. In one marriage that Weston described, the Catholic wife would invite a priest to come to the family home when she felt it was time for her family to receive the sacraments. "At the same time she begged her husband to be away from home that day, so that the priest would be at ease in the house and be able to carry out his duties without restriction. From love of his wife—they belonged to different religions—the husband agreed to her wishes." Her husband—the head of household, her superior, and the religious authority within the home—had to leave so another man, a priest, could be comfortable assuming his role.

Once, the husband did not leave as expected because of inclement weather. The priest, however, showed up as scheduled. Because the rest of the family was upstairs preparing a room for Mass, the husband answered the door. "Though he guessed at once why [this man] had come, he welcomed him kindly, invited him in and ordered a fire to be lit so that he could dry his clothes; he showed him in fact every mark of hospitality." The husband, curious, asked whether he could attend Mass too. Although the husband was master of this house, the priest insulted him and refused to let him be present at a ritual in his own home, saying that, "Sacred things must not be given to dogs." The husband persisted, and the priest finally gave in. In the middle of Mass, however, the husband allegedly grew ill, perspiring and eventually fainting. When he came to, the priest informed him that this was God's punishment for insisting on being present in the first place. The husband then begged the priest to stay and discuss the fate of his soul with him. The priest acceded, and eventually the husband converted to Catholicism (Weston 1955, 34–36).

We must not, of course, take Weston's account at face value. His objectives in his autobiography were to chronicle his own successes as a missionary and inspire future priests on mission. Despite questionable events such as the husband's illness, immediate conversion, and obedience to a Catholic priest, his portrayal of the difficulties confronted by spouses of different faiths—and their inventive compromises to facilitate marital harmony—are consistent with other evidence (Weston 1955, 49–51, 90–91; Gerard 1959, 169).

As all these contrasting examples suggest, there was no blueprint for a mixed Catholic-Protestant marriage. As the English Lady, Dorothea's, example revealed, a Catholic wife might disobey her Protestant husband's religious leadership rather than further endanger her soul. Other wives, such as Althea Holland, chose to obey their Protestant husbands' religious directives; and although Elizabeth Cary's marriage dissolved in fact if not in law, some mixed marriages succeeded to the satisfaction of both partners, as in Weston's example.

When expectations about gender and religious responsibilities contradicted, partners in mixed marriages faced difficult decisions. In general, spouses tried to balance issues of faith with customs of gender. The scales tipped toward religious priorities when an issue directly concerning salvation was involved. If salvation was not at stake, spouses generally chose to uphold traditional gender roles in the family hierarchy. In making such choices, Catholic and Protestant husbands and wives actively and likely unintentionally renegotiated gender roles within marriage in different ways than spouses in all-Catholic marriages.

Clerics were involved, too. Clerics knew that spouses in mixed marriages arbitrated such issues, and some tried to influence this decision-making process. By trying to secure the religious loyalties of the spouses involved, they unintentionally participated in altering traditional gender roles, right along with the husbands and wives. For example, although the Catholic Church customarily championed wifely submission to husbands' religious leadership in the home, the Franciscan William Stanney wrote bluntly that Catholic wives did not need their Protestant husbands' consent to adopt certain Catholic practices. Their salvation was at risk, which warranted exceptions to usual rules of marital conduct. He even changed the entrance requirements for membership in the Third Order of

St. Francis, the lay penitential order he was encouraging Catholics to join. The original rules stipulated that wives needed their husbands' permission to enroll. That rule, Stanney claimed, applied only to people in Catholic countries. In the British Isles, where devout women routinely married Protestants, husbands were "so far from giving their consent to any virtuous course of life, that they rather seeke all means possible to withdraw" their wives from the Catholic faith and salvation. "God forbid that such devout souls, which have great need for aid and consolation, should for want of husbands' consent be deprived of so many and great comforts," as membership in his organization provided. It was all right, in this case, for wives to act on their own, without spousal consent (Stanney 1617, 228–29).

Stanney tried to sugar coat this gender "heresy" to make it more palatable. Membership in the Third Order of St. Francis, he claimed, would make these women far better wives. Becoming a member would withdraw a wife "from the pomps and vanities of the world ... & thereby joining [her] nearer to God, & not only [as] a means to keep [her] from vain company and idle expenses, but to have a greater care of her husband's good & his family also." However, in the end, Stanney told wives that it was acceptable for them to deceive their husbands on this issue for the sake of their souls (228–29).

Stanney's assumption, like many clerical writers', was that wives were submitting to male authority by following priests' printed instructions (McClain 2004, 47–48, 249–51). Even though he advised wives to disobey their husbands, his clerical masculine authority was replacing their husbands', thus preserving women's expected subordination. In the end, though, it was the wife who made the decision. Yet a woman's trust in her own judgment was precisely the conduct that writers such as Gouge and Whately discouraged. If a woman thought her preferences superior to her husband's wishes, she was wrong and should squelch any inclinations to defy him. The consequences would be dire. "Out of place, out of peace." Both sides couldn't be right.

If a wife ignored her husband's will and made her own choices, a husband theoretically should be able to call on the forces of religious and civil law as well as social pressure to compel her obedience. As the Cary example illustrated, this did not always work in the real world. Protestant husbands such as Henry Cary possessed the well-recognized right to discipline their Catholic wives for any disobedience, but they often failed to do so effectively for a variety of reasons. Ultimately, each husband had to decide what he would permit and the lengths to which he would go to enforce his will. Similarly, wives such as Elizabeth increasingly realized that they, too, had choices, however uncomfortable those choices might be. Both women and men weighed the conflicting demands of gender and religion, deciding how, when, and when not to act.

These negotiations seldom occurred in a vacuum, and as family, friends, neighbors, and even complete strangers watched, they could unintentionally exert a social pressure that influenced this re-balancing of authorities and priorities. Some of the biggest choices through which gendered and religious authority were re-shaped within marriages concerned baptism and the religious upbringing of children. One famous example involved Roger Palmer, first Earl of Castlemaine, whose Protestant wife, Barbara, was well-known to be a mistress to Charles II. Once branded the most famous cuckold in Europe, Roger chose not to discipline or leave his wife over her infidelity, probably because he gained his title and other benefits from it. Instead, it was Barbara who left him in 1662 following a dispute over how to baptize their son. A husband held the customary right to make this decision. Barbara, however, refused when he insisted that their son be baptized Catholic (Macaulay 1898, 2:36, 202–3). Rather than support Roger's masculine authority as a husband over his wife, Protestant society—people who did not even know the Palmers but who heard the news and gossip—generally supported the wife's decision, seeing it as Barbara's championing of the Protestant faith and her child's salvation. Because baptismal issues were fundamental issues of salvation, it was more important to uphold religious priorities rather than the gender hierarchy within marriage.

Once a child was christened in one faith or the other, parents in mixed marriages struggled over the rearing of the child. Some partners broke promises and trust with one another trying to save their children's souls. Althea Holland formally obeyed her Protestant husband John's command to raise and catechize their children Protestant but whispered privately in their children's ears about the one true faith that was their only path to salvation (Holland 1925, 273–74). In extreme situations, the Catholic parent might spirit a child out of the home and to the continent to receive a Catholic education without the Protestant parent's knowledge, as a York butcher's wife, Margaret Clitheroe, did with one of their sons (Mush 1849, 127, 145). A Protestant wife might lie to her Catholic husband. Alexander Gordon (1678–1728), second Duke of Gordon, had married a Protestant, Lady Henrietta Mordaunt, and the couple brought up their children in Alexander's faith. On his deathbed, he asked her to promise to continue raising their offspring Catholic. She agreed, vowing to engage a priest to continue their instruction. On the very first Sunday after Alexander's death, however, Henrietta began taking their family to the Protestant church (Blundell 1909, 1:7).

As the Gordon example illustrates, the death of one spouse in a mixed marriage often freed the other spouse to change course and raise children according to their faith. Henry Cary, for example, had limited Elizabeth's contact with their children while he lived, but after his death, she persuaded as many of their children as she could to convert to Catholicism. Archbishop William Laud complained to the king in July of 1634:

> The Lord Newburge hath lately acquainted me that Mrs. Ann and Mrs. Elizabeth Cary, two daughters of the late Lord Falkland, are reconciled to the Church of Rome, not without the practice of the Lady, their Mother. Your Maiesty, I presume, remembers what suit the Lord Newburge made to you at Greenwich; and what command you sent by Mr. Secretary Coke to that Lady, that she should forbear working upon her daughters' Consciences and suffer them to go to my Lord, their brother [Lucius Cary, a Protestant], or any other safe place where they might receive such instruction as was fit for them. The Lady trifled out all these Commands ... I have taken hold of this and according to my duty done what I could think fittest for the present. But the greatest thing I fear is that the Mother will still be practicing and do all she can to hinder. (Wolfe 2001, 386–87)

Elizabeth Cary succeeded in sending most of her daughters and sons abroad to receive Catholic educations. Her eldest son, Lucius, the family heir, was staunchly Protestant, but Elizabeth arranged to have her younger sons, Patrick and Henry, kidnapped from Lucius's home and smuggled over the Channel into France to be educated Catholic. Within days, officials questioned Elizabeth before the King's Bench and Star Chamber, where she avoided giving direct answers to their queries. Records of her interrogations reveal how, "Being again demanded where her said sons now are, she saith that she thinketh they are in France, but in what part of France she knoweth not." She practiced a form of equivocation by claiming she did not know *exactly* where her sons were (which was true), even though she had a pretty good idea. The Star Chamber knew that she was trying to obstruct their attempts to recover the boys before they left England and threatened to throw her in the Tower but never did (395–99).

Patrick and Henry became Benedictine monks, and four of five Cary daughters became Benedictine nuns (Lewalski 1993, 190).

Eventually, potential spouses in mixed marriages tried to negotiate solutions to all these problems prior to marriage, spelling out expectations about the free exercise of religion and child-rearing. Each party, likely counseled by family, friends, and clerics, deliberated which issues were non-negotiable and which would be compromised. Many clerics on both sides of the religious divide discouraged such deliberations, trying to ensure the constancy of their congregations to what each saw as the true faith. Catholic Bishop Richard Challoner told of the sad mixed marriages he had seen and that "those bargains are by no means to be allowed of, by which the contracting parties agree to have the boys brought up in the religion of the father and the girls to follow the mother. God and his Church will have no such division" (Challoner 1827, 329–30).

By the eighteenth century, mixed marriage arrangements between Catholics and Protestants could be quite straightforward. By this time, over a century of experience told couples what their biggest challenges would be. For example, in his diary, the Catholic William Mawhood, Sr., a London wool draper, described his negotiations to marry his daughter, Betsey, to a Protestant, George George. He wanted Betsey to have a peaceable marriage, and religious and financial considerations, in that order, were his main concerns. In a letter from December 1786, Mawhood admitted that he had seen a great deal of marital unhappiness in mixed marriages. He asked George to be certain that he could meld his Protestant religious principles with Betsey's Catholic ones. If so, Mawhood next inquired about George's ability to maintain his daughter. Religion was Mawhood's first concern. Maintenance was his second. Two days before Christmas, George appeared on Mawhood's doorstep, prepared to satisfy both of his future father-in-law's concerns. Betsey was to have the free exercise of her religion and an estate. The couple married two months later in February 1787, first in a Catholic ceremony and two days later in a Protestant one (Mawhood 1956, 245–46, 249). True to the promises made, when Betsey gave birth to their first child, a girl, that December, she appears to have been baptized Catholic (256).

Such proactive attempts to avoid marital disharmony were obviously moot when a spouse converted after marriage, as Elizabeth Cary did. Such conversions could create a sense of betrayal, disloyalty, and disadvantage, especially when the convert was the wife. The penal laws barred husbands of recusant women from holding public office, limiting their opportunities

(3 James I, c.5; 7 James I, c.6; 3 Will & Mary, c.2; 9 Will III, c.3; 7 Geo II, c.5). Elizabeth had thus placed not only Henry's position as Lord Deputy of Ireland but his entire future career in service to the crown in jeopardy. Henry subsequently threw his masculine reputation into question by his inability to control his wife's behaviors and his own choices in refusing to provide for her. Moreover, allowing religious heresy within his household was perhaps the worst transgression possible for a husband. God would surely punish a man for his wife's sins.

However, this was unless she could convert him. This would restore his gendered and religious leadership in the home as well as her submission to his authority. Priests discussed how mixed marriages offered a spouse a prime opportunity to convert a soul. There was little hope that Elizabeth Cary could convert Henry, but the Jesuit John Gerard described, for example, how in 1604 he converted the wife of a Protestant knight, and how that wife would later convert her husband. As with Weston, Gerard's self-reported success in the mission field must be considered with a degree of skepticism, but his optimism that one spouse might convert the other rings true. In considering her own conversion, Gerard reported that the wife understood "that as soon as her husband got to know, she would suffer heavily for it. And indeed she did." She converted anyway because she believed her salvation was at risk. At first, her husband attempted gentle persuasions to guide his disobedient wife back to her traditional submissive role in the family hierarchy, such as Whately suggested (Whately 1623, 100–1). When those failed, "he used threats—he tried every way of shaking her resolution," she told Gerard. "For a long time, it looked as if there was nothing for her to do but separate from her husband and lose everything she had in the world, in order to possess her soul in peace." Her husband suffered, too, losing his public office because of her recusancy. Eventually, however, the wife convinced her husband to convert as well (Gerard 1959, 188, also 169). In some ways, this re-stabilized their family hierarchy after her initial challenge to it. From both masculine and religious standpoints, the husband was once again the head of the household now that both partners were Catholic. God had used the wife; her initial disobedience was simply a means to procure her husband's salvation. Scripture allowed for this, Challoner assured his readers, quoting 1 Pet. 3:1. Wives were subject to their unbelieving husbands, with the caveat that such wives should work to gain their husbands' souls through acts and words (Challoner 1827, 326–27). The convert husband then enjoyed masculine and religious authority within the marriage and home once again.

Most mixed marriages, however, did not produce a conversion, and spouses had to learn to live with their religious differences and negotiate new balances between gendered and religious authority. As the marriage of Margaret and John Clitheroe of York demonstrated, such marriages could be peaceful and supportive in spite of the many hurdles. Both Margaret and John, a butcher, were Protestants when they married. Two to three years into their marriage, Margaret converted to Catholicism without her husband's permission and lived as a Catholic with his knowledge for 12 years before her death (Mush 1849, 75).

Margaret Clitheroe (c. 1556–1586) was arrested and jailed many times for recusancy and is one of only three Catholic women executed for violating the Catholic penal laws. Records of her questioning remain, and her confessor, a missionary priest named John Mush, penned her story, which exists in two versions, both of which agree in the pertinent particulars. These records expose in detail Margaret's 12-year attempt to find a balance between being a good wife to John and a good Catholic. John emerges as a Protestant husband who could be critical of his wife's faith but loving to his wife in spite of her challenges to his authority. The documentation reveals a blending of the religious priorities of disobedient Catholic women discussed in Chap. 3 with the challenges that husbands faced when their authority confronted the spiritual authority of Catholic priests in the home as discussed in Chap. 4. The Clitheroes' well-documented choices reveal how some spouses understood and resolved their differences, how both Catholic and Protestant clergy viewed such changing relationships to traditional authority, and what family, friends, and neighbors thought.

For his part, her biographer/hagiographer, Mush, walked a fine line between praising Clitheroe as a Catholic and describing her disobedient behaviors as a woman and wife. Mush carefully portrayed Clitheroe as an admirable woman who conformed to social values of female and wifely comportment. She was comely, humble, courteous, and charitable. She kept an orderly household and bore her husband many children. She had a "sharp and ready wit" but was modest in her words, showing extraordinary discretion in her actions (Mush 1849, 73; also 80–85, 99–100).

These admirable feminine qualities, he explained, were due to Margaret's extraordinary religious faith and zeal. Mush wanted to show that Catholicism did not compromise or conflict with her exemplary feminine qualities. *It produced them.* It also made what would traditionally be reprehensible in a woman—deception—praiseworthy. Mush described how Clitheroe would laugh for joy at her ability to deceive heretics (108). Unfortunately, one of those heretics was her husband.

John evidently loved Margaret in spite of their differences. For example, Mush described a public fight between the two at a neighbor's house where they were attending a banquet. John had apparently been drinking, and became "liberal of tongue amongst his pots." He began criticizing and mocking Catholics in front of the revelers. After John noticed Margaret crying, he tried to reassure her that when he spoke badly about Catholics, he "meant not these words of her." She was a wonderful wife. Then the other guests joined him in comforting her, telling her he'd only been joking, after all. When Margaret related the incident later to Mush, she claimed she had not cried because he had hurt her feelings. She wept for the offense to God. One wonders if either John's or Margaret's feelings could be so easily compartmentalized (139–41).

Although her husband and neighbors knew that Margaret was Catholic, they likely did not know the extent of her devotions, support of priests, and deception. Mush knew, and he chronicled her disobedient choices as heroism for the Catholic faith, much as supporters of the disobedient daughter, Catherine Holland, had done. For example, when Clitheroe wanted to practice religious self-mortification and fasting, she asked her priest for permission but not her husband. Indeed, she lied to her husband to conceal her ascetic behaviors. Her husband, Mush reported, was a convivial man who liked to take Margaret out with him to eat and drink. She would beg off, making excuses so that while he enjoyed an evening out, she could use the time "spared from superfluous feeding the body" to "feed the soul with prayer and meditation" (116–17).

From this seemingly minor offense, Margaret's deceptions grew. Invited to the countryside for a marriage banquet by neighbors, she accepted their offer. She intended all the while to abandon her companions once they were outside the city so she could have the day free. "She would devise," according to Mush, "twenty means to serve God that day, more than any other [day] at home." In the evening, she returned home to her husband "as though she had been afeasting" and he would never know how she had actually spent the day (122). Similarly, she used midwifery as a pretense to have more time to meet with priests, and her Protestant female neighbors supported her deception. Margaret had her friends send for her, pretending that a woman was in labor and that they needed her assistance. She could then "abide the longer with her [priest] to be instructed in necessary points of Catholic religion" (122). Clitheroe even snuck out at night or when her husband was away from home to take frequent pilgrimages to an old Catholic shrine situated just a half mile from York (118).

Over time, Margaret's disobedience changed in character, and she began to challenge her husband's authority as head of household in more concrete ways. For example, she began making critical decisions about religious issues without his knowledge. She equipped two rooms so she could entertain priests and engage in other Catholic activities without John's or the neighbors' knowledge. In doing so, she brought contraband items into her husband's house. She harbored criminals and endangered the Clitheroe home and family. She trusted the children with knowledge of the secret chambers, necessitating their deception of their father (145–46). About a year before her last arrest, desperate for her children to receive a Catholic education, she sent their eldest son to the continent for Catholic schooling, in the hope that he would become a priest (127, 145). When authorities searched the home at the time of her final arrest, they discovered both a priest and an escaped Catholic schoolmaster and also found hidden Catholic books and "church stuff" (145; Add MS 151, 51r). All of Margaret's choices placed John under suspicion by the York authorities, who expected a husband to be in control of his wife and what went on within his own household (Mush 1849, 127, 145–46, 153).

Mush overlooked Margaret's lies and disobedience. Instead, he contrasted this Catholic woman's risk-taking and firm devotion with many Catholic men's feeble religious compromises. As a foil to Clitheroe's story, Mush related the martyrdom of a Catholic man, Marmaduke Bowes, whom York authorities arrested at approximately the same time as Clitheroe and for the same crimes—harboring and assisting Catholic priests in their missionary work. Bowes, a yeoman of means, was one of many husbands and fathers who feared impoverishing his family if he became a recusant. Under pressure from Protestant authorities, he faced Wodehouse's choice, and elected to attend Protestant services rather than pay the penalties. Still a Catholic by belief, he continued to harbor priests secretly and engaged a Catholic schoolmaster to teach his children. Betrayed by the schoolmaster, Bowes eventually died on the scaffold. Though he praised Bowes to some extent, Mush made clear that Bowes was not the best example of Catholic martyrdom. He had compromised. Mush devoted a few pages to Bowes's story but only as a prelude to the several dozens of pages he devoted to the female martyr, Clitheroe, who stood more firmly against Protestant authority. Not all martyrs were equal (68–72).

Clitheroe acted with full knowledge of the dangers. After the passage of the 1585 penal laws, which made it a felony punishable by death to harbor or assist priests, a Catholic male friend became concerned for Clitheroe's safety. Her Catholicism was no secret. He asked her "to be more careful of herself." Don't receive any more priests, or at least receive fewer than you have been. Don't raise your children Catholic. Above all, don't do anything of this sort "without license of [your] husband" (94).

While this man wanted to protect Clitheroe, he also prioritized male privilege over religious considerations. Clitheroe should obey her husband first and foremost, regardless of the Catholic Church's needs and directives. Clitheroe chose to navigate a more complicated path between gender and religion, between lay male privilege and clerical male privilege, than most spouses in inter-confessional marriages. Whose counsel and interests should take precedence: those of her husband and this lay Catholic adviser or of her priest? She approached her spiritual director, presumably Mush, and asked explicitly whether it was permissible for her to continue doing as she had been—supporting priests without her husband's permission. The priest did not give her a direct answer but instead asked her what she thought. Clitheroe appeared torn, trying to balance competing allegiances and gender and religious authorities.

Her top priority, she said, was to serve God and "safely walk without sin." Part of the way she had fulfilled this goal thus far was by receiving his servants, the priests. However, she continued, the reason she had been convinced that supporting the priests without her husband's approval was all right was because her spiritual director told her so. "I have put my whole confidence in you." Now she worried that the new penal laws indicated that she was not doing her duty. She questioned her confessor's advice and her choices. "Now I know not how the rigor of these new laws may alter my duty in these things: but if you tell me that I offend God in any point, I will not do it for the world." Whatever her priest advised, she would do. Obeying clerical counsel was an issue of salvation for her. Like the young Mary Ward, she was accustomed to accepting her confessor's advice as the will of God for her life. In the end, the priest counseled Clitheroe to continue receiving priests and not to tell her husband she was doing so. "It is for your husband's safety not to know of these things," unless he embraced the service of God in the Catholic faith. Ultimately, Clitheroe continued to assist priests (95–97).

This situation was about preserving male *religious* authority more so than masculine authority more generally. Mush stressed Clitheroe's need for male clerical direction. As long as she had a spiritual father near her, all was well (107–8). Mush repeatedly depicted Clitheroe as obedient to male authority, but to her spiritual father, that is, himself, rather than her husband. For example, when Clitheroe would sneak away at night to the pilgrimage site near her home, Mush emphasized how she remained dutiful to him, following his directive not to make the trip too often because of the dangers of getting caught (116–21). He freed her to aid priests by explaining that if her husband had any say in the matter, "you would not serve God at all, and in this, your necessary duty to God, you are not in any whit inferior to him" (95–97).

Interestingly, in Mush's account of this discussion, Clitheroe and the priest never mentioned a husband's authority over a wife—just a priest's authority over a layperson. It is possible that Mush did not want to confront the contentious issues surrounding one male's assumption of authority over another man's wife in that man's own home. He did, however, laud Clitheroe for providing everything so "that God might be served in her house" (105–6). He saw her primary goal as a housekeeper as serving God. Similar to Southwell's advice to householders, Mush advised that this was God's house, first and foremost, not John Clitheroe's. Mush even referred to it as "her" house, which allowed him to skirt the issue of John's authority in his own home.

However, this was a priest's interpretation of Margaret's allegiance. Margaret herself wrestled with her understanding of her gendered and religious priorities, trying to find a balance. For example, although she personally disliked buying and selling as part of her larger Catholic ascetic rejection of temporal wealth, she embraced her obligations as a tradesman's wife. Her husband trusted her with his business interests in the butcher's shop, and she saw it as part of her duty as a good wife to make sure that he got a fair price and to try to increase his wealth. This was a compromise she was willing to make that favored her gender role above faith. Of course, Margaret also indicated that if they took a business loss, she was "exceedingly merry" because she thought they had too much wealth in God's eyes anyway (126–27).

Perhaps, like Catherine Holland, Clitheroe decided to obey her male head of household in all that did not directly involve religion. In religious matters, however, Clitheroe, like Holland, followed the directives of conscience. She chose to disobey her husband to serve God, particularly—but not exclusively—when issues of salvation were at stake. She harbored Catholic priests in the Clitheroe home without her husband's knowledge and valued the counsel of her spiritual father above that of her husband, the state, and the Church of England.

Margaret crafted a personal balance between her religious and gender obligations and seemed to perceive herself as a good and obedient wife. Protestant authorities took a very different view. Examiners urged her to admit that she had been a bad wife, offending John by not submitting to his authority. They accused her of being a bad mother by her willingness to leave her children motherless if she was executed. They played on any possible guilt Margaret might feel to get her to conform. If she truly cared about her family, she would not be throwing her life away (159–60, 184). This issue loomed large in their interrogations because, in their eyes, Margaret's disobedience was part and parcel of her larger rejection of the Church of England's religious authority, the state's authority, and her proper place in the gender order.

Margaret, however, denied that she had committed any but the most usual and trivial of faults. "If I have offended my husband in anything but for my conscience, I ask God and him for forgiveness," she told her accusers. "I trust my husband will not accuse me that I have offended him at any time, except it be in such small matters as are commonly incident between man and wife." Furthermore, she claimed that she had done her duty by bringing her children up in the fear of God. Having fulfilled her obligations to her family, she was now prepared to die for her God (184–86).

Although Margaret was arrested for harboring Catholic priests, the government did not execute her on a scaffold for treason. At her arraignment, she chose not to enter a plea. She refused to recognize the government's authority to judge her (Add MS 151, 52r–v). Without a plea, there could be no trial. The penalty for such disobedience was known as *peine forte et dure*—hard and forceful punishment. The accused was pressed to death under a large weight. Women, however, typically received lighter judgments than men. According to Mush, the judge in York hesitated to sentence a woman to death, but Protestant ministers convinced him to proceed with an execution. She was, they contended, the only Catholic woman in the north defying the monarch's religious laws to such an extent, and if she were allowed to live, more like her would surely follow (57r). They wanted to send a clear message with her death.

Despite Margaret's blatant disobedience, John reportedly "acted like a madman" when he learned of her death sentence. Even though he knew that she had deceived him and broken the law, he attested she was the best wife in England and offered the authorities all he had if they would release her. They refused. He tried to visit her in jail before her execution. Again, the authorities denied his request (Mush 1849, 149, 161, 187).

On March 25, 1586, after a final three days of fasting and praying, authorities paraded Clitheroe through the streets of York to her execution at the Tollbooth prison. On a lower level of the jail, magistrates ordered Clitheroe placed on the ground, and "a sharp stone, as much as a man's fist, was put under her back." A board was placed over her chest, and "upon her was laid to the quantity of 7 or 8 [hundred pounds] at the least," all gradually piled on by beggars recruited for the task, "which breaking her ribs caused them to burst forth at the skin." She died, crushed beneath the load (Add MS 151, 64r–65v; also McClain 2004, 128–31). Mush repeatedly praised Clitheroe's patience, constancy, and cooperation with God's purpose throughout her martyrdom and likened her to the apostles (Mush 1849, 59–62, 66, 67, 79, 80, 134).

Although Mush claimed a major influence on her decisions, Clitheroe herself said that she prioritized allegiance to God and conscience above her need to submit to other forms of authority, such as her husband, priest, or government. Her duty to God warranted her disobedience to her husband, even to the point of endangering his life and property. As we saw in the cases of other Catholic women such as Holland, More, and Ward, conscience helped a woman resolve her conflicting loyalties in a manner she could live with. Margaret's duty to God justified her willingness to receive, maintain, and obey priests, but she did not see herself as their puppet. She cited God and conscience as her only judges when she refused to be tried by her country. While her examiners were sure that someone—probably a priest—had meddled with this woman's thoughts and conscience, telling her what to believe and how to act, Clitheroe assured them that she alone, guided by God, chose her path (Add MS 151, 52v; Mush 1849, 197–99). The Catholic Church canonized Margaret Clitheroe in 1970.

Clitheroe fulfilled her obligations as a Catholic. Did she also fulfill them as a woman and wife? After her execution, as her belongings were distributed among the living, her hat went to her husband, "in sign of her loving duty to him as her head" (Add MS 151, 66r). Yet Margaret had assumed many aspects of his headship by maintaining priests in his home, educating his children Catholic, and lying on numerous occasions so that she could practice her faith more freely. She was convinced that this was not in any way offensive to him or to God. Despite seemingly overwhelming evidence to the contrary, Margaret thought herself a proper wife. Knowing her deceptions and transgressions, John maintained that Margaret *was* a good wife—the best wife—all the way up to her death. Neither husband nor wife conformed to expected gender norms within marriage. Instead, they renegotiated their marital expectations in light of gendered and religious priorities. Against all odds, Margaret and John Clitheroe's mixed marriage seemed to succeed to their mutual satisfaction; and although neither Clitheroe made choices that satisfied the traditional gendered and religious demands placed upon them by society and faith, the neighbors didn't seem to mind.

"The Only Thing We Have to Fear Is Fear Itself"

Every marriage is different and, in the end, there were many ways that marriage partners worked through the conflicting demands of religion and gender in their households. Henry Cary feared this process. He was certain that the disaster of his own mixed marriage would be repeated in households throughout the British Isles. "In a short time," he worried in a December 1626 letter to Sir John Coke, "we shall have unhappy divisions made in all the families of the kingdom as is now begun in mine, to the hazard of great and manifest mischiefs and dangers" (Wolfe 2001, 271). Henry dreaded the fulfillment of Gouge's and Whately's prophecies that if society did not uphold the hierarchy of the family, the state would fall. His wife's unwillingness to submit to his masculine and religious leadership would only encourage Catholics to defy not only their spouses but the government (293–94). Yet Henry was wrong.

Instead, by the end of the eighteenth century, most men and women experienced a gradual easing of marital tensions over these issues as options were tried, discarded, or adopted. This was true in many types of marriages: those in which both partners were recusants, when one partner conformed, or when one was Catholic and the other Protestant. As the Clitheroe, Mawhood, and other marriages in this chapter demonstrate, this process of adaptation began in the first decades after Protestant reforms and continued until Catholic Emancipation.

Husbands and wives began to share leadership of their families in worldly and religious matters in an increasing variety of ways. Wives, in particular, exercised more choices on a broader array of issues, especially those involving household authority and salvation. They controlled family property, thus assuming partial responsibility for maintaining their families. They arranged baptisms and Masses, thereby undertaking elements of religious leadership in the home. They did so when their husbands were absent but also when they were present. Wives frequently expressed their willingness to act in such ways as part of their commitment to fulfilling God's will, reminiscent of Catherine Holland, Gertrude More, and Mary Ward's more detailed explanations of their renegotiations of traditional gendered and religious authorities. Women now seemed more confident ascertaining God's will for themselves, and making many decisions usually made by men—husbands, clerics, and fathers—fostered this greater confidence. Husbands, in contrast, also shared their traditional male authority in the home with other men in new ways: Catholic clerics visiting or living within their walls, or even Protestant officials who confiscated their weapons or sequestered their property. This could be a contentious process or a cooperative one depending on how the men involved understood and prioritized male privilege and religious obligation.

Most Catholic women and men undertook such burdens to cope with irreconcilable pressures and needs in their day-to-day lives, but societal attitudes took decades, if not centuries, to catch up to, and recognize, this lived reality: women trusting their consciences and making their own choices; men understanding their authority in new ways and sharing it willingly? Many men and women constrained by long-standing suppositions about gender and religion seemed unable to envision such possibilities. For example, after Protestant authorities arrested the English Lady, Dorothea, they questioned her about why she refused to attend church services. She told them simply that it was because she was Catholic. The justice seemed taken aback. "That answer is not conformable to the laws of God, the King, and the realm," he told her. She answered, "It was conformable to the laws of God and that was sufficient for me." She allowed her conscience to guide her choice. His follow-up question revealed the justice's assurance that the proper gender order and household hierarchy would fix a misguided woman's poor choice of religious non-conformity. He asked Dorothea about her marital status. Was she wife, widow, or maid? Maid, she answered. To which he replied, "So much the better, for then I hope a good husband will persuade you to change your religion" (Chambers 1882, 2:33). He then released her. Just as Protestant examiners were certain that some priest somewhere must have convinced a gullible Margaret Clitheroe to sacrifice her life for her faith, surely a man somewhere must be in authority over a woman's choices. Instead, for these women, it was God.

Men, as well, found new balances between their masculine marital priorities and their religious ones by redefining Catholic male leadership in the household. Prior to his execution as a traitor during the Popish Plot,

William Howard, Viscount Stafford's salvation was very much on his mind as he penned his memoirs. Stafford was a man, a husband, and a father, with all the gendered and religious obligations each role entailed. However, in his own mind, he was a Christian first. He trusted in "God's will be done," even if by fulfilling God's will by dying for his faith he could not fulfill his duties as a man, husband, and father.

> Thou hast said, O Lord, 'He that loves father and mother, etc., more than Me is not worthy of Me.' I acknowledge, most dear Lord, that I love my wife and children as much as a loving husband and tender father can love a most deserving wife and most dutiful children. But to show them I love them and my own life to boot, I willingly render up and forsake both … Take us under Thy protection, O Helper in tribulation! Be thou a Judge and Spouse to the Widow, a Father to the orphans, and salvation to all our souls. (S.N.D. 1929, 199)

Unlike Richard Herst 50 years earlier, Stafford did not view himself as abdicating his responsibility for his family's material and spiritual well-being. His sacrifice of his life *demonstrated* his love and religious leadership by showing them how to be worthy of God. Stafford trusted that God would fill in for him in his other duties, governing his family as judge, spouse, and father and saving all their souls.

As husbands, wives, and clerics gained experience in all-Catholic or mixed Catholic-Protestant marriages over almost three centuries, they worked through the overlapping and contradictory demands of expected gender and religious roles and unintentionally changed those roles forever. In addition, despite the fears of men such as Gouge, Cary, and Whately, government and society did not collapse. Men and women first questioned traditional understandings of masculine authority and feminine submission within marriage, using the touchstone of faith to understand the relationship between the two. This produced a contested and continuously fluctuating relationship between faith and gender. Then they restructured the relationships between women and men in marriage, reshaping the balance between personal, social, and religious expectations of authority. Each marriage provided a model to others, even to those of different social and economic classes. Because of the Carys' social rank, their conflict in all its particulars became broadly known, influencing what was thought possible between men and women, as individuals and marriage partners. However, although the Carys were of the nobility, it was not their rank that made their deviations from accepted gender roles possible. Other couples less influential than the Carys—such as the Clitheroes and the Hersts—wrestled with and resolved these issues in countless neighborhoods and villages (Mendelson and Crawford 1998, 4, 393; Tague 2002, 4–7, 95–96, 193). On this smaller scale, neighbors watched and learned, imitating one another's successes and trying not to repeat their failures. Gender roles within marriage changed. Gender roles within the Catholic religion changed, and state, church, and society did not collapse into anarchy as a result.

As the last chapters have revealed, the very foundation and stability of society and government were believed to rest upon each individual knowing their place and performing their expected roles. Gender was a cornerstone holding up society and the state. To destabilize gender roles for individuals or within marriages and families threatened the infrastructure upon which all else balanced. Family members, neighbors, and acquaintances, as well as churches and governments as institutions, reinforced gender expectations in big and small ways, through legalized rules but also through informal correctives. Such buttressing of gender norms could be intentional and overt—such as the use of a scold's bridle to tame the strident tongue of a gossip or the disinheriting of a son or daughter—or it might be more subtle and unconscious. Uncomfortable silences, sideways glances, disparaging asides, and social and professional avoidance could communicate disapproval as effectively as formal ordinances. Few individuals thumbed their noses at gender norms without a care.

Because it often proved nearly impossible to be both a good Catholic *and* a good woman, man, or spouse by traditional standards, the benchmark of acceptable behavior—the foundation upon which so much was believed to rest—had to change. Catholics in the British Isles re-defined what it meant to be good Catholic women, men, wives, and husbands in ways that allowed them to satisfy themselves and others that they were proper men and women. The Catholic Church's participation in crafting new gender standards is evident in the support it voiced in favor of women and men such as Catherine Holland and Richard Herst, who by customary interpretations of divine and natural law were disobedient daughters and poor husbands. That there were limits to acceptable change is equally evident by the Church's eventual disavowal of Mary Ward and the English Ladies.

Up to this point, we've been exploring the ways that gender played into these issues: how Catholics' understandings of what was appropriate, natural, and divinely created for each sex broadened as an unintended consequence of meeting the needs of the Church and believers during their centuries as an underground faith in the British Isles. However, that is only half the story. A building needs more than one cornerstone, more than one pillar to carry its weight. Both gender and religious norms have long supported and mutually reinforced one another as cornerstones of society and state. Just as Catholics created new understandings of what it meant to be a good woman, man, or spouse, so did they need to create new definitions of what it meant to be a good Catholic. This is the other half of our puzzle.

It was not only the gender roles and rules that transformed during these centuries of change but religious roles and rules as well. Gender and religious norms work together to offer believers different sets of opportunities based on one's sex and position within the Church. Only by laying the evolution in religious roles over the top of the gender transformations already explored can we begin to answer the puzzle of the suppression of Mary Ward's Institute and, through that, the larger issues involving changes in gender and religious roles, their limits, and consequences within the Catholic Church raised in Ward's time and the present day.

As in this first part of the book, we will begin by scrutinizing individuals' understandings of themselves. If it was difficult to fulfill traditional expectations of what made a good Catholic while living in a Protestant state, how did Catholics revise their understandings of what made someone a "good Catholic"? Then we will probe deeply into different types of Catholics' relationships with one another as laypeople and clerics, exposing how boundaries between these groups blurred over time, in response to the great needs of the Church and the faithful.

Works Cited

Add MSS (Additional MSS). York Minster Library.
Bain, Joseph, ed. 1894. *The Border Papers: Calendar of Letters and Papers Relating to the Affairs of the Borders of England and Scotland, Preserved in Her Majesty's Public Record Office, London. Vol. 1, 1560–1594.* Edinburgh: H.M. General Register House.
Bedingfeld, Katherine. 1912. *The Bedingfelds of Oxburgh.* Privately Printed.
Blom, J.M. 1982. *The Post-Tridentine English Primer.* London: Catholic Record Society.
Blundell, F.O. 1909–1917. *The Catholic Highlands of Scotland.* 2 vols. Edinburgh: Sand & Co.

Blundell, William. 1933. *Cavalier: Letters of William Blundell to His Friends 1620–1698*. Edited by Margaret Blundell. London: Longmans, Green and Co.

Broughton, Richard. 1617. *A new manual of Old Christian Catholick meditations, & praiers faithfully collected and translated, without any word altered, or added*. n.p.

CSP Dom (*Calendar of State Papers, Domestic Series*), *of the reign of Elizabeth I*. 1863–1950. Public Record Office. Series 2. London.

Cary, Elizabeth. 1630. Epistle to the Reader and Dedication in *The Reply of the Most Illvstriovs Cardinall of Perron, to the Answeare of the Most Excellent King of Great Britaine, the First Tome*, by Jacques du Perron. Douai: Martin Bogart.

Challoner, Richard. 1827. *The Catholic Christian Instructed*. London: Keating and Brown.

Chambers, M.C.E. 1882. *The Life of Mary Ward (1585–1645)*. 2 vols. Edited by Henry James Coleridge. London: Burns and Oates.

Crouch, Humphrey. 1637. *Loves court of conscience written upon two severall occasions, with new lessons for lovers. Wherunto is annexed a kinde husband's advice to his wife*. London: Richard Harper.

D'Urfey, T. 1700. *Wit and mirth: or, Pills to purge melancholy; being a collection of the best merry ballads and songs, old and new. Fitted to all humours, having each their proper tune for either voice, or instrument, many of the songs being new set. With several new songs by Mr. D'Urfey. Also, an addition of excellent poems. The second part*. London: Printed by William Pearson, for Henry Playford at his shop in the Temple-Change.

Fletcher, Anthony. 1995. *Gender, Sex, and Subordination in England 1500–1800*. New Haven: Yale University Press.

Gataker, Thomas. 1620. *Marriage duties briefely couched togither out of Colossians, 3. 18, 19*. London: William Bladen.

Gerard, John. 1959. *Autobiography of a Hunted Priest*. Translated by Philip Caraman. Introduction by Graham Greene. London: Fontana Books.

Golding, Arthur, trans. 1577. *The Sermons of M. John Calvin upon the Epistle of S. Paul to the Ephesians*. London: Lucas Harison and George Bishop.

Gouge, William. 1622. *Of Domesticall Duties: Eight Treatises*. London: John Haviland for William Bladen.

HCAB (High Commission Act Books). Borthwick Institute. York.

HCCP (High Commission Cause Papers). Borthwick Institute. York.

Holland, Catherine. 1925. "Conversion of Sister Catherine Holland." In *A Link Between Flemish Mystics & English Martyrs*, by C. S. Durrant, preface by Francis Cardinal Bourne, 272–305. London: Burns, Oates and Washbourne.

Kaplan, Benjamin J. 2007. *Divided by Faith: Religious Conflict and the Practice of Toleration in Early Modern Europe*. Cambridge, MA: Belknap Press for Harvard University Press.

Knox, John. 1558. *The First Blast of the Trumpet Against the Monstrous Regiment of Women*. Geneva: J. Poullain and A. Rebul.
Lewalski, Barbara Kiefer. 1993. *Writing Women in Jacobean England*. Cambridge: Harvard University Press.
Longstaffe, William Hylton Dyer, ed. 1858. *Acts of the High Commission Court within the Diocese of Durham*. London: Whitaker and Company for the Surtees Society, XXXIV.
Loomie, Albert, ed. 1978. *Spain and the Jacobean Catholics, volume 2, 1613–1624*. London: Catholic Record Society, LXVIII.
Macaulay, Thomas Babington. 1898. *The History of England from the Accession of James II*. 5 vols. New York: Harper and Brothers.
Mawhood, William. 1956. *The Mawhood Diary: Selections from the Diary Note-Books of William Mawhood, Woolen-Draper of London, for the years 1764–1790*. Edited by E.E. Reynolds. Newport, Mon.: R.H. Johns Ltd.
McClain, Lisa. 2004. *Lest We Be Damned: Practical Innovation and Lived Experience among Catholics in Protestant England, 1559–1642*. New York: Routledge.
———. 2014. "Elizabeth Cary and Intersections of Catholicism and Gender in Early Modern England." In *Women during the English Reformations: Renegotiating Gender and Religious Identity*, edited by Julie A. Chappell and Kaley A. Kramer, 69–89. New York: Palgrave Macmillan.
Mendelson, Sara and Patricia Crawford. 1998. *Women in Early Modern England*. Oxford: Clarendon Press.
Merrick, M.M. 1947. *James Duckett: A Study of his Life and Times*. London: Douglas, Organ.
Murphy, Cornelius. 1737. *A True and Exact Relation of the Death of Two Catholicks, Who Suffered for Their Religion at the Summer Assizes, Held at Lancaster in the Year 1628*. London.
Mush, John. 1849. *The Life and Death of Margaret Clitherow, the Martyr of York, now first published from the original manuscript*. Edited by William Nicholson. London: Richardson & Son.
Myerscough, John A. 1958. *A Procession of Lancashire Martyrs and Confessors*. Glasgow: John S. Burns & Sons.
"Notes by a Prisoner at Ousebridge Kidcote". 1877. In *The Troubles of Our Catholic Forefathers Related by Themselves*, edited by John Morris, 318–30. 3rd Series. London: Burns & Oates.
Petti, Anthony G., ed. 1968. *Recusant Documents from the Ellesmere Manuscripts*, Records Series. St Albans: Catholic Record Society, LX.
Rowlands, Marie B. 1985. "Recusant Women 1560–1640." In *Women in English Society, 1500–1800*, edited by Mary Prior. London: Methuen.
Scarisbrike, Edward. 1703. *Rules and Instructions for the Sodality of the Immaculate Conception, of the Most Glorious and Ever Virgin Mary, Mother of God*. n.p.

Southwell, Robert. 1973. "Short Rules of a Good Life." In *Two Letters and Short Rules of a Good Life*, edited by Nancy Pollard Brown. Charlottesville, VA: The University Press of Virginia for the Folger Shakespeare Library.

S.N.D. 1929. *Sir William Howard Viscount Stafford 1612–1680*. London: Sand & Co.

Speght, Rachel. 1617. *A Mouzell for Melastomus, the cynicall bayter of, and foule mouthed barker against Euahs sex. Or an apologeticall answere to that irreligious and illiterate pamphlet made by Io. Sw. and by him intituled, The arraignement of women*. London: Nicholas Okes for Thomas Archer.

Shepard, Alexandra. 2003. *Meanings of Manhood in Early Modern England*. New York: Oxford University Press.

SP Dom (State Papers, Domestic Series). Public Record Office. Kew.

Stanney, William. 1617. *A treatise of penance, with an explication of the rule, and maner of living, of the brethren and sisters, of the Third Order of St. Frauncis, comonli called of the Order of Penance, ordained for those which desire to leade a holy life, and to doe penance in their owne houses*, Part I. Douai: John Heigham.

Swetnam, Joseph. 1615. *The Arraignment of Lewd, idle, froward, and unconstant women or the vanity of them, choose you whether, With a Commendation of wise, virtuous, and honest Women, Pleasant for married Men, profitable for young Men, and hurtful to none*. London: George Purslowe for Thomas Archer.

Tague, Ingrid H. 2002. *Women of Quality: Accepting and Contesting Ideals of Femininity in England, 1690–1760*. Woodbridge, Suffolk: Boydell Press.

Underwood, Lucy. 2014. *Childhood, Youth and Religious Dissent in Post-Reformation England*. Palgrave Studies in the History of Childhood. New York: Palgrave Macmillan.

Vaux, Laurence. (1599) 1969. *A catechisme or A Christian doctrine, necessarie for children & ignorant people*. Reprint, Menston, Yorkshire: Scolar Press.

Weston, William. 1955. *William Weston: The Autobiography of an Elizabethan*. Translated by Philip Caraman. Foreword by Evelyn Waugh. London: Longmans, Green and Co.

Whately, William. 1617. *A bride-bush, or A wedding sermon, compendiously describing the duties of married persons: by performing whereof, marriage should be to them a great helpe, which now finde it a little hell*. London: William Iaggard.

———. 1623. *A bride-bush, Or, A direction for married persons Plainely describing the duties common to both, and peculiar to each of them. By performing of which, marriage shall prooue a great helpe to such, as now for want of performing them, doe finde it a little hell*. London: Bernard Alsop for Beniamin Fisher.

Wolfe, Heather, ed. 2001. *Elizabeth Cary, Lady Falkland: Life and Letters*. Cambridge: RTM Publishing.

———. 2007. *The Literary Career and Legacy of Elizabeth Cary, 1613–1680*. New York: Palgrave Macmillan.

PART II

Pushing the Boundaries of Religion

CHAPTER 6

The "Good Catholic"

"Amazons" rioted in Dublin the day after Christmas in 1629. English pressure upon Irish Catholics had been rising prior to the holiday, thanks to the displeasure of two English Protestant leaders—Henry Cary and Adam Loftus, Lord Deputy and Lord Chancellor of Ireland, respectively. According to Irish Capuchin priest Nicholas Archbold (1588/9–1650) in *Evangelicall fruict of the Seraphical Franciscan Order*, Cary and Loftus were annoyed at the growing visibility of the very Catholic practices that their government was supposed to be suppressing (Harleian MS 3888, fols. 112–15). On Christmas Day, for example, Franciscan monks celebrated a well-publicized and well-attended Mass at their regular location on Cook Street. Outraged, Dublin's mayor, its Protestant archbishop, and a contingent of soldiers planned a raid for the following day, December 26, the feast of St. Stephen. The men carefully timed their arrival so they would interrupt another Mass. They stormed through the building, tearing down images, breaking up the pulpit, and arresting two friars, before a woman—identified as the widow Nugent of Winetavern Street—organized other Catholic women of the congregation into a spontaneous uprising. The women, described as "Amazons," mounted a "fierce attack on the soldiers," striking and scratching them. The battle spilled out into Cook Street, where rural Catholics visiting Dublin on pilgrimage to St. Stephen's

© The Author(s) 2018
L. McClain, *Divided Loyalties? Pushing the Boundaries of Gender and Lay Roles in the Catholic Church, 1534-1829*, Histories of the Sacred and Secular, 1700-2000, https://doi.org/10.1007/978-3-319-73087-5_6

Well for the holiday joined the fray. Together, the women and their rustic allies rescued the friars and forced the mayor and archbishop to flee for their own safety, "pelted with stones and offal by the pilgrims, fleeing the Amazons." Shortly thereafter, Cary and Loftus's English-run government succeeded in shutting down well-known religious houses, chapels, and other Catholic gathering spots in Dublin and other parts of Ireland. The religious orders went deeper underground, as those in England and Scotland had already done (Martin 1962, 271–72).

Catholics such as these women and pilgrims and the many other women and men such as Ward, Wodehouse, Cary, and Blundell, whose stories have filled these pages, risked their reputations to serve God and the troubled Catholic Church. They did not make such choices lightly. Individuals and institutions policed gender norms doggedly just as we do now, punishing those who did not conform to conventional expectations and rewarding those who did (*Hic mulier* 1620; *Haec-vir* 1620). "Amazons," for example, were no ordinary women, but a barbarian race of warrior women from Greek mythology who lived independently under the rule of Queen Hippolyta, whose name meant "loose, unbridled mare." This imagery creates a stark contrast to William Whately's (1623) ideal of the good wife, submissive to her husband's authority like a "well-broken horse," discussed in the last chapter. These Amazons were literally soldiers fighting on behalf of the Catholic Church.

Gender and religious priorities existed in tension with one another, and it is time to shift focus to examine such confrontations through a primary lens of faith, exploring the re-negotiations of different religious roles to meet the needs of Catholics living in a Protestant state. As discussed in the first half of this book, Protestant reforms had destabilized religion in the British Isles, necessitating changes in other parts of the foundation—such as gender—to brace the whole of society and the state. However, the religious cornerstone itself needed shoring up. Religious understandings of what it meant to be a faithful Catholic would have to evolve in new directions while simultaneously being balanced with gender priorities to ensure the solidity of both. For example, while the stories of Catholic martyrs and heroes of the Reformation era are often told, rarely have they been examined in light of the overlapping new religious and gender roles they encouraged.

Any new religious roles or values would need to be orthodox and justified by scripture, as older gender and religious norms were. Luckily, New Testament scripture abounded with examples of how to overcome adversity and ill treatment, from Christ's passion to the many persecutions endured by the early apostles. Catholics looked to such archetypes for inspiration in crafting new definitions of what it meant to be good Catholics as part of an underground faith.

The most common new model of loyal Catholicism adopted in the British Isles combined the seemingly contradictory values of Christian militancy with patience. Pastoral writers encouraged both men and women, laypeople and clerics, to fight for God and the Catholic Church. Ideally the Church wanted its followers to resist with patience rather than violence, but in troubled times it lauded the unruly Amazons as well as the peaceful soldiers of Christ. While evidence does not exist to confirm whether pastoral tracts reflected the values that guided a majority of Catholics in the British Isles, the examples provided within this chapter indicate that some lay Catholics, for example the Dublin rioters, adopted the Church's exhortations to varying degrees, often struggling to resolve the seeming contradictions between militancy and patience, just as they did with the gender roles that were the primary focus of the first half of this book.

Patience and militancy were hardly new ideas within Catholicism. Christian exhortations to patience begin with Christ in the gospels. They continued through the centuries of persecutions leading up to the Roman Emperor Constantine's legalization of Christianity with the Edict of Milan in 313 and into the practices of later ascetics and monastics. A rich history of Christian pugnacity dates from Constantine's promotion of Christianity, which required the public image of Christianity to change from that of an illegal, persecuted faith to one of a strong, aggressive religion worthy of an emperor who would defend Christ and his Church.

What was novel in the Reformation years in the British Isles was the Catholic Church's increased emphasis on these ideals and the new ways that it encouraged different groups of believers to employ them. Many of the positive attributes Catholic theologians touted in these years look familiar. Loyal and humble Catholics should live in unity and obedience to the Church. They should be charitable to their neighbors and value spiritual rewards over the gains of this world.

The Church also promoted these traditional values in new ways, providing alternatives to conventional gender and religious roles. Pastoral authors, for example, increasingly encouraged laywomen, even nuns, to adopt martial qualities usually reserved for men. Lay Catholic masculinity, too, evolved into a combination of traditional masculine values, such as good husbandry and courage, with newly touted qualities such as patience, resignation, and constancy. These latter traits were traditionally associated in Catholicism with saints' lives, the masculinity of priests and monks, and femininity, but not with the masculinity of ordinary laymen.

At first glance, such combinations of religious militancy and patience and of feminine and masculine traits appear contradictory. A possible explanation for these experiments in antithesis is that Catholics realized there would be no quick, easy ejection of Protestantism from the British Isles. Resigned to the long haul, Catholics needed to combine patience with their Christian militancy. This necessity led the Church to encourage both men and women to adopt new behaviors, which had the effect, over time, of promoting a new set of attitudes, expectations, and models for how to be good Catholics.

However, while these changes fostered a more gender-inclusive understanding of the "good Catholic," they did not constitute a radical overhaul of either gender or religious roles. They caused little crisis in gender relations or faith. Instead, they allowed Catholics to push the boundaries of customary feminine, masculine, and religious behaviors to comfort themselves that they were still good men and women and good Catholics.

Ritual Under Siege

"Why aren't Catholics fighting?" many exiled Catholics asked. One writer, known only by the initials W.C., marveled at how Catholics in the British Isles could live in the midst of their enemies and yet were "so far from fighting against them" that they endangered their very souls by fraternizing with them (W.C. 1656, 10). This was not the job of a good Christian, to get along with heretics. In his preface to Robert Reade's English translation of Lorenzo Scupoli's *Spiritual Combat*, W.C. suggested:

> We have here a Combat offered us ... All we have to do, is to buckle on our Armor, and presenting ourselves cheerfully before our Captain, Jesus Christ, to promise him fidelity in this Holy war, resolving courageously under the Banner of the Cross, to pursue all our enemies even to death, not suffering any one of them to escape. (12–13)

W.C. and Reade, writing and translating comfortably from France, were among those exiled Catholics living on the continent who thought Catholics in the British Isles were not going far enough to fight for reconversion.

In reality, large numbers of Catholics *had* raised banners to fight for Catholicism, from the ill-fated Pilgrimage of Grace in the autumn of 1536 to the Norfolk Rebellion in 1569, from the Irish Rebellion and English Civil War in the 1640s to the Williamite War of the late 1680s and the Jacobite uprisings of 1715 and 1745. Catholics also tried to unseat the Protestant government through smaller conspiracies such as the Babington Plot, Throckmorton Plot, and Gunpowder Plot. Powerful Scots Catholic families such as the Maxwells and Gordons incited domestic insurrections (Blundell 1909, 1:23–24). Some Catholics of wealth, including those living in exile on the continent, offered money and soldiers to assist a large-scale invasion of England or Ireland mounted by foreign powers, such as Spain, France, or the Papacy. Protestants certainly expected Catholics to rise in arms, which is why they repeatedly disarmed Catholic men and restrained their movements, as discussed earlier. Who knew how small groups of Catholics, such as those accused in the Popish Plot, might be conspiring?

Apart from these planned and usually ineffective efforts among well-placed Catholics to create religious and political change, some ordinary laymen and clerics fought against Protestant authority in their day-to-day lives, such as the Amazons and pilgrims of Dublin or the Lancashire Catholics who felt so confident in their numbers that they banded together against a priest hunter in 1602 and forced him literally to eat his warrant (*CSP Dom* 12/283/86). Groups of Catholics not only carried but drew their weapons to defend Catholic ritual and faith, such as the Catholics who brandished rapiers and daggers against the recorder and sheriffs of London after they raided Mass at the Charterhouse in November 1576 (Lansdowne MS 23, no. 117).

Individual Catholics also raised weapons to defend their faith. William Weston described how one Catholic man had arranged for a priest to celebrate Mass at his house and wisely prepared for trouble, keeping his sword "ready for action." His worries proved well-founded when a careless servant opened the door to the knock of a group of pursuivants. Realizing her mistake, she let out a shout. Dressed in the surplice he had donned to assist the priest at Mass, the man snatched up his weapon and drove the intruders back, eventually trapping and locking them up in the lower part of his house. He returned to the priest, and, together, they stripped off the altar and their vestments. They hid the "Massing stuff," and the priest concealed himself. Only then did the man return downstairs to greet his visitors and ask them what they wanted with him. When they asked him about the surplice they had seen him wearing shortly before, he feigned ignorance. "What, I in a surplice? Do you really think I am one of those people who go about in surplices?" After he pressed gold into their hands, the searchers departed (Weston 1955, 33–34).

Not all Protestants could be bought off with a few coins, however. John Jones, the Protestant vicar of Eccles, led 400 armed parishioners to arrest the Benedictine, Ambrose Barlowe, in a barn on Easter Sunday in 1641. Barlowe reportedly was so focused on delivering his sermon to the approximately 100 assembled Catholics that he didn't even notice the mob's approach until it was too late (Rhodes 1909, iii–iv).

Physical violence against Catholics increased during the Civil War, intertwined with the political conflicts between Royalists and Roundheads. Protestant soldiers fighting for Parliament in Lancashire, for example, allegedly awoke early one morning and decided to do a little "priest hunting." Upon entering the Chaigley Hall chapel of the Holden family, they discovered a priest celebrating Mass with a small group of Catholics. The soldiers promptly beheaded the priest at the altar and threw his head over a fence outdoors (Gillow 1885, 3:330–32).

However, armed uprisings were the exceptions rather than the rule in the British Isles, particularly after 1590. Catholics who originally hoped for a quick re-conversion to Catholicism in the early decades of the Reformation had to re-orient their expectations following the defeat of the Spanish Armada and the execution of Mary Queen of Scots. Although the ascension of James VI of Scotland to the English and Irish thrones in 1603 raised Catholic aspirations, the failed Bye and Gunpowder plots during the first years of his reign left Catholic hopes unfulfilled. When Catholic convert Tobie Matthew was asked if he thought God would return his homeland to Catholicism, he replied that although persecutions were sometimes greater and at other times less, "but yet they were still always such as rather to kill our hopes of better times than to quicken them toward any expectation" of the island's reconciliation with Rome (Matthew 1931, 10). After so many attempts to reclaim the British Isles for Rome failed, many Catholics resigned themselves to a long wait and sought toleration as members of a minority faith (McClain 2004, 255–68).

Catholics then needed to re-conceptualize what they were fighting for and what their role in this holy war would be. In contrast to W.C.'s imputations, these Catholics were neither cowardly nor apathetic. They understood that this was a battle for God and souls (Scarisbrike 1703, 70–81; Fitzsimon 1881, 42–43). They just understood the fight differently than did Catholic exiles.

They needed new models for what men and women should and should not do for their faith. Such re-negotiations unintentionally yet understandably involved changes in both religious and gender roles for both men and women as a byproduct.

Catholic men and women understood themselves as actively engaged in militant defense of their faith during wartime. The language they used to describe their actions reveals how the lines between literal and figurative battle often blurred. For example, while two men began a "private voluntary skirmish" arguing about true faith, it might turn into "a public and solemn war" in print as it did for Catholic priests Thomas White and William Rushworth. Each side, White proclaimed, had an army to support him. Each side chose its weapons, preparing for the assault of the opponent. White chose the single rapier of direct discourse. Although acknowledging that his opponent's "gilded Armor shines more, and dazzles the eye, so I fear not when we come to charge, our courser steel will prove substantial and impenetrable." He planned not to waste time with "parley" but advance straight to the "close encounter" (White 1654, 1–2). Theirs was a paper war that combined martial spirit and metaphor with spiritual discourse. This military framing made it harder for men to back down from theoretical arguments while retaining their honor. Moreover, although the participants fought such battles with words, the risk of death for Catholic participants could be very real.

The lines between physical and spiritual warfare also became muddied. A man's soul, John Gerard argued, could be at risk at the same time he fought to preserve his body. Gerard counseled more than one layman to take up such gauntlets manfully. Gerard described, for example, how in 1600 the Irishman, Richard de Burgh, Baron Dunkellin, asked him to hear his confession. De Burgh had challenged another courtier to a duel over an insult to his honor. The duel was scheduled for the next day, and he wanted to confess in case things did not go well. Gerard was aghast. "Heavens," he said. "Don't you know what it means to receive the sacraments in that state?" He could not pronounce absolution over a man who intended revenge against another. De Burgh risked damnation by seeking this sacrament without a truly penitent heart.

In some ways, de Burgh's dilemma is reminiscent of Wodehouse's choice. As the challenger, he could not back out of the duel at the last moment without harming his masculine reputation. Too many people already knew about it. Gerard upbraided de Burgh for valuing his standing with worldly men who counted for nothing. "If it's your honor you're out to defend, that's not how to go about it." What was more important was his honor in God's eyes and the eyes of the Catholic Church. And, Gerard cautioned, "while you're parrying the man's thrusts at your body, the devil at every pass is working with his sword to pierce the guard to your soul." De Burgh refused to give up the fight, and Gerard refused to hear his confession. Instead, they compromised. "I'll tell you what I'll do," Gerard told de Burgh. "Here's a fragment of the true cross from my reliquary. I shall place it on an *Agnus Dei* [a wax disc blessed by the pope featuring a lamb, symbolizing Christ as the lamb of God] and you can wear it on your person." Gerard emphasized that he gave it to de Burgh not as a sign of God's favor or to "speed you in your wicked resolve," but as a prayer for God's protection "so that if you are in danger—not that I want you to be—then God may be moved to give you your life for the good will you show in honoring His cross." De Burgh had the item sewn into the shirt he wore to fight. During the duel, his opponent pierced his shirt near his heart but did not draw blood, seeming to demonstrate the protective power of the *agnus Dei*. De Burgh then wounded his foe, and seeing him on the ground, elected to spare him. He credited his victory to the power of the Holy Cross, thanking Gerard and promising repentance in the future (Gerard 1959, 180–83).

Perhaps nowhere was this mixing of physical and spiritual battle better represented than in the preface that W.C. addressed to the Catholics of England in Scupoli's *Spiritual Combat*. Although Christians had long been taught to take up God's armor against the devil's wiles, scripture made clear that these were spiritual battles, not ones against enemies made of flesh and blood (Eph. 6:10–17). W.C. addressed such issues and so interwove the language of physical combat with spiritual conflict that it becomes difficult for the reader to discern exactly what type of battle he proposed. Reade had translated *Spiritual Combat* into English in the decade after the Civil War, and the writer of this preface feared that Catholics were so traumatized by their recent losses that they would not welcome this text whose very title would seem to return them to those dark years. He explained to readers how the recent desolation and destruction on the battlefield were different from the war discussed in Scupoli's book but just as necessary to fight because without it, "there is no peace to be expected, either in this life or in eternity" (W.C. 1656, 9). This new struggle would be a guerrilla war against both foreign and domestic enemies, which W.C. first described as being like a physical battle against a tangible enemy (8–9). Then he shifted to a spiritual tack. In the Civil

War, Catholics' passions overcame them in battle, leading to calamitous losses in this life and "eternal damnation in the next" (9). However, in this new war, Catholics would conquer their passions and secure peace both in this world and the next. Under the headship of their General, Christ, Catholics should enroll themselves in this combat and resolve to faithfully fight to victory. Covered in armor to resist the continual assaults of their "mortal enemies," Catholics' souls would manage their weapons to counterattack to God's glory (9–10, 12).

Nowhere, of course, would such a blend of militancy and religiosity be better represented than among the hundreds of English, Irish, Welsh, and Scots Catholic martyrs executed under the penal laws (Gregory 1999, 6–15, 250–314; Merbeck 1999, 126–57). Building upon centuries of Christian tradition, these martyrs saw themselves as soldiers in bloody battle, both physical and spiritual. Before his execution in 1643, Franciscan martyr Henry Heath wrote to a friend that it was "the glory of a soldier to be made like his lord" as he died on the scaffold to defend his faith (Stone 1892, 172–73). Cornelius Murphy, in his account of the 1628 martyrdom of the priest Edmund Arrowsmith, gave Arrowsmith human opponents with whom to do battle and over whom to triumph (Murphy 1737, 1–32). Justice of the Peace, Pastor Leigh, was the heretic villain, always present throughout Arrowsmith's trial, imprisonment, and execution. Murphy's "Sanguinary Judge" (27) who vowed to see Arrowsmith bleed was a Puritan, almost inhuman in his persecution (8, 14, 18, 22). He manipulated the law to secure Arrowsmith's conviction and bragged to Arrowsmith about how he would see Arrowsmith's genitals hacked off and burned before Arrowsmith's face (14, 16–19, 23). On the day of Arrowsmith's execution, the judge tried to deny onlookers the display of Arrowsmith's "heroic Combat of a valiant Champion" (19) by holding the execution first thing in the morning so few people would attend. He even vowed not to eat that day until Arrowsmith was dead. The organizers, however, botched their preparations, so Arrowsmith wound up marching to his victory at midday before a good-sized crowd. Murphy described him as manfully prepared, as "a Soldier, and Apostle of JESUS CHRIST (20)" a "Christian Hero" (23). The judge, likely hungry from his delayed repast, watched the hanging, dismembering, disemboweling, and quartering from a distance. Murphy depicted the judge's eventual taking of his noonday dinner as "religious" in its cruelty. At the end of his meal, some venison was delivered to the judge as a gift, and while he admired the meat, the four quarters of Arrowsmith's body also arrived for his inspection. The judge allegedly laid Arrowsmith's bloody quarters next to the bloody venison and irreverently compared them (27).

Regardless of the factual accuracy, gendered and religious understandings of Arrowsmith as martyred man permeate this account. Arrowsmith was a soldier who manfully and bravely fought his enemies in a battle of martyrdom. His adversaries challenged his faith and his literal manhood, taunting him about his upcoming emasculation. The scaffold was the battlefield upon which his desecrated body fell. Murphy depicted Arrowsmith's opponents as gloating religiously over this fall. Like the Amazons of Dublin, Arrowsmith was a soldier of Christ, a Christian hero (5–10, 13–20, 23–24, 27, 31, 54).

Catholic seminaries on the continent trained men like Arrowsmith to understand their role as combatants both figuratively and literally. It was important to teach young people early the "Duties of Christian Warfare" in such troubled times. When William Allen began the first English College at Douai in the Low Countries, he described his students as the "scattered troops" he united. Decades later, in 1594, the 45 students from the British Isles training at St. Gregory's College in Seville appear as soldiers, walking in columns two-by-two and keeping time when they went out on the public streets. In the seventeenth century, students at St. Gregory's also competed to become Mary's champion in contests called jousts (or *justas*) that featured poetry contests, rhymes, effigies, and bequests in her honor. The students' gladiatorial spirit attracted large audiences. When students and teachers, particularly Jesuits and Dominicans, disagreed amongst themselves over the truth of the Immaculate Conception, some students erected a silver altar in the street outside the school gate, "its battlements manned by students of the college in military costume, armed with muskets which they fired as each statue [of Mary] passed beneath to a flourish of trumpets." These militant, protective roles resemble those that fighting men, not priests, were ideally supposed to assume for women through the tenets of chivalry and courtly love (Litterae Annuae 1592–1617, 19/1). Francisco de Peralta, Rector of St. Gregory's, described in an undated letter to the Jesuit Provincial of Andalusia how well such students had learned to defend the faith and "how well the seminary was training its soldiers to combat heresy" (Murphy 1992, 155).

Enthusiastic young men could take such imagery very seriously, as the future martyr Henry Heath did. His amalgamation of religious and masculine militancy colored his perception of missionary work so heavily that his superiors may have been reluctant to send him home on the mission.

For years, Heath begged to be allowed to serve the mission. In his 1641/2 letter to George of St. William, Provincial Father of the Franciscans in England, Heath sounded like a young man left behind in his village during war time, imagining the glory other young men were earning, desperate to join them.

> When I consider their unconquerable fortitude amid crosses and sufferings, and behold them so constant in the faith of Christ, so reckless of flesh and blood, so inflamed with Divine Love, I am overwhelmed with shame, that while they, like courageous soldiers, fight boldly under the banner of Christ, I remain at home in idleness and peace. (Stone 1892, 162–63)

The provincial denied his request, perhaps fearing that Heath's zeal would get him quickly killed as he threw himself recklessly into this battle (See Gregory 1999, 103–5, 286–87).

Catholic lay observers understood the martyrs in a similar light. When the London Catholic, Thomas Freke, wrote a letter to his older Protestant uncle, George, in July 1606 encouraging him to convert to the Roman faith, he tried to shame his uncle by holding up the example of the young men who had been martyred during Elizabeth I's reign for the Catholic cause. Thomas described such men as shedding their last blood in acts of heroism to become "heavenly champions" winning "prudent and courageous victories" authorized by God himself "much to the shame of their present backward elders," presumably men like his Uncle George (SP Dom 14/22/61).

Soldiers of Christ in a Holy War

Opportunities to enjoy such religious and worldly triumphs trickled down from the militancy of Jesuits and martyrs to ordinary Catholics whom writers and clerics encouraged to enlist as "warriors on behalf of the faith" (Loomie 1978, 24) and "Soldiers of Jesus Christ" (Anonymous 1690, 1–2) under Christ's captaincy or generalship to wage Christ's battles (W.C. 1656, 9–10, 12). When Benedictine Anthony Batt encouraged laypersons to pray the Office of St. Benedict, he advertised they would become part of "that glorious Army of Religious Persons, who fought under [God's] Banner" (Batt 1639a, 67–68). In Nicholas Strange's introduction to Dr. Benjamin Carier's published letter to James I explaining his recent conversion to Catholicism, Strange described how Carier,

James's former chaplain, "lifted himself into the Militia of the Roman Church" (Strange 1649, intro. 8). In his "Epistle" to his aging father, Jesuit Robert Southwell wrote that no one could "achieve to the Church Triumphant in heaven that is not a member of the Church Militant here in earth" (Southwell 1973, lines 504–5). His advice to ordinary Catholic householders in his *Short Rules of a Good Life* was that their whole lives would be ones of combat and warfare (Chap. 1, lines 53, 67, 70–74; also Gage 1652, C1r–v; Harleian MS 6211, fol. 82v).

Polemic writers repeatedly and intentionally used bold, contentious language to stir up Catholic loyalties and actions. Detailed militant imagery pervaded hymns, devotions, prayers, and rhetoric. Christians entered the lists. Catholics were "under siege" from Protestants. Christ was in his camp facing his enemies' supporters. Faith was a fortress, and Christ's Church was its armory. Christian souls armored themselves, and their sacraments, spiritual practices, and prayers were armaments against physical and spiritual foes (Batt 1639a, 52; Butler 1785, 13–14, 28; Butler 1792, 1:280–84; Anonymous 1690, 6–8, 10–11; Recusant MS B1035, 68; Vane 1648, 3–5; Herbert 1722, 3–4, 25; Crowther and Vincent 1657, 238–40).

Such writers were not encouraging ordinary Christians to seek the martyrdom of an Arrowsmith. The Church elevated martyrs precisely because their exceptional sacrifices were meant to inspire greater devotion among the faithful. However, there were other ways to take up Christ's cross. For Southwell's readers, the call to battle on behalf of Christ came down to the mundane choices they made in daily life. Catholics marched into battle by learning to resist the temptations of the world, the pulls toward Protestant conformity, and their own desires. They fought the urge to live for themselves and struggled to live for God, placing God and the Catholic Church at the center of their motivations. These everyday warriors were to sacrifice their own self-interest for love of God—waging a different type of war and experiencing a different quality of martyrdom.

Gender intertwined with warlike imagery as authors encouraged ordinary soldiers of Christ to fight the Lord's battles "manfully" and with "undaunted courage" (Anonymous 1690, 4). Society had long esteemed martial values, of course, as signs of masculinity. A fighting man sought validation of his manhood through tests of strength, skill, and heroism (Karras 2003, 1–66). Arrowsmith's hagiographer, however, drew sharp distinctions between this worldly type of bravery and achievement and the type shown by Christ's troops. Although histories and epics sang the renown of worldly heroes, their exploits no longer appeared praiseworthy once one got past all the flattery and exaggeration. "Their expeditions exhibit a Scene of Horror and Confusion: Desolated Widows, Orphans oppressed … Blood shed … Cruelty and Tyranny" (Murphy 1737, 52). These so-called worthies tarnished their accomplishments with unpunished rapes, murders, lawlessness, and injustice. Not so the soldiers of Christ! These champions were famed for their compassion, charity, and forgiveness. Whereas worldly heroes sought their own glory, preening vainly before their audiences, soldiers in Christ's army sought God's glory with self-effacing humility. Such warriors sacrificed worldly interests, faced the greatest dangers, and "challenged Death itself" (53), storming the very gates of heaven. These were the victories to which Catholics should aspire. Piety and devotion themselves were heroic. Indeed, as Murphy conjectured, "Shall I judge [these Catholic heroes] men?" Martyrs in particular, such as Arrowsmith and the lay martyr Richard Herst, were more than men. They were "Vessels of Glory, happy resemblances of the divine Original … God-like Imitations" of Christ (53, also 5–6, 43, 46–49, 54–58, 67–68).

However, writers did not frame all their martial imagery in exclusively masculine terms. Some writers, such as the former Anglican priest and Catholic convert, Thomas Vane, incorporated traditionally feminine symbols into their militant representations. Vane used passages from what is generally acknowledged to be the most feminine of Old Testament scriptures, the Song of Solomon, to describe the embattled Catholic Church in the British Isles. Outsiders looking at the Church, Vane surmised, would see it as the writer of the canticle saw his beloved: as both going forth "like the springing morn, faire as the moon, choice as the sun" but also as "terrible as an army in battel aray" (Vane 1648, 379).

This was more than mere simile. Women could become champions on the field of Christian battle, too. As a conversational partner of Tobie Matthew's put it, the Protestants may have demolished the Catholic Church, but God was supplying new building materials. These were "Workmen, yea and Work-Women" with "high and heroical Spirit" who helped rebuild the faith (Matthew 1931, 14, 16). At this time of mandatory enclosure of religious women in nunneries and the "Fight for the Breeches," Batt portrayed women active and fighting side-by-side with men, risking their reputations, the ruin of their families, and their very lives. When Batt wrote "Another Letter" to his sister in England urging her to pray the liturgy of the Office of St. Benedict regularly, he claimed that Catholics, men and women alike, needed such prayers as they made war against their own flesh, the world, and the devil. Batt included both male and female exemplars in his prayer beseeching God, Mary, St. Benedict, St. Scholastica, and all the monks and nuns who had already fought for Christ under his banner to renew the Holy Spirit of those joining the Order of St. Benedict (Batt 1639a, 61–62).

Some women referred to themselves and their actions in such militaristic terms, stretching our understanding of what was proper, acceptable behavior for Catholic women. Disobedient woman Catherine Holland, recall, described her conflicts with her Protestant father and clergy as military contests more than once. When her father repeatedly invited the Bishop of Winchester, Brian D'Uphaugh, to come to the house to convince Catherine of the truth of Protestant doctrine, she described their debates as military engagements. When her mother asked Catherine why she did not just avoid the bishop altogether, Catherine told her mother "To show him … I am not afraid of him." In fact, she recalled, "I longed for the Combat, and when the time grew near he was to come, I, to hasten his Lordship into the Field wrote to him desiring him to make Haste." In her conversion account, Holland also described as "great combats" all her machinations to leave home for the continent to join a convent (Holland 1925, 293, 300–1).

Both male and female observers represented laywomen and girls as combining heroism and piety. A Scots laywoman, Mrs. Grant of Laggan, esteemed the verses of another laywoman, the Scots Catholic poet Giles MacDonell of Keppoch (1660–1729), as blending the poetical, heroic, patriotic, and devotional (Blundell 1909, 1:11–12). Thomas Francis Walsh, who proposed a school to educate Catholic girls in England in the early 1800s, used poetry to plead his cause, calling the school and the girls a "shield of strong defense" for "Albion's cause" (Walsh 1819, 14). In their convent chronicle, the English Augustinian nuns of St. Monica's in Louvain described the laywoman Jane Wiseman with a provocative melding of traditional and non-normative gender attributes. Wiseman, the nuns recorded, excelled in the traditional Christian role of holy widow at the same time as God numbered her among his troops. The chronicler praised Wiseman's unusual strength and heroism in the face of persecution, contrasting her bravery with that of a Catholic man arraigned alongside Wiseman who "had not such courage as she" (Hamilton 1904, 1:82–3). These chronicles would not have been publicized, so such a comparison could not have been meant to shame men into equally heroic behaviors. They were penned for the encouragement and edification of women in the convent. In contrast, John Mush, the biographer of the martyr, Margaret Clitheroe, openly taunted male readers with examples of a woman's heroism. He described Clitheroe's fortitude and courage as she entered combat in defense of the Catholic faith. She fought the world, the flesh, and the devil when men were too cowardly to do so. Clitheroe herself labeled the Catholics imprisoned with her, both women and men, as "special professed soldiers of Christ" (Mush 1849, 77, 197). As Clitheroe's execution and the Irish riot in Dublin the day after Christmas demonstrated, Catholic women's battles could be both physical and spiritual.

Many writers resurrected the Church's ancient heritage of Christian militancy to spur believers of both sexes to courage and action in the present day. Irish Jesuit Henry Fitzsimon recalled for his readers "not only men of strong resolution, but also women and children" who championed Christ in the first centuries of Christianity: "Barbara, Agnes, Agatha, Cecilia, Catharina, Lucia, Dorothea, Apollonia, Margaret, Christine," and countless others. They let nothing prevent them from fighting in "Christ's quarrel" and neither should men and women of his time (Fitzsimon 1881, 42–43). The anonymous compiler of the early seventeenth-century manuscript, *The Lives of Women Saints of our Countrie of England: Also some lives of holie women written by some of the aunciant ffathers,* provided a more home-grown pedigree for women's courageous and necessary participation in this fight. Despite its title, the author highlighted approximately three dozen ancient English, Welsh, Scots, and Irish women—such as Wenefride, Keyna, Werburga, and Brigide—along with holy women praised by the Church Fathers, such as Judith, who slew the general Holofernes and whose right hand was described "with a sword in it, and all bloody, killing." Because of their prodigious faith and courage, God "armed" such women: sometimes spiritually, to spur on Christian men whose bravery quailed, but sometimes literally, with swords and other weapons, to draw blood to defend whatever needed defending. The Church upheld them as exemplars of holy living and disobedience to authority, two qualities that seemed contradictory in women, although not in martyrs. The Church applauded—even canonized as saints—women who took up arms to defend the Church against any other authority that was not religiously backed (Stowe MS 53, fols. 20r–v, 27v–28r).

Authors also adapted orthodox—yet rather obscure—depictions of the Virgin Mary to legitimate Catholic women's warrior-like actions. Mary had long served as the paragon of humility, obedience, and chastity for all Christians. Although a tradition of a powerful, bellicose Mary existed in

Eastern Christian tradition, it had been centuries since the Roman Church regularly promoted Mary in this way. Although it credited Mary with securing the Christian victory over Muslim forces at the Battle of Lepanto in 1571, Rome usually did not depict Mary as a warrior combating heretics at this time. Catholics in the British Isles, however, did (McClain 2004, 81–108).

Writers and artists promoted all the traditional, gentle Marian virtues but enlarged the list to include decidedly militant characteristics (Stafford 1635, B3v). This is a more focused example of the larger pattern noted above, whereby the Church promoted the usual list of traditional Christian virtues while adding just a few more, using them in new ways, or applying them to new groups of Catholics. Mary was now not only chaste and humble, she was the great defender. She fought for Christian souls not only in heaven but on earth as well. Mary protected Catholics from very real harm, as depicted in a votive painting of the Bedingfeld family, probably dating from the Restoration (c. 1660). In this work, Mary sheltered family members under her robes from ships at sea and from mounted men, probably soldiers from the Civil War and Interregnum (Pollen 1909, *frontis*).

As a mother, Mary safeguarded her children from all dangers, but when the Church was threatened, she became the "terror of the infidel" (Anonymous 1690, 15). The Jesuit Edward Scarisbrike called on Mary as a warrior for the Church Militant. He championed membership in the Sodality of the Immaculate Conception—a voluntary organization promoted by the Jesuits in which members took Mary as their patron. Scarisbrike openly acknowledged that religious conflict in the British Isles was "like to be of long continuance." Catholics were opposed by many adversaries and needed Mary's aid. By joining this group, it was as if the "Soul not only puts on Armor but has an outwork [a fortification to shield it] to keep the Tempter at great distance in time of trial" and protect members from the direct attacks of enemies (Scarisbrike 1703, 23, 25). Membership in the Sodality combined militancy with obedience. Sodalists would live "under command," seeking to "enlarge [Christ's] conquests." As obedient and willing Christians, their commanders expected them to meet their challenges cheerfully and to speak of victory as they "manfully" resisted and subdued their enemies (144). Despite this masculine imagery, women, such as Dorothy Lawson of Northumberland, became members.

Authors trying to describe Mary's simultaneously compliant yet warlike nature provided readers with a confusing blend of contradictory comparisons and mixed gendered metaphors. Mary, for example, was a woman with a manly heart. Authors portrayed Mary as both a lady to be won and defended as well as the mighty defender herself, "most mighty next God in heaven." Her feminine humility allowed Mary to fight (a manly occupation) and win against heresy, as pride and ego were what caused people to turn their backs on the Catholic Church (Scarisbrike 1703, 23–34, 52–54). Catholics were instructed to be "heroical" in her honor while Mary herself was described as "heroical" (16–17, 36, 70; Harleian MS 494, fols.105r–106v; Murphy 1992, 18–19).

In his treatise promoting membership in the Society of the Rosary, Jesuit Henry Garnet first equated Mary to the rainbow that God showed Noah, signifying his promise to cease flooding the world. Similarly, the Protestant heresy now flooding Britain would cease through Mary's intercession. Garnet then equated Mary to an actual bow. He seemed uncomfortable calling her a weapon, although his analogy was clear. Mary had

> Destroyed all heresies in the whole world ... From this (rain)bow there goeth none but chosen arrows taken forth from the quiver of God himself, yea, arrows of the salvation of our Lord ... arrows of salvation both in tranquility of the Church; and also against all enemies of Israel & the Church of God in this time of temptation and disturbance... . (Garnet 1596/7, A3v–4r)

Mary was a "well settled array of a pitched army," ready to face and overcome the enemy (A5v).

Catholics could fight with Mary against heresy using rosary beads. The rosary is the most popular devotion centered around the Virgin Mary promoted by the Catholic Church, and lay Catholics in the British Isles appear to have increased their use of the rosary in the sixteenth through the eighteenth centuries (McClain 2004, 81–108). Garnet lauded the beads as both armor and weapons of warfare to Catholics. They would destroy munitions, counsels, and anyone or anything contrary to the true faith (Garnet 1596/7, A3v–A4, A5r–A6r). Although Garnet likely touted the protective abilities of the *prayers* of the rosary, perhaps layman Christopher Walmsley thought of the beads themselves as literally protecting him. When he publicly confronted his religious enemies, he waved his rosary around his head "in braving manner" in the streets of Rennington, Northumberland, warding off his adversaries (Longstaffe 1858, 50).

As John Clarkson, author of *An Introduction to the Celebrated Devotion of the Most Holy Rosary,* explained, Mary was a spiritual weapon but one much more powerful than David's sling with its little missiles. She was the all-purpose weapon, "ready at hand," at all times and places. She had already obtained real-world victories for Catholics at battles in La Rochelle, Lepanto, Hungary, and more. She would now fight for Catholics of Britain (Clarkson 1737, 37, 47, 48, 72, 74).

Such writers had to be careful that their portrayals of Mary reflected Catholic orthodoxy at the same time as they expanded the scope of her capabilities. The Council of Trent had recently clarified Mary's place in the Christian hierarchy. Mary had been human, not divine. Catholics were to venerate her above the saints but not worship her in an equivalent way to God. Some authors toed the Tridentine line carefully, stating their awareness and adherence to the Council's clarified doctrines, trying not to give too much power or honor to Mary, while using a more powerful Mary to meet Catholic needs in the British Isles. (Clarkson 1737, 10–11; Challoner 1764, 1–7; Stafford 1635, B3v).

In sum, the Church reshaped a prominent feature of lay identity, encouraging laypeople to see themselves as warriors for Christ and defenders of their faith, and it promoted such militancy more adamantly than it had done in centuries. This greater stress on militancy likely changed laywomen's understandings of themselves as good Catholics more so than it did laymen's. The Church rallied laymen and women to adopt traits traditionally attributed primarily to laymen, exhorting them to show courage and do battle in a variety of ways. It would not have been much of a stretch for most men to embrace this new emphasis on a warrior-like Christianity. Laywomen, in contrast, were being asked to view themselves differently, as entitled and expected to take up arms for religious purposes. Pastoral writers legitimated women's resistance, strength, and confrontations on God's behalf by dipping into early Christian history to popularize exemplars such as St. Agatha and Judith. They magnified both the humble and the warlike qualities of the most revered feminine Catholic paragon, Mary. Christian militancy became more gender inclusive as laymen and women learned new ways to fight for their faith. What, however, of the men and women who sought the religious life?

BATTLING PRIESTS, MONKS, AND NUNS

At the time of the Jacobite uprising of 1715, a linen weaver, John Harrison, of Bodarstone, was dismayed to see a Jesuit "appear ... openly in the streets," with a sword at his side. He watched the man, later identified as

Walter Vavasour, "in the company of several persons who had all, or most of them, cockades in their hats" entering the White Bull Inn in Preston, Lancashire (Estcourt and Payne 1885, 340). The cockade was the mark of the Jacobite rebels who favored the claim to the throne of the Old Pretender, James Patrick Edward Stuart, son of deposed monarch James II, over that of George I, the first Hanoverian king. It appeared that not only would Catholic clerics and male religious encourage rebellion but that they would lead by example.

From the ninth century onward, the warlike values traditional to worldly men were alive and well among male monastics and even priests. Many fighting men were only too aware that their stock-in-trade violated God's commandment "Thou shalt not kill," and they made endowments to monastic houses so that the monks would pray for their souls. A large number of second and third sons who had little hope of inheriting family property entered the monastic life, as did many elderly knights at the end of their fighting careers. These men brought the martial values with which they were raised into the cloister. The Crusades epitomized the concept of Christian militancy and the blurring of boundaries between secular and religious masculinities, in orders such as the Hospitallers and Templars. Such men lived a mixed life, as both monastics and secular men. They were institutionally recognized warriors of God.

Although the days of the Hospitallers and Templars were long past, Catholic clerics and monastics in the British Isles resurrected the spirit and motivation of these earlier soldier-monks. Batt portrayed the members of all the religious orders as one vast army, if only they could be brought together (Batt 1639b, 55–56). Such men clearly envisioned themselves as part of Reformation-era fights, and many of them seemed to relish the chance for battle, both worldly and spiritual. In particular, as discussed earlier, Loyola established the Jesuits along the lines of a military order yet with a religious mandate, combining qualities of both traditional worldly and religious masculinities (Strasser 2008, 45–70).

It was one thing for lay Catholics to carry and brandish weapons against Protestant foes. It was quite a different matter for a monastic or cleric such as Vavasour to raise a weapon against state authority or assist others who did so. The government had already branded Catholics as traitors. To be seen with a weapon only seemed to confirm Protestant suspicions. Beyond carrying weapons, monastics and clerics were known to have facilitated communications between others engaged in actual fighting. Because many monks and clerics lived a peripatetic lifestyle, traveling surreptitiously from house to house, community to community, they were excellent conduits of information and intrigue. During the English Civil War, for example, priests volunteered to deliver messages among the Royalists, the side most closely associated with Catholics. In a 1648 letter to Rev. Robert Charnock, William Blundell detailed how priests used his home at Crosby as one of their message centers (Blundell 1933, 29–31).

Other clerics and religious men refused to involve themselves in military skirmishing and political intrigue but were perfectly willing to keep weapons nearby in case of trouble (Weston 1955, 33). They understood how Protestants would view their possession of arms, so they carefully weighed circumstances to decide when and where to draw them, as John Gerard and Roger Lee had to do in London in July 1599. Gerard was facilitating Jesuit-founder Ignatius Loyola's *Spiritual Exercises* for Lee and two other Catholics when pursuivants burst into their building. Gerard and his companions had to decide whether to fight or flee. They evidently had weapons handy, as they discussed "whether it would not be worth trying to rush down with drawn swords and force our way out, snatching the keys from the search party as we passed." Ultimately, they decided against direct confrontation, and Gerard hid in a priest hole while his companions bluffed their way through the search (Gerard 1959, 158).

Although nuns had little need to carry weapons, they saw roles for themselves in defending the Church. This might surprise those who romanticize about nuns' peaceful, prayerful lives isolated from the world's cares. Francis Bell, for example, wrote to his sister, Margaret Clare, Abbess of the Third Order of St. Francis at Nieuport in what is today Belgium, in April 1641, about how happy she and her sisters must be to escape the harshness of Catholic-Protestant hostilities. Both Bells were from Worcestershire and had taken vows as Franciscans, but Francis lived in London on the eve of the Civil War. He asked his sister to remember those Catholics living under persecution, in continual fear of loss of property and life, all to save the Catholic faith. He rhapsodized about religious women's experience being one of protected innocence, "shrouded from the world, where you see not the evils that are done under the sun, nor hear the continual inexorable blasphemies spoken and written here by the adversaries, against God's Church. Live and enjoy that happiness" until God called them home (Stone 1892, 182; also Matthew 1931, 21). In contrast to this idealized view, Catholic-Protestant conflicts often followed the nuns behind the convent walls. Consistent streams of visitors brought up-to-date news relating to politics, religion, and family matters. Most nuns wanted to help the Catholic cause in their homeland, similar to Mary Ward's desire to serve. This involved an increasing emphasis on militancy in nuns' identities.

The militant language common in male monasticism eventually permeated monastic writings directing women, as it did in the anonymously authored eighteenth-century treatise *On ye end of ye retreat*. Every day, female religious should remind themselves of why they entered monastic life. It was to "declare war … to take up the cross to follow Christ" with all humility (Recusant MS B898, unpaginated, 1st Day, 3rd Med., 1st Pt.). These "Soldiers of J[esus] C[hrist] must be humble, chaste, poor, obedient, meek, and patient"—in other words, they should embody all the traditional qualities of nuns—while simultaneously being spiritual warriors (6th Day, 1st Med., 1st Pt.).

In several daily meditations, the writer used graphic language to ask women to imagine themselves as real soldiers, fighting under Christ's banner. The author provided practical instructions for survival on the battlefield. Be always "on guard." "Always have [y]our arms in hand." Never leave your post. Since the enemy would be looking for a chance to ambush, it would not do to go about unarmed (6th Day, 1st Med., 2nd Pt.). The women's armaments were their prayers, sacraments, physical mortifications, and mental disciplines. Do not let the enemy wrest these arms from you, the author commanded (6th Day, 1st Med., 1st Pt.). Repulse any assaults, and resist any attempts to parley, because such seemingly peaceful and benign attempts to avoid battle were akin to the serpent tempting Eve with the apple. Instead, be ready to wield arms speedily and skillfully against your enemy (6th Day, 1st Med., 3rd Pt.).

The author played the role of commanding officer to these female religious, encouraging them to display the firm resolution and undaunted courage of men, as they "manfully fight the Battles of the Lord" (6th Day, 1st Med., 2nd Pt.; 2nd Med., 2nd Pt.). More than once, the author encouraged manly battle, because that was how battles were thought to be won—by men facing typically masculine challenges. Yes, there would be hardships in the field; yes, the conflicts would get terrifying; and, yes, the women would get discouraged, but these female soldiers should stay focused and obey the orders of their commander, Christ, unto death (6th Day, 2nd Med., 2nd Pt.; 8th Day, "Consideration").

Some evidence exists that nuns embraced this more masculine vision of women's role as Christ's servants. The Benedictine nun, Lucy Knatchbull, for example, called herself God's "Vassal" to whom she pledged faithful service (Matthew 1931, 135–36). In medieval feudal relationships, vassals were traditionally fighting men who owed military service to a higher lord in return for the lord's protection and maintenance. If a vassal fought well for his lord, he could anticipate favor and material rewards. Knatchbull, a female monastic, envisioned herself a vassal for God, ready to fight for her lord—THE Lord—and hoping for favor and spiritual rewards.

Nuns involved themselves in worldly Catholic conflicts in many ways. Some nuns prayed consistently for the reconversion of their country and for the success of foreign military efforts in support of this goal (Gillow and Trappes-Lomax 1910, 37; *Dominicana* 1925, 176); and just as Royalists during the English Civil War depended on Catholic priests to circulate intelligence, so did Catholics rely on communications networks involving convents on the continent to deliver messages between Catholics and their supporters, both in the British Isles and abroad. Nunneries such as the English Benedictine convent at Ghent became message centers, just as Blundell's home had been earlier. Some nuns, such as Abbess Mary Knatchbull, were knowledgeable and active in political and religious affairs inside and outside the convent walls. Knatchbull was part of the struggle for the restoration of the Stuart monarchy and Catholicism.

Ironically, gendered stereotypes about women's lesser intellectual capacity helped nuns such as the Knatchbulls participate in these movements. Because the government thought women unlikely or incapable of involvement in political affairs, the packets of letters that Mary Knatchbull sent back to England were less likely to be searched than correspondence sent by men (Walker 2000; also SP Dom 12/230/34; Glickman 2009, 81, 197–203). Their intelligence usually made it through security. These nuns may not have wielded swords as Vavasour and Gerard did, but they believed, as Ward had, that women could make important contributions to the Catholic cause in the world. The Church's great need justified their doing so.

Overall, nuns, like laywomen, learned to view their participation and contributions to the religious controversies of the Reformation era through a more militant lens. This in no way changed their obligations to fulfill their vows of obedience, chastity, and poverty. Instead, religious women were to be simultaneously obedient and humble but also aggressive and warlike in their defense of the faith, albeit from behind a convent wall. Yet as Mary Knatchbull's experience demonstrated, religious women's influence could reach outside the cloister, even if the women themselves remained behind its enclosures.

Women's ability to hold these seemingly contradictory qualities in tension were likely strained at times. Men, particularly laymen, faced a similar challenge in balancing the second characteristic of the good Catholic: patience. Patience was an attribute more commonly associated with femininity and religious masculinity than with lay masculinity. Laymen typically proved themselves men by rejecting feminine traits. They would need to reorient their gendered expectations for masculine behavior to adopt this quality that the Church so wanted them to possess.

Patient Warriors

> If we are distressed, it is for your comfort and salvation; if we are comforted, it is for your comfort, which produces in you patient endurance of the same sufferings we suffer.
> 2 Cor. 1:6

The Roman Church had long enjoined *certain* Catholics to adopt patience. Patience, or some variant of the word, appeared approximately 100 times in the English translation of the Latin Vulgate Bible known as the Douai-Rheims Bible, the Bible produced by theologians at the English College of Douai and used by many Catholics in the British Isles. In scripture, it was God who was typically described as patient in dealing with humanity, but men and servants of Christ were also encouraged to patience. In the gospels, only Luke mentioned Christ explicitly promoting patience, yet church teachings had long emphasized Christ as patient and persevering (Matthew 1931, 148). In Luke 8:15, 18:7, and 21:19 of the Douai-Rheims Bible, Christ informed his disciples that they should expect times of war and conflict, nation against nation, before the present structure of wealth and false authority was overturned. They could expect persecution for speaking Christ's truth, but should persevere with patience, because in their patience they would possess their souls. The parallel to Catholics' experiences under Protestant rule was clear.

In daily life informed by scripture and church teachings, women, of course, were the poster children for patience. They were to be patient in their marriages, patient in their afflictions, and patient like the Virgin Mary, as Anthony Stafford, a lay English Catholic author, advised women in his biography of Mary, *The Femall Glory* (1635, epistle "To the Feminine Reader," as well as 54, 62–64). Catholics lauded women who exhibited patience and resignation to God's will, particularly when sickness afflicted them (*Dominicana* 1925, 177, 185). It was not a stretch to extend such praise to women who suffered patiently for their faith (Gerard 1959, 67).

Patience was also an attribute cultivated by saints, martyrs, and monastics, both men and women, such as St. Augustine, St. Monica, St. Francis of Assisi, St. Jude, St. Rita, and St. Dymphna, although patience was more frequently associated with female saints (Coakley 1994, 91–110). Contemporary martyrologists emphasized the "invincible patience" and resignation of the new Catholic martyrs too, encouraging lay readers to emulate such qualities in their own lives, such as John Mush did in proclaiming Margaret Clitheroe's "invincible courage enter[ing] combat ... patient and joyful" to defend her faith against all foes, worldly and spiritual (Mush 1849, 197; also Murphy 1737, 1–2, 19–20, 46).

After the British Isles' break with Rome, however, Catholic writers gradually urged non-religious men to adopt patience as well. In his *Short Rules*, Southwell provided a powerful pedigree for patience, listing it as among the main virtues of Mary, the angels, saints, apostles, bishops, martyrs, patriarchs, and prophets (Southwell 1973, Chap. 11, lines 348–56). The same man who advised laymen to attain paradise through the Church Militant asked them repeatedly to adopt patience to address a variety of spiritual and worldly challenges (Chap. 1, line 62; Chap. 3, lines 51–55; Chap. 7, line 13; Chap. 9, lines 35–38; Chap. 10, lines 68–71; Chap. 11, lines 145–48). Catholic convert Tobie Matthew, in his list of reasons intended to persuade his lay readers to become Catholic, argued that Catholicism is the religion that "perfects men" using patience:

> It is yet undoubted that where there are ... the best men, most perfect in humility, purity, patience, and charity ... [that Catholicism] is the best purest and truest religion ... And this perfection of men is a most excellent argument of the truth of the Catholic religion. God only can be the author of this heroic sanctity. (Butler 1785, 33)

Batt, too, advertised the peace and salvific grace that laymen might accrue by being patient in their current afflictions in emulation of religious men of the past. "What can a man wish for more?" Batt asked (Batt 1639b, 55–56). Both Matthew and Batt enumerated the virtues typically associated with women, saints, and religious men, yet both authors were writing primarily to Catholic laymen.

Laymen encountered such exhortations to greater patience in a variety of ways. Priests on the mission sermonized on patience, as the future martyr

Ambrose Barlowe was doing on Easter Sunday—the most important service of the liturgical year—at the time of his arrest (Rhodes 1909, v). Meditation collections for use with the rosary encouraged rosarists to imitate the patience of Christ and Mary (Crowther and Vincent 1657, 228; Garnet 1596/7, 8–9, 112–13, 233; Worthington 1603, 44–45, 114). Condemned Catholics spoke to their brethren from the scaffold, encouraging them to show greater constancy and patience in their sufferings (Challoner 1839, 2:114; SP Dom 12/149/61). Prayer books provided laypeople with devotions emphasizing patience, such as the prayer to the first martyr, St. Stephen, who was stoned for defending Christ's teaching before the Sanhedrin. Catholics were to pray to learn to suffer their own persecution with patience and pray for their persecutors as Christ prayed for his. In one such book, the bold typeface chosen for certain words in a prayer for Palm Sunday emphasized these same qualities, that the devout should, by Christ's example, "learn **cheerfully** to **suffer, patiently to endure**, & **constantly to persevere**" (Harleian MS 4149, fols. 37v–38r, 41v–42r).

The Church encouraged all Christians, of course, to show patience in adversity and forgive their enemies as Christ had, but the parallels between Christ's suffering and Catholic suffering under Protestant persecution called for upping the ante. The priest, William Whichcott, newly arrived in London from Spain, described in a March 12, 1616 letter to Peralta how annoyingly difficult it was to practice Catholicism under the many restrictions in place. He marveled at the patience of Catholics in handling so many injustices as well as they did (Murphy 1992, 173–74). Catholics circulated tales of co-religionists who exercised exceptional patience, such as Edmund Campion, one of the first missionaries to be martyred, who Catholics described as another "Job for [his] patience" (SP Dom 14/32/4). John Bucke, an English priest living in exile in Louvain, warned Catholics to follow their consciences and "patiently suffer all pains" for the Catholic faith "lest thou become another [Pontius] Pilate," who went against his conscience when he turned over Jesus to be executed. All Catholics should patiently "bear the weight of our own crosses," preferring them to "false Judgement, and corruption of conscience for any fear or reward" (Bucke 1971, 28–29).

Such high ideals, however, were difficult for most Catholics to attain. In particular, Scots Catholic Alexander MacKenzie knew that Catholics sitting in jail for their faith would have their patience severely tested. He advised each prisoner "to calm his mind" and "guard himself against all

Impatience," complaining, and bitterness. Prisoners should reframe their understanding of their "Confinement to be sanctified by a Christian patience, and submission to his holy Will." Their incarceration would thereby be a holy act (MacKenzie 1764, 8). Margaret Clitheroe reportedly grew frustrated with prisoners who could not maintain this ideal. Her biographer, Mush, reported that although she went to jail regularly to help Catholics in need, "yet could she not abide to hear that in their distresses any should murmur." Mush said that he never saw "her heavy and sorrowful for the poverty, tribulation, or persecution which fell to any so long as they showed their patience and gladness to suffer," sacrificing graciously as Christ had (Mush 1849, 124–26).

Church leaders increased their emphasis on patience as an excellent quality, but could they transform it into a *manly* quality? Their success in convincing laymen to adopt this traditionally female virtue depended on their ability to rebrand it as masculine. In essence, the priest Alban Butler did just this when he described Catholics who became impatient as overly emotional—a feminine trait—and wanting in faith. In contrast, "suffering … with patience is the most heroic act of divine love," he maintained. True strength—a traditionally masculine attribute—consisted in bearing one's tribulations patiently (Butler 1792, 1:282–86).

Other pastoral writers re-cast patience as masculine by associating it with masculine bravery and pride. Catholics should exercise patience in imitation of Christ as they dealt with their religious troubles, and they were cowardly and shameful if they could not. Catholics in the British Isles must have complained a good deal about their hardships, if the number of times Catholic authors mentioning the murmuring of their brothers and sisters in adversity is any indication. The anonymous author of the *Short Treatise of the Incarnation* spelled it out in no uncertain terms. Christ's acceptance of his cup of suffering:

> ought to teach us to receive without murmuring, the Crosses which God send[s] us … and stifle in us all notions of anger, & all desire of revenge, which are raised in us when we have been offended … He has taught us by his example to look upon the persecutions of men as ordained of God, & adore his Justice in the most unjust proceedings which men may vent against us. (Recusant MS B1044, 58–59)

Love your enemies. Pardon them. Return good for evil. If you cannot, shame on you (Recusant MS B898, unpaginated, 7th Day, 2nd Med., 2nd Pt.; Mush 1849, 197).

The priest and writer, Joseph Berington, resolved any seeming contradictions between lay masculinity and feminine patience head on by equating patience with masculine good citizenship. In "An Address to Catholics" written in the late eighteenth century, Berington presented himself as a man, a fighter, defending Catholics. "I was not armed, like the champions of old, with impenetrable steel; but I had the zeal in your service and my cause was good," he proclaimed (Berington 1781, 191). He did not, however, encourage the religious zeal of past centuries. Cool heads and cool religion would prevail in his own time and thus increase Protestant toleration of Catholics (76, 108). He and his fellow Catholics were understandably exasperated after suffering under the "hundred-headed Hydra of national prejudice" for almost 300 years. The best way to decrease any unjust bias was for Catholic men to be patient and submissive to authority while still being firm and manly (192–93). Their submission should "be that of men, conscious of the integrity of their principles and the rectitude of their conduct ... The thought should animate you to the pursuit of every manly and of every virtuous endowment" (198). After all, he asked, "if you are not better men, what avails it to dissent from the religion of your country?" (195, also 128)

Berington contrasted this new secular Catholic masculinity with the clerical manhood of the missionaries arriving in the British Isles. Catholic priests, he conjectured, ought to be more manly than they had been in the last 200 years. The new priests arrived appearing suspicious, unmannerly, and ready for the rack, when they should be "regular, exemplary, & manly" (163). It was little surprise to Berington that Catholics sought priestly council less often than in decades past (161–64).

By the end of the eighteenth century, Catholic laymen's patience was meant to be seen as masculine and distinguishable not only from femininity but from clerical masculinity as well. Laymen should be patient as they fought for the Catholic faith, but not in ways that would make them appear womanly or group them with religious men, to whom they did not need to prove themselves. They needed to earn their masculine reputations in the eyes of other laymen, including Protestants, and Berington and others showed them how this was possible. They linked patience to traditional masculine values such as bravery, strength, and good citizenship, and contrasted these newly shaped, worldly expressions of patience with previous understandings of the quality. Men could be patient and still be men, just as women could be warriors and still be women.

How to Fight the Good Fight

Clearly Catholics could employ excessive militancy, as in the Gunpowder Plot, but could there also be such a thing as too much patience? In the anonymously authored pamphlet entitled *The Good Catholick no Bad Subject, or a Letter from A Catholick Gentleman to Mr. Richard Baxter*, the writer complained that Catholic men had become *too* patient. The author bristled at accusations leveled against Catholics by the Protestant theologian and pastor, Baxter, in a sermon preached before the House of Commons at St. Margaret's, Westminster, on April 30, 1660. Papists, Baxter alleged, simply could not be fully loyal to the sovereign. The "Good Catholick" refuted this, combining a discussion of patience with the imagery of militant struggle. He described how all the other Catholics he knew had adopted a "silent patience" as a "shield against the many and heavy blows" to their fame, fortunes, and religion.

However, this author thought the balance between patience and militancy had become skewed, and that Catholics' silence and patience appeared as a confession of guilt before Protestants such as Baxter. Catholics had taken patience too far, and he would have none of it. He would prove himself and his co-religionists both loyal subjects and good Catholics. He envisioned this conflict as a duel in which he would defend himself to gain satisfaction (*Good Catholick* 1660, 3). He viewed the situation through the lens of Christian militancy and added some confrontational language back into the discussion, thus crafting a better balance between patience and militancy.

The balance was the key. Too much or too little of either patience or militancy got Catholics into trouble. They ran afoul of the Protestant authorities. They risked harming not only themselves but other Catholics and the greater Catholic cause for which they were fighting. In compiling his catalog of martyrs, Thomas Worthington was determined to include only those Catholics who were executed in "Apostolical & primitive Christian-like patience, solely and directly for religion" (Worthington 1978, 11). He wrote after Catholics had involved themselves in several high-profile political plots, such as the Babington Plot, to remove Elizabeth I from the throne. Their attempts to force change through militant violence provoked the government to establish more severe legal penalties against Catholics.

However, was such a balance even possible? The final challenge in explaining this evolving and more gender-inclusive definition of the

"Good Catholic" seeks to resolve the seeming tension of the melding of Christian militancy—what one typically construes as a virtue imbued with impatience—with these new exhortations toward adopting patience—a more pacifistic quality. Batt described the need to remain within "the *militant* or *patient* Church," joining these two seemingly contradictory attributes in no uncertain terms (Batt 1639b, 36, my emphasis; also Butler 1792, 1:282, 2:269–70, 272).

Catholic writers of the time intertwined these two qualities frequently in the new Catholic ideal they preached to English, Scots, Welsh, and Irish Catholics, both males and females, secular and religious. L.P., in introductory comments to *The Right Religion Review'd and inlarg'd*, lauded English Catholics whose "many and glorious sufferings" for their faith ranked them among the "greatest Conquerors" on earth, partly because they displayed the virtues proper to men: reason, will, patience, and constancy. Protestants, he claimed, used "force and strength common to beasts," to vanquish their foes. While Protestants might defeat other, lesser men, Catholic triumphs were ultimately greater because they surmounted other conquering men and themselves. Catholic men, "brave Champions," should continue in such "patience and constancy." "Let them hammer, cut, hew you, till they are weary; they do no more than carve and fit you for the walls of Heaven." God would never abandon Catholics. "Yea, [he] marshals the very field you fight in" (Recusant MS B1039, 1742, 1–3). In *Short Rules*, Southwell discussed the need to "suffer adversity and to digest grief, especially in God's cause and a good quarrel," regaling readers with examples of others who had done so, all the while stressing how good a thing patience and constancy were. Catholic Christians were embroiled in constant warfare with worldly and spiritual enemies and thus must remain perpetually on guard, using patience to prepare both body and mind for defense and in hope of eventual victory (Southwell 1973, Chap. 9, lines 35–38, "Certain short prayers"). Irish priest Henry Fitzsimon, writing from his cell in Dublin Castle, likened Catholic-Protestant strife to a war of conquest. Catholics should run to the combat "by patience" and fight the good fight of St. Paul (Fitzsimon 1881, 15–17, 23, 42). This was the same Paul whom the priest Cornelius Murphy described as a conqueror who defied his tribulations and persecutions just as Catholic martyrs in their patience and courage did in his day, becoming Christian heroes dying in memorable combat (Murphy 1737, 4–8, 22–23, 28, 52–55). The anonymous author of *On ye End of ye Retreat* echoed this melding, instructing that "the Soldiers of J[esus] C[hrist] must be ... obedient, meek, and patient," in contrast to worldly champions who were "proud, debauched, impatient" (Recusant MS B898, unpaginated, 6th Day, 1st Med., 1st Pt.).

Both this last author, Batt, and Anthony Stafford wrote about or to women. Women could be both patient and heroic in their actions for the faith, too, sometimes more so than men. Stafford's list of Mary's feminine virtues to emulate included patience and "Valour Combatting" (Stafford 1635, B3v). Margaret Clitheroe, according to her biographer, although a woman, embodied these qualities.

> She, a woman of invincible courage, entered combat again them all, [the flesh, the world, and the devil] to defend the most ancient Faith ... where they, men, cowardish in the quarrel and faithless in their promises, labored all at once against her ... She, in every word and deed, simple and innocent; they, in everything, deceitful and mischievous. She, patient and joyful; they, furious and threatening. She, victorious. They, conquered. (Mush 1849, 197)

Clitheroe vanquished her foes, partially due to her patience. This unlikely pairing of militancy with patience becomes more understandable in light of religious developments in the British Isles as the years wore on. As discussed above, there would be no easy, quick defeat of the Protestants. Catholics were in this struggle for the long haul, and as Batt maintained in "Another letter,"

> The *Palme of Victory* cannot be achieved without *laborious battle*; give us in adversity *patience* ... so that being strengthened with thy Consolation and linked in brotherly Charity, we may serve thee with one heart, and so pass over these temporal things, that being crowned for our *victories*: we may deserve at last in the *company of those Religious troops* to attain unto those good things. (Batt 1639a, 61–62, my emphasis)

Patience was meant to strengthen believers to endure this drawn-out conflict that Catholic writers assured readers would be won in the end. The ideal Catholic joined this spiritual war, not with expectations of a quick victory but with patience and sturdiness of spirit (Gerard 1959, 90).

There are indications that some, possibly many, lay Catholics listened to these writers, but we also see the difficulty with which they embraced and attempted to find a balance between militancy and patience. Both laywomen, such as Margaret Clitheroe and Mary Ward, and religious women, such as Mary Knatchbull, pushed themselves to reconcile the patience expected of them as women with their desire to fight for God, their salvation, their neighbors, and their church. Laymen—a group that society traditionally rewarded for strength, courage, and martial success—understandably struggled more than women did with incorporating patience into their masculine skill sets. Philip, Cardinal Howard, protector of Catholics in England and Scotland from 1680 to 1688, tried to encourage Catholics toward calmness and moderation during these times but knew that reining in Catholic men's desire to fight would be difficult (*Dominicana* 1925, 3). As discussed previously, even the normally upbeat William Blundell expressed frustration as his patience wore thin during particularly difficult times such as the Popish Plot years (Blundell 1933, 203–4).

William Howard, Viscount Stafford's struggles in balancing his desire to fight with the Church's new imperative to show patience emerge from a close reading of his scaffold speech prior to his execution in 1680 as part of the Popish Plot. Stafford wrote and rewrote his final words many times. The seven extant drafts of this speech allow us to examine the changes and refinements he made as he struggled to craft just the right message (S.N.D. 1929, 198, 200–1, 212, 231). In the final version, Stafford publicly displayed the type of patience now encouraged in Catholic laymen. He twice asked God not to exact any revenge for his innocent blood either on England or upon the individuals responsible for shedding it (Corker 1682, 190–91, 196). He forgave his accusers, and the only punishment he desired was that they acknowledge and repent their false witness against him. He repented his own sins and hoped for salvation (188, 190).

While Stafford's last words appear meek and patient, militant anger lurked just beneath the surface, but only for those in the know. Stafford quoted Psalm 35:3, "Say therefore to my soul 'I am thy salvation'" (Corker 1682, 193). He spoke these innocuous words in Latin, a language likely understandable to his Catholic friends in the crowd but not the majority of Protestants (191–93). For those who understood Latin and his Old Testament reference, the remainder of Psalm 35 reminded them of King David's supplication to the Lord to avenge him against his enemies.

> Contend, LORD, with those who contend with me;
>   fight against those who fight against me.
> Take up shield and armor;
>   arise and come to my aid. (Ps. 35:1–2)

These enemies were men who plotted unfairly and gave unjust witness against David, just as Titus Oates and others had wronged Stafford. David wanted such men driven away like "chaff before the wind," shamed and disgraced. Because they came after him without cause, let them become entangled in their own net or fall into their own pit (Ps. 35:4–8).

> Lord, you have seen this; do not be silent.
>   Do not be far from me, Lord.
> Awake, and rise to my defense!
>   Contend for me, my God and Lord.
> Vindicate me in your righteousness, Lord my God;
>   do not let them gloat over me.
> Do not let them think, "Aha, just what we wanted!"
>   or say, "We have swallowed him up." (Ps. 35:22–25)

Don't let them win. Let them know ruin. "Then my soul will rejoice in the Lord and delight in his salvation" (Ps. 35:9).

Stafford's choice to quote surreptitiously from this graphic, warlike, impatient psalm suggests how hard some Catholics struggled to find a comfortable equilibrium between militancy and patience. Stafford was about to die, and his emotions ran more deeply than his words on the scaffold indicated to the casual listener. Stafford loudly proclaimed patience and forgiveness from the scaffold, but he yearned to fight back. He laboriously crafted a scaffold speech that allowed him to do both. Stafford was executed on December 19, 1680, at Tower Hill in London. The final version of this speech was printed and on sale in the streets of London by 2 p.m. that afternoon (S.N.D. 1929, 215).

These Christian virtues of patience and militancy ran deep within Catholic tradition but often on separate and parallel trajectories, which is why Stafford, the "Good Catholick," and other Catholics had so much of a struggle comfortably reconciling them. In terms of religious roles, certain Catholics, such as laywomen, saints, most monks, and clerics, were customarily supposed to be patient, while other Catholics, such as crusading monks and laymen were approved to fight. If everyone kept to their expected roles, a group of Irish Catholic "Amazons" should never have been able to successfully riot and rout a group of Protestant leaders and soldiers seeking to uphold the law of the land. The Catholic Church needed to bring these seemingly contradictory ideals together during the Reformation era to face the challenges of being an underground faith in

Protestant lands. It was willing to encourage militancy for women—even nuns. It reined in the emotions of laymen spoiling for a fight to defend the faith. By the eighteenth century, priests such as Alban Butler advertised patience as a new standard of lay masculine strength, while clerics such as Walter Vavasour carried weapons and intrigued with rebels.

These were neither easy nor uncontroversial changes. Because the security of society, church, state, and family was believed to rest on each individual staying in his or her prescribed role, any alteration in these roles and rules provoked fear. "Out of place, out of peace." Would institutions crumble? Would anarchy and godlessness prevail? For example, the Church's perceived encouragement of the Dublin widow and her rowdy Amazon associates could be viewed as threatening social disorder. Even if a laywoman or nun never started a riot or took up an actual weapon, the Church's exhortations promoted a new assertiveness and possible disobedience. Men possessed the well-recognized right to mete out discipline as husbands, fathers, and religious or civic officials. Discipline and violence kept subordinates in their place. They maintained the existing social order. Women may have used violence informally or indirectly in disciplining their peers or subordinates within their households, but society, religion, and government authorized only men to use violence in the public sphere. Now it appeared that the Church encouraged women to throw off certain aspects of subordination and gave them the authority to engage in certain types of aggressiveness and violence. Would they use it as men had to uphold the larger existing social order? No one knew, but it was a risk the Church was willing to take, within limits that will be further explored in a later chapter.

As the St. Stephen's Day riot in Dublin well illustrates, however, militancy and patience were simultaneously religious *and* gendered qualities. Catholics were being asked to adopt qualities not traditionally associated with either their own sex or religious roles and to accept these qualities in others. For all the many ways that society policed gender roles, gender was an untidy system of rules that individuals and institutions had always selectively invoked. In this case, religious needs eclipsed concerns over gender as the Church and Catholics themselves redefined what it meant to be a good Catholic. They continued to promote most of the traditionally recognized qualities of a devout believer, but there would be fewer distinctions based on sex as patience and militancy were promoted to all Catholics and not just certain ones.

In the end, weighing religious needs against gender priorities in an analytical game of "one-upmanship" distracts from the underlying issue at hand. Catholics did not need one ideal of what it meant to be a good Catholic and a separate standard for being a good woman or man. What they needed was to weave all these controversies into alternative understandings of what it meant to be a good Catholic man or woman, in which aspects of both religion and gender intertwined. A lot of attitudinal adjustments would be needed.

Beyond these broadened agreements on what defined a "good Catholic," there were other accommodations Catholics were willing to make to religious roles to strengthen the Catholic faith and its core of believers in the British Isles. Catholics were not islands unto themselves. They were part of a community of believers. Just as the Church and laypeople needed a new way to understand Catholic individual identity, so did they need to build ties to one another, ties that would function for Catholics living in a Protestant state. Catholics needed new opportunities for participation in the Church as they sought practical workarounds to the perpetual problems of a shortage of priests and sacraments and Protestant penalties and restrictions. In the process, long-standing boundaries between religious roles blurred, softening some of the distinctions between lay and priestly roles, the subject of the next chapter. Need, again, drove such changes, as Catholics and the Catholic Church adjusted to the challenges of sustaining an illegal, underground faith.

Works Cited

Anonymous. 1690. Olograph introduction to *An Instruction to Performe with Fruit the Devotion of Ten Fridays in Honour of S. Francis Xavierus, apostle of the Indies Much practised in Rome and augmented particularly of late by some most authentick miracles wrought by the intercession of this glorious saint. Vpon which score he is taken as particular patrone of allmost all Italy.* St. Omer. In copy held at the Harry Ransom Humanities Research Center. University of Texas.

Batt, Anthony. 1639a. *A Poore mans mite. A letter of a religious man of the Order of St. Benedict vnto a Sister of his, concerning the rosarie or psalter of our blessed Ladie, Commonly called the Beades.* Douai: Widow of M. Wyon.

———. 1639b. *A Short Treatise Touching the Confraternitie of the Scapular of S. Benedicts Order.* Douai: Widow of M. Wyon.

Berington, Joseph. 1781. "An Address to Catholics." In *The state and behaviour of English Catholics: from the Reformation to the year 1781: with a view of their present number, wealth, character, &c.: in two parts.* 2nd ed. London: R. Faulder.

Blundell, F.O. 1909–1917. *The Catholic Highlands of Scotland.* 2 vols. Edinburgh, Sand & Co.

Blundell, William. 1933. *Cavalier: Letters of William Blundell to his Friends 1620–1698.* Edited by Margaret Blundell. London: Longmans, Green and Co.
Bucke, John. (1589) 1971. *Instructions for the use of the beades.* Reprint, Menston, Yorkshire: The Scolar Press.
Butler, Alban. 1785. *The life of Sir Tobie Maethews. Being a posthumous work of the Rev. Alban Butler.* London: J.P. Coghlan.
———. 1792. *Meditations and discourses on the sublime truths and important duties of Christianity. Being a posthumous work of the Rev. Alban Butler.* Vol. 2. London: J.P. Coghlan.
CSP Dom (Calendar of State Papers, Domestic Series) of the of reign of Elizabeth I. 1863–1950. Public Record Office. Series 2. London.
Challoner, Richard. 1764. *The Devotion of Catholicks to the Blessed Virgin, Truly Represented.* Pamphlet.
———. 1839. *Memoirs of Missionary Priests and Other Catholics of Both Sexes that have Suffered Death in England on Religious Accounts from the Year 1577–1684.* 2 vols. Philadelphia: John T. Green.
Clarkson, John. 1737. *An Introduction to the Celebrated Devotion of the Most Holy Rosary.* London: T. Meighan.
Coakley, John. 1994. "Friars, Sanctity, and Gender: Mendicant Encounters with Saints, 1250–1325." In *Medieval Masculinities: Regarding Men in the Middle Ages,* edited by Clare Lees, 91–110. Minneapolis: University of Minnesota Press.
Corker, James. 1682. *Stafford's Memoires, or, A Brief and Impartial Account of The Birth and Quality, Imprisonment, Tryall, Principles, Declaration, Comportment, Devotion, Last Speech, and Final End of William, late Lord Viscount Stafford.* London: Langley Curtis.
Crowther, Arthur and Thomas Vincent. 1657. *Jesus, Maria, Joseph, or, The Devout Pilgrim, of the Ever Blessed Virgin Mary, in His Holy Exercises, Affections, and Elevations.* Amsterdam.
Dominicana: Cardinal Howard's Letters, English Dominican Friars, Nuns, Students, Papers and Mission Registers. 1925. London: Catholic Record Society, XXV.
Estcourt, Edgar E. and John Orlebar Payne. 1885. *The English Catholic Non-Jurors of 1715 Being a Summary of the Register of Their Estates [extracted from the Returns Made to the Commissioners by the Clerks of the Peace], with Genealogical and Other Notes, and an Appendix of Unpublished Documents in the Public Record Office.* London: Burns & Oates.
Fitzsimon, Henry. 1881. *Words of Comfort to Persecuted Catholics. Written in Exile, Anno 1607. Letters from a Cell in Dublin Castle, and Diary of the Bohemian War of 1620.* Edited by Edmund Hogan. Dublin: M.H. Gill & Son.
Gage, John. 1652. *The Christian Sodality, or, Catholick Hive of Bees Sucking Hony of the Churches Prayers from the Blossomes of the Word of God blowne out of the Epistles and Gospels of the Divine Service Throughout the yeare. Collected by the Puny Bee of all the Hive, not worthy to be named otherwise than by these Elements of his Name: F. P.* Paris.

Garnet, Henry. 1596/7. *The societie of the rosary.* n.p.
Gerard, John. 1959. *The Hunted Priest: Autobiography of John Gerard.* Translated by Philip Caraman. Introduction by Graham Greene. London: Fontana Books.
Gillow, Joseph. 1885–1902. *A Literary and Biographical History or A Bibliographical Dictionary of the English Catholics from the Breach with Rome, in 1534, to the Present Time.* 5 vols. London: Burns & Oates.
Gillow, Joseph and Richard Trappes-Lomax, eds. 1910. *The Diary of the Blue Nuns: or Order of the Immaculate Conception of our Lady at Paris, 1658–1810.* London: Catholic Record Society.
Glickman, Gabriel. 2009. *The English Catholic Community 1688–1745: Politics, Culture and Ideology.* Studies in Early Modern Cultural, Political, and Social History. Woodbridge, Suffolk: The Boydell Press.
The Good Catholick no Bad Subject, or a Letter from A Catholick Gentleman to Mr. Richard Baxter. 1660. London: John Dakins.
Gregory, Brad S. 1999. *Salvation at Stake: Christian Martyrdom in Early Modern Europe.* Cambridge: Harvard University Press.
Haec-vir: or, The womanish-man: being an answere to a late booke intituled Hic-mulier. Exprest in a briefe dialogue betweene Haec-vir the womanish-man, and Hic-mulier the man-woman. 1620. London: I. T[rundle].
Hamilton, Adam, ed. 1904. *The Chronicle of the English Augustinian Canonesses Regular of the Lateran at St. Monica's in Louvain* (now at St. Augustine's Priory, Newton Abbot, Devon) [1548–1644]. Edinburgh: Sands and Company.
Harleian MSS. British Library.
Herbert, Lucy. 1722. *Several Excellent Methods of Hearing Mass.* Bruges: John De Cock.
Hic mulier: or, The man-woman: being a medicine to cure the coltish disease of the staggers in the masculine-feminines of our times. Exprest in a briefe declamation. 1620. London: I. T[rundle].
Holland, Catherine. 1925. "Conversion of Sister Catherine Holland." In *A Link Between Flemish Mystics & English Martyrs,* by C. S. Durrant. Preface by Francis Cardinal Bourne, 272–305. London: Burns, Oates and Washbourne.
Karras, Ruth Mazzo. 2003. *From Boys to Men: Formations of Masculinity in Late Medieval Europe.* Philadelphia: University of Pennsylvania Press.
Lansdowne MSS. British Library.
Litterae Annuae Provinciae Beaticae. 1592–1617. Archivum Romanum Societatis Iesu. Jesuit General Curia, Rome.
Longstaffe, William Hylton Dyer, ed. 1858. *Acts of the High Commission Court within the Diocese of Durham.* London: Whitaker and Company for the Surtees Society, XXXIV.
Loomie, Albert, ed. 1978. *Spain and the Jacobean Catholics, volume 2, 1613–1624.* London: Catholic Record Society, LXVIII.
MacKenzie, Alexander. 1764. *The Poor Prisoner's Comforter. In a Collection of Proper Instructions and Prayers for Christians in Prison . . . To Which is added,*

Instructions and devout Exercises for a Person laying under Sentence of Death. According to Mr. Gother and other pious Authors. London: R. Balfe.

Martin, F.X. 1962. *Friar Nugent: A Study of Francis Lavalin Nugent (1569–1635) Agent of the Counter-Reformation.* London: Methuen.

Matthew, Tobie. 1931. *The Life of Lady Lucy Knatchbull by Sir Tobie Matthew.* Now first printed from the original manuscript, with an introduction by Dom David Knowles. London: Sheed and Ward.

McClain, Lisa. 2004. *Lest We Be Damned: Practical Innovation and Lived Experience among Catholics in Protestant England, 1559–1642.* New York: Routledge.

Merbeck, Mitchell B. 1999. *The Thief, the Cross and the Wheel: Pain and the Spectacle of Punishment in Medieval and Renaissance Europe.* Chicago: University of Chicago Press.

Murphy, Cornelius. 1737. *A True and Exact Relation of the Death of Two Catholicks, who Suffered for their Religion at the Summer Assizes, Held at Lancaster in the year 1628.* London.

Murphy, Martin. 1992. *St. Gregory's College, Seville, 1592–1767.* Southampton: Catholic Record Society, LXXIII.

Mush, John. 1849. *The Life and Death of Margaret Clitherow, the Martyr of York, now first published from the original manuscript.* Edited by William Nicholson. London: Richardson & Son.

Pollen, J.H., contrib. 1909. "Bedingfeld Papers." In *Miscellanea VI.* London: Catholic Record Society, VII.

Recusant MSS. Harry Ransom Humanities Research Center. University of Texas.

Rhodes, W.E., ed. 1909. *The Apostolical life of Ambrose Barlow.* Chetham Miscellanies. Manchester: Chetham Society, new series, II.

S.N.D. 1929. *Sir William Howard Viscount Stafford, 1612–1680.* London: Sands and Co.

Scarisbrike, Edward. 1703. *Rules and Instructions for the Sodality of the Immaculate Conception, of the Most Glorious and Ever Virgin Mary, Mother of God.* n.p.

Southwell, Robert. 1973. *Two Letters and Short Rules of a Good Life.* Edited by Nancy Pollard Brown. Charlottesville: The University Press of Virginia for the Folger Shakespeare Library.

Stafford, Anthony. 1635. *The Femall Glory: or The Life and Death of our Blessed Lady, the holy Virgin Mary, Gods owne immaculate mother to whose sacred memory the author dedicates these his humble endeavours. A treatise worthy the reading, and meditation of all modest women, who live under the government of vertue, and are obedient to her lawes. By Anth. Stafford, Gent.* London: Thomas Harper.

SP Dom (State Papers, Domestic Series). Public Record Office. Kew.

Stone, J.M. 1892. *Faithful unto Death: An Account of the Sufferings of the English Franciscans during the 16th and 17th Centuries, From Contemporary Records.* London: Kegan Paul, Trench, Trübner & Co.

Stowe MSS. British Library.

Strange, Nicholas. (1613) 1649. Introduction to *A missive to His Majesty of Great Britain, King James written divers yeers since by Doctor Carier; Conteining the motives of his Conversion to Catholike Religion*, by B. Carier. Reprint, Paris.

Strasser, Ulrike. 2008. "The First Form and Grace: Ignatius of Loyola and the Reformation of Masculinity." In *Masculinity in the Reformation Era*, edited by Scott H. Hendrix and Susan C. Karant-Nunn, 45–70. Sixteenth Century Essays & Studies Series 83. Kirksville, MO: Truman State University Press.

Vane, Thomas. 1648. *A lost sheep returned home: or The Motives of the conversion to the Catholike Faith, of Thomas Vane*. 3rd ed. Paris.

W.C. 1656. Preface to *The spiritvall combat: VVorthily tearmed a golden treatise of Christian perfection./Translated ovt of the truest coppies in seuerall languages by R.R.; With a letter of S. Eucherius, Bishop of Lyons . . . to his cousin Valerian à [sic] noble man: exhorting him to the contempt of the world and to embrace a truly happie and vertuous life*, by Lorenzo Scupoli. Translated by R.R. Paris.

Walker, Claire. 2000. "Prayer, Patronage, and Political Conspiracy: English Nuns and the Restoration." *The Historical Journal* 43, no. 1: 1–23.

Walsh, Thomas Francis. 1819. *Project of an Establishment designed to give a cheap education to Catholic Female Children to serve as an Asylum for orphans, and other distressed young persons, under the Superintendence of a Society for pious Ladies*. London: Keating, Brown & Co.

Weston, William. 1955. *William Weston: The Autobiography of an Elizabethan*. Translated by Philip Caraman. Foreword by Evelyn Waugh. London: Longmans, Green and Co.

Whately, William. 1623. *A bride-bush, Or, A direction for married persons Plainely describing the duties common to both, and peculiar to each of them. By performing of which, marriage shall prooue a great helpe to such, as now for want of performing them, doe finde it a little hell*. London: Bernard Alsop for Beniamin Fisher.

White, Thomas. 1654. *An Apology for Rushworth's Dialogues. Wherin the Exceptions of the Lords Falkland and Digby are answer'd: and the Arts of their commended Daillé Discovered*. Paris: Chez Jean Billain.

Worthington, Thomas. 1603. *Rosarie of Our Lady*. Ingolstadii: Ederiana apud Andreas Angermarium.

———. (1608) 1978. *A Catalogue of Martyrs in England, 1608*. Edited by D. M. Rogers. Reprint, Menston, Yorkshire: The Scolar Press.

CHAPTER 7

Sharing the Job: Cooperation Between the Priesthood and Laity

Anthony Maria Browne, 2nd Viscount Montague (r. 1592–1629) baptized his infant daughter Catholic with water from a sugar box. No priest was present, and Montague, a layman, performed the rite himself. He was convinced that it was the only way to please God and protect his child's soul.

In the process, Montague thumbed his nose at his Protestant father-in-law and the laws of the kingdom. Montague was married to Lady Jane Sackville, the daughter of Thomas Sackville, Earl of Dorset and Chancellor of Oxford University. Earlier, in 1593 when Jane gave birth to their first child, a son, Montague agreed to have the child baptized publicly in a Protestant church in front of the queen. Baptism—frequently referred to as christening—not only cleanses the stain of original sin, but through it, a church formally receives a person into the Christian faith. However, on the day scheduled for Montague's son's christening, the child unexpectedly died. A Protestant woman performed an emergency baptism just before the baby boy breathed his last.

Shocked by this sudden loss, Montague blamed himself for not insisting on a Catholic baptism. He had sinned, and his son's death was his punishment. Consequently, when his wife delivered their second child the following year, he resolved to act according to his faith. It would not be

© The Author(s) 2018
L. McClain, *Divided Loyalties? Pushing the Boundaries of Gender and Lay Roles in the Catholic Church, 1534-1829*, Histories of the Sacred and Secular, 1700-2000, https://doi.org/10.1007/978-3-319-73087-5_7

easy. Jane gave birth to a daughter, and they spent her lying-in period at her parents' home in London. When his Protestant father-in-law began suggesting Protestant godparents for the child, Montague sparked a heated argument by revealing his intention to have his daughter christened with Catholic rites. Dorset fumed, insisting that he would never allow such a thing. He was within his rights, as his daughter, son-in-law, and new grand-daughter were living under his roof. As head of household, he bore responsibility for the spiritual state of all souls under his care. Montague, however, stood his ground, arguing that he would do it without the household's knowledge. He would quietly bring in a woman, likely a midwife, he said, to do the deed. Dorset countered that he would be on guard for such a person, and if anyone tried to baptize the child, he would "pull them in pieces with [his] teeth."

Facing such vehement opposition, Montague decided to baptize the child himself. He took a small silver box of his wife's, in which she usually kept sugar. Emptying the sugar, Montague filled the box with water, creating a miniature makeshift baptismal font. He concealed the box in his hand under his hat and entered the room where his daughter lay in her cradle. The only other people in the room were his wife and a servant rocking the cradle. He sat down next to his wife and invented an errand for the servant. After she departed, he approached the cradle, offering to rock the child himself. He laid his hat, with the box underneath, on the cradle and surreptitiously put as much water as he could into his hands from the box. He poured it on the child's face and made a cross, likely on her forehead, in the traditional manner, saying, "I baptize thee, Mary, in the name of the Father, and of the Son, and of the Holy Ghost." *Ex post facto*, he left the room to announce to his Protestant father-in-law that the deed was done. Dorset wasted little time informing on his son-in-law to the authorities.

While Montague clearly valued the state of his daughter's soul above the worldly approval of his father-in-law and the state, why did he—a layman—presume that he possessed the spiritual authority to baptize? Wasn't he, in some way, thumbing his nose at the Catholic Church too? Baptism was a sacrament. Catholic priests mediated between God and ordinary believers to aid them in attaining salvation, particularly through the performance of the sacraments. Would Montague's home-based rite cleanse the infant Mary of sin? Would God welcome this infant into heaven and the Catholic faith without the priest's mediation on behalf of her soul? Moreover, wouldn't God, the Catholic Church, and its clergy be angered at this layperson's hubris in arrogating clerical authority to himself?

Montague freely admitted under questioning what he had done and why, and his answers reveal his understandings of his ability to baptize as a layperson. During his formal examination before the Archbishop of Canterbury and the Lord Keeper of London on May 22, 1584, the authorities asked him whether Rome had provided him with a dispensation, an official exception to the Church's usual rules, to baptize his own child. No, Montague answered. He acted alone. He told them why he was determined to give his daughter a Catholic christening after his son's death, and why bringing in an outsider to perform the rite was impossible given Dorset's watchfulness. In the absence of other alternatives, Montague was reasonably confident that he was allowed to baptize the child himself because it was a "case of necessity," and his daughter would not receive a true baptism otherwise (Harleian MS 6998, fol. 141; Willaert 1928, 30–35). He was both a father concerned for his child and a Catholic determined to act in accordance with his faith and who took it upon himself to perform a sacrament typically entrusted to a priest.

Montague added that he had once overheard his grandmother telling a missionary priest that she had christened a baby in her home just before it died. The priest approved of her deed. Ordinarily, a priest celebrated the sacrament of baptism, but the Catholic Church had long allowed laypeople to baptize in emergency situations (i.e., Vaux 1583, G1r–v). Based on this overheard conversation, some books he had read, and debates with other Catholic men about Catholic baptism and marriage, Montague was convinced he had also done well in baptizing his daughter (Harleian MS 6998, fol. 141; Willaert 1928, 34–35).

Through incidents such as Montague's lay baptism, we gain insight into the subtle ways that Catholics who were not clergy began to increase their participation in religious roles traditionally reserved for the clergy. Catholic clergy are individuals who have received Holy Orders as bishops, priests, or deacons through the sacrament of ordination. Ordinary Christians are not clergy, but neither are monastics such as nuns, monks, or friars who although they were called "religious" had not been ordained. Collectively, these non-ordained Christians were known as laypeople. Ordination endows clerics with a divinely instituted authority not just to perform or celebrate sacramental rites but to mediate between God and the laity through those rites to obtain salvific grace for believers (*Code of Canon Law* n.d., Canon 207).

For centuries, the Catholic Church had maintained that the clergy were a class of Christians distinct and separate from the laity, uniquely endowed by God to aid the laity's salvation. Laypeople did not possess the power to wield clerical authority—the power to save souls. The Church, in fact, historically punished laypeople who presumed to exercise clerical authority.

However, the reality of an almost 300-year dearth of clerical counsel and aid confronted laypeople such as Montague with a desperate choice: perform a role themselves or leave it undone and risk consequences as disastrous as the loss of a soul. As a result, the relationship between Catholics with different religious roles—lay and clerical—was changing. Whether baptizing in an emergency or aiding the work of priests on the mission, non-ordained people were not trying to replace priests or challenge clerical authority consciously. Rather, in the absence of clergy, laypeople saw a need, and they were willing, able, and available to fill it.

Many priests also recognized the long-term crisis taking place in the British Isles, and seemed willing to share a measure of their authority to help Catholics attain spiritual comfort and saving grace. As Montague, his grandmother, and the priest with whom she spoke understood, the Catholic Church had long been willing to bend some of its rules in times of emergency (McClain 2004, 6). This had been Mary Ward's understanding, too. It was a key reason why Ward was so sure that the papacy would bend its rules and approve her Institute. The times seemed to demand it. While Ward's ambitious gambit failed, others—men and women, both ordinary laypeople and religious, none of them ordained—were more fortunate.

The long-term consequence of this sharing was that, over time, these non-clerics understood their relationships to clergy, the sacraments, the Catholic Church, and even to God in new ways. They exercised greater autonomy in their interactions with the clergy and gradually gained confidence in their ability to work toward their own salvation in greater partnership with clergy. They understood their participation in the sacraments in new ways, expanding their role from passive observers to more active participants in the spiritual transformations believed to occur in the sacraments. By the eighteenth century, the writings of non-ordained Catholics reveal their attempts to re-define the boundaries of authority between clergy and non-clergy in both religious and worldly matters. Some lay writers placed less emphasis on priests' mediation and more significance on lay-directed efforts to create union between the believer and God. Other Catholics began to make increasing distinctions between issues in which they would allow clergy to direct them and those that they felt authorized, based on their knowledge of the Church and its policies, to make themselves. In this way the boundaries between lay and clerical roles were shifted over the course of three centuries, typically without a direct or even conscious challenge to clerical authority taking place.

It is unclear to what extent clergy willingly participated in this process of transformation. Paradoxically, as in most mission fields, the Catholic Church needed to empower laypeople to defend the faith while also asserting its God-given authority over them. Just as priests were important for the salvation of souls, laypeople were indispensable for the salvation of Catholicism in the British Isles. The Lancashire priest and president of the English College at Douai, Thomas Worthington, in his *Catalogue of Martyrs in England*, pointedly emphasized how the continued strength and presence of Catholicism in his homeland depended on the many men and women of all states and sorts who maintained their faith publicly (Worthington 1978, 8–10). Relationships between priests and laypeople changed subtly yet perceptibly under these circumstances, and the balance between religious and gendered authority also altered as a result. However, without a large-scale lay commitment to the Catholic faith and Church in both their private and public lives, the Catholic cause was doomed. The Catholic Church recognizes a similar imperative today.

Priest Shopping

Prior to reforms in the British Isles, most Christians had little choice in what church they would attend or who their priest would be. The pre-reform Church was divided administratively into parishes, each with a church. Christians were expected to attend the nearby church of the parish in which they resided. Whether they liked the priest, church, or other congregants was unimportant. The Council of Trent in its 22nd session had recently reiterated this centuries-old standard in 1562 in its "Decree concerning the things to be observed, and to be avoided, in the celebration of Mass" (Waterworth 1848, 161).

After reforms, however, Catholics in the British Isles no longer belonged to a Catholic parish. There were no Catholic churches. There was no one priest to whom they automatically owed obedience. Laypeople thus exercised a greater degree of choice in their spiritual guides than they would have prior to the break with Rome or in countries where Catholicism was legal.

This freedom of choice was greatly limited by a lack of available options. Some Catholics chose a priest from among the predictably slim selection of available missionaries (Bossy 1975, 51). Still, if they were not pleased with their present priest, some Catholics opted to change to one who would better suit their personal and household needs. After being widowed, Elizabeth Vaux of Irthlingborough, Northhamptonshire, did just that. Before he died, her husband had chosen a Jesuit priest, Richard Collins—first cousin to the Gunpowder Plot mastermind Guy Fawkes—to live in and serve the Vaux household. After his death, Elizabeth wanted a change. Collins, she admitted, was a good and pious man but was just a poor fit with the household. She said,

> she reverenced and liked him very much. Yet he had never mixed with men; he had always been absorbed in his studies, so that whenever any business or practical matter was under discussion, he could give no helpful advice. This was why some of the people in the house did not like him. (Gerard 1959, 151–52)

She chose a replacement.

Some priests expressed discomfort over this new lay autonomy. The Jesuit John Gerard called the Vaux family "ungracious." He accused Vaux and her household of not knowing how to submit properly to clerical authority. In her response, Vaux implied that if such were the case, she and her household would have already conformed to the Protestant Church. Ultimately, Vaux refused to relinquish her right to choose which priest would live in her home and serve her family (151–52). Into the eighteenth century, lay patrons such as the imperious Ann Fenwick of Lancashire expected their priests in residence to conform to their preferences. She set up a priest in Hornby Hall in 1662 and stated her standards clearly. Fenwick stipulated, for example, that if the priest "is a young man, I would have him to be very regular in every point belonging to his Function & particularly diligent in reading Pious Books" (Foley 1991, 27, 33, 34).

The future lay martyr, James Duckett, also showed a clear preference for some priests over others. Originally from Westmoreland, Duckett was a printer's apprentice in London when he turned his back on his lucrative future profession after converting to Catholicism. He remained in London, married a Catholic, and supported his family through an economy of makeshifts: tailoring and printing and trading illegal Catholic books. During a well-known leadership struggle between Jesuits and secular priests known as the Appellant or Archpriest Controversy, discussed in Chap. 8, Duckett openly preferred and promoted the interests of the priests he knew best—

the secular priests whose vestments he mended, whose books he sold, and whose Masses he attended—over their challengers. He decided that if they did not like the Jesuits, he did not either. As the conflict between Jesuits and seculars heated up, Duckett chose to print pamphlets defending the secular priests' position (Merrick 1947, 121–22, 124).

However, not all Catholics enjoyed the same level of choice in priests that a wealthy Catholic such as Vaux or a London Catholic such as Duckett did. Priests were not readily available to most Catholics living in the British Isles, especially those outside major cities. The advice, practices, and attitudes of both clerics and laypeople slowly began to change to reflect this reality, as did their relationships to each other.

In the first decades after Protestant reforms in the British Isles, most writers of Catholic catechisms and other pastoral literature emphasized the absolute necessity of laypeople's regular recourse to priests, as if Catholics in the British Isles still had parish churches in their neighborhoods and spiritual directors awaiting their visits. They made few concessions to the daily difficulties and dangers of living in a country where Catholicism was illegal. For their part, priests advertised their own authority and indispensability. They reiterated their privileged status as Christ's representatives to whom lay Catholics owed obedience. As Southwell professed in *Short Rules of a Good Life*, priests were God's "vice-regents" and "substitutes." Laypeople should treat priests as they would Christ, reiterating Christ's words, "He who heareth you [the priests], heareth me." The best route to salvation was through the direction of a priest (Southwell 1973, Chap. 3, lines 2–3, 26–30, 44–45, 51–55, 59–63; also Scarisbrike 1703, 64, 71).

Laypeople, such as William Wiseman, echoed these beliefs. While in jail in the 1590s, Wiseman penned *A Triple Farewell to the World, or Three Deaths in Different States of Soul*, a dialogue describing the prospects of salvation for three individuals on the brink of death. Although no longer extant, Gerard described the text in detail. The first person, "a man of good moral character and, in men's opinions, a virtuous man" had to resign himself to damnation. Although he had lived a principled life, "he had acted as his own guide in everything." He trusted in his own judgment rather than submitting himself to be ruled by a priest. The second, a pious woman, initially submitted "completely to direction" of her priest, but then she backslid. She was fooled by the devil and "decided to become her own director in certain matters," rather than following her priest's counsel. By repenting before her death, she managed to avoid hell. She was, however, destined to spend a long stretch in purgatory to atone for her pride and disobedience because "she had always loved her own opinion and will." Wiseman's third individual attained the holy death to which all Catholics should aspire. "He had lived in the world and was well-off and had always sought and followed the guidance of his spiritual father and manifested his soul to him for the glory of God." This man alone avoided the pains of hell or purgatory and entered paradise. Wiseman exhorted others to do the same, obeying their priestly guide in all things (Gerard 1959, 99–100).

What if, however, one had no priestly guide? By the mid-seventeenth century this situation was all too common, and most authors refined their messages accordingly. They encouraged Catholics to seek out a priest when one was available, but they also provided detailed instructions on what laypeople could do for the good of their souls when lacking priestly direction. They were changing the relationship between laypeople and the priesthood, and voluntarily sharing a measure of their clerical roles and responsibilities in an emergency situation. Some pastoral authors instructed laypeople how they could receive almost all the salvific benefits of the Eucharist without having attended a Mass (McClain 2004, 109–39). Others taught the laity how to confess and receive God's absolution for their sins if a priest were unavailable (McClain 2013). Many writers encouraged lay membership in religious confraternities, sodalities, and third orders so that Catholics could join in the salvific merits accrued by Catholic members worshiping worldwide (i.e., Scarisbrike 1703; Stanney 1617).

While making what initially appear to be unorthodox accommodations, pastoral writers preserved clerical authority as best they could. They insisted that readers submit to a priest's authority and direction whenever one was available. For example, if a reader had the opportunity to attend Mass or confess directly to a priest, they must do so rather than fall back on the instructions in a text (McClain 2004, 45–49, 55–139; 2013, 108–10). Writers tied any salvific benefits associated with a particular practice to this type of qualification. For example, "Although other Catholics may … punctually observe the Instructions laid before" official members of the Sodality of the Immaculate Conception of the Virgin Mary, "yet they partake not" of the benefits and privileges unless they were "actually admit[ed] to the organization" (Scarisbrike 1703, A4r–v). Priests had oversight of these groups. They made admission as practicable as possible for Catholics living under restrictions on worship in the British Isles, but a Catholic could not just mimic the practices of the group based on instructions in a text and hope to gain the same benefits as laypersons admitted to membership by priests. In short, if a priest was available, Catholics should make use of his mediation. If not, writers of pastoral literature presented readers with reasonable, orthodox adaptations to customary practices so Catholics could continue to work for the health of their souls.

Books were valuable tools for Catholics in need of comfort and ideas, but at some point Catholics needed performance and action. Some laypeople such as Montague engaged in ritual, liturgy, and even sacraments in new ways with very little priestly supervision. Laypeople had always participated in such religious practices. It had been common prior to reforms for a layperson to lead a household in family prayers, but such devotions had always been thought of as *supplemental* to church worship led by a priest. Now home-based, lay-led liturgies and prayers *stood in* for traditional Catholic rites. Laypeople likely did not view them as equivalent to church services, but they were clearly more than an "extra" added on to a regular cycle of religious observances led by a priest. They now formed the bulk of worship for many Catholics.

MINISTERING TO ONE ANOTHER

Increasingly, laypeople began to minister to one another, taking primary responsibility for tasks ordinarily carried out by priests. Laypeople led religious services, reading prayers publicly that would ordinarily have been read by a cleric (Gage 1652, A5r; HCCP 1597/9). Catholics instructed friends and family in how to prepare for confession. They prepared others to reconcile with the Roman Church, advising potential converts of all they needed to know or do to prepare to see a priest (McClain 2015, 449–52). Lay Catholics even began to open schools to educate the next generations of Catholics.

Women proved particularly effective at such work, being under less suspicion and risking less punishment than men if caught encouraging Catholicism. Some women gained access to potential converts through traditionally female activities such as healing and midwifery. The English Lady, Dorothea, in her 1622/23 narrative of her activities on mission, described how this built trust with the people in rural Suffolk who she hoped to serve. At times, "I tend and serve poor people in their sickness. I make salves to cure their sores … in these works of charity I spend my time not in one place, but in many." At other times, she would reside in a home for several weeks, caring for the sick. In one instance, she perceived upon first arriving that "it would not have been well taken if I had spoken of God, etc., wherefore sorting myself to their dispositions I soon gained their affections, by serving and tending them both, and making medicines and salves, and teaching them to do the same." Only later would she begin to dispense the Catholic faith along with healing, gradually introducing religion into conversations, instructing them in the faith, as a priest usually would have done. When people were ready to convert or receive the sacraments, Dorothea would arrange for folk to meet in a field or home "under the pretense of gathering herbs to make salves." She needed to gather people without raising Protestant suspicions, and her healing work provided such opportunities. Then Dorothea brought a priest (Chambers 1882, 2:28–31).

Through their work as healers, Catholic women often performed the vital task of finding priests to administer the last rites to Catholics on the brink of death. Catholics feared dying in a state of sin without this sacrament, known as the *viaticum*. For example, when a Catholic man fell ill while staying in a Protestant household in London, his caretaker—a Catholic woman— searched the city until she found the Jesuit William Weston. She brought him to the man who by that time was panicked of dying unshriven. He claimed to see thousands of "terrible black devils with fearful faces" throughout his room, ready to take him to hell. Weston eventually calmed the man, then walked him step by step through a final confession and absolution. He died the following day after receiving the last rites (Weston 1955, 142–44). While Weston wrote to underscore the dangers of dying without confession, his account highlights how without his caretaker, this man would have died without this sacrament.

Catholic women also took advantage of the long-accepted tradition of women performing charitable good works in prisons to gain access to Catholics they ordinarily would not have been allowed to see (McClain 2012, 34, 40–43). When the priest, Jasper Heywood, fell ill while imprisoned in the Tower of London and needed a nurse, his sister, Elizabeth Heywood, received permission to provide his care. In addition to healing, Elizabeth served as a courier, delivering letters between Heywood and William Weston (Weston 1955, 10; SP Dom 12/203/38i).

Unfortunately, some Protestant authorities knew about this practice and used it to entrap Catholic women. The laywoman Jane Wiseman, for example, was famous for her poultices, which she often brought to London's many jails to heal Catholic prisoners who could not afford medical care. A "hanger-on at the Gatehouse" prison, allegedly colluding with the infamous jailer Topcliffe, entrapped Wiseman by asking her to help heal an imprisoned friend of his. She agreed and tended to the man's injured leg. Unbeknownst to her, her patient was a priest, and when she was finished, they indicted her for aiding and maintaining a priest (Pollen 1908, 363; Gerard 1959, 68–69). Like Margaret Clitheroe, she refused to recognize the state's authority to judge her and was sentenced to death by *peine forte et dure*. Unlike Clitheroe, she was never executed. In an act of clemency, James I commuted her sentence.

Other lay Catholics contributed to the salvation of souls by ensuring that youth received a quality Catholic education, either by teaching or by opening schools illegally in their homes. According to the Council of Trent, tutors and schoolmasters were supposed to be clerics. Eventually the majority of the documented Catholic schoolmasters in the British Isles, however, were laymen and women. They taught formally and informally in Protestant-run grammar schools, unlicensed "hedge" schools, private homes, or mission safe houses (SP Dom 12/146/37, 12/235/68, 12/240/9, 12/243/52, 16/270/29; Beales 1963, 73, 76, 78–80, 86, 205, 207, 219–20, 229–30, 255, 264–65, 267, 271–72). The Church tolerated this widespread practice as an emergency measure, much as they did lay baptism such as Montague's (Beales 1963, 76, 86, 267).

Mary Ward and her English Ladies were laypeople who took on the education of youth as a critical part of their mission to uphold the faith. On the continent, the English Ladies opened schools at their Institute houses in the Low Countries, Holy Roman Empire, and Italian peninsula. In England, the English Ladies had to be more surreptitious. Dorothea discussed her approach to educating youth and others while on the mission:

> I dare not keep schools publicly ... but I teach or instruct children in the houses of parents, which I find to be a very good way, and by that occasion I get acquaintance, and so gaining first the affections of their parents, after with more facility their souls are converted to God. Besides the teaching of children, I endeavor to instruct the simple and vulgar sort. I teach them their *Pater, Ave,* Creed, Commandments, etc. (Chambers 1882, 2:27–28)

Dorothea's educational work was so important to her that it was the first thing she discussed in her narrative of her missionary days. Dorothea catechized students in the basic tenets of Catholicism. Even if a pupil never reconciled with the Roman Church, Dorothea described the baby steps toward conversion that such education made possible.

> Those who in ... fear of persecution, loss of goods, and the like I cannot at the first bring to ... the Catholic Church, I endeavor at least so to dispose them that they ... seldom or unwillingly go to heretical churches, abhor the receiving of their profane Communion, to ... more seldom to sin, and little by little I endeavor to root out the custom of swearing, drinking, etc. (Chambers 1882, 2:27–28)

Maybe one person went to Protestant services less often, believing the true way to salvation was the Catholic path. Perhaps another sinned less often. Her teaching opened doors of opportunity for the English Ladies' work in converting Protestants and saving souls.

Some laypeople even opened secret Catholic schools in their homes. Charles I's Privy Council, for example, was certain that Jesuits resided at the home of Anne Vaux at Stanley Grange in Derbyshire and were educating Catholic youth. They were right. Since before 1625, Vaux's school served as a preparatory school for Catholic boys, particularly those hoping to attend the English College at St. Omer. Secretary of State John Coke tried to catch the educators red-handed in 1625. When his searchers arrived at Stanley Grange, they found the doors barred. When they finally gained entrance, they found just two women in the home, neither of whom was Anne Vaux.

Although the authorities found no Catholics at Stanley Grange, they found plenty of circumstantial evidence of a secret Catholic school. This woman's house was laid out to accommodate a great many residents, more than could conceivably be part of Vaux's farming household. Never, Coke said, had he seen so many rooms and chambers in so small a space. In each room were beds and furniture to "lodge 40 or 50 persons at least." There were also two chapels. But because there were no priests or students, the searchers left empty-handed (*Manuscripts of the Earl Cowper* 1888, 1:227–29).

A decade later, in 1635, the Privy Council tried again, sending orders to local authorities to search the home and apprehend and examine any Jesuits or youth on the premises. This time, the government succeeded in exposing Stanley Grange for the illegal school it was. According to the Jesuit Annual Letters, the searchers found priests and students, all of whom they took to London along with two chests full of religious books and objects. The government sent the priests to jail but returned all students to their parents' custody (*CSP Dom* 16/214/74, 16/219/36; Foley 1875, 2:316–17; Kenny 1962, 448–50; Beales 1963, 209–13).

It is easy to understand why women such as Vaux, Dorothea, and others played such a critical role in educating Catholic youth. The government's orders for searching Stanley Grange made no mention of what to do with any women found there, nor do the records indicate whether Vaux or any other woman was present during the raid. The authorities did not deem the women's efforts as worthy of their notice. This perception provided opportunities that Catholic laypeople could exploit.

By the eighteenth century, as restrictions on Catholic activities loosened—although the penal laws remained on the books—Catholic-run schools, such as that run by Alice Harrison at Fernyhalgh, could educate youth, both Catholic and Protestant, more openly. Harrison, known affectionately as "Dame Alice," clearly structured her school to provide a Catholic education. Situated on a hill near a Catholic chapel, students prayed the rosary and litanies daily. Protestant pupils could elect which devotions they participated in. Harrison employed a female assistant, Mary Backhouse, and together they served between 100 and 200 students and sent many on to seminaries on the continent (Myerscough 1958, 247–48).

Administering the Sacraments

Lay Catholic involvement in priestly forms of work went beyond the recitation of prayers, education of youth, and other forms of basic pastoral care. Laypeople such as Montague increasingly involved themselves in the sacraments and other important rites of the Church, such as baptism and burial. With baptism, the Church allowed that when the soul of a person on the verge of death risked exclusion from the kingdom of God if a priest were not present to welcome the soul into the faith, a layperson could take on this role. To christen a person, a priest was preferable, next a deacon, then a layman, and lastly, a woman (Vaux 1583, G1r–v).

Although last in the line of preference as celebrators of baptism, women likely performed more lay baptisms than did laymen. Births were communal female experiences. Midwives attended many births in which a child's life was in peril, and laywomen other than midwives often participated in baptisms (Longley 1988, 41–42). Although the Church allowed—even trained—midwives to baptize endangered infants in the centuries prior to and after Protestant reforms, Catholics now faced additional difficulties. Protestant midwives would baptize a child according to the rites of the Church of England, which in the minds of Catholic parents would not ensure a soul's welcome into the kingdom of God. Many Catholic parents preferred Catholic midwives such as Elizabeth Cellier, known infamously as the "Popish midwife," who would be willing to send for a Catholic priest if their newborn's life appeared to be in danger. As finding a Catholic priest on short notice was not always easy, a midwife judging a newborn child to be *in extremis* often baptized the infant herself (McClain 2012, 44). Some Catholic midwives took their obligations even more seriously and traveled with unbaptized healthy children until they located a Catholic cleric to perform the sacrament (Haigh 1975, 258).

Catholic laypeople also assumed new responsibilities at burials. A traditional Catholic burial service consisted of carrying the body to the church; prayers, Mass, and absolution in a church; and burial in hallowed ground. A priest was traditionally present at each stage. In the absence of churches, Catholic burial grounds, and priests, lay Catholics struggled to provide some of the rites. In 1604, for example, Elena Bid of Wigan parish was cited by Protestant church authorities because she "did cast holy water round about the chamber at the death of Katherine Bolton" (Visitation Correction Books, EDV 1/13, fol. 102v). This would have been one of the first things a priest would have done prior to conveying Bolton's body to the church for prayer and Mass. He would arrive with holy water, which he would sprinkle on the coffin while praying a psalm, usually *De profundis*. In the absence of a priest, Bid took this role upon herself.

Catholics also needed a place for burial rites and the burial itself. Although some Catholics received public burials in Protestant churches and churchyards, many Catholics were refused burial in Protestant hallowed ground and others did not want it (Oliver 1857, 20). Prison officials at Hull Blockhouse in Yorkshire, for example, refused to allow recusants who died while incarcerated to receive Catholic rites or be buried in their Protestant churchyard. Instead, authorities interred them under the castle wall in unhallowed ground (Hirst 1913, 109). When the Protestant parson of Sefton in Lancashire refused to bury the corpse of an impoverished Catholic woman in his churchyard in 1610, her friends decided to bury her outside the churchyard on the highway. A pig rooted up the gravesite and ate portions of the corpse (Blundell 1925, 32–37; Blundell 1933, 244–45). In contrast, Edmund Smith, a recusant residing in Manchester deanery in 1611, apparently did not *want* his child buried alongside Protestants. He snuck into the chapel yard of Ellenbrough under cover of darkness and buried his child "where never awe was buried before" (Visitation Correction Books, EDV 1/17, fol. 103).

Outraged by such events, William Blundell of Little Crosby—the grandfather of the William Blundell with whom we are already familiar—set aside a piece of his own land in 1611 as a Catholic burial ground. In a letter he wrote to comfort an unnamed friend in London during an outbreak of plague there in 1665, the grandson William Blundell disclosed that among his religious books, he owned one containing the Office of the Dead. He wrote, "I have already performed [for] your deceased friend the very best Office that my Book can show me; and I will not be slow to procure from Mr. Clifford [William Clifford, a priest] a much better Remembrance," thereby fulfilling the Church's emergency precepts. Blundell, a layman, performed the office himself but clearly planned to get the rites performed by a priest as soon as he could, as his performance and the priest's were not equivalent, though Blundell's act at least gained some benefit for the deceased's soul (Blundell 1933, 109).

Although laypeople may recite these prayers at will for a specific deceased person, Blundell's ownership of the Office of the Dead combined with the burial site on his land leads to the reasonable speculation that Blundell read the office at actual burials if a priest was not available. The Blundell family formalized its responsibility, keeping a burial register of all the dead buried on Blundell land, perhaps so they could be remembered in Masses celebrated at Little Crosby. The Blundells placed a brass plate above the register, and successive generations of the family maintained the book. They recorded the names of every decedent, noting that each person had been denied burial by Protestant clerics. This perhaps legitimated the lay burials as emergency interments, satisfying God and the Church that the soul of the decedent deserved salvific merit just as Montague hoped that his emergency christening garnered salvific benefits for his child. A total of 131 Catholic burials are recorded at Little Crosby for which Star Chamber fined Blundell over £2000 (Blundell 1933, 244–46; Gibson 1887, xv, xviii–xx; Blundell 1925, 32–37).

Ample anecdotal evidence establishes a pattern that laypeople took on some of the duties officially established as clerical duties. They participated in pastoral care, sacrament, ritual, and even Catholic education in new ways and with greater frequency in the centuries after Protestant reforms. They did so to comfort and aid their own souls and those of their neighbors. Moreover, sufficient evidence exists that some clerics encouraged laypeople to do so when clerics could not be there. Together, laypeople and priests rewrote their relationships.

While clerics and Church leaders allowed and even encouraged such changes as temporary expedients in time of emergency, those "temporary" accommodations dragged into centuries. Although laypeople initially took on such responsibilities out of worry and need, their increased participation in pastoral care and sacramental activities became normalized over time. What did these new forms of religious participation in the work of the Church mean to how the laity saw their place in the larger Church and in relationship with God? Would laypeople be willing to surrender these roles when the state of emergency officially ended around the turn of the nineteenth century? One of the best ways to answer such questions is to examine closely how non-ordained people discussed their roles in liturgy and sacraments in comparison to priests' roles, particularly by the eighteenth century after these new religious roles had had time to become familiar, routine, and expected.

Overcoming Eve

While non-ordained Catholics—ordinary laypeople and monastics—continued to revere the priesthood and recognize the necessity of priests' mediation on behalf of their souls, they also saw an expanded role for themselves in sacrament, liturgy, and the process of salvation itself. For example, by exploring gradual changes in language used by non-clerics to describe how they participated in religious types of "offering"—who offered what to God and in what circumstances—it becomes clear that non-clerics notably decreased their emphasis on priests as mediators between themselves and God. Catholics in the post-reform British Isles continued to make offerings to God, Mary, and a cadre of saints in the traditional manner advocated by clerics. Believers donated their wealth to pious causes. They offered prayers and tithes as testaments to their faith. They offered themselves to God, asking for protection and grace. They offered their bodies, sacrificing their will and comfort, in return for divine favor, protection, and grace. However, non-ordained Catholics also claimed a new intimacy with God and a more active responsibility in the process of their own salvation through their role in religious offering. Most significantly, some laypeople gradually began to offer not only themselves to God but even Christ upon the altar to God in language that appears to appropriate part of a priest's role as mediator in the sacrament of the Eucharist.

This does not appear to have been an intentional grab at religious power by the laity. By the early seventeenth century, many Catholics had grown up in an environment of changing religious roles and relationships to religious authority. Just as with burials, baptisms, and Catholic education, laypeople became used to the scarcity of priests and learned to take up the slack by making some types of offerings usually made by clerics themselves. It did not require any conscious effort on the part of laypeople for broad shifts in their roles to occur.

Offerings and sacrifices to God are an integral part of Christian liturgy with roots in Judaism and earlier faiths. The most visible offering in the Roman Church is the sacrament of the Eucharist. A priest offers the sacrifice of Christ's body upon the altar on behalf of the laity. This is not a memorial of Christ's earlier sacrifice but is believed to repeat the original sacrifice in the present time. During the Eucharistic celebration during Mass, the bread and wine consecrated by the priest become the literal, physical body and blood of Christ which have just been sacrificed by the priest at the altar to redeem humanity. A cleric and the Church thus mediate between believers and God to gain salvific merits for believers in the present moment. The priest gains the authority and power to effect such a powerful transformation and repeat the sacrificial offering through another, earlier sacrament, the sacrament of his ordination. While laypeople could certainly make some offerings to God, they surely could not expect their offerings to manifest the same spiritual change and accrue the same merits toward believers' salvation as this priestly offering.

Or could they? By the early seventeenth century, some of the laity from the British Isles increasingly saw themselves in the role of "offeror," in new ways and in terms that overlapped priestly roles, and they encouraged other laypeople to do the same. The language of change is most evident in the writings of female religious from the British Isles, the nuns. This can perhaps be explained by their high rates of literacy in comparison to the general Catholic laity of the time, or perhaps by their lifestyles, which provided them more time to tease out the nuances of such issues. Monastics typically meditated on their religious roles and experiences to a greater degree than the average Catholic layperson busy with worldly responsibilities.

At first, the inclusion of the views of nuns side-by-side with those of ordinary laypeople may seem like comparing apples and oranges. Yet although monastics are distinct from ordinary laypeople, they are similar in that neither group shares in clerical authority. The Church classifies nuns and monks as laypeople in comparison to ordained clergy. Moreover, girls and women would most likely have arrived at the convent grate after growing up in the British Isles. As lay youth, they would have experienced the scarcity of priests for years and seen and possibly participated in the new duties undertaken by the laity described above. Much of their worldview was already formed. Once at the convent, they would have seen a degree of female initiative and autonomy long recognized by scholars (Bynum 1988; Johnson 1991). Although convents relied on selected priests for sacraments and general oversight, convent life was largely a "nuns-only," and, hence, a laity-only, experience because of enclosure. Benedictine Lucy Knatchbull thought of her convent as a "little surviving English world" (Matthew 1931, 131). Despite their eventual differences in daily lifestyle, nuns' attitudes were not so dissimilar to those of the laity back home.

For laywomen to participate in the more liturgical and sacramental forms of offering, they would first have to overcome a daunting obstacle: traditional teachings about women's divinely created inferiority and explicit exclusion from clerical roles. The anonymous author of *An eight days retreat for Religious* (c. 1763–1782), written for nuns to deepen their spirituality and connection to Christ, established women's favor in the eyes of God to set the stage for such a change. A frequent reason the Church gave for denying women's ability to mediate between God and believers—and, hence, to deny them clerical status and the ability to offer Christ's body on the altar—was their divinely created imperfection in comparison to men. This is part of divine law discussed previously. Theologians have often used the hierarchy of Creation established in the second chapter of Genesis to explain why men hold the priesthood exclusively. Genesis 2 held that God created man first, in the image of God, and woman later, in the image of man. Because God created only men in his own image, the argument goes, they were more suited to mediate between God and humanity.

The author of *An eight days retreat* implicitly challenged this convention right from the start by establishing as truth that God created women, too, in the divine image. In the first day's meditation, the author drew from the details of Creation found in the *first* chapter of Genesis relating how God created both men and women at the same time, both in God's image (Recusant MS B896, First Med., 1st point, 2). This elevated women's status above the more commonly repeated teachings about women's place in Creation based upon the second chapter of Genesis.

Most theologians and laypeople virtually ignored Genesis 1 to focus on Genesis 2's Creation narrative. By highlighting Genesis 1's explanation of Creation, this author wittingly or unwittingly opened a door to women's mediation between believers and God, such as making offerings, even offerings of Christ.

Women's assumption of such clerical functions was not entirely without precedent. As the Spanish Jesuit, Francisco Suarez (d. 1617), noted in his treatise *De mysteriis vitae Christi*, Mary, a woman, had provided her own substance to God to be transformed into the divine. She offered her son to be a sacrifice. Similarly, the Capuchin, Lawrence of Brindisi (d. 1619), referred to Mary as a "spiritual priest" who served in spirit up at the altar with Christ, offering the sacrament to God for salvation (Graef 1985, 2:21–24, 30).

The author's second meditation established a related principle: that God favored monastics above worldly people. They were his favorites and his friends. They obeyed his laws more exactly than did "worldlings" (Recusant MS B896, Second Med., 1st point, 1). God favored women monastics, then, both as women and as monastics, established by the intersection of their sex and their devotion. Accordingly, God bestowed more graces upon them than upon ordinary laywomen and at least as many as upon male monastics.

This was because women religious, according to the author, did not just offer themselves to God, they *consecrated themselves*, body and soul, to serving God. However, non-clerics were not authorized by the Church to consecrate! Consecration is typically an act by which a person or thing is set apart from the world and dedicated to divine or sacred purpose. Although its origins lie in pre-Christian faiths, the Catholic Church came to limit the term "consecration" to particular understandings and carefully defined ceremonies within the Church. Only certain individuals granted authority by the Church—clerics—could consecrate. Most commonly, bishops consecrate other bishops and altars, and priests consecrate the bread and wine into the body and blood of Christ during the Eucharistic celebration. Consecration involves more elaborate ceremonies than more simple offerings, blessings, or dedications of people or things to the divine. A person who has been consecrated literally has their state of existence changed from temporal existence to a more spiritual condition to best serve the divine will. The spiritual power and graces conferred by God to the consecrated person are greater than with a simple blessing or dedicatory offering. In this case, however, each religious woman participating in the spiritual retreat was instructed to "consecrate herself" and continuously sacrifice herself to God in such totality that nothing of her own would remain, just as, in transubstantiation, nothing remained of the substance of bread and wine after a priest's consecration at the altar (Recusant MS B896, Second Med., 1st point, 2; also Lawson 1765, 76–77, 81–83).

With their *bona fides* thus established, some religious women such as Lucy Knatchbull (1584–1629) and Lucy Herbert (1669–1744) began to offer. First, they offered themselves to God during Mass with similar language and apparent intent as a priest consecrated bread and wine into the transubstantiated body and blood of Christ at the altar. Second, they offered Christ to God with similar language and apparent intent as a priest sacrificed Christ at the altar. Finally, they offered such sacrifices for the salvific benefit of their own souls and also for the souls of others. Through the writings of Knatchbull and Herbert, we gain insight into the subtle ways that non-clerics began to increase their participation in rituals traditionally dominated by priestly presence and action. However, in reading such recommendations, one is frequently left wondering, "Where are the priests?"

Offering One's Self at Mass

Born in Kent, Lucy Knatchbull grew up Catholic but had little interest in a religious life until her late teens. She was received into the English Benedictine convent at Brussels in 1608 and professed in 1611 (Bowden 2009). She later played a pivotal role in establishing a new branch of the convent at Ghent. Catholic convert, priest, and diplomat Tobie Matthew chronicled her life in 1652 in *The Life of Lady Lucy Knatchbull* just a few years before his death. He included a wealth of Knatchbull's own writings, including a series of papers to a Fr. Vincent, the "Ghostly Father of the House" (Matthew 1931, 149).

In describing her own experiences at Mass to Fr. Vincent, Knatchbull explained how she offered herself to God in sacrifice. She did so prior to the priest's elevation of the consecrated host. In other words, as the priest created and prepared to sacrifice Christ's body in the Mass, she sacrificed her own body to Christ. Just as the substance of the bread and wine were annihilated and replaced with Christ's physical body and blood, Knatchbull prayed that God would make her "an entire Holocaust to him," a sacrifice in which the offering itself is annihilated (153–54). She "beseech[ed] our Lord ... to take my whole substance into himself as I received him [the Eucharist]." There should be nothing of her left (161–62). Her use of "substance" is significant. As a monastic, Knatchbull understood what happened to physical substance during the transubstantive moment of the priest's consecration. "Transform me in to thee," she prayed (151, also 162). By adding her own prayers to convert her substance, Knatchbull attempted to join the priest's sacrifice at the altar so that she, too, could be transubstantiated.

She sought greater union with God through her own offering. Following the elevation of the consecrated bread and wine—now, literally, Christ on the altar—Knatchbull described a feeling of comfort and unity with God. He was there. He asked her to "be entire to me," to be wholly part of himself. Even before she received the Eucharist—what the priest offered—she felt encompassed, encircled within the divine presence after her own offering. When she finally received the Eucharist, she "thought our Lord united my Soul with his, even as two things are made one." This was more than an idea to Knatchbull. She explained that she could feel a physical change within herself, a "sensible feeling of a kind of restlessness within myself, as if my heart had sought to pull our Lord down into it out of my mouth" (150, 153–54, 156, see also 164). She was an active participant in creating this union. She described this as more than the idea of the Real Presence of Christ as taught by the faith. Through this combination of clerical and lay actions, she "conceived a kind of certain knowledge" that Christ "gave himself entirely over into my power," giving her "free liberty to make myself (in him) as happy and blessed as I would" (146–47). In all, Knatchbull asked God to annihilate her physical substance so that she could be joined with Christ, *as* Christ, so she could know Christ beyond what the Church taught her or what the priest gave her at Mass. It required her offering, Christ's acceptance, and the priest's offering at the altar to receive these gifts.

Lucy Herbert, a Welshwoman, asked for something similar in *Several Excellent Methods of Hearing Mass*, written in 1722. Like Knatchbull, Herbert expressed a desire to consecrate and offer herself as a holocaust—specifically her heart—during Mass to unite herself with God. In contrast to Knatchbull, who wrote for primarily for herself or her spiritual director, Herbert wrote for "all good Christians," not only religious women but laypeople. She instructed readers how to consecrate and offer themselves to God as part of experiencing Mass more devoutly.

Herbert had a good sense of religious and political realities back in the British Isles. She understood what Catholics needed. When she was a child, Charles II's government arrested both of her parents on suspicion of treason during the Popish Plot. Her father, William Herbert, Earl of Powis (1617–96), was one of the five Catholic lords falsely accused and imprisoned for years in the Tower. Her mother, Elizabeth Herbert (1633–91), attempted to free him and was almost convicted of treason as well. Lucy eventually traveled to France and lived under the spiritual direction of the French Jesuit, Louis Sabran. Sabran must have respected Herbert's religiosity and judgment because he allowed her to choose which religious order she would join rather than shepherding her toward a particular convent. She selected the Augustinians at Bruges and professed in 1693. Elected prioress in 1709, she served 35 years (Durrant 1925, 307–11, 317–19). Herbert seemed to see her book as a way of fortifying the Church Militant against the "misbelieving kingdoms" so that all could be "converted to the true faith" (Herbert 1722, 79–80, also 3–4, 10, 25, 85).

Herbert urged readers to offer their bodies and souls to God with the bread and wine offered by the priest, asking that they too be changed into the body and blood of Christ (97–98). She asked God,

> What will it cost you to work this change? One word from your sacred mouth will presently change the bread and wine into the substance of the body and blood of your Son. Add one more. (51)

Many times, she asked Christ to consecrate her heart to himself, transforming it to resemble his, making it entirely holy so that nothing remained of her own. Herbert described how she elevated her heart to Jesus, in language reminiscent of priestly elevation of the host in the Mass (16–20, 40–41, 51, 65, 69, 72, 83–85, 92, 97–98, 118; see also Crowther and Vincent 1657, 490–92, 495–515). Christ would make her like himself, into himself. Jesus lived in the believer's heart, and the supplicant could directly ask Jesus to meet whatever spiritual needs they might have. This opened the possibility of petitioners relying more directly upon God's mediation rather than on the mediation of a priest (Herbert 1722, 40–41, 56, 79, 92). The believer's heart became an altar to Christ, with no priestly intermediary.

Offering Christ at Mass

However, these laypeople did more than offer themselves to God. They also offered Christ to God during the Eucharistic celebration. Herbert and Knatchbull both upheld the Mass. Herbert considered her instructions regarding the Mass as fully orthodox, even quoting from the Council of Trent's decrees in her treatise. However, priests' actions provided only the loose framework within which non-ordained people could understand their role in the sacrament. It was an issue of emphasis. Laypeople such as Herbert and Knatchbull took the focus off priests' roles and placed it on the ritual responsibilities, experiences, and results of lay believers (Herbert 1722, 14–15, 44, 58, 62). Laypeople ought to offer the sacrifice at Mass themselves, Herbert contended, because one of the most important consequences of the Mass was contrition for sins, remission of the pains of sin, and salvific grace through the merits of Christ. "Be persuaded," Herbert encouraged readers, "that you can never better atone and satisfy for your sins than by offering Christ and his sacred merits (which you possess in communion) both to his eternal Father and to himself" (71–72, also 57).

Authors never explicitly counselled laypeople that their efforts replaced that of priests'. Herbert lauded the role of the priest at the altar (34–35). But then Herbert instructed readers to "offer the sacrifice of the Mass" just as "Christ offered the bloody Sacrifice on Mount Calvary to his eternal Father and for the intention he now offers the unbloody one," the sacrifice on the altar (10).

Christ would generally be offered to God in one of two ways, neither of which mentioned a priest (50, 51, 53, 57, 65, 68, 69, 97, 102, 111, 115). First, believers were to offer Christ to God on the altar of their own hearts. Second, Christ offered himself to God the Father. For example, Herbert provided a prayer in which the supplicant accused herself of all her sins and made reparation by offering God all the merits of Christ, who would "soon *render himself* present for me on the Altar. Receive Lord, his death & Passion in satisfaction, & for the remission of my sins" (8, my emphasis). Laypeople, in effect, added their efforts to the priests' but in ways that garnered them personal access to God and his grace, seemingly bypassing a portion of one of the most significant moments of a priest's traditional mediation for believers. By assisting at the Mass—not just hearing or attending Mass—through such offering, laypeople *enriched themselves* with the merits of Christ's passion.

Herbert thus markedly, although perhaps unintentionally, diminished the priest's traditional mediating role. Herbert referred to the priest as someone the "Church sends as Embassador" to God rather than as Christ's representative on earth (80). Either way, a priest benefited believers, but by changing the origin of priestly authority (the Church sends the priest, not Christ), Herbert altered the nature of priestly power and laypeople's relationship to it. Priests do not appear in Herbert as "vice-regents," next to Christ himself (Southwell 1973, *Short Rules*, Chap. 3, lines 2–3). Herbert reminded readers repeatedly that the priest did not provide the saving grace from the sacrament directly. "We should always reflect that Christ acts as Priest, & that the priest is but his minister" (6, also 4, 12, 24, 27), seemingly a tool. Instead, the "hands of the priest" (3–4, 24) presented Christ's body and blood on the altar to God, but it was the believers who "offer[ed] him as ours," (43) who rendered themselves partakers of all the saving benefits of all the Masses said everywhere and at all times (22–24, 85).

Offerings for One's Own Salvation and Others'

Knatchbull's relationship to Christ and the Eucharist reflected a similar expanded understanding and scope for laypeople's roles in the Mass by appropriating language customarily reserved to describe clerics' religious roles and using it to portray laypeople's new roles. In her papers given to her biographer, Matthew, Knatchbull explained her private devotions involving the Eucharist during the Feast of the Presentation of Our Lady. The week before the feast, she attended Mass and received the Eucharist. Afterwards, like Herbert, she related how Christ "entered into my soul, as into his Temple, and at this selfsame time, me thought my Soul was vested with our Lord" (Matthew 1931, 129). To be vested carried two meanings. On one hand, Knatchbull felt established and secured in God. However, the better-known meaning of vesting was to be clothed specifically in ecclesiastical garb (OED Online 2017). God did not vest Knatchbull "in" himself but "with" himself. Knatchbull mentioned that she used the term "vested" in the spiritual sense which Matthew would "better understand by your own experience," rather than hers, perhaps because Matthew was a priest (129). A priest vested prior to conducting rituals and sacraments.

The next week, Knatchbull adored the Blessed Sacrament during the Feast of the Presentation of Mary, making many offerings to the consecrated body of Christ on behalf of her fellow Christians. For the feast, a priest created the Blessed Sacrament during Mass, and it was afterwards displayed and incensed. For the next 24 hours, Knatchbull, who was now vested, adored the sacrament with clear intent to mediate between God and believers and with devotions reminiscent of a priest's Eucharistic prayers. Her mediating contributions were ambitious in breadth and scope. For example, Knatchbull, through her prayers, "assembl[ed] the whole world to do homage to our Lord." In her desire for the entire world to reverence God, Knatchbull offered God "all that Honor which from the beginning of the world hath been exhibited to him by all and to all the Creatures of the world" (130). As she did all this, she felt herself united with God, which was, after all, the aim of the sacrament of the altar. But by what authority did she think that she—an un-ordained Christian— could assemble all Christians, gather all the honor ever paid to God, and offer it again?

Knatchbull likely saw herself as joining the priest in his sacred calling, rather than substituting for him. Like Herbert, she recognized that a priest was necessary to this devotion. Without a priest's creation of the Blessed Sacrament in the Eucharistic celebration, Knatchbull would have had nothing concrete to adore. However, following this creation, Knatchbull joined herself to the liturgy and to Christ in her own way without a priest's mediation and did so for the benefit of Christians everywhere, intending to mediate for them with her devotions.

Herbert went further, tying together all these strands of lay offering to explain how lay assistance at Mass benefited souls, implicitly emphasizing the effectiveness of lay mediation rather than a priest's. Herbert counseled readers to transform their substance into union with Christ to join him in offering *his* sacrifice. Offering Mass in this way was powerful, satisfying entirely for sin, just as if the believer had been present at Calvary with Mary and Jesus. It would be as if the supplicant had reached out to gather Christ's spilled blood on the cross and lifted it up in offering to God the Father. This blood was the same blood, Herbert maintained, that "we offer"—note the plural—at Mass and which obtained pardon for all sins. The blood "pleads for you" (Herbert 1722, 58–59). The supplicant was to pray:

> Eternal Father, your son has given himself to me, that I may offer him and his merits to you, to pay my debts, and purchase what I stand in need of. I then present him to you, with all the merits of his life and death; and beg by them to be discharged of the heavy load of my sins. (120, see also 37, 71–72)

The elements of the sacrifice that Herbert emphasized were that because God gave his son as a "free gift" (48) and Christ offered himself for humankind, she and other laypeople could offer Christ back to God. Herbert was certain that God would accept this offering.

> And after receiving from me a present of so great value; what return may I not hope for from you ... I dare affirm that whatever I can request, or you can give, will not be worth the victim I offer you; which raises my hopes to an assurance of obtaining what I ask for what can you deny me, when I offer you your divine son? (48)

Nothing a believer could do could better atone for and satisfy for sin than offering what believers *possessed for themselves* in this communion: Christ and his merits. In addition, laypeople could help the souls and interests of other Christians as well as their own. They could, for example, harness the "merits of all the Masses that will this day be offered throughout the whole world" toward particular causes, such as the reconversion of England (79). Again, this was the Mass, but where was the priest? The layperson was the active agent petitioning for the souls of others.

> I ask it in his name, and behold him [Christ] coming upon this Altar to join his prayers with my petition, therefore your honor [God] is engaged to hear him, and to render yourself favorable to those whom he commands to ask in his name; and to whom he communicates his merit and credit. Behold, I am one of them; honor him therefore, I beseech you, by granting me what both he and I most earnestly beg of your Divine Majesty, which is my salvation, and all the aforesaid requests. (79–80)

Such vivid descriptions of new lay roles in both offering and the Eucharist are in stark contrast to writings by continental Catholic authors who used the language of laypeople "offering" Mass as well. Their texts placed greater emphasis on the priestly role. The priest at the altar had center stage, and his understandings of Mass provided the template for laypeople to mimic in their own thoughts. The Spanish Jesuit Francis Borgia, for example, wrote his *A Short Rule How to Live Well* for a Catholic readership without restrictions on worship. He encouraged Catholics to hear Mass reverently, listening carefully to the words and paying close attention to the priest's gestures during the Eucharist. Laypeople should then join the priest in offering the sacrifice, duplicating the priest's intentions. Borgia then explained these priestly intentions in detail, rather than offering additional insights for lay readers to ponder, as Knatchbull and Herbert did. Believers then spiritually received the Eucharist while watching the priest receive corporally, and Borgia instructed them how to unite themselves with God through the effects of the sacrament celebrated by the priesthood (Borgia 1970, 123–27; also Loarte 1970). Such writers' descriptions of lay roles seem more additive to the believers' experiences of Mass rather than creative of salvific merit in and of themselves.

Put simply, Herbert and Knatchbull took the traditional teachings about believers' unification with God through the Eucharist to a new level. They placed a greater emphasis on their own, non-clerical roles in the sacrificial, sacramental moments rather than the clerics', as clerical writers like Borgia did. Herbert and Knatchbull revered the clergy, lauding their critical role at the altar, but their words clearly reflected their belief that believers brought themselves before God. It was God who taught laypeople how to assist and participate more fully in the Mass, God who transformed believers' hearts and souls.

This was a stance with which priests would agree. They were mediators, not the authors of salvation themselves. However, the role of clerics' mediation is greatly reduced simply because these lay writers so rarely mentioned priests at all. Authors such as Knatchbull and Herbert perhaps did not want to refer too frequently to priests because Catholics in the British Isles had so little opportunity to meet with one. Readers might worry more greatly for their souls if persistently reminded of the salvific aids they lacked.

However, by mentioning priestly mediation so seldom and by advertising alternatives, Knatchbull and Herbert gave laypeople new religious roles, unintentionally contributing to rewriting part of the laity's relationship with the priesthood and transforming the way laypeople understood mediation, the Eucharist, and their role in it. Perhaps nowhere was this more evident than in rituals involving the Sacred Heart of Jesus and the Church's struggle to redefine in what way people who had not been ordained could offer Jesus in sacrifice. Between 1673 and 1675, Sister Mary Margaret Alacoque, a nun at the Visitation Convent at Paray in Burgundy, received a series of visions of Christ who instructed her in how to honor his heart appropriately (Lawson 1765, 1–7). Devotions to the Sacred Heart focus upon the physical heart of Jesus as symbolic of the love that motivated him to sacrifice himself for humanity. The rites spread quickly and became particularly popular in the British Isles in the eighteenth century after authors heavily promoted them there (3–8). Authors endorsed devotions to the Sacred Heart as a way to defend Christ's and Mary's affronted honor, much in the way that Catholics had been encouraged to view themselves as soldiers and defenders of Catholicism. In return, Christ would carry believers in his heart, to the benefit of their souls (19, 38–41, 81–83).

Perhaps one reason for the popularity of these rituals was that they allowed laypeople to offer Christ—or at least a part of him—to God in a way endorsed by the Church as not transgressing a priest's sacramental role at the altar. As the Jesuit Thomas Lawson explained in his 1765 treatise defending and encouraging worship of the Sacred Heart, priests offered Christ's entire body on the altar. Laypeople who engaged in this devotion only offered Christ's heart, thus there was no usurpation of a priest's ritual powers (9–11). Yet the nature of the contrasts that Lawson made to defend the devotions reveal the Church had its concerns; one wonders how well laypeople understood the distinctions.

Lawson advertised that everything about the Sacred Heart belonged to ordinary believers because Christ's heart was "immolated" for all Christians. Lawson encouraged his readers to "make up amongst those with whom you live, your Family, Friends, and Domestics," an Association of the Sacred Heart (48). This group would draw lots daily to see who would offer the devotions. The five "winners" offered devotions on behalf of the whole association. "They are ... public Deputies or Ambassadors to the Throne of Heaven in order to obtain Favors for the rest, and to draw down particular Blessings upon each one of this Association" (45). He did not call them mediators, yet Lawson clearly intended non-clerics to fulfill a salvific role for their own souls and those of their neighbors, drawing down God's blessings on their behalf. Even a small group of Catholics, none of whom were clerics, could achieve great merit, Lawson enthused. "Take my word for it, Almighty God will look with a propitious Eye both on you and this your Assembly" (48), and nothing would be wanting for salvation (67). Devotees passed sentence on themselves for their sins rather than confessing and being judged by their priest. Then they appealed to the Sacred Heart for absolution. This heart, Lawson maintained, contained Christ's blood, the same blood that washed away the sins of humankind, the same blood sacrificed by a priest on an altar during the Eucharist. Finally, believers offered the Sacred Heart to God in satisfaction for sins and in thanksgiving for all their blessings, praying for divine grace (9–11, 40–42, 48–49, 63–64, 67). Now, however, laypeople appealed directly to God for such grace without either priest or altar (7–8, 24, 63–68).

Herbert popularized devotions to the Sacred Heart of Jesus at Bruges during her tenure as prioress (Durrant 1925, 348–50). In *Several Excellent Methods of Hearing Mass*, Herbert encouraged devotions focused on the heart of Jesus that a believer could practice in the middle of Mass. Herbert's prayers for the portion of Mass between the elevation and the division of the host—one of the most potent ritual moments of Mass—advised readers to assist at this time by offering Christ to God in the form of the heart of Jesus. Believers were to pray,

> Father of my Lord Jesus Christ: I offer you the heart of your beloved son, as he offers it himself: receive it for me with all its affections, and all the acts proceeding from it; for they are all mine, since it is for me that he Sacrifices himself. Receive them with all his merits in satisfaction for all my sins ... Receive them that thereby you may grant me all necessary graces for my salvation. (12–13, also 43, 58)

This heart, Herbert assured in no uncertain terms, belonged to the believer. The believer offered the heart of Christ and all his merits to God in satisfaction for sins. God would then grant the believer sufficient grace for salvation.

Again, where was the priest's mediation? Would readers have understood the distinction between their offering of the heart and the priest's sacramental offering of the body? Or would the many similarities with the language and prayers of the Mass increase their confidence in their own mediating abilities as laypeople? When the College of English Jesuits began an Association of the Sacred Heart just as Lawson had suggested, almost all the English Augustinian nuns at Herbert's convent enrolled (Durrant 1925, 348–50). They were not priests. They were not clerics. But presumably they would be using prayers such as Herbert's and Lawson's to offer Jesus's heart directly to God in satisfaction for sins and for salvific grace.

In sum, it was not just about doing more within a given ritual, whether it was the Eucharist, baptism, or a burial. It was about how laypeople understood their relationship to God and their priests differently because they performed these new religious roles. It was about how they reimagined their role in their own and others' salvation. For Herbert, the place where believers met Christ changed from a church and altar to Jesus's own heart. She met Jesus one-on-one rather than having her meeting mediated by a priest. Yet she was no pseudo-Protestant, denying the need for priest or altar. A priest's mediation was necessary to create the opportunity for this meeting. It was not insignificant that Jesus entered her heart at the Eucharist after a cleric created the Blessed Sacrament. But afterwards, the prayers emphasize laypersons' opportunities to know Christ and work for salvation. Repeatedly, throughout this treatise, she begged Jesus to enflame, thaw, and strengthen her heart. It was both her heart and his heart, the lines of possession blurring as Jesus changed her heart to resemble his, joining in union with the believer through the heart, through believers' participation in the Eucharist (Herbert 1722, 40–42, 56, 64, 65, 69, 70, 72, 83, 84, 85, 92, 96–98, 118). Together, laypeople joined Christ in mediating with God for the good of souls.

Authors encouraged all laypersons to re-imagine their roles. Herbert and Lawson wrote for all Christians, not just women religious. Scots Jesuit Alexander MacKenzie even encouraged Catholic prisoners to take active roles in their own and their neighbor's salvation that went beyond usual lay pastoral efforts. He composed a book, *The Poor Prisoner's Comforter*, specifically to meet the special pastoral needs of jailed Catholics. MacKenzie counseled that prison could be a blessing if prisoners used the time well to focus on faith, God, and salvation. MacKenzie would show them how.

MacKenzie urged Catholic inmates to seek out a priest for confession and spiritual direction as soon as possible but also to "be, in regard of your Fellow Prisoners, a Minister of Jesus Christ, for their eternal Salvation" (MacKenzie 1764, 17). Imprisoned Catholics were no longer just assembled communities of suffering Christians, trying to make some spiritual good out of their bad situations. MacKenzie urged them to develop their spiritual leadership, assisting their neighbors in finding opportunities to worship and grow in faith and piety. If an inmate had "a room to himself, he ought to give Leave, out of Charity, for all others to assemble in it," for meetings, study, and other religious obligations. If a cell's occupant could read, MacKenzie encouraged that person to invite fellow prisoners into the cell, where "it would be proper for him to take upon himself to read to others, and instruct those who are ignorant of any Point in the Christian Religion" (12, also 21).

MacKenzie confronted the challenges of prison life head-on, asking devout men and women literally to become their brothers' and sisters' keepers, as ministers to their fellow prisoners (10–11, 17, 32). Inmates should be on the lookout for questionable behaviors, such as too much intimacy with other prisoners, and instruct their neighbors in whatever was necessary to return to the righteous path. MacKenzie even advised prisoners how to assist women who became pregnant in jail and to dissuade prisoners from continuing in homosexual relations (14, 32–33, 37). In many ways, this was care of souls. A minister was no priest, certainly, but a minister was more than an ordinary layperson. A minister's role was distinctly linked to the idea of the priesthood and clerical leadership even prior to the Reformation.

Herbert wrote of the confidence that lay Christians would gain, putting such instructions into action. Confidence was a necessary prerequisite to lay Catholics taking on any roles and responsibilities traditionally associated with clerics—from Montague's baptism of his baby daughter and Blundell's Catholic burials to Dorothea's preparing poor people to reconcile with Rome and Knatchbull's vesting. It cannot have escaped notice that so many examples of laypeople re-imagining their place in these processes involved women. As discussed in previous chapters, pastoral authorities had begun encouraging women to trust in themselves as guided by their consciences to a greater degree. Men, both husbands and clerics, shared certain forms of authority with women that had rarely been shared, at least not with this level of sanction. Women suddenly possessed not only the confidence but the opportunities to participate in their faith and salvation as never before. The greater proportion of women re-imagining their roles in ritual and sacrament, their relationships with clerics and clerical authority, and their active engagement in procuring saving grace is likely linked to the greater proportion of openings for women created by this environment of gender and religious need and change.

Renegotiating the Bounds of Priestly Authority

In the long term, such confidence took laypeople into new, contentious territory in their relationships with clergy, eventually leading to the unintended consequence of laypeople questioning and re-drawing the boundaries of clerical authority in their lives. By the end of the eighteenth century, many of these new lay religious roles and gradual changes in relationships with the priesthood had become normalized. Laypeople no longer understood their dependence on, and obedience to, clerical authority to be as absolute as the layman William Wiseman had described it at the end of the sixteenth century in his *A Triple Farewell to the World*. In addition, whereas laypeople in the seventeenth century had allowed missionary priests to lead in both religious and worldly affairs, some Catholics in the eighteenth century now openly questioned the clergy's authority to command their absolute submission in worldly matters.

Nowhere was this more evident that when, between 1778 and 1791, a group of lay Catholics known as the Catholic Committee worked hard to craft a bill before Parliament that would revoke many of the penal laws against Catholics. Catholics had struggled under these restrictions for over two centuries, and they were tired and frustrated. These lay leaders drafted an oath of loyalty to the sovereign that they said Catholics could take without foreswearing their allegiance to the Catholic faith.

Public oath-taking was common in this era. Oath-takers proclaimed their beliefs and affirmed their loyalties by swearing an oath before God. Presumably, oath-takers risked their salvation if they swore untruly or broke their oath. From Elizabeth's reign through the eighteenth century, English, Scots, and Irish Parliaments asked subjects to swear a variety of oaths involving religion, such as their outright rejection of the doctrine of transubstantiation or their acknowledgment that the monarch sat rightfully upon the throne and could not be deposed by a pope. The intent of such oaths was clear, as in the Test Act of 1672 which carried the longer title "An act for preventing dangers which may happen from popish recusants" (25 Car. II, c. 2.) The Glorious Revolution revived pressure for Catholics to swear such oaths into the eighteenth century (Glickman 2009, 125–26). If Catholics did so, they could avoid the economic, social, and political disadvantages prescribed by almost three centuries of anti-Catholic penal laws.

What Catholics had long sought—and what the Catholic Committee sought now—was an oath that both the papacy and the government would find acceptable that would allow Catholics to be recognized as good subjects *and* good Catholics, but this was one area where the papacy refused to compromise. At first, the four bishops who exercised full jurisdiction over England's Catholics—known as the Vicars Apostolic—supported the lay efforts of the Catholic Committee.[1] Then three of the four Vicars Apostolic unexpectedly withdrew their backing, condemning the oath they had formerly supported. Committee members felt they had been quite close to rapprochement only to have their hopes dashed. The clerics gave no reason for their about-face and refused to do so later when asked. Committee members chafed because the Vicars Apostolic expected their absolute submission to priestly authority.

The Catholic Committee wrote letters to the Vicars Apostolic and to the Catholics of England protesting the clerics' actions as beyond their authority, and these laypeople possessed the confidence to define for the Vicars Apostolic exactly where pastoral authority began and ended. The Catholic Committee's resolve was built upon almost two centuries of Catholic deliberations about the boundaries of political and religious loyalties (Glickman 2009, 27–51, 90–120, 129–46, 169–74, 219). Around the turn of the eighteenth century, for example, John Belson, the Catholic controversialist, asserted that Catholics needed to beware of any presumption that they needed to "obey every order which at Rome shall be called or declared Spiritual" because *every* worldly action could be construed as having some connection to religion (Belson MS 1697, F/1/4/MS/19–20). Catholics, Belson said, should be more discerning in establishing limits to their obedience. Almost a century later, Catholic Committee members certainly were. The Vicars Apostolic, the laymen said, could claim leadership over religious issues only. As the Committee's work was not about religious issues, they were bewildered as to why they should obey what they saw as an unjustified and unfair restriction on their ability to act. If this were an issue touching salvation or religious controversy, they would have all reverence for the Vicars' directives. However, as the Committee wrote in a letter to the Vicars Apostolic on November 25, 1789, "while we respect that Authority, which the gospel of Heaven has empowered its Ministers to exercise, we cannot but recollect, that we are men and citizens, and as such have rights to claim and duties to perform" (Appendix paginated separately, 12–13).

This was not about valuing worldly interests over religious duty, they claimed. In fact, in their judgment, they had a duty to proceed in this work because, foremost, the oath would rehabilitate the reputation of the Catholic faith. It would clarify Catholic values and doctrines. It would dispel misconceptions that Protestants held about Catholic loyalties, which debarred Catholics from many of their temporal rights as men and citizens. In sum, the Committee emphasized, "WE ARE PERSUADED THERE CAN BE NO ENCROACHMENT UPON THE PASTORAL AUTHORITY" (Appendix 13).

"We conceived," they wrote, that the clerics had "extended their authority" to issues "which came not within their competency" (*A Letter* 1789, 12). "We did not neglect to acknowledge our sincere reverence for episcopal authority," they continued, "*when equitably exerted within its own sphere*. Civil concerns are evidently beyond its boundaries" (14, my emphasis). Catholics, the Committee members asserted, may have suffered a great deal over the last 200 years for their consciences, but they had also "suffered from an imprudent interference of ecclesiastical authority in civil concerns" (Appendix 13). They harkened back to the calamitous results of earlier controversies between temporal and religious concerns, such as the Oath of Allegiance controversy under James I. Again and again, the Church and clerics overstepped pastoral authority (Appendix 14–15). They "encroached upon our rights as Englishmen" (13). No more. English Catholics would render unto Caesar what was Caesar's, and render unto God what was God's. Yet the Committee members insisted that they remained good Catholics and loyal to the faith.

> One thing in particular we wish would be clearly understood:—we have invariably professed that we never conceived an idea of departing, in any one single instance, from the belief, or the acknowledged rules, of the Catholic Church. It all boiled down to confidence that in matters of fact we were convinced that the Apostolical Vicars were mistaken. (12)

Quite simply, the clergy were wrong, and the laypeople were not obliged to obey. "We declined to submit," the Catholic Committee told the Catholics of England (14).

By what power and authority did such laymen free themselves from portions of clerical authority? This is a similar question to that asked about Montague earlier. Why did Montague presume that he—a layperson—possessed the authority to baptize? The members of the Catholic Committee, Montague, and the many other lay Catholics discussed in this chapter re-drew the traditional boundary separating clerical authority from lay authority in the Catholic Church. It made no difference that the Church allowed such breaches of traditional clerical authority in times of emergency or that pastoral writers and missionary priests openly encouraged many of them as stop-gap measures to comfort and save souls. It made no difference that most laypeople did not intend to change their relationships with the Church, God, and salvation. Ultimately, their efforts changed laypeople's expectations of what they could and could not do, on who or what they could rely, and of what decisions were theirs to make or theirs to defer to a priest.

Pages ago, the questions were asked: Who exercises authority within the Catholic faith, and what legitimates it? Who submits to authority and how? Both priests and laypeople in the Catholic Church had always exercised authority, each roughly in their own separate spheres. However, with the efforts of the Catholic Committee, the clerical sphere became a bit smaller and the laity's a bit larger. As Belson had argued, for centuries, laypeople had been obliged to obey the clergy in almost all matters because the clergy had been able to define almost any issue as having some connection to religion and therefore as under their pastoral authority. These laymen re-defined the limits of priestly authority more narrowly. They explicitly defined civic concerns in which laymen had duties to perform and obligations to fulfill as exempt from clerical authority. They appealed to their rights as both Catholics and subjects to legitimate the changes.

These changes did not come out of nowhere. Catholic laypeople had been debating these issues among themselves, with the clergy, and with Rome for over two centuries. Early in this process, in the sixteenth and seventeenth centuries, the extent of lay participation in rituals, sacraments, and instruction—such as in baptism, funerals, or preparing people for conversion—formed the crux of the discussion. By the early eighteenth century, the discussion had broadened to include not only *whether* the laity would participate in fulfilling traditional clerical roles but also in defining *how* they participated, such as in Herbert's and Lawson's discussions of how exactly laypeople could offer Christ's body and heart in the Mass or MacKenzie's instructions to prisoners to minister to one another. Over two centuries of greater informal, ad hoc lay participation in pastoral care, liturgy, and the sacraments gradually changed opinions until, by the end of the eighteenth century, laypeople changed the larger structural relationship between laity and clergy. Laymen openly redefined the limits of traditional pastoral authority for all to see, in open letters addressed to every Catholic in the land. As the government gradually repealed the penal laws and removed restrictions on Catholic opportunities in the next decades, it would be difficult to turn back the clock on these changes in lay-clerical relations.

But let's be clear. This is where Catholic lay*men* drew their line in the sand. While religious relationships were being re-negotiated, gender was also in play. Notably, no women served on the Catholic Committee, and there were no women signatories to any addresses or protestations made regarding the committee's efforts. But without the earlier efforts of laywomen like the English Lady, Dorothea, and the schoolmistress, Ann Vaux, could the Catholic Committee have envisioned a more formal and permanent re-drawing of the boundaries between lay and clerical authority? By engaging in many rituals and practices formerly reserved primarily for priests and laymen, such laywomen, hand-in-hand with laymen, made blanket changes in lay-clerical relations possible. Yet when it came time to re-negotiate these larger structural changes, women had little say. Catholic women, *as women*, were excluded from both the priesthood and from making law and policy, whether for the Church or the government. We should not expect to see them as part of this public debate over clerical and civic authority. Their very invisibility, however, underscores the fact that they possessed little authority over either the religious or the patriarchal structures under which they lived, as compared to the laymen. This would make their efforts to broaden gendered and religious roles much more difficult than laymen's, as the suppression of Mary Ward's Institute proved. Gender and religion intersect differently for women than for men. If a woman such as Ward felt called by God to serve in a way not currently authorized by the Church, all she could do as a woman and layperson was appeal to authorities that were exclusively masculine and clerical. Women had no voice in making either the gendered or the religious rules, but they had to abide by them. Women's roles in the Church have, thus, expanded much more slowly than men's roles. How do we know if this is God's will or men's? By returning one last time to Mary Ward's challenge to the Church, we find clues to approach such seemingly unanswerable, un-resolvable questions.

Notes

1. The Vicars Apostolic were bishops in title only. Catholic hierarchies and administration had not been re-established in the British Isles at this time.

Works Cited

Beales, A.C.F. 1963. *Education Under Penalty: English Catholic Education from The Reformation to The Fall of James II*. London: The Athlone Press, University of London.

Belson MSS, Oxfordshire County Record Office.

Borgia, Francis. (1620) 1970. *The Practice of Christian Workes*. Translated by John Wilson. Reprint, Menston, Yorkshire: Scolar Press.

Blundell, F. O. 1925. *Old Catholic Lancashire*. London: Burns, Oates & Washbourne, Ltd.

Blundell, William. 1933. *Cavalier: Letters of William Blundell to his Friends 1620–1698*. Edited by Margaret Blundell. London: Longmans, Green and Co.

Bossy, John. 1975. *The English Catholic Community 1570–1850*. London: Darton, Longman & Todd.

Bowden, Caroline. 2009. "Lucy Knatchbull." *The Literary Encyclopedia*. www.litencyc.com/php/speople.php?rec=true&UID=12537. Accessed October 3, 2015.

Bynum, Caroline Walker. 1988. *Holy Feast and Holy Fast: The Religious Significance of Food to Medieval Women*. Berkeley, CA: University of California Press.

CSP Dom (Calendar of State Papers, Domestic Series) of the reign of Charles I, 1625–1649. 1964. Public Record Office, series 3. London: Longman, Brown, Green, Longmans & Roberts.

Chambers, M.C.E. 1882. *The Life of Mary Ward (1585–1645)*. 2 vols. Edited by Henry James Coleridge. London: Burns and Oates.

Code of Canon Law. n.d., Canon 207. http://www.vatican.va/archive/ENG1104/__PT.HTM. Accessed 25 Sept 2015.

Crowther, Arthur and Thomas Vincent. 1657. *Jesus, Maria, Joseph, or, The Devout Pilgrim, of the Ever Blessed Virgin Mary, in His Holy Exercises, Affections, and Elevations*. Amsterdam.

Durrant, C.S. 1925. *A Link Between Flemish Mystics & English Martyrs*. Preface by Francis Cardinal Bourne. London: Burns, Oates and Washbourne.

Foley, B.C. 1991. *Some People from the Penal Times (Chiefly 1688–1791)*. Lancaster: Cathedral Bookshop.

Foley, Henry. 1875. *Records of the English Province of the Society of Jesus*. 7 vols. Roehampton: The Manresa Press.

Gage, John. 1652. *The Christian Sodality, or, Catholick Hive of Bees Sucking Hony of the Churches Prayers from the Blossomes of the Word of God blowne out of the Epistles and Gospels of the Divine Service Throughout the yeare. Collected by the Puny Bee of all the Hive, not worthy to be named otherwise than by these Elements of his Name: F. P.* Paris.

Gerard, John. 1959. *The Hunted Priest: Autobiography of John Gerard*. Translated by Philip Caraman. Introduction by Graham Greene. London: Fontana Books.

Gibson, Thomas Ellison, ed. 1887. *Crosby Records: A Chapter of Lancashire Recusancy*. Manchester: Chetham Society, new series, XII.

Glickman, Gabriel. 2009. *The English Catholic Community 1688–1745: Politics, Culture and Ideology*. Woodbridge, Suffolk: The Boydell Press.

Graef, Hilda. 1985. *Mary: A History of Doctrine and Devotion*. 2 vols. London: Sheed and Ward.

Haigh, Christopher. 1975. *Reformation and Resistance in Tudor Lancashire*. Cambridge: Cambridge University Press.

Harleian MSS. British Library.

HCCP (High Commission Cause Papers). Borthwick Institute. York.

Herbert, Lucy. 1722. *Several Excellent Methods of Hearing Mass*. Bruges: John De Cock.

Hirst, Joseph A. 1913. *The Blockhouses of Kingston-upon-Hull, and Who Went There. A Glimpse of Catholic Life in the Penal Times, and a Missing Page of Local History*. Introduction by Francis J. Hall. 2nd ed. London and Hull: A. Brown & Sons Ltd.

Johnson, Penelope D. 1991. *Equal in monastic profession: religious women in Medieval France*. Chicago: University of Chicago Press.

Kenny, Anthony, ed. 1962. *The responsa scholarum of the English College, Rome*. London: Catholic Record Society, LIV.

Lawson, Thomas. 1765. *The Devotion to the Sacred Heart of Jesus, with other pious practices, devout prayers, and instructions for the use and convenience of Christians in general*. Bruges: Joseph van Praet.

A Letter Addressed to the Catholics of England, By the Catholic Committee. 1789. London: J.P. Coghlan.

Loarte, Gasparo. (1613) 1970. *Instructions and Advertisements How to Meditate upon the misteries of the Rosarie of the most holy Virgin Mary.* Translated anonymously. Reprint, Menston, Yorkshire: The Scolar Press.

Longley, Katharine M. 1988. "Blessed George Errington and Companions: Fresh Evidence." *Recusant History* 19, no. 1: 39–46.

MacKenzie, Alexander. 1764. *The Poor Prisoner's Comforter. In a Collection of Proper Instructions and Prayers for Christians in Prison By the Use of which a Prisoner may find Comfort and Satisfaction in his Poverty and Confinement, and wisely improve them to his eternal Salvation. To Which is added, Instructions and devout Exercises for a Person laying under Sentence of Death. According to Mr. Gother and other pious Authors.* London: R. Balfe.

The manuscripts of the Earl Cowper, K.G., preserved at Melbourne hall, Derbyshire. 1888. 3 vols. London: Her Majesty's Stationery Office.

Matthew, Tobie. 1931. *The Life of Lady Lucy Knatchbull.* Introduction by David Knowles. First printing from original manuscript. London: Sheed and Ward.

McClain, Lisa. 2004. *Lest We Be Damned: Practical Innovation and Lived Experience among Catholics in Protestant England, 1559–1642.* New York: Routledge.

———. 2012. "Neither Single nor Alone: Elizabeth Cellier, Catholic Community, and Transformations of Catholic Women's Piety." *Tulsa Studies in Women's Literature* 31, no. 1/2: 33–52.

———. 2013. "Troubled Consciences: New Understandings and Performances of Penance among Catholics in Protestant England." *Church History* 82, no. 1: 90–124.

———. 2015. "On a Mission: Priests, Jesuits, and 'Jesuitresses' and English Catholic Missionary Efforts in Tudor-Stuart England." *The Catholic Historical Review* 101, no. 3: 437–62.

Merrick, M.M. 1947. *James Duckett: A Study of his Life and Times.* London: Douglas, Organ.

Myerscough, John A. 1958. *A Procession of Lancashire Martyrs and Confessors.* Glasgow: John S. Burns & Sons.

Oliver, George. 1857. *Collections Illustrating the History of the Catholic Religion in the Counties of Cornwall, Devon, Dorset, Somerset, Wiltshire and Gloucester, in two parts, Historical and Biographical. With notices of the Dominican, Benedictine, & Franciscan Orders.* London: Charles Dolman.

OED (Oxford English Dictionary) Online. 2017. "vested, adj.1". Oxford University Press. http://www.oed.com/view/Entry/222891?rskey=VwRnBv&result=1&isAdvanced=false. Accessed 16 Sept 2017.

Pollen, J.H., ed. 1908. *Unpublished Documents Relating to the English Martyrs, vol. 1. 1584–1603.* London: Catholic Record Society, V.

Recusant MSS. Harry Ransom Humanities Research Center. University of Texas.

Scarisbrike, Edward. 1703. *Rules and Instructions for the Sodality of the Immaculate Conception, of the Most Glorious and Ever Virgin Mary, Mother of God.* n.p.

Southwell, Robert. 1973. *Two Letters and Short Rules of a Good Life*. Edited by Nancy Pollard Brown. Charlottesville, VA: The University Press of Virginia for the Folger Shakespeare Library.

SP Dom (State Papers, Domestic Series). Public Record Office. Kew.

Stanney, William. 1617. *A treatise of penance, with an explication of the rule, and maner of living, of the brethren and sisters, of the Third Order of St. Frauncis, comonli called of the Order of Penance, ordained for those which desire to leade a holy life, and to doe penance in their owne houses, Part I*. Douai: John Heigham.

Vaux, Laurence. 1583. *A catechisme or Christian doctrine necessarie for children and ignorant people, briefly compiled by Laurence Vaux Bacheler of Diuinitie: with an other later addition of instruction of the laudable ceremonies vsed in the Catholicke Churche. VVhereunto is adioyned a brief forme of confession (necessary for all good Christians) according to the vse of the Catholicke Churche*. Rouen: George L'Oyselet.

Visitation Correction Books. Cheshire Public Record Office.

Waterworth, J., ed. and trans. 1848. *The canons and decrees of the sacred and oecumenical Council of Trent*. London: Dolman.

Weston, William. 1955. *William Weston: The Autobiography of an Elizabethan*. Translated by Philip Caraman. Foreword by Evelyn Waugh. London: Longmans, Green and Co.

Willaert, H. 1928. *History of an Old Catholic Mission: Cowdray, Easebourne, Midhurst*. Preface by Hilaire Belloc. London: Burns, Oates & Washbourne, Ltd.

Worthington, Thomas. (1608) 1978. *A Catalogue of Martyrs in England*. Edited by D. M. Rogers. Reprint, Menston, Yorkshire: Scolar Press.

CHAPTER 8

Where the Catholic Church Draws the Line: Mary Ward vs. the Catholic Priesthood

One of the best-known tales illustrating the inappropriateness of women's assuming priestly authority and spiritual leadership was the legend of Pope Joan. The first known mention of a female pope occurs in the mid-thirteenth century in the Dominican Jean de Mailly's *Chronica Universalis Mettensis*. In subsequent centuries, other writers—including *Decameron* author Giovanni Boccaccio—took up the story, adding lurid details with each retelling. By the sixteenth century, Pope Joan's scandalous story of cross-dressing and sexual indiscretion was well-known throughout Christendom. Portrayed as a ninth-century woman of talent and learning, the mythical Joan wanted to enter the Church, study, and teach. She disguised herself as a man and assumed the name John Anglicus so she could pursue opportunities unavailable to women of her era. Joan's accomplishments were many, and she rose through the ecclesiastical hierarchy. Eventually, her colleagues elected her as their pontiff, and she served for over two years as Pope John VIII. Joan's natural, predictable womanly unchastity, however, proved her undoing and illustrated for audiences why women, no matter how brilliant and capable, should not be allowed spiritual authority or leadership. Joan took a lover and became pregnant while pope. One day, as she processed from St. Peter's to the Lateran Palace, she went into labor, collapsing on the pavement, writhing in pain. In full view of the crowd, she delivered her child. Her secret revealed, Joan died shortly thereafter (Boureau 2001, 107–296, 315–32). Century after century, the authors who retold and embellished the story of Pope Joan warned Christians about the dangers of unauthorized persons assuming clerical authority.

In the Reformation era, both Catholic and Protestant men could repudiate and laugh at the idea of women leading in religion. When the missionary priests Robert Anderton and William Marsden attempted to enter England in 1586, a fierce storm blew their vessel off course. They landed on the Isle of Wight and soon found themselves under arrest and transported to Winchester for examination. Finding the priests so young, the Protestant Bishop Thomas Cowper thought to have a little fun by disputing with them about religion in front of the assembly of justices and county gentry. Anderton and Marsden, trained in disputation at seminary, unexpectedly proved up to the challenge (Pollen 1891, 68–72). Caught off-guard, Cowper fell back upon the well-known Pope Joan myth and began to taunt the two priests with it at length. The audience hung upon every detail of the shameful story and waited to see how the priests would respond. Anderton threw the cautionary moral tale about women leading in the church back in the bishop's face. Pope Joan was an absurd lie made up by heretics, Anderton claimed. On the other hand,

> The basis of your faith, the citadel of your religion, is that you profess a woman to be the head of your Church. Surely whether we call her Pope Joan or Queen Elizabeth matters little. With what face, then, can you object that to us as an infamy which is your special glory? How can you taunt the Roman See with what you proudly regard as the bulwark of your religion? (71)

Cowper and Anderton might disagree about many religious ideals, but they found common ground in disparaging female religious leadership. Catholic leaders and priests considered it problematic for any layperson, male or female, to share in any type of authority reserved for clergy (Martin 1978, 69–74). To extend clerical authority to women *in particular* was generally acknowledged to be undesirable, if not downright dangerous.

Although Mary Ward was hardly a Pope Joan, Pope Urban VIII suppressed her life's work as decisively as authors such as Boccaccio attacked the fictitious pontiff. Urban VIII destroyed, annulled, and abolished Ward's English Ladies. He removed them entirely from the Church of

God, commanding all other Christians to consider them extinct. Ward had hoped she and her Institute might obtain an exception to strict enclosure to join in working for her neighbors' endangered souls. She was wrong.

It is time to weave religion and gender together one last time to better understand the limits of compromise and resistance negotiated between Catholic laypeople, the clergy, and the Church. From Mary Ward to the men of the Catholic Committee, laypeople and the clergy working with them interrogated and tested the boundaries of what it meant to be Catholic women and men in the British Isles. Some experiments, such as the Catholic Committee's, worked. Others, such as Ward's, did not. Throughout this extended process, it did not require a conscious effort on anyone's part to reshape Catholic expectations and practices over such a long period. The times seemed to demand flexibility and adjustment to make Catholicism work amid Protestant restrictions. The Church had always been willing to bend some of its rules temporarily in emergency situations. As the many examples in earlier chapters well illustrate, the Church became tolerant of large-scale exceptions to its policies in the British Isles, even institutionalizing some of the permissive changes. Much of this process was evolutionary rather than revolutionary, however, and prone to tension and controversy, especially when changes in gender roles accompanied religious changes. It is finally time to more fully answer the puzzle of Mary Ward and her treatment by the papacy, exploring the overlaps of male, female, lay, and clerical issues at stake not just in Ward's time but in our own.

Keeping Peter's Ship Afloat: The Doctrine of Apostolic Succession

On one hand, if the Church's primary goal was to strengthen the mission and sustain Catholics in the British Isles, the Church seemed to run counter to its own interests by suppressing Ward's Institute. The English Ladies gained some converts, provided access to priests, and helped priests in their missionary labors. The Institute, in its own limited way, was succeeding. On the other hand, if the women's violation of enclosure and the gossip and controversy that accompanied such unconventional women's behavior was the crux of Catholic opposition, Urban VIII should not have smoothed the way for Ward's return to England, as he did just a few years later. Her gender hadn't changed. She and her companions were still living together unenclosed. Their presence was likely to continue dividing Catholics.

Something bigger than reclaiming the British Isles for the Catholic Church must have been at stake. Something bigger than these women's rejection of enclosure and traditional gender roles spurred the Church to act with such severity. That "something" was the women's perceived violation of one of the most fundamental doctrines of the Catholic Church: *apostolic succession*. This doctrine recognizes ordained clergy as the only individuals able to exercise sacramental authority in the Church. The person authorized to perform the sacraments mediates between God and humanity to access God's saving grace for believers. These sacraments are some of the most important tools of salvation in the Catholic faith. The Reformation-era Council of Trent (1545–63) heavily emphasized the doctrine of apostolic succession in the sixteenth century, and the Catholic Church still does.[1] This issue is fundamental because it concerns access to the sacred and the source of religious authority and salvific grace.

By focusing upon the language contained in critiques of Ward, the prominence of Catholic concerns about women assuming apostolic and priestly activities comes to light. It becomes clear that the decisive issue driving the suppression of the Institute was *not* whether Mary Ward and the English Ladies were acting beyond their female capacities, assuming male privileges in a broad sense. It was whether they might be perceived as assuming a particular type of gendered and religious authority: apostolic authority. To more fully understand the conundrum posed by the papacy's harsh suppression and later promotion of Ward's work, we must weave her into our understanding of long-standing debates not only about gender but also about the nature and limits of divine authority itself and to whom it gets given. As shall become clear, the boundaries of apostolic succession did not encompass Pope Joan and the English Ladies, but they also failed to admit certain types of men to certain types of religious work.

In Ward's case, the papacy refused to set the precedent of violating the doctrine of apostolic succession, even if it meant sacrificing an effective part of the Roman Church's efforts in the British Isles. While the Holy See was willing to bend many gender norms and religious rules around domestic relationships and charitable and ministerial works, it set firm limits protecting the clergy's sacramental authority. It drew the line at condoning even the perception that it would extend apostolic, clerical, sacramental authority to women. It continues to do so.

Particularly in its early years, the Institute's efforts to educate girls, catechize families, perform good works, and support missionary priests garnered some praise in the British Isles, on the continent, and even from Rome, as discussed earlier. What are important to explore now are the statements of critics who found something objectionable in the women's underground evangelism. These nay-sayers increased in number, volume, and impact by the 1620s. Critics branded the women as useless and as "chattering hussies" and "galloping nuns" (Wetter 2006, 25).

The perceived success of the Institute's activities drew some of the criticism. Archbishop of Canterbury George Abbot reportedly claimed that Mary Ward alone "did more harm than six Jesuits" (Kenworthy-Browne 2008, 21; Chambers 1882, 1:406–7). Catholic leaders in England agreed. In a memorial sent to Rome in 1622 known as the *Informatio*, the secular clergy of England, led by the opinions of Archpriest William Harrison, asserted that the Institute had "made such progress in a very few years that its disciples have come together into England in great numbers" (Chambers 1882, 2:183). Letters written by lay Catholics in England mirrored the clergy's opinions. In June 1619, for example, a parent, A.B., complained about a daughter who wished to join the Institute. The parent opposed her choice, describing how the Institute's members "scattered through almost all the island" were a harmful influence on young women, Jesuits, and Catholic unity (1:444–46).

In the midst of better-known gendered criticisms were accusations suggesting that the English Ladies engaged in apostolic or priestly work. For the Church, this was the real crux of the problem. Harrison, for example, described the English Ladies as professing "the offices of the Apostolic function" and "to be devoted to the conversion of England, no otherwise than as priests themselves who are destined to this end by apostolic authority." Harrison was appalled that "such vain designs of weak women, supported by no ecclesiastical authority" had proven so successful (2:183–84). Whereas many scholars have focused attention on Harrison's disparagement of women as vain and weak (Ellis 2007; Lux-Sterritt 2011), it is the latter half of Harrison's statement—"as priests themselves" and "supported by no ecclesiastical authority"—that truly damned Ward's efforts. Harrison claimed it his duty to protect the Catholic religion from this threat (2:183).

Ecclesiastics possess authority thanks to the early, foundational church doctrine of apostolic succession. Based on the Gospels of Mark and Luke, apostolic succession specifies how the Catholic Church acquired its authority and ability to save souls through formal, divine sanction (Mark 3:14; Luke 6:13). God gave the power of salvation—to bind and loose souls—

to Christ who shared it with 12 male apostles. When the apostles later chose their successors, the first bishops, they passed the power of salvation on to these bishops through the sacrament of ordination. Through ordination, bishops have endowed priests with their salvific authority all the way to the present day. In an apostolic hierarchy that resembles a genealogical lineage (see below), generations of priests trace their descent as "heirs" of the first apostles who were given their power by Christ himself.

How Authority to Save Souls Is Passed Through the Catholic Church
(Apostolic Succession)

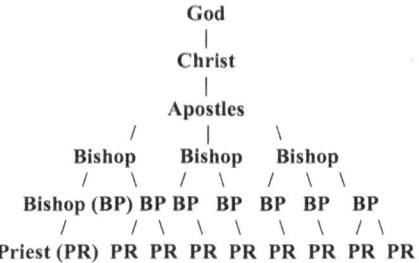

The arguments supporting this hierarchical interpretation of clerical authority date back to the first and second centuries and are the subject of much contemporary debate. In these early centuries, Christianity was illegal, and martyrs were made. There was not yet an institutionalized Christian Church, a formal priesthood, or even a Bible. Although Christ, in his lifetime, spoke often about what believers should do to please God, he left behind no obvious blueprint for any type of institution or church to lead believers toward heaven. Different groups of Christians thus felt free to structure their communal and ritual lives according to members' needs, guided by their knowledge of Christ and the Holy Spirit. There were few agreed-upon doctrines, scriptures, rituals, or leadership structures. Instead, isolated groups of Christians ringed the Mediterranean, worshipping underground while hiding from the authorities (Brock 2003; King 2003).

Such religious choice troubled Christian thinkers such as Clement, a first-century Bishop of Rome, and Irenaeus, a second-century Bishop of Lyon. Surely not all these churches with their diverse practices could lead believers to heaven. Jesus, they wrote, must have left one true path to salvation. In the absence of clear direction, Clement, Irenaeus, and others decided to trace this one path through the apostles (Bettenson 1963, 63, 68–70).

The doctrine of apostolic succession was the linchpin in early attempts to organize a uniform Christian "church" as an institution. It created a formal clergy: a small group of carefully chosen people separate from ordinary believers who held the keys of heaven. The path to salvation led through the clergy who themselves were organized through the hierarchy of apostolic succession into the one true church. Eventually, only ordained priests were authorized to celebrate the sacraments, a key source of God's grace and salvific merit. Any person could pronounce ritualistic words over bread and wine, but unless that individual had the authority of the apostles, transferred to him by one of the apostles' recognized successors, the bishops, that bread and wine would not be transubstantiated into Christ's body. Unauthorized persons who tried to perform the sacraments were thieves, stealing the chance of salvation from the Christians they duped.

Apostolic succession confers legitimacy not only on sacraments but on ministry, teaching, and other activities performed on behalf of the Roman Church. The word apostle, from the Greek *apostolos*, means one who is sent forth or someone entrusted with a mission. The term implies that one does not go off oneself with a divinely inspired purpose but must be sent out by someone in authority. By the later fifth century, the Pope was that authority.

More recently, leaders at the Council of Trent reinforced apostolic succession and clerical status and privilege in session after session. Decision-makers placed the sacraments and other tools necessary to Christian salvation more incontrovertibly under the control and supervision of men authorized under the hierarchy of apostolic succession to save souls (O'Malley 2000, 52–53).

It is easy to see why issues of apostolic authority were on the minds of Catholics during the Reformation. Rome excommunicated and rescinded the apostolic authority of bishops and priests who joined Protestant state churches. The Catholic position was that all future priests ordained within those churches possessed no apostolic authority because the bishops who ordained them were no longer heirs to the apostles. The Protestant position in England, Ireland, and Wales was that their bishops' place within the hierarchy of apostolic succession could not be retroactively severed. The Presbyterian Scottish Kirk rejected apostolic succession and its role in salvation altogether when it broke with Rome in 1560.

The challenges of practicing Catholicism under Protestant rule bore remarkable resemblance to the circumstances that produced Clement's and Irenaeus's arguments in support of apostolic authority. The institutional church was forbidden, and small, underground Catholic communities functioned beneath Protestant radar as best they could. Protestant clergy were the new thieves of salvation, their sacraments allegedly useless to procure God's saving grace. Catholics and Protestants argued over who the true heirs to apostolic authority were, and, indeed, whether apostolic succession even mattered to salvation.

Even among Catholics in the British Isles, chains of hierarchy and authority, particularly episcopal ones, were unstable and contested. With many different types of priests working in relative isolation from one another on the mission, it was not always clear who was in charge of whom. In Ireland, for example, energetic resident bishops attempted to supervise the clergy and care for the spiritual needs of Ireland's Catholic majority, but priests in the monastic orders, who were immensely popular with ordinary Catholics, often forged an independent path. No bishop could lead openly, and each lacked the authority produced by the usual episcopal apparatus.

England, Scotland, and Wales often lacked Catholic bishops altogether, so in 1598 the papacy appointed an archpriest. Archpriests are not bishops; they are simply the top-ranked cleric in a region. In theory, this established clear leadership of the clergy. Jesuits, however, operated under direct papal authority. This led to the Appellant/Archpriest Controversy, a decades-long, inconclusive struggle for control between the two parallel command structures. Finally, in 1623, at the same time that churchmen were debating Ward's plans for the Institute, the papacy abandoned the archpriest system and began ordaining Vicars Apostolic. Vicars Apostolic were bishops with full jurisdiction over Catholics yet without the usual cathedral, administration, or revenues. This theoretically provided Catholics with a more clearly defined place within apostolic succession as someone held the title of bishop, but anger and confusion over these issues of hierarchy and authority continued. The system of Vicars Apostolic lasted until 1850.

In light of such uncertainties, many Catholics clung to the rock of apostolic succession. Descriptions of contemporary missionaries and martyrs as heirs of the apostles fill the writings of laypeople and priests in the British Isles. Missionary priests took their place in the hierarchy of apostolic succession at their ordination. Through conversion of souls, they imitated the apostles, performing all their functions. Through their trials, they suffered like the apostles. They lived apostolic lives and were labeled "Apostolical" men, soldiers, and apostles of Christ (Worthington 1608, 11; *CSP Dom* 14/21/48; Lansdowne MS 75, fols. 44–44v; Gibson 1887, xix–xx; Murphy 1737, 4, 11, 19–20, 26, 29, 32, 56–57; Challoner 1839, 2:94, 145, 153, 192). The Jesuit William Weston emphasized the apostolic character of the mission when he described it as "Peter's ship," linking the mission not only to the apostles but to Rome's authority. In a modification of apostolic succession known as the Petrine Doctrine, the popes claimed themselves heirs of the apostle Peter, the first bishop of Rome, whom Christ allegedly delegated authority over all other apostles. Peter was the rock on which Christ would build his church and the apostle to whom Christ first gave the keys of heaven (Weston 1955, xxii).

Those who wanted to serve on the mission had to be sent by someone above them in the Catholic Church's hierarchy of apostolic succession. God "sent and deputed" men in God's name to make his will known, as Jesuit James Blake preached at the chapel of the Spanish Ambassador in London on the Feast of Corpus Christi in June 1686. Those men, he said, proved themselves credible so that no man could doubt their "Mission and Deputation from God unto us (as all that are sent from him for the Conversion of Nations unto his Holy Faith, have done, and still do)" (*A Select Collection* 1741, 395). When Protestant authorities asked the future martyr Thomas Bullaker whether the pope had sent him into England, Bullaker affirmed that although the pope had not sent him personally, people to whom the pope had given authority had sent him (Stone 1892, 141).

Men such as Henry Heath formally requested permission to go on mission from those with apostolic authority. Heath was the same enthusiastic Franciscan who refused to accept a set of ordinary laymen's clothes in which to travel to England, choosing instead to have a tailor alter his habit into the appearance of layman's clothing. Potential missionaries such as Heath attempted to prove their worthiness to "exercise the apostolic office," alluding to their formal and official understanding of that role. Not everyone who wanted to go on mission was approved (Stone 1892, 162–63). Sometimes, as with Heath, it took several tries for a man to convince his superiors within the Church to send him.

Once Heath was on mission, he clearly envisioned himself as heir to the apostles. Heath's superior, Fr. Angelus of St. Francis Mason, preserved Heath's own words describing his arrest and trial in *Certamen Seraphicum Provinciae Angliae pro Sancta Dei Ecclesia* (Douai 1649).

After authorities quickly apprehended Heath in London—he was literally sitting on the doorstep of what he hoped would be his safe-house the day of his arrival—the Mayor of London questioned Heath as to why he had come to England. Heath replied that he "came to save souls like Christ Himself came down from Heaven to save souls and like Christ sent his Apostles, bidding them teach all nations." When asked why he went about in poor men's clothing, Heath said he did it because Christ "made himself poor for us, and the Apostles of Christ, following in His footsteps left all." Sentenced to death, Heath told his judges and a French observer, de Marsys, that he was about to die like Christ, his apostles, and the martyrs (Stone 1892, 168–69). Following Christ's example was Heath's primary aim, but the apostles appear inextricably intertwined with Heath's understanding of his goal. He was following an example passed down from Christ to Heath's superiors and to Heath himself via apostolic succession.

Lay Catholics believed that the constancy of this visible, lawful succession of apostolic authority demonstrated the truth of their church over newer Protestant ones. Catholics such as the anonymous author of the 1778 pamphlet who claimed to be an "Old Fashion Farmer" and the future martyr, Margaret Clitheroe, defended priests, claiming that they were sent by God, commissioned by God, for the good of the faithful. The Old Fashion Farmer mocked the Church of England because he did not see how the Protestants could claim to be the holy and apostolic church of God unless God had worked a miracle and sent them some of the apostles *ex post facto*, which he was certain God never did. No, the Old Fashion Farmer scorned, theirs was a new and upstart church (*Old Fashion* 1778, 30–31, 36–37, also 130, 140–41, 189). Clitheroe laid out the doctrine of apostolic succession for Protestant ministers when she told them that the true church was the one Christ "left to his Apostles and they to their Successors: ministering the seven sacraments" (Add MS 151, 53v, 58r). This chain of unbroken apostolic authority clearly mattered to the author who labeled himself a "Good Catholick" who maintained his loyalty to the Catholic faith as "preached by the Apostles, and from them derived to me by the ministry of those persons his sacred wisdom has appointed to succeed them" down through the ages to his own time (*Good Catholick* 1660, 1).

Catholics reiterated the hierarchy of apostolic succession in testimony and in text after text, calling it the very foundation of the Church. God, they believed, sent Christ who sent out the apostles who would send out others to teach, baptize, and celebrate the sacraments. This had been a constant since Christ's time on earth. As the anonymous author of the early eighteenth-century treatise, *The Importance of enquiring into ye marks of ye true Church of Christ*, maintained, it was important to commit truths to carefully chosen, faithful men, as had been done in the decades after the crucifixion (2 Tim. 2 and 2 Thes. 2), and as Church doctrine had done since, through its written and unwritten apostolic traditions (Recusant MS B1043, 11, 12, 20, 28). Priests writing for lay Catholics hammered home the importance of apostolic authority, liberally peppering their writings with the term "apostolic" or some variant thereof (Hay 1783, 317–46). "Where no priest is, there is no God" (Butler 1570, Aiv). Anyone who rejected this standard of apostolic legitimacy was of a false faith.

Christians could not simply assume, or as the Catholic convert Thomas Vane termed it, "usurp," such authority themselves, and this was true for missionaries. Quoting numerous scriptural passages, Vane reproved individuals who went on mission without having been lawfully *sent*. Not only would their preaching, teaching, and sacraments be illegitimate, they would be dangerous to the salvation of the ones receiving them (Vane 1649, 208–9). The Catholic author who identified himself only as L.P., a gentleman, opened his 1742 treatise, *The Right Religion Review'd and inlarg'd*, with the words of Ez. 13, castigating those who sent themselves out to do the Lord's work without having been sent. "Woe be to Foolish Prophets, that follow their own Spirit; they see nothing but vain Things, and divine Lies, saying, the Lord: whereas the Lord hath not sent them" (Recusant MS B1039, title page, 1). Indeed, as the Old Fashion Farmer lamented, there was so little reverence for obedience and apostolic authority anymore that "tinkers, cobblers, and chimney-sweepers now pretend to be as able to conduct and teach their neighbors the road to Heaven, as the greatest Pope, or learned Bishop in the Universe" (*Old Fashion* 1778, 143, also 141, 188–89). As Robert Persons advised, Christians must obey authority and uphold divinely established apostolic hierarchies if they wish to be saved (Persons 1754, 215–16, 359–62). Otherwise they were enemies of religion (Lawson 1765, 273).

Amid such concerns, Ward's request to join in the work of the mission and for her Institute to be exempt from episcopal jurisdiction as the Jesuits were must have raised red flags and increased uncertainties over authority, particularly apostolic authority. Despite Mary Ward's best intentions to serve the Catholic Church, Ward unintentionally placed her Institute at the heart of such issues. Rome shut her down.

Apostolic Viragoes and Galloping Nuns

Ward was aware of the tightrope on which she walked, balancing over a net of gendered and religious concerns, particularly over apostolic authority and the priesthood. From Ward's perspective, God had commissioned her to create the Institute. However, Ward never called her Ladies "apostles." Instead, in a short collection of spiritual instructions, she inspired them to have the "zeal of Apostles" combined with the "spirit of hermits" (Chambers 1882, 1:467). In an early plan for the Institute, the *Ratio Instituti* of 1616, Ward suggested that as men were already working as "Apostles" on the English Mission, the female sex should be allowed "also in its measure" something "more than ordinary" in this common cause, but she clearly indicated that such works would be charitable in nature rather than apostolic (1:376). By the time of her revised 1621 plan for her Institute, known as the *Institutum*, however, Ward indicated her Ladies' willingness to go abroad wherever the pope might send them. She clearly recognized the importance of being sent on mission by proper religious authority. In a letter to Antonio Albergati, papal nuncio in Cologne, that same year, she explicitly referred to "what God by diversity of sex hath prohibited"—presumably the priesthood for women. She was aware of limitations to her mission but at the same time asked the papacy to approve something beyond the ordinary in light of the needs of the times (Kenworthy-Browne 2008, 144–48). She pushed against those limits, but the Church held firm.

Not everyone was drawing such fine distinctions between gender and religious issues as Ward was. As early as 1615, the Spanish Jesuit, Francisco Suarez, commented upon the Institute, which had only been active in England for several years. He expressed serious concerns about the women's desire to travel about England "ordained and directed towards the salvation of souls." Suarez's choice of the term "ordained" likely referred to his concerns about Ward and her colleagues assuming priestly responsibilities for the care of souls. The sacrament of ordination placed individuals within the hierarchy of apostolic succession with the power and authority to help save souls. These women's desire to be ordained to this work, Suarez observed, appeared to be against both scripture and canon law, but only the pope, he cautioned, could make such a determination (Mother M. Salome 1901, xii–xiii).

Those closer to the action circulated rumors that the women openly violated apostolic succession. Reports arose in St. Omer by late 1614 that the English Ladies had "undertaken Apostolic Missions in England" (Chambers 1882, 1:318–24). From within England in 1621, Archpriest Harrison's memorial provided seven arguments justifying why the pope should not approve Ward's Institute. The first claimed that it was unheard of for women to discharge apostolic office, implying that the women were doing just that. Later, the memorial asserted that, indisputably, "the Catholic faith has been propagated hitherto in no other way than by apostolic men of approved virtue and constancy." The women's rejection of enclosure was the second reason offered why Rome should reject the Institute, indicating the importance of this issue. But it *was* second (2:183, 185).

Although it is important to investigate the archpriest's emphasis on "men," it is of equal importance to analyze the qualifier "apostolic" and the implications of "apostolic office." This is not to suggest that previous scholars have been off-track in emphasizing enclosure, but that additional aspects of gender and its intersections with religious authority may more fully explain the puzzle of the papacy's suppression of the Institute but later support of Ward and her companions. Authors employ this descriptor, "apostolic," frequently yet uncritically to describe Ward's and her companions' work (Gallagher 1999, 209–11; Lux-Sterritt 2006, 192, 201, 204, 206–7, 211; Lux-Sterritt 2001, 638, 644; Wetter 2006, 20). Confusion over the term is understandable. For centuries, many Christians imitated the lives of the first apostles as a means of spiritual fulfillment. They turned their backs on the demands of the world and the wealth and pomp of the Catholic Church to be closer to Christ. To varying degrees, they devoted themselves to piety, voluntary poverty, and service for the good of souls.

As understood in Ward's time, however, to *be* an apostle or to participate in the apostolate was to participate in, and exercise, divine authority through fulfilling a religious appointment such as the priesthood. It was not simply an adjective used to describe a holy person or their work. It carried the sanction of the Church and the ability to access salvific grace.

Harrison clearly recognized this. He revealed his anxieties over the blurring of apostolic authority and gender as he described the English Ladies as Apostolic Viragoes. (Chambers 1882, 2:186). Harrison claimed to know that Institute members "presume and arrogate to themselves authority to speak of spiritual things before grave men and even sometimes when priests are present to hold exhortations in an assembly of Catholics and to usurp ecclesiastical offices" (2:185). When the Catholic Church's Secretary of Propaganda, Francesco Ingoli, recommended in

1630 that harsh measures be taken against the Institute, one of his key justifications was that the women "arrogat[ed] to themselves spiritual jurisdiction" (Wetter 2006, 59–60). Certainly, gendered language pervaded these documents, as Harrison's comments demonstrate, but gendered language was as much the vehicle used to express fears over perceived threats to clerical authority and apostolic succession as it was the source of those fears.

Rumors about the English Ladies' assumption of clerical authority circulated among ordinary laypeople and low-level clergy in England as well. In April 1622 in Suffolk, for example, a Benedictine missionary, Palmer, criticized the English Ladies in front of a woman he did not realize was a member of Mary Ward's Institute. He, "in a jesting manner," asked the woman, Dorothea, if she might like to become one of those "galloping nuns" or "a preacher" (Chambers 1882: 2:38–39). Further, in 1626, a particularly disturbing allegation arose in a paper by "Bencora, afterwards secretary of the Pontifical Embassy to the Congress of Munster," that Ward "preached in a public street before an altar" and read theology (2:170). Preaching before an altar carried the implicit charge that Ward had presented herself as a priest. Whether these accusations were true or not, Ward appeared to be usurping a particular type of religious authority that had not been given to her by those who possessed such authority. She and her Ladies, critics asserted, needed to be stopped.

Some Catholics and most Protestants in England greeted news of the papacy's suppression of Mary Ward's Institute with joy. A version of the 1631 bull, *Pastoralis Romani Pontificis,* was published in pamphlet form in English the same year under the provocative title *The Suppressing of the Assembly of the Pretended Shee-Jesuites.* The pamphlet corroborated critics' earlier judgments about these women and their activities. "No Laborers shall presumptuously intrude themselves into the Vineyard without being lawfully called and elected." These women had "boldly and presumptuously taken upon themselves the name of Shee Jesuites, without the consent and approbation of the Holy Apostolical Chair ... Ascribing and taking upon them such power and authority as seemed good unto themselves ... under this Cloak and pretense of promoting souls' salvation" (*Suppressing* 1631, 3, 5).

The word "apostolical" or some variant thereof appears repeatedly throughout the pamphlet. Mary Ward's English Ladies did not respect the "Apostolical See," the pope called on his "Apostolical Authority" again and again as he issued this "Apostolical Edict" from his "Apostolical

Chair" (4–6, 12). In a more careful, modern translation of the bull, Urban VIII also provided his "Apostolic blessing," issued his "Apostolic mandate" using his "Apostolic authority." Urban cited "the Apostle," and referred to St. Peter's Basilica as the "Apostolic Palace" and "the Basilica of the Prince of the Apostles in Rome (Wetter 2006, 213–18).

Of course, some reference to apostolic authority is expected in a document composed by the papacy, but it is the sheer *number* of references in the document that stands out. It was this apostolic authority that Ward's Institute threatened. It was this apostolic role that needed to be unambiguously denied to Ward and women of her Institute through the suppression. The evidence suggests that Urban was upholding the Council of Trent's many decrees regarding apostolic succession at least as much as the one about female enclosure.

That is not to say that gender was not at issue. Both religious and gender issues were in play. The upholding of apostolic authority as male authority was clear as Urban VIII explained how he made his decision. He suppressed Mary Ward's Institute after "mature consideration with our venerable brothers, Cardinals of the Holy Roman Church, specially deputed by the same See" to root out "heretical depravity" (214). He instructed "by Apostolic mandate each and every one of our Venerable Brothers and beloved sons, the Nuncios of the Apostolic See, and also Patriarchs, Primates, Archbishops, Bishops, and all local ordinaries" to publish and enforce the order for suppression of Ward's Institute immediately (217). Brothers, sons, patriarchs: each of these ecclesiastical officeholders was male.

When Ward and her companions returned to England in 1639, they were still women, living together, unenclosed, working to propagate the Catholic cause in their home country. However, now they did so with papal support even though the papacy had condemned and crushed the Institute. The key difference in Ward's position and treatment was that any ambiguities and possible misperceptions *vis-à-vis* apostolic succession had been clarified in no uncertain terms through the suppression. Although Ward still worked and lived with female companions, the papacy had officially defined them as laywomen. There was no Institute, thus enclosure was no longer an issue, but more importantly there could be no confusion over any perceived clerical or apostolic activity. By defining their roles as non-apostolic, the Roman Church defended apostolic succession. As important as the re-conversion of the British Isles was, and as effective as the Institute's previous efforts appear to have been, the papacy determined that it was not worth endangering the core doctrine which authorized and empowered Catholic clergy. The Church wanted to draw a clear boundary restricting access to the types of authority granted by apostolic succession, and gender demarcated one aspect of that boundary.

If Mary Ward Had Been a Man

Which raises the question, would a lay*man* have stood a chance of getting a plan for a similar Institute of English Gentlemen approved by the papacy? Such an inquiry is more than hypothetical. In contrast to Ward's difficulties, the papacy blessed a group of laymen who had proposed to serve the faith in a similar manner decades earlier. It did so with little difficulty or debate. A young Suffolk gentleman, George Gilbert (c.1559–1583), organized the Catholic Association in 1579. Members were laymen who would imitate the apostles and aid priests on mission.

There were many parallels between the proposed work of Ward's Institute and Gilbert's Catholic Association. Like the English Ladies, Catholic Association members were to be laypeople: single, pious, from good families, and free from worldly attachments so they would be free to serve God and Church. Like the English Ladies, the men aimed to live in imitation of the apostles and devote themselves to the salvation of souls and conversion of their Protestant countrymen. Both groups kept houses in London where priests could celebrate Mass and provide the sacraments for Catholics in surrounding areas. Members of both organizations prepared laypeople for conversion and obtained priests for formal reconciliation. Like the English Ladies, Catholic Association members aided priests on mission, frequently adopting disguises to avoid detection. On April 14, 1580, Pope Gregory XIII blessed the Catholic Association. The next year, however, the Catholic Association was defunct, the men's efforts quashed by a rise in persecution of Catholics (Foley 1873, 147–211; Gillow 1885, 1:298).

But this conundrum goes deeper than simplistic contrasts of "male versus female" in the Catholic Church. Gilbert's association was too short-lived to draw any firm conclusion that the only pertinent distinction between the papacy's decision-making about Ward's and Gilbert's organizations was gender. Given time, these laymen's works may have drawn similar criticisms as Ward's.

Instead, this was, at its heart, about authority: who possesses it, who gives it, and what legitimates it. Gender was an important part but not the entirety of this conversation. Intersecting the well-known gendered conflicts of the Reformation era was the much longer-standing issue of how religious authority and ability to save souls was passed through the Roman Church. As mentioned above, Jesus of Nazareth never sat down with his followers to lay out a detailed game plan to continue his work after the crucifixion. There were leadership controversies among both male and female disciples for generations. Approximately when and under what circumstances certain disciples were explicitly designated "apostles," numbered as 12, and selected as all-male is a subject of historical and theological debate. Additionally, scriptural and other evidence exists that women served as missionaries, priests, deaconesses, and even bishops in the first centuries of Christian practice (King 1998; Brock 2003; Torjeson 1993). The Church gradually excluded women from ordination and activities associated with apostolic authority (*Didascalia Apostolorum* 1929; Donaldson 1886; Macy 2008).

While the Church eventually decreed that only men could pursue apostolic activities, it also denied apostolic authority to most men. In contrast to women's blanket exclusion, the criteria regarding which men could exercise apostolic authority took centuries to develop. Sometimes ordained men succeeded in excluding or limiting other men's participation in Church leadership and decision-making. For example, Ambrose, Bishop of Milan, successfully thwarted Roman Emperor Theodosius's efforts to lead the Church. Laymen, Ambrose argued, cannot make decisions for the Church. Only men on the hierarchy of apostolic succession were divinely authorized to lead it (Potter 1994).

Laymen, however, did not relinquish religious authority or roles easily. At times, circumstances allowed mighty laymen to reclaim powers from the Church. Four centuries after the disputes in Milan, the Holy Roman Emperor Charlemagne (r. 800–814) made decisions for the Church during chaotic times of invasion and disorder in the papacy and the Italian peninsula (Einhard 1880, 26–28, 50–69). The following century, Emperor Otto I (r. 962–973) called a church synod in which participating clergy sought the emperor's assent before deposing a pope. Otto did not determine church policy and administration directly, but he was behind the scenes pulling many strings (Liudprand of Cremona 1930, 215/829). For powerful men below the rank of emperor or king, participants in the eleventh-century Investiture Controversy debated whether any worldly leaders should be allowed to invest bishops with the symbols and authority of their office. The Church claimed this right exclusively. Unless a bishop was invested by one of the apostles' recognized successors, they argued, there was no transferal of divine authority and the power of salvation.

The Church even limited the activities of devout laypeople who simply wanted to live in imitation of the apostles. By the twelfth century, laypeople could not simply preach or teach about Christianity without the approval of someone with apostolic authority. For example, a former Lyonnaise merchant, Peter Waldo, (c. 1140–c.1218) and his followers, known as the Waldensians, wanted to preach spiritual simplicity and poverty. They were part of a broader movement among Christians in this era to imitate apostolic poverty, evangelize, and encourage penitence. The Waldensians were not trained for such ministry, and the Church refused to send them. The Waldensians, convinced that they were doing God's work, refused to disband. The Church excommunicated Waldo, and the Fourth Lateran Council condemned the Waldensians by name in 1215, declaring them heretics (Audisio 2007).

The full history of the evolution of sacred authority and to whom it is given is detailed, complex, and beyond the scope of this book. At their heart, however, these conflicts were about who could wield authority within the Church and over salvation (Martos 1981). From the Church's standpoint, leaders worried that unauthorized laypeople—whether emperors, lords, or poor men trying to live in apostolic poverty—could lead the Christian Church and its followers astray, imperiling both the institution and believers' souls. Such laypeople might popularize heresy or jeopardize believers' salvation by trying to perform sacraments that contained no saving grace. Punishments for men who violated apostolic succession included excommunication, charges of heresy, interdict, declaration of war, and the suppression of male-run religious organizations.

However, the Church's later position in the British Isles during the Reformation era was precarious. It could not enforce its large institutional priorities in nations lacking episcopal hierarchies, clerical discipline, and authority. The Church desperately needed the loyalty of laypeople if the faith were to survive. This situation allowed laypeople greater opportunities to re-define their short- and long-term relationships with the Church over the course of almost three centuries. From lay perspectives, debates over the boundaries of authority encompassed gendered, religious, social, political, and economic concerns well beyond those raised by Church leaders. Laypeople gradually displayed an increasing confidence in their ability to identify and balance competing priorities for themselves. When their experiments brought them face-to-face with issues of traditional apostolic authority, however, sparks could fly. As mentioned earlier, this could be a contentious or a cooperative process depending on how the priests involved understood and prioritized male privilege and religious obligation.

Laypeople were not rejecting their faith or the clergy, however. As the many stories told thus far reveal, the Catholics who renegotiated so many of these changes, such as the Christmas rioters in Dublin, Francis Wodehouse, and Lucy Herbert, were devout believers who sacrificed a great deal to remain loyal to Rome. These changes tended to be evolutionary rather than revolutionary, and many were the unintentional byproducts of Catholics' accommodations to the challenges of practicing an underground faith in a Protestant land.

Ward's attempt to found a new form of women's religious life is particularly significant because the controversy it caused exposed so many of the fissures between ordinary believers' priorities and Rome's. Ward's first concern was to fulfill God's will as communicated to her through her visions. She believed that God told her to found an organization similar to the Society of Jesus to work for the salvation of souls, which she understood as a fulfillment of Jesus's scriptural direction to focus on loving God and her neighbors above all else (Matt. 22:35–40; Mark 12:28–31). In what better way could she do both than to help her neighbors know God's true church, access saving grace, and further their hopes of salvation? In what has been described as naiveté, Ward thought it obvious that the pope would prioritize souls and encourage her Institute (Wetter 2006, 36–37, 46, 54, 62, 73).

The needs and priorities of Christian laypeople such as Ward, however, can be different from those of clergy. Ideally, both groups work together to fulfill God's will, but in this situation, they did not. Roman Church leaders understood their priority to be the fulfillment of God's will as communicated to the Catholic Church through scripture, centuries of interpretation of scripture, and corresponding tradition. To them, the doctrine of apostolic succession was God's will.

Both the laywoman, Ward, and the cleric, Pope Urban VIII, acted to fulfill what each understood as God's will. Both claimed God's sanction— the ultimate source of legitimacy—for their activities. Whose understanding of God's will would carry the day?

Medieval theologian Thomas Aquinas gave Catholics a well-regarded means to resolve such disagreements. Aquinas asserted that contradictions and conflicts such as these come from God. God challenges humans to confront both their knowledge of God and their poverty of understanding in light of God's omniscience and omnipotence. No one is sufficient unto themselves to comprehend the entirety of God's will. If humans unite, however, and share their different perspectives on the Holy Spirit's call, they stand a chance of hearing more of God's message (Aquinas 1947, 2a2ae, qq. 1–9, 16, 29). The Church was one way that humans united to discover God's will. Individual seekers who relied on the Holy Spirit as revealed to them through conscience, like Ward, were another. Aquinas also spoke of situations where competing interpretations could not be reconciled by human means. These, he argued, must be approached with a leap of faith, coupled with acceptance that contradictions were simply evidence of the limits of human understanding of a greater divine plan.

However, differing perspectives on the divine will frightened many laypeople and clerics. They complained about Ward, concluding that this woman's discernment of God's will, especially her motivation to participate in the missionary work usually reserved for male clerics, must be incorrect in light of Church tradition and doctrine. Aquinas himself addressed the contradictory evidence regarding whether women might instruct other Christians. On one hand, he affirmed that God gave gifts of speech, wisdom, and grace to women. He presented scriptural proof that God expected Christians to use God-given gifts on behalf of their neighbors. Then he contrasted this evidence with that found in other scriptures, particularly 1 Tim. 2:11–15 and 1 Cor. 14:34–35, that stipulate that women should not presume to preach or teach but should remain submissive and silent, asking men for instruction instead. Ultimately, Aquinas privileged the epistles attributed to Paul as well as divine and natural laws justifying the submission and inferiority of women. He concluded that women could teach privately but not publicly on behalf of the Church (2a2ae, q. 177). Aquinas never directly addressed whether women should hold the priesthood.

As Aquinas's conclusion demonstrates, those on the hierarchy of apostolic succession have a distinct advantage when laypeople's and clerical leaders' understandings of God's will collide. The pope was known as Christ's vicar or substitute on Earth, and ordained clerics were Christ's representatives. Who would most Christians believe to be better qualified to know God's will: Christ's substitute and representatives on Earth or a young, untrained woman such as Mary Ward? Also, which side has the authority to enforce their opinion? Those given apostolic authority possess the authority of salvation. Theirs is the ability to literally bring back God upon the altar at the Eucharist or exclude troublemakers from the feast. The pope privileged his understanding of the divine and told Ward and the Christian world that she misunderstood God's intentions and that her efforts were against God's will. Ward would have to accept his judgment or risk her salvation.

From one perspective, Church leaders can be commended for their unwillingness to bend or break a foundational doctrine of the Catholic faith as an expedient to address their problems in the British Isles. From another, Ward's understanding of God's will did not restrict the inspiration of God while the papacy's appeared to limit it. Like Catherine of Siena, Ward fostered the vocations of Christians who felt called by God to pursue a particular type of service for God, the Church, and for souls. By suppressing Ward's Institute, Urban VIII not only told these lay Christians that their discernment of their calling was wrong but, in so doing, refused to entertain the possibility that God wanted something new or different from traditional church protocols. In protecting apostolic succession, the Church told Ward and all Christendom that God either would not or could not choose women for these roles.

Leading the Flock in a Different Direction

The door had not yet opened in the early seventeenth century for laypeople, especially a lay*woman* such as Ward, to re-negotiate relationships with the Church hierarchy. By the eighteenth century, however, the lay*men* of the Catholic Committee succeeded in changing the boundaries between lay and clerical authority, as discussed at the end of the last chapter. What changed? Oath-taking, remember, was at the heart of the conflict between the committee and the Vicars Apostolic. Catholics had long sought an oath that would allow them to be recognized as good subjects *and* good Catholics. By delving into debates over oath-taking, we spotlight not only how laymen began questioning the limits of apostolic authority in their lives but also how lay initiative and capacity to alter the terms of lay-clerical relations grew over time, particularly for men.

Since the reign of Elizabeth, people at all levels of the Catholic hierarchy—laypeople, missionaries, clergy in exile on the continent, and papal administrators in Rome—debated the issues of authority and obedience involved in the taking of such oaths to the monarch and state. The papacy was understandably reluctant to make any concessions that might further erode their proclaimed authority over nations, rulers, and subjects. Rome instructed Catholics that they could not, on the health of their souls, take these oaths under any circumstances. Institutional needs trumped pastoral ones.

The reality on the ground within the British Isles looked different. Some priests were sympathetic to the struggles of the laity and collaborated with them to devise acceptable compromises. Their shared goal was to craft an oath through which the oath-taker professed a worldly loyalty to the monarch without in any way damaging the apostolic authority of the pope. Many Catholics, including priests, believed that they had succeeded, as did the 13 signatories to "A Protestation of Allegiance" to Elizabeth I in 1602 (Tierney 1841, 3:clxxxviii–cxci). In later decades, other laypeople and priests penned their own oaths or allowed Catholics to equivocate by taking public oaths with their own private understanding of what they were swearing (the same practice that caused Henry Garnet so much trouble). Low-ranking clergy approved these measures in direct contradiction of papal policy to help the troubled laypeople they served. They thought it was the right thing to do in the eyes of God (McClain 2004, 257–68). Some clerics went further, working toward rapprochement between Catholics and the Protestant government in open contradiction of Rome's directives. The Irish Jesuit missionary, William Malone, for example, negotiated without papal approval with Ireland's Protestant government and religious leaders for over three decades during the reigns of James I and Charles I. He tried to secure toleration for Irish Catholics in return for allegiance to the crown (Gaffney 1989). In their own eyes, these compromisers believed that they had found a way for Catholics to be both good Christians and good subjects.

Few in authority, however, were satisfied. A succession of popes condemned all efforts at compromise, even stripping some priests of their sacramental functions, while Protestant monarchs continued to distrust their Catholic subjects. Divisions among Catholics in the British Isles and the community of exiles on the continent grew.

Although the hierarchy of apostolic authority theoretically prohibited such innovations by laypeople and low-ranking clergy, the surreptitious nature of bishops' and priests' work and the lack of clearly defined chains of command opened spaces in which laypeople renegotiated lay-clerical relationships in the long-term (Glickman 2009, 158–88). Historically, English, Welsh, Irish, and Scottish loyalty to Rome and the dictates of the papacy had never been absolute. Even before Henry VIII's and the Scottish Kirk's breaks with Rome, native churchmen and laypeople sometimes ignored papal policies and financial exactions. Rome was simply too far away for the Church to do much about it (Brentano 1988). It was even more difficult for Rome to enforce its will when the majority of its administrative structures were dismantled and priests and believers forced underground.

By the end of the eighteenth century when the Catholic Committee debated the limits of clerical authority in laypeople's lives, more than a century had passed since the pope's suppression of Ward's Institute. Relations between laity and clergy had evolved. Generations of lay Catholics and priests had gradually grown accustomed to sharing some of their different responsibilities. Laypeople and low-ranking clerics thus succeeded in shifting the boundaries of apostolic authority in ways that were not possible in Ward's day, either for a layperson or for a woman.

As in Ward's case, laypeople and clergy differed on interpreting God's will, and issues involving apostolic authority were at stake. Trying to pave the way for emancipation, laymen on the Catholic Committee judged the oaths of loyalty required by the two Catholic Relief Acts to be reasonable promises that any good Catholic could make. Many low-ranking clerics evidently agreed with them, if the signatures of support they attached to "The Declaration and Protestation Signed by the English Catholic Dissenters in 1789: With the Names of Those Who Signed It," are any indicator (*A Letter* 1789, Appendix no. III, 16–19).

The Vicars Apostolic disagreed, claiming authority over this issue. Officially, they rejected the oaths on behalf of all Catholics under their jurisdiction, ordering Catholics not to take them. Since the Vicars Apostolic ranked higher on the clerical chain of command established through the doctrine of apostolic succession, their decision should have resolved the issue.

However, this time, laymen refused to back down, and they had a degree of support from low-ranking priests, although such clerics would not have tolerated any direct attacks upon the doctrine of apostolic succession. Committee members argued that the Vicars Apostolic were being overly strict and could claim leadership over religious issues only. They did not deny apostolic succession. They only debated the limits of apostolic authority. In 1792, laymen went further, creating a new lay Catholic organization, the Cisalpine Club, whose members vowed to "resist any ecclesiastical interference which may militate against the freedom of English Catholics" (Gerard and D'Alton 1912). Just as had happened many times among Catholic men, the boundaries of lay and clerical authority had been redefined, but this time without Rome's authorization and as more than a temporary expedient.

Catholic Committee members' confidence in their right and ability to redefine lay relationships with clerical authority did not emerge from nowhere at the end of the eighteenth century. Traditional balances between lay and clerical authority had been thrown askew by Protestant reforms for some time, as discussed in previous chapters. Some of the changes affected laymen and women similarly. Clergy no longer featured as prominently in most Catholics' daily lives. The visible manifestations of the clergy's sacramental and institutional authority were no longer present through churches, ecclesiastical courts, and other public displays. Catholic priests no longer had a parish home and were instead dependent upon the hospitality of laypeople. Laypeople took on larger roles in sacrament and ritual.

However, laymen had also made additional adjustments to both gender and religious authority in which women could not participate. Laymen shared their religious authority within their own homes with the priests who visited and sometimes came to stay. Laymen grappled to renegotiate their masculine responsibilities, the loyalty they owed to worldly leaders, and their obedience to their faith, church, and clergy. Combined with political developments of the seventeenth and eighteenth centuries that emphasized natural rights over natural laws and rule with the consent of the governed (Harrison 2002), we begin to understand how gender and religion intersected with other factors to provide laymen with the confidence and means to redefine their worldly and religious obedience during the three centuries in which Catholicism was an underground faith.

So What Happened Next?

In essentials unity, in nonessentials liberty, and in all things, charity.
Motto of Pope John XIII[2]

Shortly after Catholic laymen redrew the boundaries between lay and clerical authority, the practice of Catholicism became legal throughout the British Isles with the Roman Catholic Relief Act of 1829. This theoretically ended the great need that catalyzed so many of the changes discussed throughout this book. The "devout outlaws" were no more. However, unlike after World War II and the short-term Rosie the Riveter and Bletchley Park situations, Catholics could not simply "return to normal." There was no normal left to which to return. After so many generations, people's practice and understanding of Catholicism could hardly be expected to recreate their previous medieval traditions nor play catch-up to conform to the path taken by other Catholic countries. Nor could the evolutions in gender roles and in lay/clerical relationships spawned by necessity and normalized over centuries simply be undone.

It is tempting to wonder whether the deviations from gender and religious tradition wrought by the men of the Catholic Committee, Ward, William and Ann Blundell, Catherine Howard, Elizabeth Cary, Francis Wodehouse, and others are partially responsible for sparking the vibrant debates about changing gender roles and lay and clerical authority within the Catholic Church today. In the following brief discussion of such issues in the present era, it is difficult to ignore the prevalence of English, Irish, American, Canadian, and Australian Catholics among the devout outlaws of our day, at the forefront of calls for further evolutions in how the Church understands the nature and limits of divine power and authority and to whom it gets given. Such a conclusion, however, would be too simplistic. It would require taking up the thread of this story after 1829 and following it an additional two centuries to the present day following a global and post-colonial odyssey that spans continents—a valuable suggestion, to be sure, but one beyond the scope of this story.

However, perhaps searching for a direct cause-and-effect relationship between the changes described in this book and contemporary concerns is the wrong goal. It may be more useful to think of gender and religion not as clearly defined sets of roles and rules but as large patterns of events and relationships among overlapping interest groups. At times, these patterns are self-reinforcing and restrictive and at other times generous in inclusivity. Such an understanding leaves room for acceptable stability, compromise, and change in gendered and religious authority and traditions (Cadden 1993, 9–10, 53, 226, 258, 280).

In the centuries since Ward's death, the authority of the Catholic Church and its relationships with its members, both lay and clergy, male and female, have metamorphosed worldwide. Since Pope Leo XIII's Constitution *Conditae* of 1900 and subsequent Regulations of Canon Law in 1901, for example, the Catholic Church no longer requires nuns to live and worship under enclosure in monasteries, making new forms of religious life and service possible for women. The Church now encourages and celebrates such women who serve the faith, including women who later followed Ward's path. Urban VIII may have suppressed her Institute, but he did not suppress Ward's vision. Her companions resurrected a new form of the Institute in England in the later seventeenth century. In 1699, its leader, Mary Anne Babthorpe, submitted the Institute's Rules to the papacy, carefully concealing any connections to Ward and her former organization (Lux-Sterritt 2011, 94). Four years later, in 1703, Pope Clement XI approved this new Institute and, in the nineteenth century, Catholic women in Ireland established their own distinctive and vibrant branch of the organization.

This second institute spread throughout six continents and continues in the present day under the name of the Institute of the Blessed Virgin Mary (I.B.V.M.), or Sisters of Loreto, a reference to the Italian shrine dedicated to the Virgin Mary where Ward was known to have prayed. Their best-known member was Mother Teresa of Calcutta, who was a Sister of Loreto serving in the Loreto Schools in India from 1928 to 1950 before beginning her Missionaries of Charity. The Catholic Church has since fully restored Ward's reputation, and I.B.V.M. members now proudly and publicly claim Mary Ward as their founder (Wetter 2006, 203–11). In 2003, the Roman branch of the I.B.V.M. fulfilled a final aspect of Ward's vision to "Take the Name of the Society" when members adopted the Constitutions of the Society of Jesus and a new name, *Congregatio Jesu*, or Congregation of Jesus.[3] In 2009, Pope Benedict XVI declared Mary Ward "Venerable," the first of the three steps toward canonization. These organizations are just a few among the many women's religious and lay groups established over the two centuries since Catholic emancipation in the British Isles.

Although observers frequently refer to such work as a women's apostolate, the foundational Catholic doctrine of apostolic succession remains unaltered and fiercely protected. Although many Catholics request or demand that the Church extend additional leadership and ritual roles, such as responsibility for the homily, to laypeople, nowhere is the pressure on apostolic succession more heated than surrounding the ordination of women to the Catholic priesthood. Even after the exclusion of women from apostolic succession was formalized in the third and fourth centuries, women's sacramental and leadership roles within Christianity continued to be discussed. The advent of the women's movement for gender equality in the 1960s and 1970s, however, provided people of faith with both gender and religious frameworks from which to discuss such issues publicly and persuasively (Henold 2008; Cochran 2005). It is no coincidence that the Congregation for the Doctrine of the Faith, the branch of the Roman Curia that upholds Catholic doctrine, felt the need to officially address the issue of admitting women to the priesthood in 1976 with its declaration,

Inter Insigniores. The Church proclaimed that in loyalty to the model left by Christ to his followers (in other words, apostolic succession), Church tradition forbids the ordination of women.

While tradition has not wavered on this point, the Church's justifications for that tradition have changed. Prior to the Reformation era, explanations for refusing women a place in the hierarchy of apostolic succession revolved around women's inherent sinfulness and inferiority to men. Just as Eve invited Adam to eat the fruit of knowledge in violation of God's commands, women were inclined to seduce others to sin, it was argued. If women were to stand before men to either preach or celebrate sacraments, their mere presence would inspire men to lustful thoughts. Moreover, only men were created in God's image, and thus men were more likely to understand the divine will than women. Finally, as clergy were of superior status to the laity, it would be incongruous for women, who by divine law and natural law were created inferior to men, to be raised above some men as clergy (Humbert of Romans 1982, 223; Aquinas 1947, 1, q. 92).

The Church no longer supports such reasoning, though it does still exclude women from apostolic authority on the basis of sex. As the Congregation for the Doctrine of the Faith explained in *Inter Insigniores*, the priesthood and the power of salvation involve mysteries established by Christ himself. The Church thereby considers itself bound by Christ's manner of acting. Since Christ was incarnated as male and by church tradition all 12 original apostles were male, the Church declares that God meant for males alone to exercise the priesthood. Catholic decision-makers expressed certainty that this was the "entirety of God's plan as God himself has revealed it" (Sacred Congregation 1976). For centuries, the Church has taught that the priest acts at the altar not as himself but as Christ. To exercise the apostolic function, a priest must be able to represent Christ to the point of being his very image, particularly during the Eucharist. In such circumstances, the Church argues that it would be difficult for believers to see the image of the male Christ in a woman at the altar. The Church does not consider the extension of ordination to women to be an issue of individual human rights or gender equality but one of fulfilling the divine will, with which there can be no compromise nor accommodation.

However, if the Church could back away from its ancient and medieval justifications backing apostolic succession and institute new reasoning to legitimate it, many Catholics believe that the Church could also alter its understanding of the doctrine to welcome Christians of any sex in a way that would not undermine the basics of the doctrine itself: the idea of God delegating the power of salvation to certain, chosen, ordained representatives in a hierarchy of authority. Is the heart of the doctrine about salvific authority given by God or about sex? Just as the Catholic Committee did in 1792, such Catholics do not deny or attempt to diminish apostolic succession. They debate its boundaries.

Catholics and non-Catholics around the globe have strong opinions on this controversial issue. The last three pontiffs, Popes John Paul II, Benedict XVI, and Francis I, have reaffirmed Catholic doctrine that women should not be ordained, and the defense of apostolic succession as male is front and center within their justifications. In 1994, John Paul II issued the Apostolic Letter *Ordinatio Sacerdotalis* (Priestly Ordination) in which he declared that all Catholics should hold as definitive belief that the Catholic Church has no authority to ordain women. Benedict XVI, when he was still Cardinal Joseph Ratzinger, explained further that the constant and unbroken tradition of a male-only priesthood in the Church makes the Church's ban on women priests an infallible decision. He asked believers to reframe their understanding of the issue. Catholic women, he asserted, do not need to be admitted to holy orders to demonstrate their equality to men in the Church. Instead, he asked Catholics to consider men's and women's roles within the Church as complementary. Both sets of roles are vital to the Church, but they are not identical nor do they need to be (Allen 2015, 122–34). All work, however, was not created equal. Certain status, authority, privilege, and access to resources accompanies certain roles, usually not the type held by women (Lorber 1994, 1–36; Johnson 2014, 26–47).

Since his elevation to the papacy in 2013, Francis I has repeatedly and unequivocally stated that the Church should not, and indeed cannot, ordain women. It "is not a question open to discussion" (Francis I 2013, 103, 104). Speaking at the World Meeting of Families in Philadelphia in September 2015, the pontiff called women the future of the Catholic Church, praising their contributions to the Church and making specific reference to the lay nature of those roles. "We know that the future of the church, in a rapidly changing society, now calls for a much more active engagement on the part of the laity," Francis said. "In a particular way, it means valuing the immense contribution that women, lay and religious, have made and continue to make to the life of our communities." Later in his U.S. visit, he thanked women for their strength, fight, and "that spirit of courage which puts you on the front lines in the proclamation of the

Gospel ... "I wish to say 'thank you,' a big thank you ... and to tell you that I love you very much" (Barbato 2015). During a press conference held on a flight to Rome, Maria Sagrarios Ruiz de Apodaca, a correspondent from Radio Nacional de España, asked the pope directly, "Will we one day see women priests in the Catholic church as some groups in the U.S. ask, and some other Christian churches have?" The pope upheld apostolic succession as male while confirming his commitment to women as important lay contributors to the faith.

> [O]n women priests, that cannot be done. Pope St. John Paul II after long, long intense discussions, long reflection said so clearly. Not because women don't have the capacity. Look, in the Church, women are more important than men, because the church is a woman. It is "la" church, not "il" church. The Church is the bride of Jesus Christ. And the Madonna is more important than popes and bishops and priests. I must admit we are a bit late in an elaboration of the theology of women. We have to move ahead with that theology. Yes, that's true. (Catholic News Agency 2015)

He has also promoted women's education and greater inclusion of women in the workplace and society more generally. In sum, Francis I appears to support women filling a greater number and variety of authoritative, decision-making lay positions in the church—almost all roles except the clergy. That door, he says, is closed (Allen 2015, 122–26; Catholic Women Speak Network 2015; Wills 2015).

Yet opinion in favor of re-drawing the boundaries between lay and clerical roles in the Catholic Church, including but not limited to women's ordination, is mounting. This controversy does not pit laypeople on one side against priests on the other. Just as some priests in Ward's and the Catholic Committee's times joined ordinary laypeople in their efforts to meet an evolving set of Catholic needs, so are some laypeople, monastics, and priests placing concerted public pressure on Rome to question its interpretation of divine will and tradition. Predictably, as in Ward's day, this is producing controversy and division.

Much of the pressure to ordain women comes from within the Church, from devout and loyal Catholics who allege that the Church's refusal to ordain women is legitimated by traditions of sexism rather than those of scripture or divine institution to which defenders of refusal appeal. One of the best-known proponents of greater gender inclusivity has been Joan Chittester, an American Benedictine nun, author, and activist for human rights. She is the former prioress of the Benedictine Sisters of Erie, PA, and past president of the Leadership Conference of Women Religious in the United States. She gained international attention and almost became a devout outlaw in her own right in 2001 after she refused to obey a Vatican order not to advocate for women's ordination at a conference held by Women's Ordination Worldwide (WOW) in Ireland. Chittister risked excommunication and possible expulsion from her monastery if she spoke out. Prior to the conference, the Vatican pressured her prioress, Christine Vladimiroff, to enforce Chittester's monastic vow of obedience and compel Chittester to stay home. Vladimiroff refused and risked Rome's discipline herself. She contrasted Benedictine understandings of monastic obedience within community to the type of obedience the Vatican asked her to impose upon Chittester (Vladimiroff 2001). Their monastic community voted in overwhelming support of Vladimiroff's decision to support Chittester, and 127 of the 128 sisters signed Vladimiroff's explanatory letter to the Vatican. Nuns in 22 other monastic communities wrote to Rome in support of Chittester. The Vatican let the matter drop. Chittester spoke at the WOW conference in Dublin, where she commented, "The Church that preaches the equality of women but does nothing to demonstrate it within its own structures is dangerously close to repeating the theological errors that underlay centuries of Church-sanctioned slavery" (Bonavoglia 2002, 311).

Since 2001, WOW has continued to advocate for women's ordination. The organization held its international conference in Philadelphia just days before Francis I arrived to speak to the World Meeting of Families as part of his 2015 visit to the United States. According to Miriam Duignan, a WOW leader, the group hosted an international contingent of delegates from countries as diverse as Canada, Sri Lanka, Palestine, and Poland. WOW members kept up their pressure by picketing the pope to pressure him to address women's ordination after he arrived in Washington D.C. (Siddiqui and Gambino 2015).

Men, both clerics and laymen, have also spoken out in support of women's ordination. Greg Reynolds, a former Australian Catholic priest, has spoken publicly in favor of women's ordination since 2010, saying that to deny women the priesthood was "obstructing the work of the Holy Spirit" ("The Outsider" 2013). In 2013, Reynolds, the founder of Inclusive Catholics, which advocates for women's ordination and same-sex marriage, became the first priest excommunicated and defrocked by Pope Francis I. In a letter to other priests in his archdiocese of Melbourne, Archbishop Denis Hart explained that Reynolds was excommunicated primarily "because of his public teaching on the ordination of women" (West 2013). Similarly, Irish layman Jon O'Brien, President of Catholics for Choice, an organization that supports abortion rights, criticized what he viewed as Francis's disregard for Catholic women's priorities. "Women can wait while he takes care of more important issues" (Allen 2015, 123).

Modern change-makers point to a body of evidence that women did hold clerical roles in the first centuries of Christianity before being excluded from these positions by male clerics in the third and fourth centuries. To ordain women would thus not be a frivolous or unwarranted accommodation to modern proclivities but a return to original Christian tradition. In addition, some Catholics openly question whether denying women the priesthood may thwart God's will. They sift through detailed documentation and arguments, and, as members of the Catholic Committee did centuries before, make reasoned determinations for themselves on this issue rather than accepting Rome's claim to monopoly of interpretation. Like Ward, however, they have no official authority to change Rome's opinions or doctrines.

Arguing whether such change should or should not occur is not the purpose of this book. Still, should change come, it will most likely be instigated by coalitions of committed laypeople collaborating with lower-ranking members of the clergy, much as it was with the Catholic Committee. Also, because women have more influence in society today than they did in Ward's and the Catholic Committee's time, they are much more likely to be a part of this process.

Such cooperation between men and women, both laypeople and clerics, can succeed in gradually changing the opinions of high-ranking churchmen. During the Vatican's Synod on the Family in 2015, Canadian Archbishop Paul-Andre Durocher encouraged his fellow synod participants to condemn interpretations of scripture that justify men's dominion over women and to expand women's opportunities for leadership and decision-making, including ordination to the diaconate. This, Durocher advocated, would "clearly show the world the equal dignity of women and men in the Church." A former president of the Canadian bishops' conference, Durocher said, "I think we should really start looking seriously at the possibility of ordaining women deacons because the diaconate in the church's tradition has been defined as not being ordered toward priesthood but toward ministry." Deacons—along with bishops and priests—are one of the three ordained "orders" of ministers in the Catholic Church. They are not priests, but they may preach and teach, lead in prayer, and perform works of mercy. Durocher was careful to distinguish between the sacramental roles versus ministerial functions that such ordained women might perform. According to tradition, Durocher claims, deacons are directed *non ad sacerdotium, sed ad ministerium* ["not to priesthood, but to ministry"] (McElwee 2015). As ordained ministers, deacons exercise a variety of sacramental duties typically denied to laypeople, such as being able to preside at baptisms, marriages, and funerals. Durocher thus continued to reserve the most important apostolic powers—those dealing with salvation—to ordained male priests and bishops. Durocher also suggested extending a greater level of authority to laypersons—both men and women—by granting permission for laypersons to deliver the homily at Mass. The homily, or sermon, explains and expounds upon scripture to teach a congregation, and this role is presently reserved for ordained clergy (*Institutio Generalis Missalis Romani* 2002, 65–66).

The future of women's ordination and greater sharing of liturgical, ministerial, and sacramental roles between clergy and laypeople has yet to be decided. As almost two millennia of back-and-forth wrangling over apostolic authority—from Clement and Irenaeus to Bishop Ambrose of Milan and Theodosius, from the eventual exclusion of women from leadership roles in early Christian churches to Pope Joan, from the Council of Trent to Vatican II and through the present day—demonstrate, a significant number of gender and religious roles intersect and fluctuate according to stressors present within a given environment. The British Isles were the locus of one intense, concentrated renegotiation of such roles. In times of instability or uncertainty such as occurred over the protracted period between 1534 and 1829 in England, Ireland, Wales, and Scotland, the strict enforcement of traditional gender roles or between lay and clerical roles may not be the Church's top priority. Individuals are able, and even encouraged, to perform new roles either by choice or necessity. The negative social consequences usually associated with transgressing custom diminish, and there may even be positive rewards.

However, in contrast to the modern situations—such as Rosie the Riveter and fundamentalist Islamic sects' use of women suicide bombers in direct contradiction of social and religious mores—that sparked this inquiry, the 300-year example of Catholicism practiced illegally within the British Isles highlights the Catholic Church's firm commitment to apostolic succession, even in the face of great need and possible great benefit. Rome pragmatically compromised on many gender and religious issues as long as one particular line was never crossed, as long as such accommodations did not threaten apostolic succession, a core doctrinal belief of the Church. As Ward's example demonstrates, the Church was willing to risk losing its foothold among Catholics in the British Isles rather than set the precedent *or risk even the perception* that women had been given any type of apostolic authority, whether as missionaries or priests. Given the Church's history, apostolic succession appears to be a line the Catholic Church will not cross easily, if at all, even today.

Gender and religious systems and the unacknowledged inequalities and privileges that accompany one's place within these systems are uncomfortable topics for discussion. We live in a partially changed world: our own "new normal." However, just as Catholics in the British Isles struggled to reconcile and re-negotiate the seemingly incompatible demands of gender and religious roles 300 years ago, so do people of faith today, often taking for granted the many changes in attitudes and institutional practice that have already occurred since Ward's day. Most modern Christians, for example, now view the myth of Pope Joan as proof of medieval sexism rather than evidence of women's unsuitability to be spiritual leaders. The Catholic Committee proved that laypeople could change the balance between lay and clerical authority without rejecting apostolic succession. And Mary Ward's Institute, although initially suppressed, exists in several forms today without fear that members are trying to assume the functions of priests. Mary Ward herself—the devout outlaw whose story provided the framework for this larger exploration of changing gender and religious roles in the Catholic Church—is on the road to possible canonization. Many Catholics expressed fears that changes such as these would weaken the foundations of the Church, the family, and society, but these fears never materialized.

With every crisis and every dispute over apostolic authority, lessons are learned—in advocacy, community, rhetorical debate, and interpretation of scripture, certainly, but also in justice and humility before one another and before God. Profits are shared by all sides in the debate. Although it comforts many Christians to believe that they profess an unchanging faith and belong to an unchanging church, any assertions of changelessness are illusions. Such claims are a rewriting not only of history but of theology as well. Christians are far from alone in confronting these realities. Aquinas claimed that God is the source of such challenges: that it is God's will for humans to grapple with contradictions and uncertainties. As no one is capable of comprehending the entirety of God's will, Aquinas taught that believers stand a better chance of hearing more of God's message by uniting and sharing their different perspectives on the Holy Spirit's call

(Aquinas 1947, 1, q.1, art. 1). As contemporary deliberations over the limits of apostolic authority and gender roles progress, both Church leaders and ordinary believers engage with one another to discover new evidence, perspectives, and insights that deepen faith and, hopefully, encourage constructive dialogue. There will be experimentation, there will be evolution, and there will be growth and change. In Ward's time, as now, this is a question of how the Catholic Church will live out its values. How will it encourage or restrict Catholics' ability to follow conscience and what they perceive to be God's calling in their lives? What path follows the example of Christ and the will of God? Aquinas never said it would be easy.

Notes

1. Session 25 of the Council of Trent reinforced the medieval mandate regarding female enclosure. Substantially more sessions, canons, and decrees of the council, however, mention and reinforce apostolic succession and call upon it to justify other mandates. For example, Session 22, ch. 1 and ch. 4, Canon 4 especially reinforce apostolic succession, but other decrees clearly rely on apostolic succession to reinforce Church authority, hierarchy, and jurisdiction. See especially Session 5, "Decree on Reformation," ch. 2, on the authority to preach which helps establish the threat of Ward and her Ladies possibly preaching publicly; Session 6, Canon 29 and "Decree on Reformation," ch. 1; Session 7, Canon 10 and "Decree on Reformation," ch. 13; Session 13, ch. 3; Session 22, ch. 1 and Canon 2 (*Decrees of the Ecumenical Councils* 1990).
2. From the Latin, "*In necessariis unitas, in non-necessariis libertas, in utrisque caritas.*" Ironically, Marco Antonio de Dominis, in *De Republica Ecclesiastica* (1617), 4: ch. 8, first articulated this idea in a text critical of the papacy. A Catholic bishop, he fled to England during a dispute with the Pope, and the Church of England welcomed him. He eventually returned to Italy and the Roman Church but died under imprisonment in the Castel Sant'Angelo in 1624.
3. The Irish branch adopted the Constitutions but not the new name.

Works Cited

Add (Additional) MSS. York Minster Library.
Allen, John L., Jr. 2015. *The Francis Miracle: Inside the Transformation of the Pope and the Church*. New York: Time Books.
Aquinas, Thomas. 1947. *Summa Theologica*. Translated by the Fathers of the English Dominican Province. New York: Benziger Bros.

Audisio, Gabriel. 2007. *Preachers by Night: the Waldensian Barbes, 15th–16th centuries*. Leiden: Brill.
Bar Convent Archives. York.
Barbato, Lauren. 2015. "Pope Francis Says Women are the Future of the Church, So Where are They?" *Bustle*. http://www.bustle.com/articles/113294-pope-francis-says-women-are-the-future-of-the-church-so-where-are-they. Accessed December 3, 2015.
Bettenson, Henry, ed. and trans. 1963. *Documents of the Christian Church*. 2nd ed. London: Oxford University Press.
Bonavoglia, Angela. 2002. "The Church's Tug of War." In *Nothing Sacred: Women Respond to Religious Fundamentalism and Terror*, edited by Betsy Reed, 310–16. New York: Thunder's Mouth Press/Nation Books.
Boureau, Alain. 2001. *The Myth of Pope Joan*. Translated by Lydia G. Cochrane. Chicago: University of Chicago Press.
Brentano, Ralph. 1988. *Two Churches: England and Italy in the Thirteenth Century*. Berkeley, CA: University of California Press.
Brock, Ann Graham. 2003. *Mary Magdelene, The First Apostle: The Struggle for Authority*. Cambridge, MA: Harvard Divinity School.
Butler, Thomas. 1570. Introduction to *A Treatise of the Holy Sacrifice of the Altar, called the Masse*. Translated by Antonio Possevino. Louvain: Ioannem Foulerum.
Cadden, Joan. 1993. *Meanings of Sex Difference in the Middle Ages: Medicine, Science, and Culture*. Cambridge: Cambridge University Press.
Catholic News Agency. 2015. "Full Transcript of Pope Francis's inflight interview from Philadelphia to Rome." http://www.catholicnewsagency.com/news/full-transcript-of-pope-francis-inflight-interview-from-philadelphia-to-rome-60499/. Accessed 19 Sept 2015.
Catholic Women Speak Network, eds. 2015. *Catholic Women Speak: Bringing Our Gifts to the Table*. New York: Paulist Press.
Challoner, Richard. 1839. *Memoirs of Missionary Priests and Other Catholics of Both Sexes that have Suffered Death in England on Religious Accounts from the Year 1577–1684*. 2 vols. Philadelphia: John T. Green.
Chambers, M.C.E. 1882. *The Life of Mary Ward (1585–1645)*. 2 vols. Edited by Henry James Coleridge. London: Burns and Oates.
Cochran, Pamela D.H. 2005. *Evangelical Feminism: A History*. New York: New York University Press.
CSP Dom (Calendar of State Papers, Domestic Series) of the reign of Elizabeth I. 1863–1950. London: Public Record Office, series 2.
Decrees of the Ecumenical Councils, vol. 2, Trent to Vatican II. 1990. Edited by Norman P. Tanner. Original text established by G. Alberigo, J.A. Dossetti, P.-P. Ioannou, C. Leonardi, and P. Prodi, in consultation with H. Jedin. Washington, D.C.: Georgetown University Press.

Didascalia Apostolorum: the Syriac version translated and accompanied by the Verona Latin fragments, with an introduction and notes by R. Hugh Connolly. 1929. Oxford: Clarendon Press.

Donaldson, James, trans. 1886. "Apostolic Constitutions." In *Ante-Nicene Fathers, Vol. 7*, edited by Alexander Roberts, James Donaldson, and A. Cleveland Coxe. Buffalo, NY: Christian Literature Publishing Co. Revised and edited for New Advent by Kevin Knight. 2009. New Advent. http://www.newadvent.org/fathers/0715.htm. Accessed Feb 5, 2015.

Einhard. 1880. *The Life of Charlemagne*. Translated by S.E. Turner. New York: Harper and Bros.

Ellis, Pamela. 2007. "'They are but Women': Mary Ward (1585–1645)." In *Women, Gender and Radical Religion in Early Modern Europe*, edited by Sylvia Brown, 243–64. Leiden: Brill.

Foley, Henry. 1873. *Jesuits in Conflict, or, Historic facts illustrative of the labours and sufferings of the English Mission and Province of the Society of Jesus by a member of the Society of Jesus.* London: Burns & Oates.

Francis I. 2013. *Evangelii Gaudium*. http://w2.vatican.va/content/francesco/en/apost_exhortations/documents/papa-francesco_esortazione-ap_20131124_evangelii-gaudium.html. Accessed Dec 10, 2015.

Gaffney, Declan. 1989. "The Practice of Religious Controversy in Dublin, 1640–1641." In *The Church, Ireland and the Irish*, edited by W.J. Shields and Diana Woods, 145–58. Oxford: Basil Blackwell for the Ecclesiastical History Society.

Gallagher, Lowell. 1999. "Mary Ward's 'Jesuitresses' and the Construction of a Typological Community." In *Maids and Mistresses, Cousins and Queens: Women's Alliances in Early Modern England*, edited by Susan Frye and Karen Robertson, 199–219. Oxford: Oxford University Press.

Gerard, J. and E. D'Alton. 1912. "Roman Catholic Relief Bill." *The Catholic Encyclopedia*. http://www.newadvent.org/cathen/13123a.htm. Accessed Feb 2, 2015.

Gibson, Thomas Ellison, ed., 1887. *Crosby Records: A Chapter of Lancashire Recusancy*. Manchester: Chetham Society, new series, XII.

Gillow, Joseph. 1885–1902. *Biographical Dictionary of the English Catholics from the Breach with Rome, in 1534, to the Present Time*. 5 vols. London: Burns & Oates.

Glickman, Gabriel. 2009. *The English Catholic Community 1688–1745: Politics, Culture and Ideology*. Woodbridge, Suffolk: The Boydell Press.

The Good Catholick no Bad Subject, or a Letter from A Catholick Gentleman to Mr. Richard Baxter. 1660. London: John Dakins.

Harrison, Ross. 2002. *Hobbes, Locke, and Confusion's Masterpiece: An Examination of Seventeenth-Century Political Philosophy*. Cambridge: Cambridge University Press.

Hay, George. 1783. *The Sincere Christian Instructed in the Faith of Christ from the Written Word in Two Volumes*. Dublin: P. Wogan.
Henold, Mary J. 2008. *Catholic and Feminist: The Surprising History of the American Catholic Feminist Movement*. Chapel Hill, NC: University of North Carolina Press.
Humbert of Romans. 1982. "Treatise on the Formation of Preachers." In *Early Dominicans: Selected Writings*, edited by Simon Tugwell, 179–370. New York: Paulist Press.
Institutio Generalis Missalis Romani. 2002. http://www.eucharistiefeier.de/docs/igmr2002.htm. Accessed Dec 20, 2015.
Johnson, Allan. 2014. *The Gender Knot: Unraveling our Patriarchal Legacy*. 3rd ed. Philadelphia: Temple University Press.
Kenworthy-Browne, Christina, ed. 2008. *Mary Ward 1585–1648: A Briefe Relation with Autobiographical Fragments and a Selection of Letters*. Rochester, NY: Boydell and Brewer for the Catholic Record Society.
King, Karen L. 1998. "Prophetic Power and Women's Authority: The Case of the Gospel of Mary (Magdalene)" In *Women Preachers and Prophets through Two Millennia of Christianity*, edited by Beverly Mayne Kienzle and Pamela J. Walker, 21–41. Berkeley, CA: University of California Press.
———. 2003. *What is Gnosticism?* Cambridge, MA: Harvard University Press.
Lansdowne MSS. British Library.
Lawson, Thomas. 1765. *The Devotion to the Sacred Heart of Jesus, with other pious practices, devout prayers, and instructions for the use and convenience of Christians in general*. Bruges: Joseph van Praet.
A Letter Addressed to the Catholics of England, By the Catholic Committee. 1789. London: J.P. Coghlan.
Liudprand of Cremona. 1930. *The Works of Liudprand of Cremona*. Edited and Translated by F.A. Wright. New York: E.P. Dutton.
Lorber, Judith. 1994. *Paradoxes of Gender*. New Haven: Yale University Press.
Lux-Sterritt, Laurence. 2001. "An analysis of the controversy caused by Mary Ward's Institute in the 1620s." *Recusant History* 25, no. 4: 636–47.
———. 2006. "Mary Ward's English Institute: The Apostolate as Self-Affirmation?" *Recusant History* 28, no. 2: 192–208.
———. 2011. "Mary Ward's English Institute and Prescribed Female Roles in the Early Modern Church." In *Gender, Catholicism, and Spirituality*, edited by Lux-Sterritt and Carmen M. Mangion, 83–98. London: Palgrave Macmillan.
Macy, Gary. 2008. *The Hidden History of Women's Ordination: Female Clergy in the Medieval West*. Oxford: Oxford University Press.
Martin, Gregory. (1619) 1978. *The Love of the Soule. Made by G.M. Whereunto are annexed certain: Catholike questions to the Protestants. With a new addition of a catalogue of the names of Popes and other professors of the ancient Catholike faith: and a challenge to Protestants to shew (if they can) a like catalogue of the names of the professors of the Protestant faith*. Reprint, Menston, Yorkshire: Scolar Press.

Martos, Joseph. 1981. *Doors to the Sacred: A Historical Introduction to Sacraments in the Catholic Church*. New York: Doubleday.

Mason, Fr. Angelus of St. Francis. 1649. *Certamen Seraphicum Provinciae Angliae pro Sancta Dei Ecclesia*. Douai.

McClain, Lisa. 2004. *Lest We Be Damned: Practical Innovation and Lived Experience among Catholics in Protestant England, 1559–1642*. New York: Routledge.

McElwee, Joshua. 2015. "Canadian archbishop's full remarks to Synod on women deacons." *National Catholic Reporter*. http://ncronline.org/blogs/ncr-today/canadian-archbishops-full-remarks-synod-women-deacons. Accessed Dec 4, 2015.

Mother M. Salome. 1901. *Mary Ward: A Foundress of the 17th Century*. London: Burns & Oates.

Murphy, Cornelius. 1737. *A True and Exact Relation of the Death of Two Catholicks, who Suffered for their Religion at the Summer Assizes, Held at Lancaster in the year 1628*. London.

The Old Fashion Farmer's Motives for Leaving the Church of England and Embracing the Roman Catholic Faith. 1778. n.p.

O'Malley, John W. 2000. *Trent and All That: Renaming Catholicism in the Early Modern Era*. Cambridge, MA: Harvard University Press.

"The Outsider". 2013. *Sydney Morning Herald*. http://www.smh.com.au/national/people/the-outsider-20131103-2wvjt.htm. Accessed Dec 4, 2015.

Persons, Robert. 1754. *A Christian Directory, Guiding Men to Their Eternal Salvation*. Liverpool: John Sadler.

Pollen, John Hungerford. 1891. *Acts of English Martyrs Hitherto Unpublished*. London: Burns and Oates Ltd.

Potter, David. 1994. *Prophets and Emperors: Human and Divine Authority from Augustus to Theodosius*. Cambridge, MA: Harvard University Press.

Recusant MSS. Harry Ransom Humanities Research Center. University of Texas.

Sacred Congregation for the Doctrine of the Faith. 1976. "Declaration on the Question of Admission of Women to the Ministerial Priesthood." http://www.vatican.va/roman_curia/congregations/cfaith/documents/rc_con_cfaith_doc_19761015_inter-insigniores_en.html. Accessed Dec 4, 2015.

A Select Collection of Catholick Sermons Preach'd before Their Majesties King James II. Mary Queen-Consort, Catherine Queen-Dowager, etc. Vol. 1. 1741. London.

Siddiqui, Sabrina and Lauren Gambino. 2015. "Protesters urge pope to ordain female priests and stop 'legitimizing sexism.'" *The Guardian*. http://www.theguardian.com/world/2015/sep/23/pope-francis-female-priests-catholic-church-sexism. Accessed Dec 3, 2015.

Stone, J.M. 1892. *Faithful unto Death: An Account of the Sufferings of the English Franciscans during the 16th and 17th Centuries, From Contemporary Records*. London: Kegan Paul, Trench, Trübner & Co.

The Suppressing of the Assembly of the Pretended Shee-Jesuites. By the Edict of our most holy Father and Lord, Urbanus, Dei Gratia. The eight (of that name) now Pope of Rome. Translated out of the Low-Dutch. 1631. London: Printed for Nathaniell Butter and Nicholas Bourne.

Tierney, M.A. 1841–1843. *Dodd's Church History of England from the Commencement of the Sixteenth Century to the Revolution in 1688.* 5 vols. London: Charles Dolman.

Torjeson, Karen Jo. 1993. *When women were priests: women's leadership in the early church and the scandal of their subordination in the rise of Christianity.* San Francisco: Harper San Francisco.

Vane, Thomas. 1649. *A lost sheep returned home: or The Motives of the conversion to the Catholike Faith, of Thomas Vane.* 3rd ed. Paris.

Vladimiroff, Christine. 2001. "Regarding Deliberations with the Vatican." http://womensordinationworldwide.org/dublin-2001/2014/2/2/statement-of-benedictine-prioress-sr-christine-vladimiroff. Accessed 18 April 2016.

West, Ed. 2013. "Pope Francis excommunicates Australian priest." *Catholic Herald*. http://www.catholicherald.co.uk/news/2013/09/27/pope-francis-excommunicates-australian-priest/. Accessed Dec 4, 2015.

Weston, William. 1955. *William Weston: The Autobiography of an Elizabethan.* Translated by Philip Caraman. Foreword by Evelyn Waugh. London: Longmans, Green and Co.

Wetter, M. Immolata. 2006. *Mary Ward: Under the Shadow of the Inquisition.* Translated by M. Bernadette Ganne and M. Patricia Harriss. Oxford: Way Books.

Wills, Garry. 2015. *The Future of the Catholic Church with Pope Francis.* New York: Penguin.

Worthington, Thomas. (1608) 1978. *A Catalogue of Martyrs in England; 1608.* Edited by D. M. Rogers. Reprint, Menston, Yorkshire: Scolar Press.

Index[1]

A
Allen, William, 127, 166
Amazons, 157–159, 161, 166, 188, 189
Apostolic, confusion over meaning and use, 247
Apostolic succession
    Catholic Church's firm commitment to, 266–267
    Catholic loyalty to, in British Isles, 242–245
    Catholic vs. Protestant views, 241–242
    confusion of episcopal hierarchies among Catholics in British Isles, 242–243
    debates over women's ordination to the priesthood, 260–265
    development of doctrine and tradition, 239–241, 250–252
    exclusion of some men, 250–252
    Mary Ward's perceived violation of, 238, 239, 246–250
    power dynamics when lay and clerical priorities differ, 253–255, 260–265
    status of doctrine today, 260–261
Apostolic Viragoes, 247
Aquinas, Thomas, 268
    on how to know God's will, 253–254
    views on women's roles in the Church, 253–254
Archpriest/Appellant Controversy, 18, 200–201, 242
Arrowsmith, Edmund, 165–166, 168

B
Babington, Anthony, 90
Baker, Augustine, 53, 59, 61, 62, 68, 76

---

[1] Note: Page numbers followed by 'n' refer to notes.

Baker, Augustine (*cont.*)
  instruction of Gertrude More, 54
  trial, 58–59
  views on women, 54
Baptism, 33, 89, 130, 135, 195, 197, 205, 207–208, 223, 225, 229
  Browne, Anthony, 195–197
  emergency baptism, 195, 197; women's roles, 207–208
Barlowe, Ambrose, 162, 181
Baxter, Richard, 104, 107, 108, 184
Blaes, Jacques, 68
Blundell, Ann, 26, 106, 127–128
Blundell, William, 26, 85, 91, 96, 111, 126–128, 176, 187
  challenges to masculinity, 26–27
  sword, 28, 29, 105, 106, 108
Browne, Anthony, 85, 195
  baptizes own child, 195–197
Burial, 33, 89, 207–209, 223
  burial ground, Little Crosby, 209–210
  lay roles, 208–209
Butler, Edmund, 31
Butler, Richard, 28, 30

C
Cary, Elizabeth, 117–119, 129, 133, 135, 137, 148
  attempts to educate children Catholic, 136–137
Cary, Henry, 117–119, 129, 134, 138, 146, 148
  death, 136
  Dublin riot, 157–158
Catherine of Siena, 255
Catholic Church
  administration in British Isles, 17, 242
  attempts to reclaim British Isles (*see* Plots; Rebellions)
  bend gender and lay rules, 24, 73–76
  exceptions to usual rules, 21, 44
Catholic Committee, 32, 103, 225, 226, 228, 229, 237, 255, 257, 258, 267
  redrawing boundary between clergy and laity, 225–228, 255–258
Catholic Relief Acts, 33, 257
  Roman Catholic Relief Act of 1829, 258
  See also Emancipation
Children
  baptism in mixed marriages, 135
  Catholic schools in British Isles, 205–207
  parents' attempts to educate Catholic, 44, 136–137, 141
Chittester, Joan, 263–264
Christening, *see* Baptism
Church papism, 88–90
Civil War, English, 20, 25, 26, 28, 30, 33, 34, 44, 69, 82, 92, 93, 96, 105, 127, 161, 162, 164, 165, 172, 176, 178
  communications carried by priests and monastics, 175–176, 178
Clergy
  changing relationship with laity, 195–230
  distinction from laity, 197–198
  necessity of clerical mediation, 201–203
Clerical authority, 201
  limited by laity, 225–228
  sharing with laity, 236
Clerical privilege
  challenges to, 56, 59–63
Clitheroe, John, 146, 149
Clitheroe, Margaret, 75, 135, 139, 145, 147, 149, 171, 180, 182, 186, 205, 244
  marriage, 139–146
Congregatio Jesu, 260

Conscience, 42, 43, 45–55, 57–64, 66, 68, 71–75, 118, 131, 143–145, 147, 181, 254, 268
  distrust of women's conscience, 58, 74
  Protestant understanding, 42
Constable, Barbara, 62
Council of Trent, 15–16, 174, 199, 205, 217, 238, 241, 249, 266, 268n1
Coverture, 15, 34, 127

D

de Burgh, Richard, 163–164
Deceptions, 94–95
  dissimulation and equivocation, 98–104, 256
  in mixed marriages, 140–142
  property, 20, 91–92, 97
Disguises, 1, 95–97, 99, 250
  cross-dressing, 96–97
Dissimulation, 98–104
Divine authority
  development of debates over, 250–252
  See also Clerical authority
Divine law, 15, 34, 42, 212, 261
  Genesis 1 & 2 on women, 212–213
Dorothea, Sister, 69, 70, 132, 133, 147, 203–205, 207, 225, 229, 248
  See also Institute of English Ladies
Dublin riot, 157–158, 171, 188, 189, 253

E

Emancipation, 32–33
  Roman Catholic Relief Act, 5, 33, 258
Emergency situation, 7, 34, 69, 198, 210

Emigrants/exiles, 17, 26, 32, 52, 126, 127, 160, 161, 181, 255, 256
  return under James II, 29
Enclosure, 2, 15, 73
  Ward's/English Ladies' violation of, 247
English College, *see* Seminaries
English common law, 15, 20, 34, 42
Equivocation, 98–104, 256
  women's, 136–137

F

Fight for the Breeches, 43, 67, 123, 169
Fitzsimon, Henry, 23, 171

G

Galloping girls/nuns, 25, 63–73, 239, 246–250
Garnet, Henry, 7, 23, 24, 72, 95, 101–103, 173, 256
  Gunpowder Plot, 101–102
Gender, 189, 250–253
  intersections with religion, 149–150, 158, 189–190, 229–230, 247–250, 258, 262, 266, 267; divine authority, 250–252
Gender norms, 21, 23, 34, 35, 41–43, 48, 63–73, 81–89, 92, 94–107, 165, 166, 185
  common willingness to transgress, 3–4
  evolutions in, 4–5
  men, 80–82, 163; financial difficulties, 92; good husbandry, 82–89, 94; protect family, 105–107; Protestant and Catholic attacks on masculinity, 82, 165, 166, 185; tensions between lay and clerical

Gender norms (*cont.*)
    masculinities, 82–87; "true" man, 81, 94–105
    obedience to priests, 71
    policing, 149, 158
    undermining gender norms undermines society, 149, 189, 267
    women, 42; Catholic Church approves deviations, 41–43; less suspected of criminal behavior, 21; renegotiating women's gender roles, 23, 48, 63–73
Gerard, John, 68, 84–86, 95, 96, 101, 138, 163, 164, 176, 178, 200, 201
Gilbert, George and the Catholic Association, 250
    parallels with Ward's Institute, 250
Glorious Revolution, 29, 30, 33, 34, 226

H

Harrison, William, 35, 68, 71, 125, 174, 239, 247, 248
Hartlib, Samuel, 93–94
Heath, Henry, 95, 165–167
    understandings of work and martyrdom, 243–244
Henry VIII's break with Rome, 13
Herbert, Lucy, 7, 96, 253
    devotions to Sacred Heart, 222–224
    writings on offering, 214–221
Herbert, William, 89, 120, 216
Herst, Richard, 119–120, 149, 169
Holland, Althea, 44, 47, 48, 50, 120, 133, 135
Holland, Catherine, 41, 43–53, 63, 66, 73, 104, 120, 140, 143, 147, 149, 170
    debates Protestant bishop, 50
    running away, 48–51
Holland, John, 44, 47, 48, 50
Howard, William, 148
    last speech, 187–188

I

I.B.V.M., *see* Institute of the Blessed Virgin Mary
Institute of English Ladies, 1–3, 5, 8n1, 8n2, 14, 16, 18, 19, 23–25, 36, 37n1, 41, 43, 65–73, 75, 132, 150, 198, 205, 237–239, 242, 245, 246, 248–249
    advantages over men on mission, 20, 25
    criticism of, 2, 66–68, 246–250
    deceptions (*see* Deceptions)
    mixed life, 1–2, 16, 65, 69–70
    revived, present day, 25, 259–260
    successes/praise for, 24, 239
    suppression, 1–2, 36, 43, 230, 237, 245; Shee-Jesuites pamphlet, 248–249
    work of the Institute, 16, 18, 24
Institute of the Blessed Virgin Mary (I.B.V.M.), 259–260

J

Jesuits, 18, 22–24, 33, 49, 85, 105, 172, 174, 175, 206
    debates over partiality to British Isles (*see* Seminaries)

K

Knatchbull, Lucy, 177
    writings on offering, 214–221
Knatchbull, Mary, 178, 186

L

Laity/laypeople, 203–205, 207, 224, 229–230, 255–259, 265
  Catholic Committee limits clerical authority, 225–228
  changing relationship with clergy, 195–230, 252–253; change over time, 255–258; contemporary debates and issues, 259; importance of support from low-ranking clergy to effect change, 256–257, 265; women's exclusion from the debate, 229–230, 265
  choice of priest, 199–201
  distinction from clergy, 197, 198
  expanding women's role in sacraments, 24
  laymen's vs. laywomen's ability to effect change, 255–258
  ministering to laypeople, 203–207; in prison, 224; women's effectiveness, 203–207
  monastics as laypeople, 211–212
  taking on roles in liturgy and sacrament, 195–197, 207–210
Laws against practice of Catholicism, 18–20, 27, 31, 33–34, 88, 142, 226
  fifth column, 104–105
  irregular enforcement of, 26
  marriage partners, 138
  Penal Code, Ireland, 31
  penal laws, 18–19, 26, 82
  Recusancy Acts, 19, 26
  suspension of, James II, 29
Lee, Roger, 68, 176
Loyal subjects, 17, 20, 27, 28, 30, 32, 82, 90, 104–109, 118, 120, 226, 256–258, 261

M

Man with Brass Bowels, 79–80, 109–110
Marriage, 6, 69, 81, 89, 111, 117, 118, 120–123, 125, 126, 129, 130, 132, 133, 135–140, 142, 146, 148, 197, 264
  ballad Poor Anthony, 123–124
  Cary, Elizabeth and Henry, 117–119
  Catholic priests loosen wives' obedience, 133–134, 142–143
  church papist/one partner conforms, 125, 131
  mixed-Catholic & Protestant, 44, 117–119, 125, 131–146; deceptions within, 140–142
  one spouse converts the other, 138–139
  Palmer, Roger and Barbara, 135
  Protestants support wives challenging roles within, 135
  recusant, 119–120, 125–127
  religious headship, 124
  renegotiation of marital roles, 117–149
  traditional gendered roles within, 121–124
  undermining family hierarchy undermines society, 121–123, 146, 148, 149
  Widdrington/Reeveley, 125–126
  women's religious leadership, 130–131
Martyrs, 20, 21, 28, 52, 83, 103, 125, 141, 162, 165–166, 168, 169, 171, 180, 181, 187–188, 200, 243
  Arrowsmith, Edmund, 165–166, 168
  Barlowe, Ambrose, 181

Martyrs (*cont.*)
  Clitheroe, Margaret, 144–145, 170–171, 244
  Heath, Henry, 165, 243–244
  heirs of the apostles, 245
  Herst, Richard, 119–121, 169
  Howard, William, 147–148; last speech, 187–188
Mary, Virgin, 171–174
  militant, 171–174
  as spiritual priest, 213
Matthew, Tobie, 162, 169, 180, 214
Mawhood, William, 137
Militancy, Christian, 169–171, 177–179
  actual violence, 161–162
  exiles, 160, 161
  history, 159, 174–179
  language, 160, 163–169; women, 169–171, 177–178
  Mary, Virgin, 171–174
  militancy and patience combined, 159
  priests and monastics, 174–179
  training at seminaries, 166
  what's new, 159–160
  women, 157–158, 171, 186
Mission, 14, 15, 17–19, 21, 22, 24, 25, 36, 37n3, 65, 66, 69, 95, 127, 133, 138, 166, 180, 198, 199, 203, 205, 236, 237, 242, 243, 245, 246
  missionaries as heirs of the apostles, 244, 245
Montague, *see* Browne, Anthony
More, Gertrude, 7, 42, 44, 52–63, 73, 147
  contemplative, 54
  ideas spread to other nuns, 54, 59–61
  obedience to clergy, 55–61
  patience, 62

Mother Teresa of Calcutta, 260
Mush, John, 18, 139–145, 171, 180, 182
  Priestly role in Clitheroe marriage, 146

N
Natural law, 15, 20, 34, 42, 73, 149, 261
Nuns, 1, 2, 15, 25, 48, 51–53, 59, 62, 63, 65–67, 73, 137, 170, 176–178, 189, 197, 211, 212, 223, 259
  Augustinians, Bruges, 48, 51, 89, 216; devotions to Sacred Heart of Jesus, 222–223
  Benedictines, Brussels, 214
  Benedictines, Cambrai, 52, 58–63
  consecrating selves, 213–214
  Poor Clares, 14
  shared gender and religious pressures as laywomen, 52

O
Oathtaking, 104, 255–257
  Catholic Committee, 225, 226
Offering, language of, 210–223
  contrast with continental Catholic language, 220–225
  offering Christ at Mass, 214–218
  offering for salvation of one's self and others, 216–221
  offering one's self at Mass, 214–216
  offering the Sacred Heart of Jesus, 221–224

P
Pastoralis Romani Pontificis, 1, 248
Patience, 174–183

for laymen, 180–182 (*cont.*)
  Mary, Virgin, 179
  as masculine quality, 182–183
  in prison, 181–182
  in saints' lives, 180
  in scripture, 179
  too much patience, 179–184
Patience and militancy combined, 184–189
Periculoso, 15, 16
Persons, Robert, 24, 104
Plots, 17, 20, 30, 34, 99, 100, 161, 162
  Babington Plot, 17, 90, 99, 100, 161, 184
  Gunpowder Plot, 17, 20, 23, 95, 101–102, 161, 162, 184
  Titus Oates Plot/Popish Plot, 27, 102–103, 107, 147, 161, 187–188
Pope Joan, 235–236, 238, 266
Prisons, 100–101, 181–182, 205
  prisoners ministering to one another, 224
Protestant Ascendency, 30–31
Protestants
  distrust of Catholics, 27
  growing trust of Catholics in eighteenth century, 32
Pursuivants/priest hunters, 20, 161, 176

R
Rebellions, 20, 161–179
  Jacobite uprisings, 32, 174
Restoration, 27, 45, 48, 104
Riots, 34
  Dublin riot, 158, 171, 188, 189
  Gordon Riots, 33
Rosary, 45, 89, 173–174, 181

S
Sacred Heart of Jesus, 221–224
Seminaries, 14, 22, 23, 127, 166, 207
Sisters of Loreto, *see* Institute of the Blessed Virgin Mary (I.B.V.M.)
Society of Jesus, *see* Jesuits
Southwell, Richard, 86, 87
Southwell, Robert, 83, 86, 87, 98–101, 124, 143, 168, 180, 185, 201
Sword, 28, 105, 106, 108, 122, 161, 164, 171, 174, 176

T
Toleration, 225–228
  Toleration Act, 29

U
Urban VIII, 1–3, 5, 36, 236, 237, 249, 253, 255

V
Vicars Apostolic, 226–227, 242, 255, 257
Vitelleschi, Mutio, 22, 23, 72
Vladimiroff, Christine, 264

W
Ward, Mary, 1, 2, 5–8, 13–15, 18, 20, 21, 23–26, 33, 36, 41–44, 63–74, 76, 96, 186, 198, 205, 236–238, 245, 249–250, 260
  challenges to clerical direction, 68–69
  criticisms of, 66–68, 238–240
  death, 25
  deceptions (*see* Deceptions)
  disobedient woman, 63–73

Ward, Mary (*cont.*)
  early life, 14, 63–64
  If Mary Ward had been a man, 250
  mixed life, 69–70
  not trying to violate apostolic succession, 246
  perceived violation of apostolic succession, 238, 239, 246–250
  plans for the Institute, 69, 246
  questioning clerical authority, 63–64
  return to England after suppression, 2, 25; puzzle solved, 249–250
  revelations, 15, 64, 246, 253
  road to canonization, 260
  Ward vs. Urban VIII, 253–255
Weapons, 105–106, 161–162, 175–176
  rosary, 173–174
Weston, Richard, 92–94
Weston, William, 79, 90, 95, 99, 100, 110, 131–133, 161, 204, 243
Widdrington, Roger, 125–126
Wigmore, Winefrid, 37n1, 72
  challenge to papal authority, 73
  See also Institute of English Ladies; suppression
Williamite War, 30, 31, 161
Wiseman, Jane, 170–171, 204–205
Wiseman, William, 84, 201, 225
Wodehouse, Francis, 7, 79, 80, 82, 83, 88–90, 92, 109–111, 127, 131, 141, 158, 163, 253
Women's ordination to the Catholic priesthood, 264–265
Women's ordination to the diaconate, 266–267

The manufacturer's authorised representative in the EU is Springer Nature Customer Service Centre GmbH, Europaplatz 3, 69115 Heidelberg, Germany. If you have any concerns regarding our products, please contact ProductSafety@springernature.com

Printed and bound by CPI Group (UK) Ltd, Croydon, CR0 4YY

23/03/2026

02076672-0012